Immigration and Conflict in Europe

Contemporary debates give the impression that the presence of immigrants necessarily spells strife – yet as *Immigration and Conflict in Europe* shows, the incidence of conflict involving immigrants and their descendants has varied widely across groups, cities, and countries. This book presents a theory to account for this uneven pattern, explaining why we observe clashes between immigrants and natives in some locations but not in others and why some cities experience confrontations between immigrants and state actors while others are spared from such conflicts. The book addresses how economic conditions interact with electoral incentives to account for immigrant–native and immigrant–state conflict across groups and cities within Great Britain as well as across Germany and France. The author highlights the importance of national immigration regimes and local political economies in shaping immigrants' economic position and political behavior, demonstrating how economic and electoral forces, rather than cultural differences, determine patterns of conflict and calm.

Rafaela M. Dancygier is Assistant Professor of Politics and Public and International Affairs at Princeton University. Her work has appeared in the *American Journal of Political Science* and in edited volumes.

D0904319

Cambridge Studies in Comparative Politics

General Editor
Margaret Levi *University of Washington, Seattle*

Assistant General Editors
Kathleen Thelen *Massachusetts Institute of Technology*
Erik Wibbels *Duke University*

Associate Editors
Robert H. Bates *Harvard University*
Stephen Hanson *University of Washington, Seattle*
Torben Iversen *Harvard University*
Stathis Kalyvas *Yale University*
Peter Lange *Duke University*
Helen Milner *Princeton University*
Frances Rosenbluth *Yale University*
Susan Stokes *Yale University*

Other Books in the Series

David Austen-Smith, Jeffry A. Frieden, Miriam A. Golden, Karl Ove Moene,
 and Adam Przeworski, eds., *Selected Works of Michael Wallerstein: The
 Political Economy of Inequality, Unions, and Social Democracy*
Andy Baker, *The Market and the Masses in Latin America: Policy Reform
 and Consumption in Liberalizing Economies*
Lisa Baldez, *Why Women Protest: Women's Movements in Chile*
Stefano Bartolini, *The Political Mobilization of the European Left,
 1860–1980: The Class Cleavage*
Robert Bates, *When Things Fell Apart: State Failure in Late-Century Africa*
Mark Beissinger, *Nationalist Mobilization and the Collapse of the Soviet State*
Nancy Bermeo, ed., *Unemployment in the New Europe*
Carles Boix, *Democracy and Redistribution*
Carles Boix, *Political Parties, Growth, and Equality: Conservative and Social
 Democratic Economic Strategies in the World Economy*
Catherine Boone, *Merchant Capital and the Roots of State Power in Senegal,
 1930–1985*

Continued after the Index

Immigration and Conflict in Europe

RAFAELA M. DANCYGIER

Princeton University

CAMBRIDGE
UNIVERSITY PRESS

CAMBRIDGE UNIVERSITY PRESS
Cambridge, New York, Melbourne, Madrid, Cape Town, Singapore,
São Paulo, Delhi, Dubai, Tokyo, Mexico City

Cambridge University Press
32 Avenue of the Americas, New York, NY 10013-2473, USA

www.cambridge.org
Information on this title: www.cambridge.org/9780521150231

First published 2010

Printed in the United States of America

A catalog record for this publication is available from the British Library.

Library of Congress Cataloging in Publication data
Dancygier, Rafaela M., 1977–
Immigration and conflict in Europe / Rafaela M. Dancygier.
  p.   cm. – (Cambridge studies in comparative politics)
Includes bibliographical references and index.
ISBN 978-0-521-19907-0 (hardback)
1. Europe – Emigration and immigration.   2. Ethnic conflict – Europe.   3. Europe – Race
relations.   4. Europe – Ethnic relations.   5. Immigrants – Cultural assimilation – Europe.
I. Title.   II. Series.
JV7590.D36   2010
304.8′4 – dc22   2010006623

ISBN 978-0-521-19907-0 Hardback
ISBN 978-0-521-15023-1 Paperback

For my parents and Jason

Contents

List of Figures and Tables

Figures

Tables

Acknowledgments

I could have not written this book had it not been for the help and support that I received from numerous colleagues, friends, and family members.

This book had its origins as a doctoral dissertation in political science at Yale University, and I owe great debts to my graduate school mentors and friends who generously offered their help and guidance during my time at Yale. Frances Rosenbluth and Ken Scheve shared excellent insights and provided kind encouragement throughout the research process. Their incisive comments undoubtedly helped sharpen the argument, and I am very grateful for their continued support. I would also like to thank Don Green and Stathis Kalyvas whose outstanding advice proved invaluable in shaping the conceptual and empirical development of this book. Together, these scholars not only helped me with the research that forms the basis of this book; along the way, they also showed me what it means to be a teacher and a scholar, and I thank them for that.

At Yale, I was fortunate to lean on a group of friends and colleagues for intellectual stimulation as well as moral support. I wish to extend very special thanks to Dan Galvin, Elizabeth Saunders, and Beth Addonizio, who were tremendously helpful throughout the research and writing process. I also very much benefited from the useful comments of David Cameron, Katie Glassmyer, Harris Mylonas, Tom Pepinsky, and Nawreen Sattar.

The Politics Department and Woodrow Wilson School at Princeton University provided an excellent environment in which to complete this book. I wish to thank Mark Beissinger, Carles Boix, Evan Lieberman, Gwyneth McClendon, Sophie Meunier, Jonas Pontusson, Ezra Suleiman, and Deborah Yashar for offering extremely helpful insights and suggestions.

For their constructive feedback and valuable advice, I would also like to thank Erik Bleich, John Eade, Anna Grzymala-Busse, Dan Hopkins, Michael Keith, Anthony Messina, Dan Posner, Shamit Saggar, Shanker Satyanath, Gurharpal Singh, John Solomos, Steven Wilkinson, and Marie Zwetsloot. Furthermore, I would like to acknowledge the very good comments I received from workshop participants at Yale University, University of California at Irvine (Institute on International Migration), University of California at Berkeley, University of California at Los Angeles, New York University, and at meetings of the American Political Science Association.

At Cambridge University Press, Lewis Bateman, senior editor of political science and history, was exceptionally supportive and patient in guiding me through the production process. Anne L. Rounds provided very helpful and friendly editorial assistance. I thank them both. I would also like to thank Margaret Levi for her support of this project and three anonymous reviewers for their perceptive comments and penetrating criticism.

All of these individuals immensely improved this book; any shortcomings that surely remain are mine.

Several institutions and individuals facilitated the research on which this book is based. I am very grateful for generous financial assistance from the Yale University Center for International and Area Studies, the Yale University Leitner Program in International and Comparative Political Economy, the Horowitz Foundation for Social Policy, and the Princeton University Committee on Research in the Humanities and Social Sciences. My thanks also go to archivists at the National Archives in London, the Labour History Archive and Study Centre in Manchester, and the Bundesarchiv in Koblenz (especially Elke Hauschildt) as well as the helpful staff of Ealing and Leicester city governments, the Metropolitan Police Service, and the Yale University Library for providing me with important data. I am grateful as well to current and former political officials in England who agreed to be interviewed for this book. For their warm hospitality in England, I wish to thank Mayling Birney, Naomi Baar, Diana David, Edith Endzweig, and Selin Kurlandski.

Finally, I would like to express my deepest gratitude to my terrific parents, Henryk and Hellena Dancygier, who always encouraged me to pursue my intellectual interests, even if they have taken me thousands of miles away from them. Most of all, I wish to thank my wonderful, loving husband, Jason Rogart. His many compromises in support of my scholarly endeavors, as well as his quiet but unyielding encouragement, have meant the world to me.

PART I

GENERAL INTRODUCTION AND THEORETICAL FRAMEWORK

1

Introduction

What explains immigrant conflict? Why do we observe clashes between immigrants and natives in some locations, but not in others? When do cities experience confrontations between immigrants and state actors? Why are some immigrant groups likely to become targets of native opposition, while others are more often engaged in conflicts with the state? What accounts for change in immigrant conflict within locales over time?

This book explains why, where, and when immigration leads to conflict in the areas of immigrant settlement. Immigration has been changing the faces of neighborhoods, cities, and countries across Europe, North America, and beyond. The large-scale inflow and permanent settlement of migrants is no longer confined to traditional immigration countries. In 2005, the share of foreign-born residents reached 12.5 percent in Austria and 12.1 percent in Germany, compared with 12.3 percent in the United States. In many other European countries approximately one in ten residents is born abroad (see Figure 1.1). Moreover, countries that have long been exporters of labor, such as Spain and Italy, have begun importing foreign workers and their families in large numbers. The magnitude of immigration manifests itself even more strikingly at the local level: Amsterdam, Brussels, Frankfurt, London, and New York are just some of the cities whose foreign-born residents constitute more than one-fourth of the population (Migration Policy Institute 2008).

Immigration is unlikely to abate in the near future. Confronting declining fertility rates, ailing pension systems, and pressing labor market needs, advanced industrialized economies provide the "pull" factors that drive international migration, while economic hardship and political unrest in less developed countries furnish the necessary "push" factors. Moreover, amid ongoing, sizeable migrant movements across borders, millions of previously settled immigrants are becoming permanent members of their adopted home countries; the number of foreign residents acquiring citizenship has followed an upward trend in

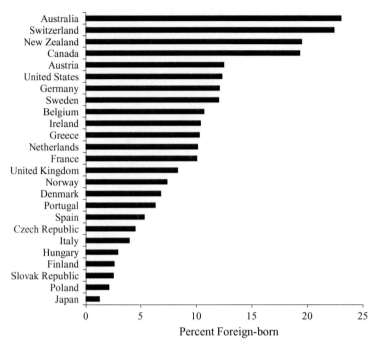

FIGURE 1.1. Percentage of foreign-born residents in selected countries of the Organisation for Economic Co-operation and Development (*Source:* OECD 2008).

many Western democracies.[1] Immigration is thus bound to have an enduring impact on the political systems and social fabrics of receiving societies.

As immigration and migrant settlement continue to be important, so will the need to recognize the conditions and mechanisms that link migration to conflict. While contemporary debates can give rise to the impression that the presence of immigrants and the ethnic communities they build necessarily spells strife, the incidence of immigrant conflict has in fact varied widely across settings and over time.[2] To help us understand why immigrant conflict occurs, this book begins with the observation that not all confrontations involving immigrants are the same. As I elaborate more fully in Chapter 2, I group immigrant conflict into two phenomena: immigrant–native conflict and immigrant–state conflict. *Immigrant–native conflict* involves the sustained confrontation between members of the immigrant and the native populations in a given locality. It consists of violent and nonviolent native opposition against immigrants, such as the local electoral success of xenophobic parties or physical attacks directed against

---

[1] Chapter 8 discusses these trends at greater length.

[2] I use the terms "immigrant" and "ethnic minority" interchangeably. I use the term "native" to refer to the white indigenous population who has lived in a given country for many generations. For a discussion of these labels, see Chapter 2.

migrant settlers. *Immigrant–state conflict* involves the sustained confrontation between members of the immigrant population and state actors in a given locality. Low-level flare-ups as well as major disturbances between immigrant-origin minorities and state actors, most often the police, are common indicators of this type of conflict.

Both faces of immigrant conflict display considerable variation across groups, cities, and countries. Concerning immigrant–native conflict in Great Britain, which is the main focus area of this book, the arrival of postcolonial migrants prompted the rise of the xenophobic National Front in London's East End. Nevertheless, many ethnically diverse western London boroughs as well as immigrant destinations farther north, such as Manchester or Liverpool, did not witness an electoral backlash against the newcomers. In the summer of 2001, major disturbances between Pakistani-origin youths and white residents hit the streets of Bradford; when Pakistanis first arrived, however, the city had been lauded as "the standing refutation of the argument that multi-racial communities are inevitably beset by racial troubles" (Spiers 1965, 154). Concerning immigrant–state conflict, large-scale confrontations between immigrants and the police shook British inner cities in the 1970s and 1980s. As I show in later chapters, however, not all ethnically diverse urban areas were affected, and not all immigrant groups participated equally in these clashes: Migrants of West Indian descent have tended to be involved in confrontations with the state, while their South Asian counterparts have been more likely to be targeted by native white Britons.

Compared to developments in Britain, the arrival and settlement of guest workers in Germany – another case discussed later in this book – has been associated with relatively lower levels of organized resistance on the part of the indigenous population. Large-scale riots between these migrants and their German neighbors or local electoral victories of the far right have been less pronounced. The same cannot be said, however, of the brief but vicious local campaigns that coincided with the migration of ethnic Germans[3] and political refugees in the late 1980s and early 1990s. The other face of immigrant conflict, confrontations between immigrants and state actors, has generally not been extensive in Germany, especially when they are placed in comparative perspective. Nevertheless, in the early 2000s, relations between the police and minority residents became strained in Berlin and elsewhere.[4]

Such variation in immigrant conflict outcomes is not unique to Britain and Germany. In France, for example, both types of conflict reveal checkered patterns. The far-right *Front National* has served as a model to many anti-immigrant movements in Europe. Its success, however, has fluctuated over the years and across towns. Furthermore, clashes between immigrants and the forces of law and order have not spread evenly throughout the country. Such

---

[3] Ethnic German migrants (*Aussiedler*) hail from Eastern Europe and countries in the former Soviet Union, but they are of German descent. See Chapter 7 for a more detailed definition.
[4] *Die Tageszeitung*, "Jugendliche fallen über Polizisten her," November 16, 2006.

violence first surfaced in the 1970s, appeared on a larger scale in the early 1980s, and erupted most forcefully in the fall of 2005 – yet some towns have largely escaped these confrontations. Marseille has generally not produced violent antistate disturbances, and much media attention indeed focused on the port city's record of relative calm during the 2005 riots. Just over a decade earlier, however, anti-immigrant activities had turned the city into the "racist capital of Europe."[5]

In neighboring Belgium, violent disturbances between the police and immigrant youths have taken place in some Brussels municipalities, while local anti-immigrant mobilization has been particularly striking in Antwerp, where the racist *Vlaams Blok* represented the largest party on the city's council between 1994 and 2006 and racist murders provoked riots and public outcries.[6] But while the xenophobic vote has enjoyed spectacular results in Flanders, in the Walloon region the racist *Front National* never achieved such success, despite similar shares of non-EU immigrants across regions.[7]

Beyond Europe's borders, local anti-immigrant mobilization and hate crime gained momentum in the United States in the 2000s. Public agitation led some towns to enact ordinances aimed at stopping the arrival of Hispanic migrants. At the same time, so-called sanctuary cities welcomed these newcomers with immigrant-friendly policies.[8] South Africa became the site of anti-immigrant killings in 2008, when a "spasm of xenophobia" hit its cities. A series of gruesome attacks against Zimbabweans, many of whom had settled in the area years ago, swept Johannesburg neighborhoods.[9] In sum, immigrant conflict has varied widely within and across receiving countries. Although clashes between immigrants and natives, as well as between immigrants and the state, continue to claim lives, cause property damage, and impede the integration of immigrants more generally, we still know very little about what causes these confrontations to emerge.

The rest of this chapter is organized as follows. In the first section, I present a brief overview of the book's theory of immigrant conflict. I then situate the argument in the existing theoretical and empirical debates in the second section (Chapter 2 contains a more extensive treatment of the theoretical framework and the state of the literature). In the third section I identify some of the main problems that scholars face when they attempt to explain the causes of

---

[5] See Singer (1991, 376). Chapter 8 follows immigrant conflict in France more closely.

[6] In 2002, the murder of a teacher of Moroccan origin by a white neighbor sparked off riots on Antwerp's streets; four years later, renewed racist killings led over 15,000 local residents to stage a protest march through the city. See *Süddeutsche Zeitung*, "Belgier demonstrieren gegen Rassismus," May 26, 2006.

[7] In 2000, 2.2 percent of Flanders' population and 2.1 percent of Wallonia's population were non-EU citizens; the total share of noncitizens is higher in Wallonia (10.1 percent) than it is in Flanders (4.9 percent); see Martiniello and Rea (2003).

[8] On the political debate about sanctuary cities, see *The New York Times*, "A Closer Look at the 'Sanctuary City' Argument," November 29, 2007.

[9] See, e.g., *The New York Times*, "South Africans Take out Rage on Immigrants," May 20, 2008.

immigrant conflict. The final section indicates how this study seeks to overcome these limitations by presenting an overview of the remaining chapters.

The Argument in Brief

This book develops a theory to explain why, where, and when immigrant–native and immigrant–state conflict occur. I argue that the interaction of two variables – economic scarcity and immigrant electoral power – accounts for the incidence of immigrant–native and immigrant–state conflict. Both kinds of conflict only occur in the context of local economic scarcity, when immigrants and natives compete for goods whose supply is relatively fixed in the short term. Differences in immigrants' electoral clout in turn lead to variation in the *type* of conflict we observe. When immigrants can back up their claims for scarce economic goods with pivotal votes, local politicians will allocate these resources to this new constituency. Natives are in turn likely to protest such distribution by turning against immigrants, producing immigrant–native conflict.

Conversely, in the absence of political leverage, immigrants are left with few resources during times of economic shortage. This state of affairs may leave natives content, forestalling immigrant–native conflict, but it is more likely to cause immigrants to engage in conflictual relations with state actors, producing immigrant–state conflict. Immigrants who do not possess the local political power to commit local politicians to disbursing scarce goods to them hope to effect a more favorable distribution of resources by inflicting costs on the state in the form of property damage and injury. Finally, I maintain that both types of conflict are more likely to occur when the state (rather than the market) is in charge of disbursing scarce goods; state actors are more sensitive than market actors to the costs that anti-immigrant (and obviously antistate) activities impose. The next chapter develops these propositions more fully.

Focusing on economic scarcity and immigrant electoral power in the local areas of migrant settlement yields a parsimonious model of immigrant conflict. A set of institutional and behavioral variables, however, shapes the ways in which these two key economic and political variables unfold locally. As I spell out more extensively in Chapter 2, immigration regimes may affect the degree of *economic scarcity* through their impact on the supply of, and demand for, economic goods in local immigrant destinations. While migrants generally tend to navigate toward areas where employment is plentiful, states may vary, for example, in the extent to which they match the recruitment of foreign labor with the supply of local physical infrastructures, such as housing or schools, leading to variation in local economic scarcity across countries. When governments encourage (or tolerate) immigration but do not take steps to help localities absorb the inflow of migrants, differences in economic conditions across cities and towns within countries will prove crucial. This situation characterizes post-war migration from Britain's former colonies to the mother country as well as much of the undocumented migration into the United States in the 1990s and 2000s.

Immigration regimes can also affect the level of migrant demands for economic goods. All else being equal, the same number of immigrants will put greater strains on local resources when the immigrants are parents and children as opposed to individual labor migrants. Political refugees arriving as families, for instance, are likely to place more demands on social and educational services than are young, single guest workers. Over time, however, primary economic migrants often reunite with their families in the host country, leading to increased demands on economic resources well after initial settlement.

National political institutions may also produce different levels of *immigrant political power*. Laws governing the acquisition of citizenship and access to local voting rights open up the potential for immigrant electoral influence. The ease with which immigrants can turn into citizens varies considerably across countries and, within countries, over time (Brubaker 1992; Howard 2006). Furthermore, some countries allow foreign nationals to cast votes in local elections, while others restrict this right to specific national-origin groups or citizens only (Bauer 2007). When immigrants and their descendents are entitled to participate in local elections, local electoral rules as well as immigrants' ability to mobilize co-ethnics may additionally impede or help their quest for local political power. Institutional and behavioral variables are therefore at work in molding patterns of immigrant political power. As I demonstrate in later chapters, South Asian migrants in Britain have often been able to draw on networks of kin and clan to facilitate impressive get-out-the-vote efforts, which – given this group's geographic concentration and Britain's ward-level elections – has made this group politically powerful in many British local authorities.

Synthesizing this information, I state that the variation in political institutions interacts with behavioral features of immigrant groups to generate systematic predictions about the likelihood of local immigrant political power. Furthermore, differences in economic institutions (i.e., the ways in which immigration regimes affect the supply of and demand for local economic resources) influence levels of economic scarcity in immigrant destinations. Together, immigrant political power and economic scarcity explain the incidence of local immigrant–native and immigrant–state conflict.

The book's main interest lies in explaining why some cities witness sustained confrontations between immigrants and longer-settled native residents or continued clashes between immigrants and the state, while relations between immigrants, natives, and state actors remain peaceful elsewhere. As a result, it must be attuned to the *local* dynamics that shape these conflict patterns. At the same time, I maintain that *national* immigration and citizenship regimes bear on these outcomes by influencing the potential for local economic shortages and immigrant electoral behavior. As these national institutions change, so should the incidence of local immigrant conflict. Within-country variation in immigrant conflict therefore exists alongside aggregate national differences, or country effects. As later chapters will show, British cities have varied considerably in their experience with the two types of immigrant conflict, and we can only make sense of these differences by isolating the economic and political dynamics that cause local conflict or peace. Nevertheless, we also observe country effects: Overall levels of local conflict involving postcolonial migrants in Britain exceeded overall levels of local conflict involving guest workers in Germany. I argue that policies that guided guest-worker migration (e.g., the provision of local resources, or the conditionality of migration and settlement on employment and housing) reduced the likelihood of competition over economic goods and hence lowered the incidence of immigrant conflict in the areas of settlement. Such regulations were largely absent in directing postwar migration into Britain. Differences in national institutions thus produce differences in local conflict outcomes across countries.

Existing Arguments

The purpose of this book is to identify the variables that cause local-level immigrant–native and immigrant–state conflict. It aims to show how differences in national immigration regimes and political institutions shape and interact with differences in local economic conditions and immigrant political behavior to yield systematic variation in the occurrence of immigrant conflict across groups, cities, and countries. In this way, this book contributes to our understanding of immigrant conflict specifically and to ethnic conflict more generally. In examining why immigrants come to be involved in two types of conflicts, the book also generates insights about the social and political implications of large-scale immigration in advanced industrialized democracies.

The scholarship linking immigration to domestic conflict has thus far mostly focused on clashes between immigrants and natives; comparative research explaining confrontations between immigrants and state actors in the contemporary period is still in its early stages. In both cases, however, there have been surprisingly few attempts to systematically and comparatively study conflicts involving immigrants as these conflicts take shape on the ground. While there is a vast literature covering the incidence of ethnic conflict across the globe, only a small number of comparative works actually study the occurrence of such conflict in localities of immigrant arrival.[10] Numerous single-case histories provide rich accounts of the local immigrant experience, and this book draws on many of these. But these narratives generally do not aim for generalizable explanations. Even in the context of ethnic minority relations in the United States, a widely studied topic, "there have been remarkably few comparative studies that bring... locally specific work together" (Jones-Correa, 2001a, 2).

Although comparative research on the local manifestations of immigrant conflict remains scarce, scholars have addressed the topic at different levels of aggregation. Much of the research explaining domestic opposition against immigration thus speaks to variation at the national or at the individual level. Cross-national studies show how macrolevel variables such as unemployment

---

[10] For exceptions, see Weiner (1978), Olzak (1992), Karapin (2002), and Hopkins (2010).

rates, immigration levels, economic restructuring, and electoral institutions can account for the success and failures of national far-right, xenophobic parties.[11] Moreover, survey research has employed political economy models to examine individual responses to the distributional consequences of immigration.[12] I follow these studies in focusing on the economic winners and losers of immigration, but I also identify the conditions under which native residents find it necessary to protect their economic welfare by mobilizing against immigrants in their neighborhoods. In doing so, I show that the extent to which immigration has an impact on natives' (as well as immigrants') material well-being hinges on systematic features of immigration regimes that may lead to local resource shortages and on electoral variables that may enable immigrants to make economic claims at the expense of native residents.

Examining individual attitudes, scholars have also argued that identity-based fears can outweigh economic anxieties and point to the cultural threats that cause individuals to reject the inflow of ethnically distinct newcomers.[13] The public debate about immigrant integration has also often focused on the alleged incompatibility between the behavioral norms and cultural values (as well as the skin colors) of migrant newcomers and those of the host country's majority population. In the United States, for example, Benjamin Franklin expressed serious concerns that "Palatine Boors... herding together... will Germanize us instead of our Anglifying them, and will never adopt our Language or Customs, any more than they can acquire our Complexion" (cited in Fraga and Segura 2006, 280). Several hundred years later, Hispanic immigrants have taken the place of German settlers in the United States. Across the Atlantic, public discussion has singled out Islam as the main impediment to native acceptance and immigrant assimilation, prompting the question, "can one be Muslim and European?" (cf. Zolberg and Woon 1999, 6; Sniderman and Hagendoorn 2005).

This book's emphasis on the economic dimensions of immigrant conflict challenges arguments that locate the main source of conflict in immigrants' racial, cultural, or religious backgrounds. Ethnicity, broadly understood, clearly matters in shaping social relations, such as friendship, marriage, or business transactions, both between immigrants and natives and among immigrants

---

[11] Cross-country studies of far-right parties include, e.g., Kitschelt (1996), Golder (2003), Carter (2005), Givens (2005), and Norris (2005). Scholars have begun to extend this line of work to within-country variation in the electoral performance of the extreme right; see, e.g., Kestilä and Söderlund (2004).

[12] See, e.g., Scheve and Slaughter (2001) and Hanson, Scheve, and Slaughter (2007) for the U.S. case and Mayda (2006) for a cross-national analysis. See Freeman and Kessler (2008) for a review of the political economy of migration and migration policy.

[13] Sniderman, Hagendoorn, and Prior (2004) demonstrate that both economic and cultural threats drive hostility toward immigrants among Dutch citizens. Hainmueller and Hiscox (2007) and Sides and Citrin (2007) find that economic factors matter less in shaping European attitudes toward immigrants than cultural values and beliefs, which in turn are mediated by respondents' educational attainment. Fetzer (2000) also addresses both cultural and economic bases of opposition.

themselves. Indeed, although my central argument centers squarely on the primacy of economic interests in the production of immigrant conflict, I do not claim that ethnic identities are irrelevant. In my account, however, group identities are not the drivers of sustained conflict. They matter in so far as they help immigrants mobilize politically to bolster economic demands; failure to organize politically may cause economically deprived immigrants to protest against the state, while successful mobilization in economically hard times may invite a native backlash. By themselves, though, ethnic difference or the strength of ethnic ties do not produce sustained conflict. I thus do not argue that identity-based differences between immigrants and natives are inconsequential in the social realm or even in the political arena.[14] Rather, as I elaborate in the following chapters, on their own, immigrants' ethnic or religious backgrounds cannot explain the wide variation in both faces of immigrant conflict we observe within and across countries.

Studying Immigrant Conflict

Demonstrating that the economic needs and political strategies of ethnically distinct migrants bring about immigrant conflict requires an empirical approach that can pull apart ethnic identities, economic shortages, and electoral mobilization. Moreover, any convincing explanation of local immigrant conflict must be firmly rooted in an understanding of local processes. For theoretical and practical reasons, much of this book therefore seeks to explain differences in the occurrence of both types of conflict in local immigrant destinations within one country, Great Britain. But it does so without losing sight of the importance of national frameworks in structuring the inflow and settlement of migrants: The book also contrasts immigrant conflict in Britain with an analysis of developments in Germany, and it briefly examines broad patterns of subnational conflict and calm in France.

Studying Immigrant Conflict within and across Countries
From a practical standpoint, studying within-country variation in immigrant conflict outcomes allows us to better isolate the variables that cause these clashes. Even within countries, immigration regimes and citizenship laws can vary across immigrant groups and over time. In France, for instance, postwar labor migration coincided with inflows of refugees that fled the war in Algeria. In Germany, migrants of German lineage from Eastern Europe and the former Soviet Union were granted automatic access to citizenship, but regulations were successively tightened in the mid-1990s. By contrast, the guest-worker population initially faced stringent naturalization requirements that were later liberalized. Moreover, the skills and economic resources of earlier ethnic German migrants generally surpassed those of later waves, while the

[14] On the distinction between ethnic salience and ethnic conflict, see Laitin (1986), Chandra (2001), and Fearon (2006).

socioeconomic profiles of descendents of guest workers have also become more differentiated. Countries may thus simultaneously receive inflows of immigrants who vary in their capacity to participate in the electoral process; differ in the amount of pressure they put on local economic resources; and diverge in their ethnocultural backgrounds. Within countries, this diversity may provide us with excellent research opportunities. In a comparison across countries, these differences will be magnified and further coincide with potential competing explanations (such as national political cultures and institutions or historical legacies) that could conceivably influence immigrant conflict. Convincingly identifying which variables cause multiethnic conflict or harmony cross-nationally is thus challenging.

Furthermore, measuring immigrant conflict consistently across countries is extremely difficult. Data sources that exhaustively catalog immigrant–native riots within or across countries and over a substantial period of time are still lacking, although there have been related efforts.[15] Systematic, over-time and across-space information on large-scale confrontations between immigrants and the state is also currently not available. Reports on the smaller clashes and flare-ups that make up the anatomy of everyday immigrant–state conflict tend to come to light only once major disturbances have taken place, if at all. Since state actors are involved in these confrontations – as the target audience and direct participants – one good data source for these lesser events is government archives, and this book draws on archival evidence from Great Britain and Germany.

Data on smaller-scale events pertaining to immigrant–native conflict are not as challenging to obtain, but nevertheless pose problems with regard to cross-national comparability. While figures on racist violence have been collected for a set of countries in the very recent past, different legal definitions on what constitutes hate crime more generally and racist violence in particular (as well as widely diverging collection and dissemination procedures) make it inadvisable to compare these statistics across countries. As Mudde (2007, 286) notes on the cross-national analysis of racist violence, "serious comparative studies are at this stage impossible, given the huge inconsistencies in data collection between European countries." Indeed, the European Monitoring Centre on Racism and

---

[15] Susan Olzak (1992) tracks "ethnic collective action" in seventy-seven cities in the U.S. from 1877 through 1914. Ron Francisco has assembled an excellent data set covering protest and coercion events across twenty-eight European countries from 1980 to 1995 (see http://web.ku. edu/ronfran/data/index.html). Since the data were not collected with the specific aim of capturing immigrant conflict, the categories do not map onto the conflict dimensions I study here. The innovative MERCI project (Mobilization over Ethnic Relations, Citizenship and Immigration) has gathered very interesting data on so-called political claims making by ethnic minority actors or those in the migration and ethnic minority relations field (including political actors opposing immigrants), covering Germany, the United Kingdom, France, the Netherlands, and Switzerland from 1992 to 1998. See http://ics.leeds.ac.uk/eurpolcom/research_projects_merci. cfm and Koopmans, Statham, Giugni, and Passy (2005) for an encompassing account of the findings generated by MERCI. All three sources are based on the coding of newspaper articles.

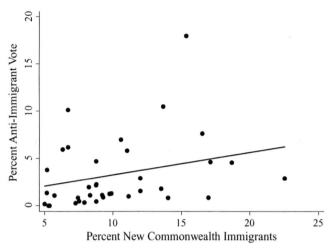

FIGURE 1.2. Immigration and the local anti-immigrant vote, Great Britain, 1970s.

Xenophobia advises researchers to analyze trends in racist violence within but not across countries, which is also the approach adopted in this book.[16] Finally, we need to proceed with caution when comparing anti-immigrant parties across countries. The National Front in Britain, for example, is a more extreme, neofascist party than the more populist *Front National* in France (Golder 2003). Though both parties clearly espouse anti-immigrant platforms, the more extremist appearance and rhetoric adopted by the British Front might suppress overall levels of support when compared to its French counterpart. To arrive at valid conclusions about the scale and intensity of immigrant–native conflict across countries, we would thus have to take into account additional indicators, such as anti-immigrant rallies or riots.

Given these constraints, this book first examines within-country conflict dynamics in Great Britain before moving on to other national contexts. The initial focus on the British case has the advantages of allowing for valid measurement and holding constant potentially confounding variables that diverge cross-nationally, while still leaving us with a significant amount of variation in the local political and economic features of immigrants and immigrant destinations, producing remarkable differences in conflict patterns. A first glance at the local electoral fortunes of anti-immigrant parties in Great Britain illustrates some of this local-level diversity. Figure 1.2 depicts the correlation between the share of New Commonwealth immigrants (originating mostly from the Indian subcontinent and the West Indies) and local election results of xenophobic parties in immigrant destinations over the course of the 1970s.[17] As is visible from

[16] See European Monitoring Centre on Racism and Xenophobia (2005, 158–159). For a more detailed discussion of racist violence data, see Chapter 4.
[17] Specifically, Figure 1.2 includes localities where immigrants from the New Commonwealth and Pakistan constituted at least 5 percent of the overall population (according to the 1981 census)

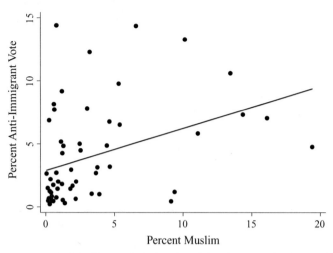

FIGURE 1.3. Muslims and the local anti-immigrant vote, Great Britain, 2004.

the figure, the presence of ethnically distinct residents does not necessarily pro-voke a negative native response at the ballot box. Anti-immigrant candidates foundered in several local authorities with a high percentage of immigrants. The relationship between the immigrant presence and the anti-immigrant elec-toral backlash is not particularly strong (the correlation is $r = .27$, $p = .12$, and falls to $r = .18$, $p = .30$, once the observation displaying the highest vote share is removed).

On their own, these correlations of course do not constitute a test of the argument that ethnic difference causes intergroup conflict. Collective anti-immigrant mobilization can manifest itself in additional ways not captured in this simple graph. Moreover, it might be the case that identity-based threats are more intensely felt once immigrants have settled for longer periods of time and have had a chance to express their religious beliefs and pursue their cul-tural practices in the public realm, for example through the building of mosques and temples and the enactment of multicultural policies. Indeed, as Figure 1.3 illustrates, more recently the relationship between the xenophobic vote and the Muslim presence seems to be stronger ($r = .38$, $p = .004$), apparently sup-porting those who fear that a clash of civilizations will fracture Europe's cities. However, it is also the case that Britain's open citizenship regime, as well as Muslims' capacity to get out the community vote, has turned this group into a pivotal electorate in many localities. To examine whether Muslims' electoral

and shows the highest vote share that the National Front received over the course of the 1970s. In one case (Bradford), I use vote shares of the "Yorkshire Campaign against Immigration." Election data come from Rallings, Thrasher, and Ware (2006); demographic data are available at www.nomisweb.co.uk.

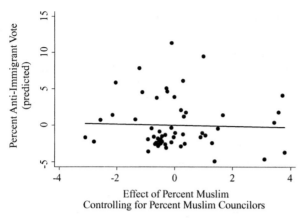

FIGURE 1.4. Muslims and the local anti-immigrant vote, controlling for Muslim political power, Great Britain, 2004.

clout provokes xenophobic opposition at the polls, I coded all elected councilors according to their religious backgrounds.[18] As revealed in Figure 1.4, once we take into account localities' share of Muslim councilors, the relationship between the Muslim presence and the far-right vote vanishes completely.[19]

These figures serve to illustrate patterns and to raise questions, rather than to test or refute arguments. Although they should instill a dose of skepticism among those who favor essentialist explanations for immigrant–native strife, on their own they cannot rule out the notion that identity-driven threats matter in producing conflict: In Great Britain, residential concentration can translate into local political power, at least for groups that mobilize on election day. Ward-level elections and geographically concentrated, high-turnout Muslim electorates therefore produce a very high correlation between the share of Muslims in the local population and the share of councilors this group elects.[20] Looking at snapshots only thus makes it tricky to identify whether religion, elections, or both cause conflict. Selecting contexts in which the immigrant

[18] Figures 1.3 and 1.4 are based on election results in the 2004 British local elections in the local authorities where candidates of the British National Party (BNP) ran. I chose the 2004 contests because (at the time of data collection) information on the first and last names of candidates and councilors (which allows for more reliable coding than reliance on last names alone) was available electronically only for 2004 (see www.andrewteale.me.uk/2004/index.html). I first coded all names according to their religious background (Muslim or non-Muslim) myself and next repeated the exercise with the name-coding software program ONOMAP, with the help of Pablo Mateos (see also Mateos 2007). The correlation between these two measures is $r = .99$. The share of the Muslim population, first measured in the 2001 census, is available at www.nomisweb.co.uk.

[19] The straight line in Figure 1.4 represents the slope coefficient of percentage Muslim, which drops to $b = -.08$ ($SE = .33$), once percentage of Muslim councilors is controlled for.

[20] In the present sample the correlation is $r = .94$ ($p = .000$, based on 56 observations); the full sample (including local authorities where the BNP did not run) shows a correlation of $r = .88$ ($p = .000$, based on 144 observations).

presence does *not* lead to immigrant electoral power would get us closer to the true sources of conflict. More fine-grained evidence that tracks local processes over time would further reveal how and if immigrant political behavior links up with conflict outcomes and whether immigrant electoral mobilization is a cause, rather than an outcome, of xenophobic opposition.

Still, students of immigrant conflict may encounter additional difficulties. Migrants' economic characteristics, for instance, often correlate with their national and ethnic backgrounds. Compared to other faith groups, Muslims in Great Britain are most likely to live in economically deprived areas and to suffer from unemployment and low earnings themselves (Office of the Deputy Prime Minister 2006; Saggar 2009). Similar trends are present elsewhere. In France, the employment rate of those born in Portugal is 72 percent, compared with 50 percent among those born in Morocco, while in Norway this figure reaches 48 percent among Pakistani-born residents, 60 percent among those born in the former Yugoslavia, and 79 percent among migrants from Denmark (OECD 2008, 128–129). More generally, the fact that the degree of ethnic distance between a particular group of migrants and the majority population often coincides with the group's degree of economic disadvantage (at least in the contemporary European setting) casts doubt on accounts that, without taking into consideration these economic realities, view cultural predispositions or religious beliefs as the principal drivers of immigrant–native and immigrant–state conflict. Such arguments gained currency in the aftermath of the 2005 French disturbances (cf. Schneider 2007). Across the channel, a common view also held that the cultural background of West Indian youths was to blame for this group's involvement in the antistate riots of the 1980s (see Chapter 3). This book aims to show that such analyses are misguided.

Empirical Approach

Without probing the political and economic circumstances that immigrant groups face locally, inferences about the relationship between culture and conflict are difficult to sustain. Moreover, the snapshots just given here cannot disentangle whether ethnic difference, electoral behavior, economic conditions, or their interactions are behind immigrant conflict. To overcome these problems, I adopt a set of empirical approaches that, when taken together, aim to isolate the causes of immigrant conflict. Within Great Britain, I study the incidence of both types of immigrant conflict across groups that share many characteristics, but that vary in the degree of political power they wield locally. I do so by analyzing cross-group patterns of immigrant–native and immigrant–state conflict as well as by examining the dynamics that underlie smaller-scale acts of racist violence. To better identify the processes that link economic shortages and immigrant electoral clout to conflict outcomes, I further investigate the occurrence of immigrant conflict in four locations over time. In the first pair of cases, immigrants are politically powerful but economic scarcity varies; in the second pair, economic conditions are held constant but immigrants differ in their electoral clout. Additionally, in two cases in which immigrant groups are politically pivotal, economic conditions, and as a result immigrant–native conflict, change over time, giving us more confidence that the variables identified by the theory – as opposed to unobserved city-level factors – generate conflict outcomes. Moving beyond Great Britain, we see that an examination of immigrant conflict in Germany demonstrates the significance of immigration regimes in influencing economic scarcity in local immigrant destinations, while a briefer investigation of the French case reveals the important interactions between economic shortages and immigrant electoral power in shaping local conflict outcomes.

Finally, though the theory advanced in this book is meant to apply to many democratic settings, I should mention why I chose the countries I did. First, for the purposes of the study of immigrant conflict, Great Britain is a good case because it provides researchers with wide variation in local economic conditions, as well as with differences in ethnic minorities' political behavior. As mentioned, Britain's postwar immigration regime initially did not impose strict rules and guidelines; postcolonial arrivals were not subject to settlement restrictions within Britain and central government did not provide immigrant-receiving localities with much support. As a result, immigrants faced varied local economic conditions.

Second, while unemployment rates among two of the major immigrant groups (those originating from the West Indies and the Indian subcontinent) were quite similar during the first decades after initial arrival and these two groups' destination locales exhibited comparable economic conditions (see Chapter 3), levels of local electoral participation and hence political power varied significantly across the two groups. More generally, it is thus also not the case that migrants' local electoral participation hinges on economic contexts. Migrants have failed and succeeded to mobilize in settings where economic goods are undersupplied; local turnout is not correlated with economic conditions (see Chapter 2).

Third, studying British localities offers practical advantages, in that qualitative and quantitative data tend to be more readily available when compared with that of other countries. I was thus able to draw on a host of town histories and reports dealing with local experiences of immigrant settlement as well as ward-level data on residents' country of birth and their ethnic self-identification (the latter since 1991). Information on residents' ethnicity is generally much more difficult to obtain in other European countries. Finally, and again in contrast to many other countries, detailed data on racist violence are available at the level of the local authority, albeit only for more recent years, and are also deemed to be of higher quality than those collected by most other European countries (Oakley 2005; Goodey 2007).

In terms of the cross-national comparisons, Germany and Great Britain make for a good pairing. The two countries share a host of similarities: Both opened their borders to large-scale immigration in the postwar period, resulting in the settlement of immigrant communities that are ethnically, culturally, and religiously distinct from the indigenous population and, on average, of lower socioeconomic status than their native counterparts. While Germany is a federal system and Great Britain formally a unitary state, local government has significant discretion over the allocation of public resources in both settings. Local electoral laws differ across countries – based on proportional representation in Germany and plurality in Great Britain – but should, if anything, make it easier for small, anti-immigrant parties in Germany to gain votes; for most of the period under study, this has not been the case. The main relevant features that distinguish the two countries are the economic foundations of their immigration regimes and the stringency of their citizenship laws, and it is these differences that account for the observed cross-country variation in local immigrant conflict. The next section provides an overview of the book and lays out the empirical strategies in greater detail.

Plan of the Book

The rest of this book is organized as follows. In Chapter 2, I present the central theoretical framework in greater detail. I discuss my conceptualization and measurement of immigrant–native and immigrant–state conflict; provide fuller definitions of economic scarcity and immigrant political power; and explicate the logic that links local economic scarcity and immigrant political power to the two faces of immigrant conflict. I next clarify the assumptions that underlie my explanatory model and the conditions under which I expect it to hold. The chapter also spells out how this book speaks to the wider scholarship on immigrant and ethnic conflict.

The second part examines the occurrence of the two types of immigrant conflict across groups and economic conditions in Great Britain. In Chapter 3, I study how the incidence of immigrant–native and immigrant–state conflict has differed across immigrant groups and over time, from 1950 until 2008. Disaggregating immigrant conflict in this way reveals intriguing patterns of variation. First, when looking at large-scale immigrant–native and immigrant–state riots, we observe that the majority of both types of conflict have occurred during economic downturns and in economically deprived settings. Second, in comparing South Asians and West Indians, I show that immigrant groups who share many characteristics (such as economic characteristics at the level of the individual and the settlement locality or prejudicial attitudes directed against them), but who vary in the extent to which they have been able to translate their presence into local political power, also differ with regard to their involvement in immigrant conflict. In addition to laying out these patterns, the chapter presents an overview of Great Britain's postwar immigration and citizenship regime as well as politicians' approach to the new electorate, thus providing the local political and economic contexts in which immigration and hence immigrant conflict are embedded.

Chapter 4 focuses on explaining one indicator of immigrant–native conflict, smaller-scale acts of racist violence. The aim here is not to argue that racist violence strictly adheres to the logic of immigrant–native conflict proposed here, but rather to show that individual acts of racist violence can be part of the larger fabric of such conflict. To do so, I first demonstrate that this type of hate crime covaries with the success of anti-immigrant parties across Britain's local authorities. Next, the chapter employs data on racist violence in Greater London's thirty-two boroughs (local authorities) to establish that the in-migration of politically powerful South Asian migrants provokes increased attacks against this group, which are further compounded by rising levels of economic deprivation. Conversely, in-migration of politically less powerful migrants of Caribbean an African origins has no effect on the victimization of this group. Differences in economic conditions across boroughs magnify these effects.

Part III presents structured comparisons of four cases to test my theory of immigrant conflict.[21] Whereas Chapters 3 and 4 show that variation in the economic and political factors that I highlight coincides with variation in immigrant conflict patterns, Chapters 5 and 6 deploy local-level evidence to trace the processes and causal pathways connecting local economic conditions and immigrants' electoral leverage to conflict outcomes. The case selection and over-time study pulls apart economic conditions, immigrant political power, and immigrant ethnic backgrounds, while the narratives contain the in-depth, microlevel information that links causes to effects and establishes that immigrant electoral mobilization is not a product of xenophobic agitation.

The first two cases, that is, Ealing and Tower Hamlets, are two London boroughs that were both characterized by immigrant political power and economic scarcity in the first two decades of settlement. Whereas pressures on state-controlled resources did not persist in Ealing, though, the shortage of such goods intensified in Tower Hamlets. As a result, Ealing has overcome immigrant–native conflict even as the electoral power of its immigrant population has expanded. Tower Hamlets witnessed a deterioration of intergroup relations over the same time period, and, moreover, immigrant–native conflict has varied within the borough as a result of a decentralization experiment that resulted in varied housing-allocation rules across wards. I next contrast two Midlands cities, Leicester and Birmingham, that shared similar economic trajectories but have varied in immigrant political power. In the first decades of immigrant arrival, amidst increasing economic scarcity, immigrants in Leicester were politically powerful, while their counterparts in Birmingham lacked electoral clout, leading to immigrant–native conflict in the former and immigrant–state conflict in the latter. Additionally, economic scarcity declined in Leicester over time, easing intergroup tensions and earning the city its reputation for multicultural harmony.

Covering immigrant groups of different backgrounds, these cases show that economic conditions and immigrants' political behavior, rather than national or ethnic origins per se, account for conflict outcomes. The major immigrant groups in Ealing and Leicester are of Indian descent and include Sikhs and

---

[21] On structured comparisons in case study research, see George and Bennett (2005).

Hindus, while the largest minority group in Tower Hamlets consists of Bangladeshis (most of whom are Muslim). Birmingham is home to sizable shares of Indian, Pakistani, and West Indian migrants (the latter are predominantly Christian). As I discuss later, other sources of variation and similarity, such as residential concentration or demographic balance, also fail to map onto conflict dynamics.

Part IV takes a step back and addresses national differences in immigrant conflict. In Chapter 7, I apply my theory of immigrant conflict to the German context. Here, guest-worker migration is associated with lower levels of local conflict than both the inflow of political refugees (asylum seekers and ethnic Germans) into Germany and the postcolonial migration into Britain. I argue that the regulations that guided guest-worker migration reduced the likelihood of local economic shortages and hence the incidence of immigrant conflict. Such guidelines were largely absent in the two other migration regimes. Chapter 8 investigates how the features of France's postwar immigration regime interacted with the country's political institutions to produce high but varying levels of both immigrant–native and immigrant–state conflict. This analysis is followed by a discussion of recent trends in immigration, naturalizations, economic scarcity, and decentralization across European countries, developments that influence the likelihood of the two faces of conflict. Chapter 9 concludes by restating the main findings and discussing some of the book's theoretical and policy implications.

In advancing my argument, I exploit different sets of sources, such as government and party archives, local and national newspapers, census statistics, elite interviews, and the secondary literature. Quantitative sources include data on racist violence and xenophobic party vote shares, surveys measuring immigrant political behavior, and native attitudes. Interested readers can find more details on my use of respective sources in the upcoming pages.

2

A Theory of Immigrant Conflict

In this chapter, I present an in-depth overview of the book's theory of immigrant conflict. I begin by providing my conceptualization of both types of conflict, immigrant–native and immigrant–state conflict, and go on to describe their indicators. I next address the two key independent variables, economic scarcity and immigrant political power. In specifying when and where immigrant destinations are likely to be affected by economic scarcity, I pay particular attention to the role of national immigration regimes. The rules and regulations that govern the arrival, recruitment, and settlement processes of migrant newcomers, I argue, can have important effects on the supply of and demand for economic resources at the local level. In my discussion of immigrant political power, I highlight the importance of national political institutions – citizenship regimes, voting laws, and local electoral systems – as well as the political behavior of immigrant-origin ethnic minorities. Having established the conceptualization of the key variables, I turn to an exposition of the book's theory of immigrant conflict. In spelling out the logic that underlies the central argument, I further draw attention to the importance of state actors – rather than market actors – being in charge of disbursing material goods that are in short supply. Moreover, I state the assumptions on which the book's theoretical model of immigrant conflict rest. In the final section, I consider how the book's argument contributes to the existing literature on intergroup conflict and the domestic consequences of immigration.

Immigrant Conflict

To understand the incidence of contemporary immigrant conflict, I start with the premise that not all confrontations involving immigrants are the same. I group immigrant conflict into two theoretically and empirically distinct phenomena: immigrant–native and immigrant–state conflict. *Immigrant–native conflict involves the sustained confrontation between members of the immigrant and the native populations in a given locality.* While minimal, this definition nevertheless clarifies a great deal of what immigrant–native conflict does and does not capture. First, my conceptualization involves a temporal and a spatial dimension, in that intergroup conflict has to be sustained, covering a period of at least five years, and it must occur in a given locality. In my definition, a series of confrontations (subsequently defined) in a specified location add up to a situation that can be characterized as immigrant–native conflict. I select a lower threshold of five years to exclude short-term anti-immigrant agitation that commonly accompanies initial immigrant settlement. Rapid demographic change associated with immigration often provokes antagonism among a small cross-section of the native population; I investigate under what conditions such hostility becomes entrenched over time and a cause for collective opposition.

Confrontations between immigrants and natives must be hostile if they are to constitute intergroup conflict, but they need not be violent. The local electoral performance of xenophobic parties with fiercely anti-immigrant platforms is thus an indicator of intergroup conflict, as is the formation of social movements that campaign for anti-immigrant policies (such as compulsory repatriation or exclusion of immigrants from public services) as well as groups that organize to defend immigrants' physical safety. Violent attacks and nonviolent demonstrations directed against individuals, groups, or properties based on their membership status as immigrant-origin minorities or natives count as indicators of immigrant–native conflict.

Empirically, these indicators tend to occur together. Grievances that lead some to vote for anti-immigrant parties may lead others to commit violent acts against immigrants.[1] In addition, right-wing parties and pressure groups legitimize or even foment racially motivated attacks, and street demonstrations by pro-immigrant lobbies to protest racist assaults that start out peacefully may be disrupted by racist agitators, turning into violent disorders. Together, these measures are meant to capture both the incidence and the severity of immigrant–native conflict. I pay particular attention to intergroup violence and local collective action. For example, a situation in which political elites try to foment anti-immigrant sentiment by injecting xenophobic rhetoric into political debates, but in which local anti-immigrant organizations do not emerge, xenophobic parties fail at the polls, and violence against immigrants does not ensue does not constitute immigrant–native conflict.[2]

While violent protests directed at immigrants are indicators of immigrant–native conflict, care must be taken to differentiate "homegrown" violence (which counts) from "imported" violence (which does not necessarily count). A street disturbance instigated by skinheads who traveled from elsewhere in

---

[1] Drawing on cross-national racist violence data, Koopmans (1996) suggests that the success of anti-immigrant parties effectively substitutes for nativist attacks. I maintain that these two conflict indicators tend to coincide and address this point empirically in Chapter 4.

[2] See Brubaker, Feischmidt, Fox, and Grancea (2006) on the importance of distinguishing between elite-level ethnonationalist discourse on one hand, and the resonance of this type of rhetoric among local populations on the other.

the country to invade the immigrant area of a town is thus not a reliable sign of local immigrant–native conflict; it depends on the extent to which the local population takes part. Similarly, well-publicized hate crimes or acts of antistate violence have been shown to inspire copycat acts.[3] As long as such acts remain singular events and are not preceded or followed by similar actions, it is not appropriate to characterize a location that has witnessed a copycat incident as ridden with immigrant conflict.

Whereas immigrant–native conflict encompasses the sustained confrontation between members of immigrant and native communities, *immigrant–state conflict involves the sustained confrontation between immigrant communities and state actors in a given locality*. Similar to my conceptualization of immigrant–native conflict, my understanding of immigrant–state conflict is based on the manifestation of antistate behavior in a particular location over time. Antistate behavior can take peaceful and violent forms, and it can be small scale and large scale in nature. Nonviolent manifestations of immigrant–state conflict may involve, for example, the dissemination of views opposing the state's actions and expressing distrust in state institutions. Smaller-scale violent incidents often include low-level flare-ups between immigrant-origin youths and state actors, but they have also been shown to be targeted at social workers and other public officials. Antistate violence can further include property damage inflicted on public buildings, such as fire stations, police headquarters, and public schools as well as *indiscriminate* attacks (i.e., not selecting on the basis of ethnicity) on private property, such as automobiles. While major disturbances represent the most destructive and visible instances of immigrant–state conflict, smaller-scale attacks by immigrant-origin youths on public buildings or employees and ongoing battles with local police and local state institutions tend to comprise the less widely publicized anatomy of immigrant–state conflict in which these larger events are embedded (e.g., Benyon 1984; Garbaye 2005; Wieviorka 2005; Mucchielli and Le Goaziou 2006).

As I discuss in Chapter 3, where I address some of the empirical hurdles involved in correctly identifying rioters' actions, the measurement of large-scale incidents of immigrant–state and immigrant–native conflict presents researchers with difficulties. It is therefore crucial to place these large, complex events in context and to study the smaller-scale instances that precede major riots. In my investigation of immigrant–state conflict in Great Britain (and in Birmingham specifically), archival records and local histories from the early 1970s show that altercations between migrants and state actors were commonplace in many inner city areas before riots erupted in the 1980s. Likewise, scholars have shown that antistate riots in France followed a series of more minor confrontations between migrant youths and the forces of law and order (e.g., Zancarini-Fournel 2004); and that strained relations between African American residents, the police, and city hall were harbingers of the "Black

---

[3] See Green, McFalls, and Smith (2001, 495–496) for a brief review of the potential importance of media-based demonstration effects in the commission of hate crimes.

Rebellion" in the United States during the 1960s (e.g., Sugrue and Goodman 2007). These studies, as well as the evidence presented in this book, suggest that the police often act as the local representative of a state that is perceived to act in discriminatory ways. Conflictual relations between immigrant groups and the police thus indicate immigrant–state conflict.

I turn next to a discussion of the two variables that together determine whether local immigrant destinations will experience confrontations between immigrants and natives, confrontations between immigrants and the state, or no confrontations at all.

Economic Scarcity and Immigrant Political Power

The main focus of this book is the study of immigrant conflict as it occurs in the localities where immigrants settle. Local immigrant integration does not, however, occur in a vacuum. National institutions crucially determine the recruitment and settlement of immigrants and shape immigrant incorporation into domestic economic structures. Immigration regimes vary in all of these dimensions. Some countries deliberately follow economic rationales and carefully plan and execute the immigration and settlement of foreign labor by integrating this workforce into their labor market institutions and welfare states. Others might also open their borders to economic migrants, but they may take few measures to assist these workers in their search for housing or employment. Still others might pay less attention to the economic needs for foreign labor but allow large-scale inflows of migrants for political reasons, for example because of historical obligations arising from colonial or wartime experiences.

Once settled in the new country, migrants also have differential access to political rights. Some countries bestow these newcomers with enhanced political privileges, allowing them to participate in local elections or to naturalize as citizens of the destination country, while other countries set strict limits on the scope for immigrant political behavior. Countries differ widely in the laws that govern whether, when, and which immigrants can become citizens. Moreover, there is variation within and across countries (as well as within countries across immigrant groups) with respect to the extension of the local franchise to noncitizens. The ways in which the state allocates economic and political goods to immigrants thus varies across immigration regimes and political institutions. These differences in the national economic and political frameworks further shape and interact with variation in local *economic scarcity* and *immigrant political power* to produce varied paths of immigrant integration and conflict on the ground.

National Immigration Regimes and Local Economic Scarcity
This section presents how features of immigration regimes may influence economic scarcity in the local areas of immigrant settlement. In the context of this study, "economic scarcity" characterizes a situation in which there is a

shortage of goods desired by both immigrants and natives. Clashes over these goods will be especially fierce if their supply is not easily expanded in the short term, resulting in zero-sum competition. Shortages in education or housing, for example, might be addressed only once new constructions are built. As immigration expert Card (2007, 21) notes, "Although most of the existing research on the economic impacts of immigration has focused on the labor market, immigrant inflows can have other effects on the quality of urban life." The population increase caused by immigrant inflows can thus have significant effects on the availability and cost of housing, education, health care, and other local goods, particularly those that are subject to congestion effects.

As we will see in later chapters, the accessibility of material goods that are in demand among both immigrants and natives varies across countries, and part of this variation can be traced back to immigration regimes. Furthermore, the effects of immigration on local economic scarcity also differ across local immigrant destinations within countries. This type of local variation is especially likely when national immigration regimes do not manage immigrant settlement across cities and towns, adhering to a uniform set of policy guidelines; in this scenario, preexisting local economic conditions will be particularly significant.

I define immigration regimes as the official and unofficial rules that guide the recruitment, arrival, and settlement processes of immigrants.[4] Official rules can, for example, stipulate migrants' skill level, industry, employment conditions, and housing and health care options. They can also specify the rules that delimit the migration of family members, such as making the arrival of dependents conditional on adequate income or housing. These aspects of immigration regimes will have clear domestic economic consequences and influence levels of local scarcity. When immigration regimes are based on noneconomic political or humanitarian criteria, they can also affect local economic outcomes, as countries may grant individuals originating from designated countries refugee status, regardless of how these migrants' skill sets map onto domestic economic needs.

Immigration regimes can have considerable economic repercussions even if they are not based on officially codified rules. States may allow, or even promote, substantial inflows of immigrants without declaring this strategy to be official immigration policy. In France, for example, authorities believed that market signals would be more efficient in attracting foreign labor than state regulations, and therefore they tacitly encouraged the unregulated entry of European and North African migrants in the 1950s and 1960s. These migrants would generally obtain work permits and legal status after they had arrived.[5] In

---

[4] This definition is related to but distinct from Soysal's more wide-ranging conception of "incorporation regimes," which further includes "patterns of policy discourse" in addition to other aspects, such as the political and cultural rights of migrants as well as their associational lives (1994, 32).

[5] See Sturm-Martin (2001, 98–99). On the economic efficiency of illegal immigration, see Hanson (2007).

the United States, employers and migrants circumvented immigration restrictions and border controls throughout the 1990s and 2000s. Even though undocumented workers have become a vital part of the U.S. economy, the lack of an official immigration policy has been associated with high costs for migrants and natives alike (Massey 2007). More generally, from the perspective of local economic scarcity, the unguided arrival of immigrant newcomers often means that localities do not have a chance to adapt their infrastructures to absorb a sizable population increase in a timely manner, and they are also less likely to receive logistical or financial assistance from higher levels of government.

Given the complexity of immigration regimes, one way to think about these regimes' local economic implications is to consider their impact on both the *supply of* and *demand for* material goods at the local level. On the supply side, efforts by government, at times supported by employers, to expand municipal services and infrastructures can prove essential in structuring local economic scarcity. A good that is crucial to the economic welfare of immigrants as well as to natives is access to housing: "Lack of adequate housing has perhaps been the single most persistent and controversial problem related to the issue of social services for migrants" (Freeman 1986, 59). While (labor) migrants tend to initially locate in areas where employment is abundant, housing is often less plentiful. Moreover, the population increase caused by immigration may raise rental prices and housing values.[6] If immigrants place a premium on benefiting from being plugged into social networks (e.g., Waldinger 2005), they might be more sensitive to proximity to friends and family than to housing conditions or prices, creating further strains on the housing market, at least in the short run.[7]

Across countries, we observe significant differences in the extent to which immigration regimes incorporate housing. Some countries prepare for the arrival of immigrants by setting aside vacant housing or constructing new dwellings for these newcomers. While postwar migration to Great Britain was not accompanied by any such measures, German authorities devised programs that would expand the supply of accommodations for guest workers. France also enacted specific policies in the housing field, but, in contrast to its German neighbor, the implementation was insufficient and ad hoc, leading to "chaotic conditions" in the housing market.[8] Cross-national differences also emerge in

---

[6] Investigating American cities, Saiz (2007) finds that immigration has a much larger impact on rental and housing prices than it does on wages.

[7] In the medium to long run, native and immigrant residents may respond to an increase in housing prices by moving, and new dwellings may be built. See Saiz (2007) for a model that incorporates these factors.

[8] Frey and Lubinski (1987, 86). German authorities compiled information on how the housing of immigrants compared to measures undertaken in other European countries; see B134/37467: Federal Ministry of Land Use Planning, Building Industry and Urban Development, October 15, 1972.

the quality of immigrant accommodations.[9] Although early and recent immigrants in Europe have tended to face poorer housing conditions than have their native counterparts, important distinctions across settlement locations and immigrant groups remain (Spencer 2006, 37). As I show in subsequent chapters, the extent to which immigration regimes address housing has been critical across cities in Europe.[10] From the standpoint of the existing, native population, an expansion of the housing supply implies that immigration will not impinge on native housing needs, at least in the early years of settlement. Seen from the perspective of immigrants, easy access to housing (that is of decent quality) is an important aspect of economic welfare.

The variable supply of other goods, such as education, health care, and social services, can also be tied to differences in immigration regimes. Postwar labor migration to Europe, for example, was accompanied by notably different measures in this regard. In the late 1980s, the Dutch "minorities budget," which included employment, education, housing, social welfare, and health, was almost twice as high as that of its French counterpart, despite France's considerably larger immigrant population. In Sweden, municipal authorities set up centers that helped migrants obtain social services and health care, as well as education and housing. Compared to the Netherlands and Sweden, the British government took far fewer measures to address potential supply shortages in local immigrant destinations.[11] In Spain, the massive rise in both legal and illegal immigrants that began in the 1990s prompted the government to embark on ambitious integration plans several years later. In 2002, these programs had a budget of $1.3 billion, with the majority earmarked for health care, education, and reception centers.[12]

Immigration regimes may also influence the level and type of *demand* that migrants place on local economies. Immigrants' skills and their demographic structure are important factors here. Generally speaking, immigrants who are selected according to skill criteria will have more favorable labor market outcomes than immigrants who arrive for other, noneconomic reasons, such as family reunification or political asylum.[13] Employment obviously directly impacts immigrants' economic welfare, but it also has important implications for local economic scarcity: As immigrants' unemployment risk decreases and

[9] For a brief comparative analysis of immigrants' housing conditions in several European countries in the 1970s and 1980s, see Frey and Lubiniski (1987, 85–89).

[10] In the United States, where there have been few coordinated attempts to address housing pressures caused by immigration, the local impact of immigration on housing markets has also been significant (Ottaviano and Peri 2006; Saiz 2007).

[11] See Soysal (1994, 45–83) for a very useful discussion of what she terms "instruments of incorporation" in the context of postwar labor migration to Europe. See also chapters in Hammar (1985).

[12] As a result of the large degree of regional autonomy in Spain, there are also important local variations in the administration of integration measures. See Calavita (2005, 94–97).

[13] See Bauer, Lofstrom, and Zimmermann (2000) on the link between selection criteria and labor market outcomes.

their earnings increase, they will put fewer pressures on some local economic goods, such as public housing or social services, reducing levels of economic scarcity for a given level of supply. (The same is of course true for natives.) Nevertheless, it is also important to keep in mind that as the character of domestic economies change, so will the effects of skill-based policies on immigrant employment outcomes. Rising unemployment levels and rapid deindustrialization across Europe have meant that many low-skilled labor migrants who initially faced favorable employment conditions would later be out of work or in low-paid jobs.[14] This development also suggests that, over time, the domestic economic consequences of immigration regimes will change.

Turning to the native population, the effect of migrants' skills on native economic welfare (and, by implication, the effects on the demands natives will place on local economic goods) is less clear-cut. According to economic theory, low-skill (high-skill) migrants should put downward pressures on the wages of low-skill (high-skill) native workers.[15] But immigration regimes might again be important in mediating these effects. Guest-worker migration in Germany, for example, was conditional on immigrants being paid the same wages as German workers, a moderating provision that was not in place with regard to postcolonial migration into Britain. Empirically, however, there has been little evidence that immigration has produced significantly lower (or higher) wages among natives, in both the European and American contexts. Neither has it been shown that immigrants tend to displace native workers, a scenario that would be more likely to materialize if, for example, the employment of immigrants at fixed wage levels prompted employers to reduce the overall number of workers.[16] Notwithstanding these findings, one needs to draw distinctions between the aggregate effects of immigration on native wages and employment on the one hand and the distributional effects across localities and individuals on the other. Overall gains can mask individual losses.[17]

The demographic structure of migrants also significantly affects the demand that newcomers will place on local economic goods. In the early stages of labor migration, immigrants are often young and arrive without spouses or children. They will therefore generally make less use of local public resources, such as kindergartens, schools, and hospitals. Moreover, being employed, they

---

[14] See Brücker et al. (2002) for a review of the skills and labor market performance of migrants in Europe.

[15] This prediction is consistent with two prominent models, the Heckscher–Ohlin Model and the Factor-Proportions Analysis Model. For a brief review of both, as well as the assumptions they make and their relevance in explaining immigration preferences in the United States, see Scheve and Slaughter (2001). See also Mayda (2006) for a cross-national analysis of the relationship between native and migrant skills and native opposition to immigration.

[16] For reviews on the findings on immigrations' wage and employment effects and the methodological difficulties involved in arriving at valid estimates, see Brücker and collaborators (2002, 26–31) on Europe, and Borjas (1994) and Card (2005) on the United States. See Dustmann, Fabbri, and Preston (2005) and Pischke and Velling (1997) for analyses of the British and German cases, respectively.

[17] See Straubhaar (1992) on the implications of this distinction for immigration policy.

contribute to the tax base, allowing the state to reap the fiscal benefits of immigration. European guest-worker migration was indeed based on the premise that immigrants would put more in than they would take out (Freeman 1986). As we see later in Chapter 7, this was especially true in the German context.

In many cases, however, primary labor migrants are joined by family members after a stay of several years in the host country. The demands for local economic goods will tend to increase with family reunification, while the per capita tax revenues collected from the immigrant population will likely decrease, since dependents are less likely to be employed than primary labor migrants. Immigrants that arrive for noneconomic reasons, such as political refugees, are also more likely to arrive as complete family units. Furthermore, in many countries, political refugees are entitled by law to access state-provided goods. From the perspective of local economic scarcity, we can thus expect the immigration of political refugees to have a more immediate impact on local economic resources, especially when compared to labor migrants (holding supply constant). As we see later in Chapter 6, the influx of Asian-origin refugee families in Leicester put local schools under pressure. Similarly, the inflow of refugees into Germany in the late 1980s and early 1990s was accompanied by significant resource constraints. Survey research has shown that migrant families who represent fiscal burdens are likely to provoke native opposition[18]; if the arrival of migrants puts additional strains on local infrastructures, such opposition will be compounded. Table 2.1 summarizes some of the implications for local economic scarcity that are associated with various immigration regime features.

Note that immigration regimes can also play a role in dampening the potential negative repercussions that immigration may have on public goods provision. Alesina, Baqir, and Easterly (1999) maintain, for instance, that local electorates vote to lower the share of spending allocated to public goods, such as education, welfare, or health, as their surroundings become more ethnically fragmented: Members of one ethnic group may oppose paying for resources that are shared by members of another ethnic group.[19] Nevertheless, if centrally funded immigration regimes supply these goods, such tensions will be defused locally (though they may gain salience at the national level).[20]

Lastly, if immigration regimes influence local economic scarcity and hence conflict outcomes, they may also change in response to these local developments (Money 1997; Karapin 1999). Policy makers may want to impose stricter entry

---

[18] Hanson, Scheve, and Slaughter (2007) find that differences in the fiscal costs that individuals expect to bear as a result of immigration inflows – which in turn are a function of state tax systems and individual skills – explain variation in attitudes toward immigration policy in the United States.

[19] See Gilens (1999) and Luttmer (2001) for research on individual preferences toward redistribution that is consistent with this argument. For contrasting accounts, see Habyarimana, Humphreys, Posner, and Weinstein (2009) and Hopkins (2009).

[20] On the consequences of immigration for national redistribution, see Roemer, Lee, and Van der Straeten (2007).

TABLE 2.1. *Immigration Regimes and Implications for Local Economic Scarcity*

Features of Immigration Regimes	Implications for Local Economic Scarcity (*holding all else constant*)
Immigrants' employment status	Immigrants who are permitted to work will be in need of fewer state-subsidized goods and will generate higher tax revenues than immigrants who are not permitted to work.
Immigrants' skills	If immigrants with lower skills earn lower incomes and have lower employment rates than immigrants with higher skills, lower-skilled migrants will be in higher need of state-subsidized goods and will generate lower tax revenues than more highly skilled immigrants.
Immigrants' demographic composition	The per capita demand for local resources (e.g., education, health, and social services) will be lower and the per capita tax revenues will be higher for economically active migrants than for children, the elderly, and other economically inactive migrants.
Entitlements for immigrants	Immigrants whose status entitles them to access specific state-provided goods will make higher use of these goods than immigrants who do not enjoy such entitlements, putting pressures on these goods.
Provision of resources	Immigration regimes that adjust the supply of local resources to match the additional demands generated by an inflow of immigrants reduce local resource shortages compared with immigration regimes that do not take such steps.
Resource conditionality	Immigration regimes that make the arrival of immigrants and their dependents conditional on immigrants' employment status, adequate income, or housing reduce pressures on local resources compared with immigration regimes that impose no such restrictions.

requirements or alter migrants' skill mix if the existing regime produces negative local consequences. Yet, scholars who have analyzed the determinants of immigration policy making have tended to paint a more complicated picture of legislative outputs. In addition to local labor market and fiscal effects, legislators' ideology and partisanship (Gimpel and Edwards 1999; Milner and Tingley 2009), interest group lobbying (Freeman 1995), or legal and moral constraints (Joppke 1998) may prevent politicians from retrofitting existing immigration regimes to account for local economic and conflict outcomes. Nevertheless, it should be noted that there could be feedback effects whereby one immigration regime is designed to address the failures of the previous one. Much of this book, however, addresses the effects of postwar immigration regimes that were not developed with countries' earlier immigration experiences in mind. New Commonwealth mass migration to Britain was unforeseen and facilitated by the expansive citizenship code embedded in the 1948 British Nationality Act (Hansen 1999), while a series of bilateral agreements in the 1950s and 1960s between Germany and sending countries provided the foundation of guest-worker migration. Though Britain enacted restrictive immigration legislation beginning in the 1960s, these laws did not effectively address the resource shortages associated with local immigrant conflict (see Chapter 3).

This discussion has emphasized the importance of immigration regimes in determining levels of economic scarcity. Additional dynamics that are not directly related to national immigration regimes, such as expansions and contractions of the economy; slum clearance and urban redevelopment; increases or cutbacks in social spending; or the relocation of both immigrants and natives to escape resource scarcity will also have important implications for the local economic conditions that immigrants, their descendents, and native residents will face.[21] In a similar vein, the labor market outcomes and access to economic goods of later-generation immigrants, and the ethnic minority communities they give rise to, will be contingent on additional factors not captured by the immigration regimes that recruited their ancestors. How destination countries' political economies and welfare states allocate local economic goods across groups will therefore become increasingly critical as time passes.[22]

Summing up, I state that immigration regimes may significantly shape levels of local economic scarcity by having an impact on the supply of, and demand for, local economic goods that both immigrants and natives desire. If such regimes do not contain specific measures that provide localities with the infrastructural capacity to absorb the potential costs and congestion effects sometimes associated with immigration, then much will depend on the ways in

---

[21] The organization of immigration regimes may in fact parallel the organization of political economies. As suggested by Freeman (2004), scholars have not yet explored whether and how "varieties of capitalism" (Hall and Soskice 2001) may lead to variation in immigrants' economic incorporation.

[22] It is also important to bear in mind that I have addressed some of the *local* economic implications of immigration. However, decisions about immigration policy tend to be controversial in part because immigration's economic impacts are distributed unevenly across different levels of government. While the national government may welcome immigration for its presumed beneficial effects on pension systems or inflation, for example, localities may be less enthusiastic, as they could bear the costs of infrastructural facilities that are rising in immigration. Usher (1977), Simon (1999), and Freeman and Kessler (2008) discuss some of these effects.

which local economies are equipped to cope with the population increases that are produced by an inflow of migrants. In addition to immigration regimes, general economic trends and government-spending decisions will affect local economic scarcity and therefore have consequences for the economic welfare of natives and first- and later-generation immigrants.

National Political Institutions, Political Behavior, and Immigrant Political Power

This book seeks to demonstrate that when the demand for local economic resources exceeds their supply, the capacity of immigrants to claim valuable material goods will be crucial in determining the nature of immigrant conflict. As I argue in subsequent text, immigrants' political power often represents the key mechanism that allows these newcomers to obtain scarce goods.

I consider an immigrant group to be politically powerful if its vote is influential in deciding the outcomes of local elections. Access to voting rights is a necessary precondition for political power, but the competitiveness of elections and the extent to which parties rely on the immigrant vote to keep them in power also determine whether a given immigrant voting bloc will be pivotal. This definition of immigrant political power thus privileges formal political participation of immigrant-origin ethnic minorities who can vote in local elections over informal, pressure group activity by immigrants who are barred from casting ballots in these electoral contests.

Sociodemographic characteristics of immigrant groups interact with these formal laws to determine immigrant political power. While national immigration regimes play an important role in determining the availability of economic resources in local immigrant destinations, national political institutions may widen or restrict the scope for immigrant political power at the local level. Moreover, behavioral differences in immigrant groups' ability to turn out in great numbers matter in translating sheer numbers into pivotal votes.

Citizenship laws present the most obvious gatekeepers in allocating rights to electoral participation. Some countries grant their immigrant residents citizenship after several years of legal status, while in others citizenship acquisition represents a long, arduous, and sometimes impossible process. More generally, citizenship laws tend to follow the two broad principles of *ius soli* – whereby those born in the national territory can become a citizen – or *ius sanguinis* – which connects naturalization to ethnic or national descent.[23] For instance, France and Germany have been held up as opposite extremes, with the former embracing a relatively liberal citizenship code based on *ius soli* and the latter imposing more restrictive conditions, tying citizenship to German ancestry (Brubaker 1992). More recently, Germany has brought its citizenship laws more in line with less stringent rules followed in France, Belgium, the Netherlands, Ireland, and the United Kingdom (Howard 2006).

---

[23] In addition, states may consider residence and a spouse's citizenship as grounds for naturalization (Weil 2001).

But not everywhere is citizenship a necessary prerequisite for local electoral participation and hence political power. Within the European Union, for example, EU citizens are entitled to vote in local elections in all member states. Several countries (e.g., Ireland, the Netherlands, Denmark, Belgium, and Sweden) additionally allow citizens of all nationalities to cast ballots in these local contests (Bauer 2007). In sum, the ease with which noncitizen immigrants can acquire citizenship or become eligible to vote in local elections varies across countries; these differences will have implications for the potential of local immigrant political power and, in turn, will help shape the occurrence of immigrant conflict.

While national laws govern access to voting rights, local electoral rules interact with immigrant political behavior to determine whether a given immigrant group will possess local political clout. Electoral rules can be helpful or harmful in promoting immigrants' pursuit of local political power. Immigrant groups that are residentially concentrated may find it easier to elect group members when local elections are contested at the ward level, as opposed to the city at large. In ward-level elections, a municipality is divided up into a number of smaller-sized wards or districts, each of which elects one or more representatives to the city council. In at-large elections, the entire city represents one electoral district, and each voter selects from the same list of candidates. In the study of ethnic minority representation in U.S. cities, "One of the most persistent findings... is that single-member district elections increase descriptive representation of underrepresented racial and ethnic groups on city councils."[24] At-large elections, by contrast, have been found to be less favorable for boosting ethnic minority representation. As we see in future chapters of this book, ward-level elections in Great Britain have been especially advantageous for the political representation of groups that tend to be both geographically concentrated at the ward level and well organized. In France's municipal elections, though, which operate according to at-large rules, geographic concentration does not deliver a comparable advantage to migrant communities (Bird 2005; Garbaye 2005).

These electoral institutions further interact with behavioral characteristics of immigrants to produce local immigrant political power.[25] For example, the capacity of immigrant candidates to induce their co-ethnics to turn out and vote may vary across groups. We also observe that ethnic minority voters differ in the extent to which they use existing electoral institutions and social networks to gain access to city hall. In Denmark, for instance, electors may cast personal votes for their preferred candidates; some well-organized immigrant communities have used this option to great effect, electing fellow migrants to

---

[24] Trounstine and Valdini (2008, 555). The authors provide a brief review of this literature and further find that district-level elections in American cities will increase diversity on city councils when minority groups are concentrated and constitute a sizable share of the population.

[25] For an account that also considers institutional and behavioral variables in the production of immigrant political behavior, see Bloemraad (2006).

many city councils, while others do not draw on their common heritage for electoral purposes (Togeby 2008).

In the preceding paragraphs, I have outlined how differences in immigration regimes and wider economic trends can shape levels of economic scarcity in local immigrant destinations. I have further indicated how national political institutions and immigrant behavior can help or hinder in turning immigrants into pivotal local political actors. The next section brings together these two central variables – economic scarcity and immigrant political power – to develop a theory that explains when and why immigrant–native conflict and immigrant–state conflict occurs.

A Theory of Immigrant Conflict

Immigrant–Native Conflict

The theory of immigrant–native conflict proposed in this book is based on the following propositions. I begin with the assumption that the native population will be more likely to engage in sustained anti-immigrant behavior if such actions are believed to be effective in deterring immigrants from acquiring scarce resources. This assumption in turn implies that the actor who controls the disbursement of these goods is sensitive to anti-immigrant agitation, or that the costs that such confrontations inflict on immigrants themselves are sufficiently high to discourage them from accepting these scarce goods, or both.

A corollary of this implication is that immigrant–native conflict is more likely if the state, rather than the market, allocates scarce resources. When economic goods are distributed by the state, deserting ruling parties in favor of candidates that advocate anti-immigrant policies is intended to increase the costs associated with pro-immigrant resource allocation borne by the governing party. Anti-immigrant organizations and rallies are meant to bring attention to the grievances caused by immigration to politicians and ruling parties. They are also intended to reach a broad public audience, some of whom will abandon incumbents unless policies that appear to favor immigrants are changed. Additionally, anti-immigrant violence and ensuing cycles of reprisals cause some voters to seek out parties who advocate repatriating immigrants, which, these parties claim, would decrease the incidence of violence.[26]

When competition centers on goods that are allocated by the market, the scope for *effective* anti-immigrant activity, though present, is more limited. Not only are market actors, such as employers or private landlords, less sensitive to local voting patterns; during economic downturns they also generally face few incentives to give into demands for resource allocations that favor natives, especially when migrants are willing to accept a lower wage or a higher price.

---

[26] The National Front in Britain adopted this strategy in the 1970s and 1980s (Taylor 1981); the British National Party has also disseminated reports of immigrant-on-native violence during election campaigns (see Chapter 4).

At times, employers will act in the economic interests of natives, but this tends to occur when native and employer interests overlap. For instance, when European economies slowed down and deindustrialized in the 1970s, many employers had an interest in sending back excess low-skilled migrant labor and even provided subsidies for the return journey. Employers did so not because they responded to native pressures, but because they no longer had a need for immigrant workers, whom they perceived to be an impediment to the modernization of production.[27] In other instances, private providers of resources can often benefit from competitive markets. Accounts of local immigrant settlement commonly relate how large numbers of migrant newcomers crowd in single-family homes – a practice that is profitable for landlords who demand excessive rent payments from each tenant – in spite of protests by longer-settled neighbors. Similarly, the indigenous population may object to having realtors sell houses to immigrant families. Nevertheless, as we see in Chapters 5 and 6, realtors benefit from the rising property prices that sometimes follow immigration and thus overcome their own and native neighbors' resistance to sell to immigrants: "Despite a general reticence, white vendors may well sell to coloured households if it seems in their economic interests," wrote a geographer about Leicester's housing market in the 1970s (Phillips 1981, 115).

Given these facts, I expect that competition over scarce resources that are allocated by the state will be more likely to lead to sustained immigrant–native conflict than competition over scarce resources allocated by market actors. Note that I am not arguing that market-based competition will not lead to economic grievances and ensuing anti-immigrant attitudes. In fact, as I mentioned earlier, a growing body of research documents links between individuals' position in the economy and their preferences over immigration policies. I simply claim that *acting* on these grievances will, on the whole, be less effective in bringing about the desired outcomes if the market is solely responsible for the allocation of resources. For anti-immigrant activity to have a payoff, harassment and violence directed against migrant settlers would have to impose sufficiently high burdens on immigrants for them to refrain from taking up private housing or jobs, which may in turn threaten their livelihoods as well. This outcome is certainly conceivable, especially if we consider earlier historical periods.[28] Nonetheless, when local government is responsible

---

[27] For a similar argument in the context of low-skilled migration to the United States, see Chiswick (2006).

[28] Natives have mounted resistance against immigrants well before the advent of systematic state intervention in the allocation of economic goods. When one is applying the argument put forth here to earlier decades and centuries, it is important to keep in mind that variables that are held relatively constant in postwar democracies may change. These include, for instance, the effectiveness of law enforcement and individuals' related anticipated costs of engaging in antistate or anti-immigrant violence; politicians' reliance on the vote to stay in power; or norms about the public use of violence (see Horowitz 2001, 560–565 on changing tastes for violence in twentieth-century democracies). Nevertheless, one could probe whether engaging in anti-immigrant activities was considered even more effective in earlier time periods when

for distributing goods to immigrants, natives who stand to lose such goods to newcomers can use votes and violence to make it costly for both local politicians and immigrants to shift resources away from natives and toward immigrants.

It is further important to underscore that the analytical distinction is not based on the type of goods per se, but on the actor who has control over the disbursement of these goods. State-owned housing, public employment, or area-based government grants are goods that are often linked directly to local government control. The state, though, especially at the national level, also affects resource allocation among immigrants and natives through, for example, regulations that give natives preferential treatment in obtaining jobs or through ethnically based training and employment quotas.[29]

If natives engage in anti-immigrant behavior to protest the state's allocation decisions, what determines these distributional choices in the first place? I begin with the simple assumption that ruling political parties charged with allocating resources to their constituencies will disburse scarce goods to immigrant groups if the expected gains exceed the expected losses associated with such actions. This implies that political parties will only appeal for immigrant votes on the basis of material resources if they assume that the impact of the potential electoral backlash of such action is smaller than the boost delivered by the new immigrant voting bloc. In calculating this trade-off, ruling parties take into account actions of the opposition parties who may pander to natives and thereby increase the electoral backlash associated with pro-immigrant resource allocation.

In the case of immigrants who have access to local voting rights, this calculation is in turn based on the size and concentration of the immigrant vote relative to the relevant electoral boundary and on the organizational capacity of immigrants to induce their co-ethnics to turn out on election day. As we see in subsequent chapters, Labour and Tories thus routinely compared the size of their electoral margins on the one hand with the estimated size of the immigrant vote and educated guesses of prospective native losses in case of immigrant recruitment on the other. However, if immigrants are barred from the ballot box, or if they are eligible to vote but do not do so in significant numbers, ruling parties do not court immigrants' support by distributing scarce goods to them at the expense of their native constituents. Note also that

governments, rather than market forces, were in charge of disbursing material goods, such as, for instance, patronage jobs.

[29] Jones-Correa (2001b) has argued that interethnic strife is often based on competition for state-based goods because their supply is usually relatively fixed and competition as a result is zero sum in nature. I agree that, in the context of state-based resource allocation, zero-sum competition further increases the odds of immigrant–native conflict, but I also suggest that it is not the zero-sum character alone that leads to sustained conflict. See also Hardin's discussion of ethnic conflict and the importance of positional goods (i.e., public office) in the allocation of distributional goods, especially during economically hard times (1995, 57–58).

political parties enjoy much greater leeway when appealing to immigrants on the basis of goods that are not in short supply or not desired by natives.[30]

The identification of group claims is thus critical. In the context of this book, which focuses on immigrant conflict in advanced democracies, immigrant–native confrontations emerge when immigrants make costly material demands to which political parties are responsive. In studies focusing on the electoral incentives behind ethnic conflict in other settings, this may not be the case. For example, Wilkinson's theory of Hindu–Muslim riots in India is based on the important assumption that Muslim minorities "will be willing to 'bid low' in terms of what they demand from majority parties across most issues in order to maximize their security" from Hindu attacks (2004, 140). Being an electorally pivotal group making cheap demands therefore buys government protection from attacks. When it comes to immigrant conflict in advanced democracies, I maintain that natives will not have a reason to engage in such attacks if the presence of immigrants does not reduce their material welfare.

Immigrant–State Conflict

If immigrant political power induces intergroup conflict when resources are scarce, I argue that it is the absence of such power during economically trying times that is likely to compel immigrants to engage in violent and nonviolent conflict with the state. As with immigrant–native conflict, this proposition rests on the assumption that local political actors will only address immigrant needs in times of resource scarcity if the gains associated with the immigrant vote exceed the losses incurred by the anti-immigrant vote that such resource allocation might trigger. I also assume that engaging in antistate actions on the part of immigrants can be intended to highlight the grievances that are seen to have been caused by state neglect. Since the local political process is less receptive to demands by groups that cannot reward politicians at the polls, and local politicians cannot make credible commitments to these groups, acting against the state represents an alternative channel to articulate demands.

By engaging in antistate behavior, actually disenfranchised immigrants who cannot vote or effectively disenfranchised immigrants who fail to translate their presence into electoral power may thus hope that local government will listen to their concerns and initiate a change in state allocation practices.

---

[30] At first blush, national parties do not appear to behave in the same way, as left parties have been shown to be more likely to favor immigrant-friendly policies than their right-of-center counterparts (Lahav 2004; Givens and Luedtke 2005). But the left's support of immigrant interests has varied, and this variation has in part been due to strategic electoral calculations (e.g., the French Socialists' backing away from proposals to grant noncitizens local voting rights in the face of rising anti-immigrant forces in the 1980s, or the German Social Democrats' acquiescence to asylum restrictions in the 1990s). Moreover, in the context of this book, an appropriate comparison of local and national party approaches would have to investigate whether left parties have appealed to immigrant voters on the basis of undersupplied goods desired by natives.

As one youth who was involved in the 1991 disturbances in the ethnically diverse Brussels municipality of Forest proclaimed, "Now we have been heard. The mayor knows that we exist."[31] I thus reject the hypothesis that "greed" will *cause* immigrant-origin ethnic minorities to engage in antistate behavior. For instance, while looting certainly occurred during antistate riots in Britain, research has shown that, in most cases, looters were not locals or ethnic minorities, but were whites who traveled from outside to take advantage of an ongoing riot.[32] Looting also did not feature significantly in the 2005 French riots (Waddington, Jobard, and King 2009).

Why should antistate action pay? Violent antistate behavior is intended to impose direct costs on the local state through property damage and police injury and more general costs in the form of social instability. Incumbents fear a reduction of the local tax base caused by property damage as well as a decline in future investment in areas that are prone to violence. An official dealing with immigrant integration in Frankfurt, Germany, acknowledged, for example, that one reason why the city's mayor tried to keep immigrants "happy" was to prevent riots that would cause investors to flee.[33] Moreover, some voters might punish incumbents for their failure to keep the peace.

To avoid future violence, state actors will consider taking immigrant demands into account. This expectation – that violence could buy politically marginalized groups leverage – has been articulated in the aftermath of the American race riots of the 1960s: "When we sat down at the bargaining table," a black community activist remembers Newark's post-riot political landscape, "an unnamed person sitting with a brick was with us ... The most important weapon was that there had been a riot and the powers that be were afraid of us. They would do anything to keep a lid on black anger" (A. Jacobs 2007, 19).

Everyday violence on a smaller scale, as well as the threat of it, has also been shown to be used by immigrant-origin minorities to extract concessions from local officials in Great Britain (Fitzgerald 1988) and France. On the basis of ethnographic fieldwork in a Villiers-sur-Marne housing project in the Paris region, Mohammed (2009, 166) finds that "violent breakdown has always been seen and feared by local political elites as *the* means of expression by the [ethnic minority] youths and constantly likely to occur" (emphasis in the original). Moreover, Mohammed's fieldwork nicely illustrates the development of politicians' and youths' strategic interactions and is worth quoting at length. After a group of immigrant-origin youths had been suspected of attempting to

---

[31] Rea (2001, 24), citing a quote from *Le People*, May 15, 1991; author's translation.

[32] See Keith (1993). The "greed versus grievance" question has been extensively debated in the context of civil war; see Fearon and Laitin (2003), Collier and Hoeffler (2004), and Kalyvas (2006).

[33] Interview with the author, Frankfurt, Germany, October 2005.

set fire to a municipal building, concessions – rather than punishment – from the mayor's office were forthcoming:

The [youths] did not immediately realise the extent of the local political 'clout' they were now able to exercise. However, it was on the basis of experiences like this that the idea gradually dawned that, by causing social unrest, they were able to achieve collective benefits for themselves.... [Some] ... readily understood that a reputation based on a notorious delinquent past ... could offer the basis for local power and give rise to such benefits as improvements in local housing, jobs, and investment ... such manipulation of the fear of disorder has always enabled about 15 delinquents and known ex-delinquents to carve out a place for themselves in the local government or secure municipal accommodation via a process of patronage. (2009, 167)

This account is revealing for several reasons. First, it demonstrates the logic of immigrant–state conflict in action as antistate violence substitutes for political power. Second, it shows how seemingly random violent events can nevertheless set off strategic immigrant–state interactions and be conducive to the rational pursuit of objectives. In this way, it supports other research that has shown how French minority youths "became fluent in the idiom of bargaining daily social peace against minor services with prominent and powerful city councillors" (Garbaye 2005, 171). Finally, the account, which mentions the targeting of benefits to just over a dozen individuals, is also consistent with the conclusion that immigrant–state conflict, large and small, though prompting politicians to consider immigrant needs, has generally not effected a significant redistribution of resources. This outcome follows from the electoral incentives just clarified: Not only would a native backlash ensue if local elected officials were to respond to such violence by transferring substantial amounts of resources away from their native constituents, but native desertions from ruling parties would also not be balanced against a large enough immigrant vote to secure safe reelection.

British national policy makers recognized this balancing act of assuaging immigrants who may engage in antistate violence without triggering protests from the native population as well (Chapter 3). Indeed, national politicians may also serve as an audience for those who initiate local violence. Antistate behavior can send a signal to higher levels of government concerned with the maintenance of law and order and social peace. As Chapters 3 and 7 show, national policy makers fear the emergence of potentially militant nonstate actors and are inclined to address these actors' grievances in order to forestall violence. In contrast to local politicians, national governments might also be better able to internalize the locally occurring native backlash that could arise if immigrant grievances are addressed, or they can prevent conflict altogether if resources from the center enlarge overall levels of local supply. But national politicians, of course, face electoral realities of their own, which may in turn thwart such actions.

On the whole, then, antistate behavior may generate confined, short-term benefits for ethnic minorities but does not tend to shift resource allocation patterns significantly or in the long run. Unless local economic scarcity declines through an expansion of supply or a decrease in demand (e.g., through the infusion of central government monies, economic growth, or improvements in immigrants' or natives' economic status), thereby allowing local politicians to allocate goods to both groups without impinging on the economic welfare of either, local officials will generally be reluctant to disburse scarce economic goods to a group that cannot return the favor at the polls. Similarly, attacking natives who receive resources that immigrants desire is likely to backfire even in the short term. In this scenario, local politicians still face no electoral incentives to distribute goods to the migrant community, but the size of the electoral backlash by an attacked native population in the event of resource allocations that would favor immigrants would likely be even larger. Furthermore, if natives perceive that antistate violence also hurts their interests – for instance, if indiscriminate targeting turns out to result in the destruction of a large number of native-owned cars – the state must tread very carefully in addressing immigrant grievances.

Finally, in line with my conceptualization of the use of violence (explicated in the subsequent text), I do not claim that all actors involved in violent antistate actions intend to impel the state to change its behavior, but that such intentions represent an important component of immigrant–state conflict.

The causal logic of the propositions just given here is encapsulated in Figures 2.1 and 2.2. Figure 2.1 depicts how national immigration regimes influence and interact with local political economies to generate distinct conflict outcomes. When one is trying to understand when immigration may lead to local conflict, it is useful to examine whether national immigration regimes supply economic goods, helping local infrastructures adjust to the population inflow. If that is the case, then no significant shortages ensue and neither does immigrant conflict. If national immigration regimes do not supply these goods, then we next determine the extent to which incoming migrants demand local economic resources (note that the analyst could also begin by first establishing the demand side). As I discussed earlier, migrants' skill profile and demographic structure play important roles here. When migrants' economic demands are low, neither type of conflict emerges. By contrast, when these newcomers are in need of economic resources, such as social services, housing, and employment, the abundance of these goods in the destination locality will decide whether the locality will witness immigrant conflict. Finally, if local economic resources are underprovided and immigrants face high economic needs, then it is the level of immigrants' electoral clout that will tell us which *type* of conflict will emerge.

The diagram in Figure 2.1 incorporates the national institutions, local conditions, and political behaviors that together yield distinct local conflict patterns. Figure 2.2 displays similar information in very simplified form, from the perspective of the locality and immigrant group. Recall that I have defined *economic scarcity* to describe a situation in which there is a shortage of goods desired by both immigrants and natives; this shorthand definition thus subsumes the aforementioned supply-and-demand components that produce this

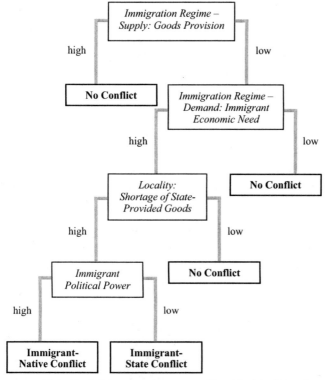

FIGURE 2.1. Explaining immigrant conflict: National immigration regimes and local political economies.

outcome. The evidence will further illustrate that it is specifically when goods allocated by the state are in short supply and high demand that the likelihood of conflict rises.

The top row of Figure 2.2 indicates that neither type of immigrant conflict is likely to emerge when economic resources are generally available. In this

		Immigrant Political Power	
		Low	High
Economic Scarcity	Low	No Conflict	Immigrant Mobilization; No Conflict
	High	Immigrant-State Conflict	Immigrant-Native Conflict

FIGURE 2.2. Explaining immigrant conflict: The local level.

scenario, incumbents can disburse material goods to the immigrant-origin constituency without fear of a native backlash: Distributing goods to immigrant minorities does not come at the expense of natives. Moreover, immigrant electoral mobilization does not lead to conflict (upper-right box). In the lower-left box, when immigrants lack electoral leverage and economic goods are scarce, ruling parties will refrain from allocating limited resources to a new, nonpivotal constituency, for this would hurt their existing voter base. Native residents will thus refrain from mobilizing against their immigrant neighbors, but immigrant-origin minorities are likely to protest state neglect by turning against local government. Finally, when immigrants do possess the political clout to induce local politicians to allocate scarce resources to them, and this distribution impinges on the welfare of natives, natives will punish incumbents and immigrants by voting for anti-immigrant parties and by engaging in other forms of immigrant–native conflict (lower-right box). Given this logic, we should not observe both types of conflict occurring in the same locality at the same time, unless it is home to multiple immigrant groups that display low and high levels of political power, respectively, in the context of economic scarcity. The empirical chapters that follow bear out this prediction.

This theory of immigrant conflict explains the varied incidence of immigrant–native and immigrant–state conflict across immigrant groups, localities, and countries. Postcolonial immigration to Great Britain occurred in the relative absence of state intervention, and it was instead facilitated by the fact that Commonwealth migrants were part of the former British Empire. As British subjects, immigrants from the former colonies initially faced few immigration restrictions, but they also generally had to find accommodation and employment without state assistance. In the absence of regulated state recruitment and settlement policies, differences in local political economies played a large role in immigrant integration. Because postcolonial migrants had access to citizenship upon arrival, the variation in the use of this electoral potential and differences in economic conditions on the ground together explain the varied patterns of immigrant conflict across groups and areas of settlement.

A comparison between West Indian and South Asian immigrants will demonstrate that the settlement of immigrants from the West Indies, while concentrated in particular cities and towns, is quite dispersed at the level of the electoral ward. In contrast, Indian, Pakistani, and Bangladeshi migrants have settled in close-knit communities that are concentrated both across and within towns. Moreover, strong ethnic ties among South Asian minorities – much less in evidence among their West Indian counterparts – have contributed to this group's ability to deliver the "ethnic vote." In short, South Asians tend to possess local political power (putting them in the right column of Figure 2.2), but political clout tends to elude West Indians (putting them in the left column).[34] When economic resources are scarce, South Asian immigrants are much more likely than their Caribbean counterparts to acquire these valued goods and

---

[34] On differences in political participation across these two groups, see also Maxwell (2008).

in turn become targets of anti-immigrant agitation, resulting in immigrant–native conflict (lower-right box in the figure). Absent political power, immigrants are much less likely to claim economic resources distributed by the state, leading them to protest against state neglect (lower-left box). As Chapters 5 and 6 demonstrate, variation in immigrant electoral power and economic conditions also explains the incidence and type of immigrant conflict across locations, holding constant the immigrant group in question. The structured, over-time comparisons of four British local authorities further allow me to rule out the idea that dense social networks and concentrated settlement – rather than the electoral power they give rise to – drive conflict outcomes within Britain.

Investigating immigrant conflict across countries sheds further light on the importance of immigration regimes and political institutions in producing immigrant conflict outcomes on the ground. Chapter 7 shows that the institutions underlying Germany's guest-worker migration put the country's immigration experience in the upper-left corner of Figure 2.1 and the upper-left box of Figure 2.2. Guest workers were recruited during times of economic prosperity, and the state, together with employers and unions, assisted in their settlement, accommodation, and employment. The immigration regime aimed for economic integration, but citizenship and voting laws ruled out political incorporation; guest workers could not vote in local elections and German citizenship remained elusive. When resources became scarce as a result of economic downturns, competition between natives and immigrants in the settlement locations was significantly reduced – especially when compared to Great Britain – as the state followed the guidelines of the guest-worker scheme that put native economic needs explicitly ahead of those of the migrant workforce, and immigrants lacked the political leverage to induce state actors to disburse economic goods to them. Moreover, Germany's immigration regime alleviated economic deprivation among migrants and therefore helped prevent instances of antistate behavior because its stringent regulations forced or persuaded economically unsuccessful migrants to leave the country. Lower levels of conflict were thus traded off against (involuntary) departures.

As time passed, the rules that had initially guided the guest-worker regime began to lose some of their relevance, the German economy experienced a lasting recession, and steps were taken to naturalize guest workers and their descendents. The probability of both types of immigrant conflict increased as a result. Finally, while my main focus is on the guest-worker regime and its effects on immigrant conflict, I also show how the sudden influx of migrants (ethnic Germans and asylum-seekers), whose status gave them privileged access to state resources during a time when these goods were in short supply, caused brief but fierce local-level anti-immigrant mobilization. In this particular case, such regulations effectively substituted for immigrant political power – but the general absence of such power also meant that, once the rules were changed, migrants lost many of their entitlements.

Assumptions, Concepts, and Scope Conditions

Before delving into the empirical study of immigrant conflict, let me first clarify some of the assumptions and conceptualizations that underlie the book's model of immigrant conflict, and let me indicate how this book contributes to the existing literature on immigration and ethnic conflict.

Assumptions

As just laid out, the logic of immigrant conflict makes several assumptions pertaining to the relationship between immigrant political representatives and their constituencies and between local government, local goods, and immigrant groups. First, groups that possess political power are assumed to make claims for economic goods if their members are in need of such goods. This is often, but not always, the case. If ethnic minority groups are in need of economic resources, but they do not believe or expect that the state should provide these resources, then both types of conflict are much less likely to occur.

May such expectations vary across settings? One could imagine, for example, that immigrants of the second generation, having been born in the "host" country, are more likely to be outspoken in their demands than their immigrant parents. If true, the incidence of immigrant conflict would rise with generational succession, holding all else constant. Empirically, of course, not all is held constant. First-generation (labor) migrants tend to arrive when employment is available and as single workers, relieving pressures on local resources. Even so, the historical record does show immigrants of the first generation petitioning for valued material resources. By the late 1960s, immigrants in France, for instance, had begun making vocal demands as they went on strikes to lobby for higher quality housing, albeit with limited success (Lequin 2006a, 416). In Germany, first-generation immigrant workers were involved in industrial disputes and strikes, sometimes joining their native counterparts, other times going it alone (Kühne 2000, 56; Göktürk, Gramling, and Kaes 2007, 42–44). Chapters 5 and 6 also show first-generation immigrants campaigning for economic resources in Britain.

Expectations about the state's delivery of economic goods could also vary across immigrant groups. If groups do not want to claim economic resources from the state even though they might be in need of them, then the occurrence of immigrant conflict should decrease. One group that may fall in this category is migrants of Chinese origin in Britain. Only about one in five ethnic Chinese casts their ballots in local elections; this group has not made advances in local electoral representation; and it has also not voiced significant demands.[35] As one local official put it, the "Chinese never ask for anything... they point blank

---

[35] Turnout rates are based on my analysis of the 2003 Home Office Citizenship Survey. See Appendix B for details.

will not accept any support from the council."[36] A local councilor also lamented the lack of involvement among the Chinese in his town, where councilors could not tell which party they would vote for.[37] Reports of Chinese involvement in either type of immigrant conflict are largely absent.

But what happens if immigrant groups *do* want state-based resources, but their representatives are unable to supply them? This brings me to the second assumption: The use of political power refers to substantive and not merely descriptive representation. Political power indicates that immigrants and their descendents receive the goods they lobby for.[38] Nonimmigrant politicians can thus represent the interests of their minority constituents if the latter use their electoral leverage to induce them to do so. By contrast, immigrant leaders who are elected into town halls but who, intentionally or unintentionally, fail to deliver goods to their co-ethnic constituents do not in fact use their group's electoral muscle to attain valued resources. In this case, natives have few reasons to stage anti-immigrant campaigns, and immigrants have more reasons to protest against the political leadership and take part in immigrant–state clashes, even if it contains co-ethnics.

Finally, the model assumes that local government exercises control over the distribution of state resources. Empirically, many goods that are in demand among both immigrants and natives, such as state-subsidized housing, access to local public services, types of public-sector employment, and area-based government grants, are indeed under local control, or, in the case of some central or federal government programs, require considerable assistance from local elected officials.[39] However, when local government actors have no discretion over the disbursement of these goods, immigrants' local electoral power will matter much less in affecting patterns of resource allocation and hence immigrant conflict. The same is true at the level of the immigrant group. Some migrants are entitled to certain government goods and local officials are required by law to allocate these goods to them, even if the former have few political rights. In this case, immigrant status stands in for electoral leverage. According to the general logic of the argument, natives should also object to such allocation rules in settings when such goods are scarce and when the state

---

[36] Interview with the author, Leicester, England, March 2005. This official thought that the Chinese stayed neutral and unengaged in political affairs because of their desire to maintain good relations with China.

[37] Interview with the author, Oxford, England, November 2004.

[38] See Pitkin (1969) for a distinction between substantive and descriptive representation and Mansbridge (1999) for a discussion of how the latter can enhance the former.

[39] The goods that fall under the purview of local government do vary across time and countries, variation that produces implications for the incidence of immigrant conflict (see Chapter 8). However, even in the United States, where powers of local government have been said to be limited (Peterson 1981), recent research suggests that city halls have exercised discretion over the distribution of a wide range of goods and services (Trounstine 2008). On linkage mechanisms between voters and politicians more generally, see Kitschelt (2000).

might prove responsive to native claims (see the discussion of ethnic Germans in Chapter 7).

Summing up, the central theme running through these assumptions is that the mechanism linking immigrant-origin minorities to conflict is their capacity to claim scarce economic resources from the state that are desired by both immigrants and the native, majority population. In democratic settings, electoral power is often the precondition for this ability.

Concept: Immigrants and Ethnic Minorities

In addition to these assumptions, the theory developed here and tested in the following pages encompasses conceptualizations of immigrants, violence, and immigrant mobilization that have to be spelled out in some detail. This book uses the term "immigrant" to apply to both first- and later-generation immigrants. It also uses the term "ethnic minority" to signify immigrant populations, reflecting both common parlance and the fact that many of the numerically sizable minority groups in advanced democracies of the past half-century have recent immigrant origins.[40]

Should we maintain the immigrant or ethnic minority labels across generations for the purpose of studying local-level immigrant conflict? To assess whether the immigrant label is appropriate beyond the first generation, one could investigate how long different generations identify with their countries of origin. Along this metric, immigrant status can be quite sticky. In the United States, for example, surveys conducted over the course of the 1970s showed that only 13.5 percent of the population either indicated no ancestral country or stated "American" as their ethnic ancestry. The vast majority of whites who fell in this category – 97 percent of so-called unhyphenated whites – had been in the United States for at least four generations (Lieberson 1985, 172–175). In other words, identification with the ancestral country – at least in a traditional country of immigration – may persist for a long time.

Most of the material in this book, however, tends to deal with first- and second-generation immigrants. The book covers the occurrence of immigrant conflict involving populations that dominated immigration flows from the postwar years to the end of the twentieth century. In Britain, these include migrants from the subcontinent and the Caribbean.[41] In Germany, the largest single group of guest workers hailed from Turkey, with smaller contingents originating from Southern Europe, while immigration beginning in the late 1980s was dominated by ethnic Germans from the former Soviet Union as well as by refugees from Eastern Europe and the former Yugoslavia.

---

[40] I acknowledge that some find the terms "immigrant" as well as "ethnic minority" offensive and have instead opted for the term "person with a migration background," a terminology I will not use for stylistic reasons.

[41] By 1981, the population born in the New Commonwealth and Pakistan was two and half times larger than the population born in Ireland, four times the size of those born in the European Community, and ten times larger than the foreign-born hailing from the Old Commonwealth countries of Australia, Canada, and New Zealand (see www.nomisweb.co.uk).

In the case of Britain, one might wonder whether selecting a time period in which predominantly nonwhite groups arrived on the island's shores prevents us from studying the effects of skin color on conflict. Migrant groups that are racially similar to the majority population and who might, as a result, be less prone to be involved in immigrant conflict than darker-skinned newcomers are not the focus of the British case examined here. Yet, as Benjamin Franklin's earlier quoted statements about the inassimilability and complexion of German settlers illustrates, similar skin colors have not necessarily ensured cross-ethnic solidarity. In Britain, natives also considered white migrant populations of earlier decades to be ethnic outsiders. When Irish migration was at record highs in the mid-nineteenth century, the Irish were regarded as both racially and, more obviously, religiously distinct. Newspaper articles reflected racial stereotypes. They depicted members of this group as having "the unmistakable width of mouth, immense expanse of chin and 'forehead villainous low' so characteristic of the lowest Irish" and derided their "ape-faced, small-headed" features.[42] The Irish, who tended to live in squalid conditions and occupied the lowest rung on the socioeconomic ladder, also became the target of sustained anti-immigrant activity. Accounts of their reception in the nineteenth century talk of "racial savagery between Irishman, Englishman, and Scot" (Foot 1965, 82), pervasive "work-related anti-Irish violence" and "serious rioting" (MacRaild 1999, 166, 168). The decreasing involvement of the Irish in local conflict over the years must thus be seen not in light of their outward appearance but in the context of Irish socioeconomic improvement, a pattern that is also consistent with the upward mobility and conflict trajectories of Jewish and, more recently, of Indian immigrant-origin communities.[43]

Returning to the discussion about the terms employed in this book, using the term "immigrant" to go beyond the first generation captures the notion that the immigration regime that recruited the first generation has an impact on the life experiences (such as the economic integration) of the second and perhaps even the third generation.[44] Employing the terms "immigrants" and "ethnic minorities" interchangeably further conveys that immigrant status is meant to also denote minority status: In the time period spanned here, postwar immigrants and their descendents do indeed constitute numerical minorities

---

[42] Handley (1947, 105, 108), quoting undated articles appearing in *The Guardian*, most likely published in the 1840s or 1850s.

[43] As another group of white immigrants, East European and Russian Jews also encountered considerable resistance among sections of the British population (see, e.g., Foot 1965, 85–102; Fishman 1997). Over the course of the twentieth century, both the Irish and Jews experienced significant upward mobility (Hornsby-Smith and Dale 1988; Godley 1997) and have become much less likely to fall victim to xenophobic mobilization. By the end of the twentieth century, the socioeconomic position of British Indians had also improved markedly, and this group's participation in immigrant conflict has declined.

[44] The belief that parents' immigrant status influences the social and economic integration of their French-born children has motivated unofficial data-collection efforts based on "foreign origin" and "ethnic belonging" in France, where official statistics may not record citizens' ethnic or national ancestry (Kastoryano 2004, 69).

in their settlement cities. Conversely, immigrant groups that had arrived in previous decades and centuries may by now identify as being part of the larger "native" majority population in many urban settings – at least with reference to more recent immigrant groups. Nevertheless, as cities turn into majority-minority areas amid continuing new migration, who counts as an immigrant, a native, or a member of an ethnic minority community – and the roles of each in the production of immigrant conflict – must be reevaluated in studies that examine "immigrants" and "ethnic minorities" in the twenty-first century.[45]

Concepts: Violence

Violence is one important component of immigrant conflict. In the present study of immigrant conflict (which occurs in otherwise peaceful settings), I assume that the causes of violence, directed against immigrants or natives on the one hand and state institutions on the other, are similar to the causes of other indicators of immigrant conflict. My analysis thus assumes that individuals who engage in anti-immigrant or antistate violence do so in a goal-oriented way.

Ascribing rationality to violence is contentious. The interdisciplinary literature on hate crime identifies both expressive and rational motivations in the commission of such violence. On the basis of research in Scandinavia, for example, Björgo (1993, 40) labels anti-immigrant attacks comprising arson, bombings, and shootings as "terrorist violence," to underscore that these types of attacks are meant to achieve a specific objective. He goes on to state, however, that "in most cases these various [expressive and instrumental] motives are woven together in a complex way."[46] Others have depicted how hate crime in 1950s urban America was employed systematically to drive out black neighbors: "The violence that whites unleashed against blacks was not simply a manifestation of lawlessness and disorder. It was not random, nor was it irrational.... It involved thousands of whites, directly affected hundreds of blacks... and indirectly constrained the housing choices of tens of thousands of blacks fearful of harassment and physical injury" (Sugrue 1996, 233). Even if some individual whites may have acted on irrational impulses, their actions were part of a larger grassroots campaign that pursued specific, well-articulated goals.

In the context of the ethnic riot, Horowitz sums up the tension between expressive and rational motivations as follows: "Since the riot involves passion and calculation, the sources of explanation reside in realms appropriate sometimes to psychological and sometimes to strategic behavior. Violence has

---

[45] The analysis of racist violence in Chapter 4 uses data from 1999 to 2005. As a result, I control for the share of preexisting ethnic minorities in a local authority, a variable that does affect victimization patterns.

[46] See Dancygier and Green (2010) and Chapter 4 on the motives driving hate crime. See also Petersen (2002) on the role of emotion in ethnic violence and Kalyvas (2006, 23–28) on the varied aims of political violence.

so many wellsprings of action that the varied repertoire of the fox, rather than the single-mindedness of the hedgehog, is more appropriate to the explanatory task" (2001, xiv). While individual perpetrators may thus be driven by emotion and rationality, collective actors, such as xenophobic political parties, may foment this type of bigoted violence strategically, aiming to further expose the costs associated with immigration (Taylor 1981; van Donselaar 1993, 52).

Though I acknowledge its multifaceted nature, I also assume that violence can be one element of a larger strategic objective. First, in the context of immigrant conflict, violence directed against ethnic groups or state institutions often serves a specific communicative function. The empirical evidence will illustrate, for example, that natives can commit attacks against immigrants to deter the latter from appropriating "their" resources and to send a message to political actors that they disapprove of having to share scarce goods with immigrant-origin minorities. Similarly, evidence presented in Chapter 6, as well as the research cited earlier on antistate violence in France, shows that immigrants may engage in confrontations with state actors or participate in antistate riots to signal their dissatisfaction with state practices and to wrest concessions from the state. Second, violent acts do not occur in a vacuum but are embedded in specific political contexts, economic conditions, and social environments. In the case of violence targeted against ethnic minorities, criminologists, sociologists, and anthropologists have demonstrated that such attacks are part of a larger process of victimization and proliferate when the attacks enjoy the tacit or explicit support of a wider cross-section of the "perpetrator community" whose racist resentment, I will show, is in turn a function of the local political economy.[47]

In a similar vein, minority communities may express solidarity with those who attack property and are battling the police. For instance, Rea's ethnographic work has shown this to be the case in the context of immigrant–state conflict in Brussels, where a sense of solidarity and "neighborhood consciousness" (*conscience du quartier*) sanctioned the rioters' behavior (2001, 68). Likewise, in Birmingham, post-riot reports show community leaders to be sympathetic to rioters' actions (see Chapter 6).

While my analysis of minority violence against state actors will thus also demonstrate that such behavior follows a systematic pattern that is tied to the articulation of collective grievances on the part of immigrant-origin groups, I do not maintain that all those who engage in violent antistate behavior operate according to identical motivations. For example, riots in France exhibit signs of both "protest and delinquency." Nevertheless, though they generally lack organization, "This does not mean that they lack in rationality. The young rioters, for instance, are violent but they are rather careful with ordinary people. They burn cars or buses, they fight with the police, but they don't attack

---

[47] See, e.g., Björgo (1993), Bowling (1993), Pinderhughes (1993), Sibbit (1997), and Foster (1999). On the importance of tacit support in sustaining Islamic extremism in the West, see Saggar (2009).

people" (Wieviorka 2005). I follow those who conceptualize antistate violence as an instrumental action,[48] but I do not aim to propose an all-encompassing, macrosociological or social-psychological theory of political violence. While an abundance of such theories on this topic exists, it has been generally acknowledged that the wide reach of the phenomena that they seek to explain, ranging from revolutions and secessions, to riots and strikes, has resulted in a poor fit between theoretical predictions and empirical outcomes.[49] Furthermore, I do not group immigrant–state conflict under the rubric of social movements, as they have been conceived in the literature. Though larger instances of such conflict constitute contentious collective action, they tend to lack the organization and network structures said to underlie full-fledged social movements (Tilly 1978; Tarrow 1998, 6).[50] Rather, I combine both structural and rationalist approaches of contentious action (McAdam, Tarrow, and Tilly 2001, 20–22) in specifying under which conditions we are likely to observe immigrant conflict, and I assume that individuals pursue certain objectives when they engage in such conflict.[51] At a minimum, these structural conditions can be shown to be conducive to violence; at best, they can be shown to motivate individual decisions to engage in violent behavior. In short, this study does not argue that violent behavior on the part of natives or immigrants is never expressive or follows only one motivation, but it does claim that the strategic use of violence by groups and individuals represents a crucial feature of immigrant conflict.

Concepts: Mobilization

Immigrant conflict is distinct from immigrant *mobilization*. More generally, ethnicity can be socially or politically mobilized without producing ethnic conflict or violence (Laitin 1986; Olzak 1992; Chandra 2001, 2004; Lieberman 2003; Fearon 2006; Beissinger 2008). Rather, ethnic mobilization – the organization of groups along ethnic lines – is a necessary condition for ethnic conflict to occur. Indeed, scholars have argued that the relative ease of mobilization of ethnic groups who share the same language, territory, culture, or preferences contributes to the emergence of ethnic conflict (Bates 1983). However,

---

[48] On rationality in riot behavior, see, e.g., Piven and Cloward (1971) and Fording (1997) for the American context and Wieviorka (1999, 2005) for the French case.

[49] Horowitz (2001, 34–42) reviews these theories (e.g., frustration-aggression theory, relative deprivation theory, and resource mobilization theory) and provides a critique.

[50] Research on Great Britain (Scarman 1982, 74–77) and France (Cesari 2005; Wieviorka 2005) concludes that antistate riots have lacked organization. The Kerner Report, which investigated over twenty U.S. inner-city riots, "found no evidence that all or any of the disorders or the incidents that led to them were planned or directed by any organization or group – international, national, or local" (Kerner Commission 1968, 89).

[51] Scholars studying the major disturbances involving African Americans during the 1960s have also sought to identify the city-level characteristics and community conditions that may prompt individuals to engage in violent behavior. See Spilerman (1970, 1976), Olzak and Shanahan (1996), and Myers (1997). See Thompson (2000) for a review of literature that also covers the 1992 Los Angeles riots.

we observe ethnic mobilization for nonethnic as well as for nonconflictual purposes. The U.S. Democratic Party's recruitment of immigrant electorates in the 1930s thus certainly occurred along ethnic lines, but this mobilization served to build a coalition in support of the New Deal (Gamm 1989).

Ethnic mobilization for ethnic purposes is also a routine occurrence in plural democracies, but such action need not impinge at all upon members of ethnic out-groups. In the case of immigrants this is especially likely to be true, as this group requires specific goods and services, such as assistance with the setting up of cultural and religious infrastructures, or with access to local and state bureaucracies and immigration authorities, all of which are more easily achieved through organization at the group level and through connections with these organizations and their leaders at the level of the individual. As one Pakistani-origin councilor in Bradford put it, "Pakistani councillors here have to do ten times as much work as white councillors because we have to help people who do not understand the British system."[52] Writing about contemporary immigration in the United States and Canada, Bloemraad finds that "Newcomers believe that coethnic politicians better understand the interests of the community and take these interests to heart" (2006, 55).

In brief, being linked to one's ethnic group "provides a convenient handle for political organization to press claims on government and to interpret government to group members" (Horowitz 1985, 81). Scholars have thus attributed the link between ethnic mobilization and political machines in the United States to immigrants' need for a "buffer against an unfamiliar state and its legal minions." At the same time, ethnic mobilization of this kind familiarized immigrants with the American party system and "fostered their integration into American life" (Cornwell 1964, 30, 33), thus sowing the seeds of its own destruction. For this reason, ethnic leaders of immigrant groups might even intentionally stall the assimilation of their co-ethnics, since the status of these intermediaries is inversely related to their groups' assimilation to the new country.[53]

Empirically, ethnic mobilization can of course trigger immigrant–native conflict when the pursuit of these ethnic goods constitutes a threat to native interests. The building of a mosque may thus be presented as a threatening proposition, taking away funds and land or undermining the native population's sense of identity, for example. By the same token, ethnic mobilization for nonethnic purposes, such as gaining access to certain occupations traditionally held by

---

[52] *The Times*, "Asians seize on fast route to Westminster," September 30, 1994. This councilor went on to argue that the special needs of migrant communities and their co-ethnic representatives' appreciation of these needs required the election of co-ethnic MPs.

[53] This relationship between ethnic leaders and their constituents also extends to the economic arena. See Kwong's account of Chinese entrepreneurs in New York City who draw "a veritable color line that keeps their [Chinese] workers from all external contacts" and who use their economic status to "maintain social and political control of the community" (2001, 83–84). See also Laitin (1998) on the impact of "in-group status" on assimilation decisions in the linguistic realm.

natives only, can become framed in zero-sum terms. In sum, ethnic mobilization for ethnic goods can lead to ethnic conflict as can ethnic mobilization for nonethnic goods. Nevertheless, it is necessary to draw analytical and empirical distinctions between ethnic mobilization and ethnic conflict and to investigate under which conditions the former induces the latter.[54]

Furthermore, electoral mobilization does not depend on economic conditions; the two central independent variables – immigrant political power and economic scarcity – do not move in tandem. It is not the case, for instance, that immigrants only lobby councils and try to boost community turnout when their economic welfare is at stake, or that economic hardship necessarily prompts get-out-the-vote drives among immigrant-origin minorities. In Deptford, southeast London, for example, a borough characterized as "grim, grimy, dilapidated, with the mark and even the smell of poverty everywhere," election observers concluded that "immigrants are difficult to reach or organize, and prefer to keep out of politics" (Sherman 1965, 106, 118). Similarly, in nearby economically challenged Brixton, there was a "strong impression . . . that most West Indians do not vote" (Sharpe 1965, 28). In Birmingham, shortages in education, housing, and social services also did not lead to successful political campaigning among the city's ethnic minority electorate. On the flip side, electoral participation and the election of immigrant-origin candidates continued in Ealing and Leicester as economic conditions improved (see Chapters 5 and 6), while in Bradford, representatives of the Pakistani-origin electorate made strong showings in local elections, but these politicians did not tend to lobby for much-needed economic concessions and instead concentrated on delivering religious goods to their constituents (Dancygier 2007a). Quantitative analyses of 1997 British survey data further reveal that unemployment – both at the ward and at the individual level – does not lead to increased turnout during elections among immigrant-origin voters.[55]

Finally, it is not the case that immigrant voters only make an impact at the polls when native voters stay at home, or that the competitiveness of elections significantly determines their mobilization efforts.[56]

---

[54] Chandra (2001) provides a very useful discussion along these lines, clarifying the conditions under which demands made by ethnic groups may lead to ethnic conflict.

[55] To obtain these results, I ran probit analyses employing data from the Ethnic Minority Survey that was part of the 1997 British General Election Study (Heath and Saggar 2000). When disaggregated by group, however, too few Black Caribbean and Bangladeshi respondents lived in local authorities holding council elections in 1997 (a precondition of being asked about turnout at the local level) to generate results. Other surveys containing ethnic minority oversamples (e.g., the 2003 Citizenship Survey; see Chapter 3) do not tend to disclose respondents' locality, thereby making it impossible to test the importance of contextual factors in determining turnout.

[56] In the four locations studied in Chapters 5 and 6, immigrants did not organize effectively in Birmingham even though the city's average turnout rates were the second lowest among the four. Moreover, I performed statistical significance tests that confirmed that turnout rates in Birmingham as well as electoral competitiveness (the vote margin between the two largest parties) were not significantly different from those in the comparison city of Leicester, where immigrants did mount effective mobilization campaigns. Ealing, where Indian migrants became

Scope Conditions

In light of these assumptions and conceptualizations, I expect my argument of immigrant conflict to hold in *democratic settings where immigrants settle legally*. The majority of immigrants that settled in Western Europe during the postwar decades fall within these scope conditions. For obvious reasons, electoral leverage cannot be a factor in immigrant conflict in nondemocracies. Some regimes combine autocratic forms of government with wealth distributions that are strongly skewed toward small immigrant-origin ethnic minority populations in control of key sectors of the economy, an outcome that tends to anger the impoverished majority. In such settings, the political leadership – not relying on the majority's vote to remain in office but expecting to reap financial benefits from the minority's economic prowess – has at times clamped down on antiminority activity while at other times allowing riots to occur and using the resented minority as scapegoats when convenient (Rakindo 1975; Chua 2004). Compared with their democratically elected counterparts, autocratic elites may thus more directly influence the anticipated costs of engaging in antiminority violence. Such costs could also deter immigrants from engaging in antistate behavior.

Another important scope condition refers to the actual settlement of migrant groups in the specific locations and their relationships with indigenous communities and political actors in these areas. Migrants that are perpetually in transit or that settle for a short period of time only, such as political refugees whose claims for asylum have been denied after a brief stay, do not fall in this category. Furthermore, it follows that the theory does not account for the success of far-right parties if it were to occur in areas that are largely devoid of immigrants. Motivations other than dissatisfaction with local ethnic diversity and its repercussions cause voters to opt for such parties in these settings.

Finally, the theory applies to legal immigrants, but it might be less accurate in predicting immigrant conflict when it comes to illegal settlers. Illegal status greatly reduces the scope of immigrant behavior. Undocumented immigrants might not claim resources for fear of native reprisals and the unwanted exposure that ensues. Their illegal status and fear of deportation could also inhibit them from participating in violent or nonviolent antistate behavior.

Implications

The book's theory of immigrant conflict produces several implications for the study of intergroup conflict, ethnic politics, and the domestic consequences of immigration. First, the book shows that it is important to disaggregate

politically powerful, registered the highest overall turnout rates but the borough is statistically no different from Birmingham when it comes to electoral competitiveness (importantly, the average vote margins in Leicester, Ealing, and Birmingham do not mask skewed distributions; their standard deviations are very similar). Tower Hamlets' margins and swings are more erratic, but the increasing electoral competitiveness was in part a product of Bangladeshis' mobilization, rather than inducing immigrant turnout (see Chapter 5). These calculations are based on data contained in Rallings, Thrasher, and Ware (2006).

contemporary immigrant conflict into the two types proposed here. This distinction is warranted on empirical grounds. But it also sheds light on the operation of "racism" or "prejudice" in contemporary democracies. So far, I have not said much about the role of racism, either at the level of the individual or within the functioning of governmental and nongovernmental institutions. This is not because I dispute its relevance. Indeed, individual countries as well as the European Union have implemented laws to combat both kinds of racism and to facilitate the incorporation of immigrants and ethnic minorities on a more equal footing with the majority population. Rather, I seek to uncover how differences in national and local contexts produce varied incentives for individuals and groups to behave in racist ways, which in turn lead to different outcomes: immigrant–native conflict, immigrant–state conflict, or no conflict at all. My approach is thus not necessarily inconsistent with macrosociological theoretical accounts that trace the origins of race and racism and their construction in contemporary societies,[57] but it illuminates how, even within the confines of one larger historical backdrop, behavioral manifestations of prejudice vary as individuals respond strategically to given contexts.

This conceptual framework links up with the study of ethnic conflict more generally, where contextual factors have been shown to exert important incentives on group behavior, whereas the association between prejudice and conflict still remains tenuous.[58] It also speaks to recent scholarship on the operation of racism in the American context, which recognizes the institutional and organizational underpinnings of racist *actions*. Here, scholars have criticized the field's preoccupation with studying racism as an irrational, social-psychological phenomenon at the level of the individual on the one hand, or as a deep-seated, structural component of American society and institutions on the other. There remains, however, "surprisingly little theoretical or empirical analysis of what leads individuals to commit racist acts."[59] This study aims to do just that.

In doing so, the book not only takes into account the actions of natives but also takes seriously the behavior of immigrants. I build on the work of others who show that environmental and institutional factors importantly shape the political behavior of ethnic groups (e.g., Laitin 1986; Fearon 1999; Chandra 2004; Posner 2005; and Yashar 2005) and of immigrant groups specifically (e.g., Ireland 1994, 2004; Koopmans and Statham 2000; Koopmans et al.

---

[57] For an introduction to these theories, see Back and Solomos (2000) and Winant (2000).

[58] In a review of the scholarship on prejudice and ethnic conflict, Green and Seher (2003) document that the establishment of an empirical association between bigoted beliefs and bigoted actions still eludes the field.

[59] See Frymer (2005, 373). See Bonilla-Silva (1997) and Frymer (2005) for a review of macrosociological theories of racism, a critique of the existing scholarship on race and racism, and for calls to view racist behavior as a rational response to specific institutional environments. For recent research that takes contextual determinants of *attitudes* toward ethnic out-groups into account, see Oliver and Mendelberg (2000), Gay (2006), and Bowyer (2009). Bowyer's interesting results, which disaggregate white English opinion by out-group, are consistent with the main findings presented in this book.

2005; Garbaye 2005; cf. Marrow 2005; Bloemraad 2006). But I also show that within the same institutional environment, differences in the social organization of ethnic groups matter in producing distinct political outcomes. In combining ethnographic and sociological insights with institutional analysis in the context of ethnic politics, I take up the call to study the "micro-contextual factors [that] tend to be particularly decisive in determining the electoral success of ethnic minority candidates" (Bird 2005, 431).

The book also contributes to the comparative study of intergroup conflict as it unfolds on the ground. Comparative studies of locally occurring ethnic conflict have produced important theoretical insights in our understanding of interethnic violence (e.g., Brass 1997; Varshney 2002; Wilkinson 2004). With a small number of exceptions (Weiner 1978; Olzak 1992; Karapin 2002; Hopkins 2010), however, scholars have not yet examined local intergroup conflict between immigrants and natives by using the comparative method. Moreover, there have also been few attempts to systematically explain local variations in the incidence of immigrant–state conflict. As mentioned in Chapter 1, opposition against immigration is most often analyzed at the individual level, using survey research, or at the national level, investigating, for example, the rise and fall of xenophobic parties across countries and over time.

These accounts provide important theoretical insights on which the following chapters build, but we should not assume that the national success of far-right parties necessarily reflects an accumulation of entrenched conflicts in local areas of immigrant settlement. For instance, the stunning 2002 presidential election success of Jean-Marie Le Pen – France's most well-known xenophobe – occurred just after his party had suffered substantial declines at the municipal level. Similarly, variation in individual attitudes is most likely not linearly related to variation in collectively organized local immigrant conflict. Furthermore, local problems often do not match up with their dissemination and perception nationwide. In Ireland, for example, where large-scale immigration is a relatively new and much-discussed phenomenon, only 8 percent of the population considered racist violence "not [to be] a problem at all" but when asked about their local area, 61 percent of Irish respondents held this view. In Denmark, the rise of the xenophobic Danish People's Party is often linked to Islam and its feared effects on Danish society. Nevertheless, researchers who have studied the party's local campaigns have found platforms to focus on mundane issues, such as public transport and care for the elderly. The recent success of the British National Party in several London boroughs also has less to do with the threat of Islamic terrorism in the wake of the London bombings on July 7, 2005 (known as the 7/7 bombings); election leaflets instead focused on the shortage of public housing allegedly caused by recent immigrants.[60]

---

[60] On perceptions of racist violence in Ireland, see the Equality Authority & National Consultative Committee on Racism and Interculturalism (2005, 20). For a brief review of research on
the Danish People's Party, see Documentation and Advisory Centre on Racial Discrimination
(2005, 15). On the British National Party's exploitation of the housing shortage in Barking and

These examples are meant to highlight the potential disjuncture between local and national events, rather than rule out feedback between the two. As I have argued, national immigration regimes interact with local conditions to shape the incidence of immigrant conflict on the ground. Local conflicts can, in turn, gain the attention of national elites who, depending on incentives of their own, politicize immigration and the problems it produces on a nationwide scale. In doing so, political rhetoric (as well as media coverage) might reflect the content of local conflicts, or it might distort them. While local events can thus aggregate upward to attain national salience, it is less likely that national discussion of immigration and immigrants can, *on its own*, produce lasting and organized conflict at the local level. Local grievances sustain local conflicts. Assessing the extent to which the economic, social, and political repercussions of local immigration reverberate throughout a country to produce national outcomes (or the extent to which national discussion of the topic filters down locally) is important but different from investigating what determines these effects in the first place.[61]

The book further adds to the debate about the relative role of economic motivations versus identity-based claims in structuring interethnic conflict. This debate has a long pedigree and has not been resolved. Realistic conflict theory states that conflicting material interests between social groups – themselves products of individuals' self-interested calculations about the costs and benefits of membership – trigger intergroup antagonism. These processes are said to be especially pronounced when members of the dominant group, who have appropriated certain material goods as their own, have to share these resources with minority groups.[62] Social identity theory, by contrast, does not conceptualize shared material interests as a precondition for group identification or conflict; rather, it views such membership as a natural outgrowth of individuals' desire for enhanced self-esteem, which, in turn, leads to the categorization of groups and to a need to perceive the in-group as superior to out-groups.[63] At a theoretical level, both theories present cogent alternatives, and, empirically, many studies find evidence in support of both. For example, most investigations of anti-immigrant attitudes that highlight the role of economic considerations acknowledge that individual levels of tolerance also matter (e.g., Mayda 2006; Hanson et al. 2007). Likewise, studies that draw attention to the importance of identity-based threats in determining opinions about immigrants tend to

---

Dagenham and the local Labour MP's ensuing endorsement of a policy to put the indigenous population first, see *The Guardian*, "Hodges Locals Take Softer Line on Migrants," May 22, 2007.

[61] See Hopkins (2010) for an argument focusing on the interaction between demographic change at the local level and the national politicization of immigration in driving local conflicts.

[62] On rational sources of group identification, see Hardin (1995). See Sherif (1966) for an early social psychological account of the nexus between group membership and competition and Hechter and Okamato (2001, 195–197) for a review of the literature that links economic modernization and labor market stratification to ethnic conflict. For classic American texts on the relationship between racial threat and conflict, see Key (1949) and Blalock (1967).

[63] On the social psychology of intergroup relations, see Tajfel (1982). See also Horowitz (1985).

find that economic concerns also shape these opinions, but their effects are shown to be smaller in magnitude (e.g., Sniderman et al. 2004; Sides and Citrin 2007).[64]

The present study finds that competition over economic goods has been more significant in shaping on-the-ground conflict than struggles over identity-based claims. Nonetheless, it also draws attention to the ways in which groups actually attain such resources. The book therefore does not dismiss the role of group identity, as the previous section on immigrant political mobilization indicates. Shared immigrant experiences often matter in the election of ethnic minority politicians, who are considered to better represent their fellow migrant-origin constituents. By itself, however, group identity and the political representation it may facilitate do not provoke sustained native resistance. It is only when groups use their electoral success to acquire scarce material resources that native residents will engage in conflict with their immigrant neighbors. The general logic of this theory might thus also hold in contexts other than immigration. As long as individuals are able to mobilize electorally as groups and subsequently gain access to valued and scarce goods, those who are excluded may retaliate. Similarly, if (nonimmigrant) groups are systematically marginalized from the local political arena and therefore also neglected in the allocation of resources, they may turn against the state.

Finally, demonstrating empirically that economic conditions outweigh cultural differences is not the same as proving theoretically that economics should trump identity in the production of ethnic conflict. Rather, the analytic significance lies in specifying the conditions and mechanisms that make economically driven conflicts more likely than identity-based rivalries. More generally, one productive way to adjudicate between the relative importance of material incentives on the one hand and cultural motivations on the other is to ask what general conditions and specific mechanisms will make economically based individual and collective action against ethnic out-groups more effective than organizing around identity-based claims, and vice versa.[65] For example, in the context of this study, the fact that immigrant conflict occurs within democratic settings that recognize both individual and group rights in the areas of

---

[64] A few studies explicitly argue that both economic and cultural motivations impact opinions about immigrants and ethnic minorities; see, e.g., Citrin, Green and Wong (1997) and Sniderman and colleagues (2000). Note that tolerance and the individual characteristics that lead to variation in economic interests, i.e., education and skills, tend to be correlated and economically driven opinions about immigration and immigrants might themselves influence tolerance judgments; these endogenous relationships are rarely explored (but see Hainmueller and Hiscox 2007).

[65] For an example of such an approach, see Mughan and Paxton's study of voting for the One Nation Party in Australia, which finds that anti-immigrant attitudes will only prompt right-wing voting if there is a party that "promises to translate [native] fears into remedial government policy if elected to office" (2006, 357). This necessary fit between attitudes, policy preferences, and party platforms may explain why the ecological literature on right-wing voting has not yet produced conclusive results (cf. Golder 2003, 433; cf. van der Brug, Fennema, and Tillie 2005, 540).

religion and culture matters in limiting the content of and scope for effective anti-immigrant actions. At the same time, the fear of Islamic terrorism
has opened up avenues for restricting the cultural and religious practices of
Muslim communities within Europe, which might also have implications for
the local manifestations of future immigrant conflict.

Conclusion

This book argues that the interaction of economic scarcity and immigrant
political power lies at the heart of the two faces of contemporary immigrant
conflict. Though parsimonious, the book's theoretical framework rests on a
set of assumptions, most of which convey the notion that politically pivotal
immigrant groups in fact use their electoral clout to obtain scarce economic
goods from local government, and that local government in turn has discretion over the allocation of such goods. According to the theory, the ability of
immigrant-origin minorities to claim goods during economically trying times
invites a native backlash, while failure to do so will generate minority resentment against a state that is seen to be unresponsive to minority needs. Why
would such actions be effective? When natives engage in anti-immigrant behavior by attacking immigrants and voting for xenophobic parties, their audience
not only consists of members of the migrant community who bear the burden of
verbal and physical attacks, but also includes local politicians, who lose votes
to anti-immigrant parties: Violence and votes thus effectively express native
dissatisfaction with having to share limited resources with newcomers. When
immigrant-origin minorities turn against the state, they also communicate their
discontent with the status quo; engaging in violent behavior is meant to impose
sufficiently high costs on local government to prompt a consideration of ethnic
minority needs in the disbursement of economic goods.

The theoretical model incorporates two key variables, but their varied manifestation in local areas of migrant settlement may result from a number of features. In this chapter, I have clarified how immigration regimes may influence
the supply of and demand for economic goods in local immigrant destinations,
causing differences in local levels of economic scarcity. I further highlighted
some of the political institutions and behavioral characteristics that may help
immigrant-origin minorities become pivotal local voters, or preclude them from
doing so. Countries may simultaneously follow more than one immigration
regime – for example, the recruitment of labor migrants may occur alongside
the arrival of political refugees – and immigrant groups may also vary in their
propensity to turn out on election day. Moreover, economic developments
within countries, as well as differences in the ways in which economic goods
are allocated across countries that are unrelated to immigration regimes, shape
levels of local economic scarcity. In light of this complexity, Chapters 3 through
6 are devoted to testing the theory by exploiting subnational variation in one
country, Great Britain.

INTRODUCTION TO PART II

This book argues that the interaction of local economic scarcity and immigrant political power is at the center of immigrant conflict. As discussed in Chapters 1 and 2, the simplicity of this assertion belies the empirical complexity that one encounters when assembling evidence in support of this claim. One challenge pertains to the isolation of these two central variables. To be convincing, the account offered in this book will have to distinguish economic and political variables from competing factors that may plausibly produce conflict patterns. It will also have to provide good measures of immigrants' political behavior, local economic scarcity, and conflict outcomes.

The evidence put forth in Chapters 3 and 4 represents the first steps in these endeavors. The main goal of these chapters is to show how immigrant groups that share many characteristics, but that have differed in their capacity to amass local electoral clout, have followed different conflict trajectories. West Indian and South Asian migrants arrived in Great Britain around the same time; were subject to the same immigration regime and wider economic trends; enjoyed the same formal political rights; and have occupied similar socioeconomic positions and lived in economically similar towns. Moreover, both groups are ethnically distinct from the majority population and, as I will show, British attitudes were no more acceptant of West Indians than they were of South Asians. Drawing on a variety of local accounts of immigrant electoral mobilization, as well as on quantitative survey data, I demonstrate that the key difference that sets these two groups apart from the perspective of immigrant conflict is the extent to which they have gained electoral leverage at the local level. While Chapter 3 catalogs large-scale instances of immigrant–native and immigrant–state conflict from the 1950s to the present, Chapter 4 continues the cross-group analysis by focusing on one indicator of immigrant–native clashes, the incidence of racist attacks in Greater London, from 1999 to 2006.

In addition to laying out differences in groups' involvement across conflict *types*, a second goal of Chapters 3 and 4 is to demonstrate the correlation between economic conditions and *levels* of conflict, regardless of conflict type.

Put simply, large-scale confrontations between immigrants and natives, as well as between immigrants and the state, have been more likely to occur during economic downturns than in times of prosperity and in local areas that have been particularly hit by economic scarcity than in those that have fared better. Similarly, the statistical analysis shows that smaller-scale acts of racist violence tend to increase along with economic resource pressures. Together, Chapters 3 and 4 thus establish the central roles that immigrant electoral behavior and local economic conditions play in generating conflict patterns across groups, time, and place. Later chapters (Chapters 5 and 6) provide the microlevel evidence that more fully fleshes out the causal chain connecting immigrants' political behavior and local economic resources on the one hand to conflict outcomes on the other.

While I attempt to isolate the variables that cause immigrant conflict by focusing on similar groups that face similar circumstances, Chapters 3 and 4 also employ a range of qualitative and quantitative data to measure immigrant political behavior and economic scarcity. I further make use of a number of different data sources to arrive at measures of the two types of immigrant conflict. In Chapter 3, I collect data on major instances of immigrant–native and immigrant–state conflict, beginning in 1950 and proceeding up to the present day. To assemble my list of these large-scale violent incidents, I rely on secondary sources as well as on newspaper articles (see Appendix A for more detail). I break down riots according to conflict type, location, and the ethnicity of participants (South Asian or West Indian). Some readers might disagree with the resulting list; perhaps I omit instances that some would count as "major," while including events that others deem to be "minor." Moreover, as I discuss in Chapter 3, large-scale disturbances are complex events and can thus be subject to coding errors.

One rationale for choosing major events that have been discussed in the literature and in newspaper articles is to avoid misclassifying riots. Nevertheless, in light of the difficulties that may arise in generating a comprehensive list of large-scale violent conflict events, it is prudent to also gather information on the less conspicuous manifestations of immigrant conflict. By supplementing information on major disturbances with data on the lower-intensity events that generally precede and follow such major outbreaks, we can increase our confidence that the results that emerge from my compilation of large-scale events – that is, the striking differences in the involvement in the two conflict types across groups – are not due to significant measurement errors. Indeed, archival evidence confirms that West Indian migrants were more likely than their South Asian counterparts to be engaged in low-level flare-ups with the forces of law and order. Furthermore, crime surveys have found that minorities of South Asian origin have been disproportionately victimized by acts of racist violence.

Much of the secondary literature as well as the media do not cover the less sensationalist and less egregious developments that constitute the everyday nature of immigrant conflict. This is especially true for low-level immigrant–state conflict. Confrontations between immigrant-origin youths and the state usually have to cross a certain threshold of destructiveness and violence to be noticed by a wider audience. By contrast, governments are – for obvious reasons – quite interested in the relationship between minorities and state actors. Government archives are thus a good source for collecting data on these lesser flare-ups. In Chapter 3, my investigation of British archival sources indeed documents the emergence and entrenchment of small-scale immigrant–state conflict prior to the occurrence of major disturbances and further confirms the group differences that turn up in my catalog of major riots.

Furthermore, public officials tend to be eager to learn about the causes of immigrant–native conflict, especially if the electoral backlash associated with such conflict threatens politicians at the polls. I therefore also investigate government and party archives to collect information about immigrant–native conflict.[1] In addition to archival sources, the chapter also reports findings on immigrant–native attacks that further line up with the group differences identified by the riot count. Chapter 4 provides additional evidence that the determinants of such violence differ across target groups and economic conditions.

Placed within one national context but drawing on a diverse set of data sources, the cross-group, over-time, and cross-sectional analyses of both conflict types presented in Chapters 3 and 4 provide the first set of tests of the book's theory of immigrant conflict.

---

[1] I conducted research at the National Archives (London) and at the Labour History Archive and Study Centre (Manchester). I also draw on files from the Conservative Party Archive (Oxford). I did not visit this archive and thank Jeremy McIlwaine for pointing me to the relevant documents.

3

Patterns of Immigrant Conflict in Great Britain

Great Britain has witnessed large-scale violence involving first- and later-generation immigrants both as targets and as active participants in every decade since the 1950s. What accounts for this violence? In this chapter I present patterns of collective violence involving minorities of South Asian and West Indian descent and provide an explanation for its varied incidence across time, space, and groups.

I begin by cataloging major events of collective violence involving immigrant populations from 1950 until 2008 and classify them into two categories: episodes of immigrant–native conflict and instances of immigrant–state conflict. The most striking pattern that emerges from this compilation is the significant difference in involvement in such conflict across immigrant groups: Whereas immigrant–native violence has tended to occur between South Asians and whites but much less so between black Caribbeans and whites, immigrant–state violence has been associated with minorities originating from the Caribbean islands but to a much lesser degree with South Asians. Scholars studying immigration and race relations in Britain have surely not missed this difference. Nonetheless, as a result of a tendency to emphasize the common "black" (i.e., nonwhite) immigrant experience of racism, analytical distinctions between immigrant groups or conflict types, especially in the period covering the contentious 1970s and 1980s, are rare.[1]

I next turn to an explanation of this phenomenon. I first present an overview of the broad contours of Britain's postwar immigration regime. Immigration to Great Britain occurred without much state planning and was instead a product of its liberal citizenship laws, which allowed free movement and settlement within the former British Empire. State authorities made few provisions for the recruitment, settlement, and employment of migrant workers, but they did bestow them with full political rights. In the absence of central state involvement, local economic and political conditions played a vital role in structuring

---

[1] For exceptions, see Joshua, Wallace, and Booth (1983) and Keith (1993).

immigrant integration on the ground. I next turn to archival correspondence produced by politicians and public officials who themselves tried to understand the causes and dynamics of immigrant conflict. These sources are particularly useful for my purposes, since they contain, draw on, and aggregate multiple local accounts produced by a variety of sources from throughout the country. Distilling these reports into an overall assessment of immigrant conflict, public officials and the police were unanimous in their verdict: Economic competition between natives and immigrants was the main source of conflict between these two groups, while economic deprivation and discrimination suffered by immigrants and perceived to be perpetuated by the state and its representatives were the primary causes of immigrant–state conflict. I further show how this understanding of immigrant conflict paralyzed effective policy making: Failure to address the economic needs of immigrants, policy makers realized, may cause this group to turn against the state, while focusing too much attention on the demands of these newcomers may provoke natives to turn against their immigrant neighbors.

But policy makers failed to understand why this trade-off would affect two of Britain's major immigrant groups differently. Archival records reveal that public officials began to recognize important variation across groups in the involvement of immigrant conflict, differences they themselves acknowledged they were unable to explain. I argue that local immigrant political power is the missing link in accounts that focus solely on the economic bases of immigrant conflict. I employ qualitative and quantitative indicators to demonstrate how close ties of kin, caste, and clan have produced concentrated settlement and enabled effective organization among South Asian migrants, attributes that have helped this group gain political clout at the local level. By contrast, as a result of weaker networks among minorities of West Indian origin, this group's settlement in Britain has been more dispersed and its capacity for mobilization less pronounced – developments that in turn have diluted this group's influence in local politics. As a result, minorities of Indian, Pakistani, and Bangladeshi descent have more often been the targets of xenophobic campaigns than have their Caribbean counterparts, while settlers hailing from the West Indies have been more likely than South Asian migrants to engage in antistate behavior.

Immigrant Conflict and Large-Scale Violence: Patterns and Puzzles

In this section, I map out national trends in instances of major violent immigrant conflict. The incidence of highly visible events, such as disturbances involving immigrants as participants, is often taken as a barometer for the quality of intergroup relations nationwide or as an indicator of minorities' integration into the institutions of the host society. Along this metric, the 1980s are considered a low point for race relations, as the number of disturbances spiked and the Thatcher government's stance toward ethnic minorities was marked by indifference, if not outright hostility. It is certainly true that, in many areas, the 1980s represented a low-water mark for race relations. If we paint with too broad a brush, though, we also risk obscuring nuances. Specifically, violent events have to be disaggregated into instances of immigrant–native conflict and episodes of immigrant–state conflict, but many accounts do not do so explicitly. This problem is apparently not just confined to the study of immigrant conflict. According to Horowitz, "There has been a tendency, particularly in the literature on turmoil, to merge antigovernment and intergroup violence" (2001, 7–8).

In the study of collective violence involving immigrants and ethnic minorities, ideological leanings and the political climate at the time of writing often inform the portrayals of these phenomena, and immigrant–native clashes and immigrant–state conflict are lumped into one. For example, academic accounts of the 1980s (often written from a neo-Marxist perspective and in strong opposition to Thatcher's neoliberal orthodoxy) draw attention to the predicaments of the urban underclass, while neglecting the disturbances' ethnic component; "uprisings by entire inner-city populations" (Fryer 1984, 395) or "urban violence" (Hiro 1991, 80) are thus common labels. Closer inspection reveals, however, that these descriptors are somewhat misleading. Such inaccuracy is particularly egregious in the context of investigating ethnic conflict, since the labeling of these events is often highly contentious, reflecting the dynamics of the wider conflict itself. As King notes, "The rhetorical battle for control over defining the event can thus be as much a part of the contestation as violence itself.... Labeling...is a political act" (2004, 449, 452). Similarly, Brass observes that "The struggles to gain acceptance for particular constructions of violent and riotous behavior are inherently political, with important consequences for state policies and resource distribution. The constructions that become officially or broadly accepted are usually far removed from the actual precipitating incidents and from local interpretations of them" (1997, 5).

This tension has most recently come into view in the characterizations of the 2005 French riots. Some considered these events to be indicative of a wider, homegrown Muslim "intifada" and branded them as such, while others, concluding that socioeconomic realities loomed large, eschewed religious labeling.[2] Returning to the scholarship in Britain, I find that, in contrast to accounts that attempt to outline national trends, journalistic and anthropological research that is primarily concerned with the morphology of these episodes is very useful for the purposes of this study, for it identifies participants, their actions, and the sequence of events.[3] Drawing on these sources, I embed these events into the political and economic contexts that allow them to emerge.

As a first step, I catalog major events involving immigrants that have been variously labeled urban or racial, ethnic, or immigrant violence, disorder,

---

[2] According to Cesari (2005), American media have been much more likely to perceive the riots as a manifestation of a European Muslim "intifada" or "jihad," while the French and wider European coverage has mostly focused on the disturbances' social and economic dimensions.

[3] On collective violence involving ethnic minorities in Great Britain, see, e.g., Keith (1987, 1993) and Rowe (1998); also see the sources listed in this chapter in Table 3.1.

unrest, uprising, or riot. The goal of this compilation is twofold. First, it sets up an empirical baseline of the time, location, and character of these events. Second, by distinguishing between instances of immigrant–native and immigrant–state conflict, it establishes variation in one component of each dependent variable.[4] Collective violence is of course a complex social phenomenon, reflecting a multitude of internal and external dynamics (Brubaker and Laitin 1998). Even leaving aside ecological and ideological biases, such events are difficult to study from a purely empirical standpoint. They depend heavily on eyewitness accounts, but different pairs of eyes witness different parts of the same event and may also interpret the same observation in different ways (Clare 1984, 48). Identifying the motives of rioters tends to be even more difficult than establishing their identities. In his review of the literature on riots in the United States, McPhail lists the most commonly mentioned reasons for participating in riots, including "to see what people are doing...to protest 'the precipitating incident'...to loot" or even "to advocate non-violence" (1994, 11).

In short, a host of empirical and conceptual ambiguities plague the study of collective violence. Despite these difficulties, it is possible to classify most instances of collective violence involving immigrants in postwar Britain as representing acts of immigrant–native conflict or acts of immigrant–state conflict, as these categories are still very broad and their observational implications are distinct. I pay particular attention to precipitating trigger events, to the ethnic identity of the participants, and to the selection of their targets. For instance, if police behavior, which members of an ethnic minority group perceive to be discriminatory, sparks a riot in which members of this group attack the police and property but leave white natives unscathed, such an event is coded as an instance of immigrant–state conflict. Note that white natives may also participate in these events, but their presence does not automatically turn an act of antistate behavior into a show of cross-ethnic, class-based solidarity and protest.[5] For example, Keith (1987, 1993), rejecting the notion of the "average rioter," has shown that whites' participation in several British riots in the 1980s was often quite opportunistic, as they traveled from outside to loot unguarded stores, while ethnic minorities tended to live much closer to the scene of the riot.[6] In contrast, an instance of immigrant–native violence may be one in which members of the immigrant-origin population fight members of the indigenous population on the streets or when natives seek out and destroy immigrant-owned property.

---

[4] To keep the distinctions clear and the focus on violence, the following classification does not include demonstrations and counterdemonstrations organized by political parties of the extreme right and left. I also leave instances of violence between different ethnic minority groups – a relatively recent phenomenon – for future study.

[5] An official inquiry into the 1981 Brixton (South London) riots produced evidence that showed "certain white people" assisted in the manufacturing of petrol bombs in a "makeshift 'factory'" (Scarman 1982, 75–76).

[6] Others have also noted that looters formed a distinct group in 1981 (Greaves 1984, 68; Nally 1984, 57).

With these caveats in mind, Table 3.1 presents a classification of the major acts of collective violence involving South Asians and West Indians in Britain, starting in 1950, when large-scale immigration to Great Britain took hold, up to 2008. I gathered these data by using the extensive secondary literature on race relations and "urban" violence and newspaper articles published by *The Times* and *The Guardian* (see Table 3.1 for selected sources; see Appendix A for the decision rules I used in coding these events). The purpose is to generate a list of major instances of violent immigrant–native conflict and immigrant–state conflict in postwar Britain, keeping in mind that collective violence is only one component of immigrant conflict. This classification thus does not indicate whether or not a locality can more generally be characterized as being stricken with immigrant conflict; it simply presents us with one empirical slice of the phenomenon to be studied. Moreover, by focusing on events that have been widely covered because of their scale, I do not include series of minor altercations that, when added up, might also constitute a situation of sustained immigrant conflict. The archival materials that I subsequently draw on do, however, address these more minor incidents and indeed establish a relationship between the slow buildup of low-level tensions and the eventual outbreak of large-scale violence in the case of immigrant–state conflict. Finally, later chapters provide a fuller and more fine-grained picture, relating these major events to the state and dynamics of immigrant conflict in specific localities and disaggregating the events themselves.

Immigrant Conflict and Economic Conditions

Even in this pared-down version, several patterns stand out. One clear trend relates to timing. Most events occur in clusters, most obviously in the spring and summer of 1981, coinciding with a serious nationwide macroeconomic downturn. Between 1979 and 1981, Britain's national unemployment rate had almost doubled from 5.6 to 10.6 percent and the country's gross domestic product fell by 2.2 percent in 1980 and by a further 1.1 percent in 1981 (Hall 1986, 120). The economic indicators in the areas affected by rioting were even direr, especially among the male population. In Lambeth and Islington (two London boroughs) for example, 14 percent of men were seeking work; in Birmingham and Coventry, this share rose to 17 percent and in Liverpool it shot up to 22 percent. In the individual wards within these areas where some of the rioting took place, male unemployment also came close to or exceeded the 20 percent mark.[7] Nevertheless, it is also the case that major disturbances occurred in Oldham, Burnley, Leeds, and Bradford in 2001, when the country's economy was quite healthy. An investigation of the economic indicators in these northern towns reveals, though, that their economic situation compares unfavorably to conditions in the rest of the country. The towns stand out for

---

[7] These figures are based on my calculations of unemployment figures from the 1981 census (Table 5, "Economic Position"), available at www.nomisweb.co.uk.

TABLE 3.1. *Large-Scale Collective Violence Involving Immigrants, Great Britain, 1950–2008*

	Date			Location		Participants		Type of Event	
Year	Month	First Day	Region	Local Authority	Area	West Indian	South Asians	Immigrant–Native	Immigrant–State
1958	9	1	London	Kensington & Chelsea	Notting Hill	x		x	
1958	8	23	E. Midlands	Nottingham	St. Ann's Well Rd.	x		x	
1962	7	31	W. Midlands	Dudley	"Coloured Quarter"	x		x	x
1975	11	5	Yorkshire & the Humber	Leeds	Chapeltown	x			x
1976	8	30	London	Kensington & Chelsea	Notting Hill	x			x
1978	6	11	London	Tower Hamlets	Spitalfields		x	x	
1979	4	23	London	Ealing	Southall		x	x	
1980	4	2	South West	Bristol	St. Paul's	x			x
1981	3	3	London	Lewisham	Deptford	x		x	
1981	4	10	London	Lambeth	Brixton	x			x
1981	5	23	W. Midlands	Coventry	various	x	x	x	
1981	7	3	North West	Liverpool	Toxteth	x			x
1981	7	3	London	Ealing	Southall		x	x	
1981	7	7	London	Haringey	Wood Green	x			x
1981	7	9	London	Kensington & Chelsea	Notting Hill	x			x
1981	7	9	London	Hackney	Stoke Newington	x			x
1981	7	9	London	Wandsworth	Battersea	x			x
1981	7	10	London	Lambeth	Brixton	x			x
1981	7	9	North West	Manchester	Moss Side	x			x
1981	7	10	W. Midlands	Birmingham	Handsworth	x			x
1981	7	10	London	Waltham Forest	Walthamstow		x	x	
1985	9	9	W. Midlands	Birmingham	Handsworth	x			x
1985	9	28	London	Lambeth	Brixton	x			x
1985	10	1	North West	Liverpool	Toxteth	x			x
1985	10	6	London	Haringey	Broadwater Farm	x			x
1995	6	10	Yorkshire & the Humber	Bradford	Manningham		x		x
1995	12	13	London	Lambeth	Brixton	x			x
2001	5	26	North West	Oldham	various		x		x
2001	6	5	Yorkshire & the Humber	Leeds	Hareshill	x	x	x	
2001	6	23	North West	Burnley	various		x	x	
2001	7	7	Yorkshire & the Humber	Bradford	various		x		x

Source: Rex (1982), Scarman (1982), Joshua et al. (1983), Clare (1984), Nally (1984), Benyon (1986), Jacobs (1986), Benyon and Solomos (1987), Keith (1987, 1993), Pilkington (1988), Forman (1989), Graef (1989), Bradford Congress (1996), Rowe (1998), Hansen (2000), Ouseley (2001), Ritchie (2001), Farrar (2002), Bagguley and Hussain (2003), King and Waddington (2004), and Hussain and Bagguley (2005). Note that these are selected secondary sources.

67

their overall levels of economic stress and also for containing large pockets of severe deprivation.[8]

In spite of this correlation between economic stress and immigrant conflict, both in space and time, the twin faces of the phenomenon prevent us from drawing a straight causal arrow from economic disadvantage to violence. The clustering of events during times when Britain experienced a sharp recession and in areas that have suffered from economic pressures certainly suggests that economic conditions did play a crucial role in generating intergroup and anti-state violence. Nevertheless, placing emphasis on economic conditions alone still leaves the causal mechanisms that link grievances to immigrant–native or immigrant–state conflict unspecified. Some have pointed to the role played by the far left in instigating immigrant–state violence.[9] While others reject conspiracy theories that view leftist revolutionary groups as the masterminds of the 1981 disorders, they draw attention to the fact that a number of such groups, like the Workers' Revolutionary Party – a "fundamentalist and secretive Trotskyist group" – had been actively campaigning in Brixton in the months before and after the April riot (Shipley 1981, 195). These operations may have heightened the awareness of shared economic grievances, but it is also the case that ethnic minorities have often viewed activities of white left-wingers with great suspicion.[10]

It is also interesting to note which locations did not make it to the immigrant–native violence list. In Birmingham, for example, discrimination against "coloured people" was reported to be commonplace in the first decade of immigrant settlement (Rex and Moore 1967). An opinion poll of 1,000 "Brummies" held at the Labour Party Archives reveals an extraordinary amount of prejudice against the city's nonwhite newcomers: 98.5 percent reported that they would not "take a coloured person into [their] home as a lodger;" 98.1 percent would "object to a coloured worker being in charge of [them];" and 64.3 percent thought that "on average the intelligence of coloured people here [was] . . . less . . . than that of white people." [11] Nevertheless, the city did not experience large-scale immigrant–native violence. In fact, as Chapter 6 shows, Birmingham should not be characterized as a city ridden

---

[8] See the 2004 *Indices of Deprivation* (Department for Communities and Local Government [DCLG] 2004), which contain, among other indicators, measures of income, employment, and the availability of housing and services.

[9] Margaret Thatcher thought, e.g., that "racial tension and bitter hostility to the police . . . [in Liverpool was] encouraged by left-wing extremists" (Thatcher 1993, 144). Sir David McNee, the Commissioner of Police for the Metropolis, also "stated with certainty that the [Brixton] disorders were instigated by extreme left-wing political agitators," but he claimed that these revolutionaries came "from outside" (Greaves 1984, 68).

[10] Articles in the magazine *Race Today*, published by a Brixton-based cooperative run by ethnic minorities from the 1960s through the 1980s, tend to voice this mistrust. White leftists were seen to want to advance the cause of the working class without appreciating the additional disadvantages associated with racial discrimination.

[11] LAB: The (undated) document, produced by the Working Party on Racial Discrimination, shows poll results that are published in *Colour and Conscience*, published in 1957 (no author named).

with immigrant–native conflict, especially when compared with other British cities. Similarly, Brixton (an area in the South London borough of Lambeth) has been the site of immigrant–state but not large-scale immigrant–native conflict. Early observers did not characterize the native population as less prejudiced, but they did note that "Brixtonians prefer, on the whole, to keep their antipathy to immigrants outside party politics" (Sharpe 1965, 19).

Immigrant Conflict across Groups

Finally, we observe noticeable intra-immigrant differences. While West Indians are involved in twenty-two major events, only four can be categorized as constituting immigrant–native violence, with the remainder falling into the category of antistate violence, generally addressed against the police. Turning to the South Asian population, we observe a quite different pattern. South Asians are involved in fewer events overall (ten) and their involvement is generally restricted to major instances of intergroup violence. These events are not confined to one national or religious group, and they include minorities originating from India (e.g., Ealing, Coventry), Pakistan (e.g., Waltham Forest, Bradford), and Bangladesh (e.g., Tower Hamlets, Oldham).

Summarizing these figures, I find that among events involving black Caribbeans, 82 percent are episodes of immigrant–state conflict and 18 percent constitute immigrant–native conflict. Among South Asians, this pattern is reversed: only 20 percent of events are confrontations between immigrants and the state, while 80 percent can be classified as large-scale clashes between immigrants and natives. Further research into these events shows that of the four immigrant–native incidents involving West Indians, only one, the clashes in Deptford (Lewisham, South London), were part of more sustained immigrant–native confrontations. The violent riot between West Indians and whites in Nottingham was not followed by overt conflict, and some observers even commented on the city's display of racial harmony soon afterward.[12] Similarly, no sustained immigrant–native conflict followed the violence in Notting Hill, London; the fascist candidate, Sir Oswald Mosley, campaigned heavily but was disappointed with his electoral performance in the general election of 1959 in which immigration did not become an issue (Walker 1977, 32–33; Tompson 1988, 65). In Dudley, no anti-immigrant parties campaigned in the years preceding or following the riot and "race relations... were probably rather better than in many other West Midland areas."[13] Interestingly, it is in Deptford, where intergroup violence appears to be part of a larger pattern, that the

---

[12] Lawrence summarizes these views. He rejects the characterization of Nottingham as a beacon of racial tolerance but nevertheless observes a "relative absence of conflict" (1974, 9).

[13] See *The Times*, "Dudley's Youth Problems as a Factor in Colour Riots," August 13, 1962. During the riot, a police officer reportedly said, "I just cannot think why all this hooliganism should be taking place. It was supposed to be a race riot, but last night two Jamaicans in a car drove down the road between two groups of youths and they were cheered" (*The Times*, "Police Stand By in Dudley," August 3, 1962). For local election results, see Rallings et al. (2006).

borough council was forced to grant immigrants equal access to public housing, after it had been found guilty of violating antidiscrimination statutes (see subsequent text) by favoring white native households over needier immigrant families. According to Husbands (1983, 62), "This policy change may have made some whites erroneously believe that blacks were receiving preferential treatment and it may account for some of the quite remarkable success of the National Front and National Party in Deptford in 1976."

Among South Asians, clashes with natives are often indicative of sustained immigrant–native conflict. Probing deeper into the circumstances surrounding these events, as later chapters will do, we observe that these incidents indeed tended to be part of a larger confrontation between South Asian minorities and white natives. Tower Hamlets, a borough in London's East End, has been the site of ethnic conflict between predominantly Bangladeshi immigrants and white working-class natives since the early years of the Bangladeshi settlement in the late 1960s; it was the first district (but not the last) to elect a member of the racist British National Party to its council in 1993. Local anti-immigrant political organizations and their violent followers also fought prolonged battles with the Indian population in Southall, located in the outer London borough of Ealing. By the 2000s, though, Southall had become known for its interethnic harmony, while Bradford in the north (a city with a large Pakistani-origin population) traversed the opposite path. Once a model of peaceful intergroup relations, it turned into a flash point of interethnic strife.

In addition to the results produced by my list of major violent events, other sources point to similar findings. Some observers have noted, if only in passing and without explanation, that "The Asian population has been the target of racialist violence and British Movement or National Front-inspired attacks, while the West Indian community does not appear to face the same degree of threat" (Shipley 1981, 197). In its first survey on racial violence published in 1981, the Home Office also noted that Asian immigrants were significantly more likely than their West Indian counterparts to be targeted by such attacks (cited in Lawrence 1987, 154). Government-sponsored investigations uncovered similar patterns in 1986 and again in 1989, when 70 percent of the victims of recorded racial harassment in London were of Asian origin and the perpetrators were usually white teenagers (Anwar 1998, 85).[14] Indeed, the colloquial label that has been attached to these attacks is "Paki-bashing." Others have also pointed out that "The attitudes of Asian people towards the police appear to be more favourable than those of Afro-Caribbeans, but they are particularly critical of police behaviour in respect of racial attacks.... The incidence of unprovoked attacks, especially on Asian people, appears to have increased considerably since 1976" (Benyon 1986, 249). In short, the group differences that turn up in my nationwide count of collective violence do reflect a more general phenomenon.

---

[14] This result is not a product of differences in the groups' population shares in London; see Chapter 4.

The varied incidence of immigrant conflict across immigrant groups is puzzling, for the two groups have much in common. Migrants from the Caribbean and from the Indian subcontinent arrived in Britain around the same time and were thus subject to the same cultural, social, and political traditions. As Commonwealth citizens, they were equally affected by immigration and citizenship laws, and as nonwhites, they were ethnically distinct from Britain's predominantly white population.

Moreover, immigrants from South Asia and the West Indies are economic migrants in the classic sense. They came to Britain to increase their earnings and, for the most part, intended to return once they had amassed enough capital to establish a better life for themselves and their families in their home countries.[15] In the end, this "myth of return" (Anwar 1979) did not materialize for the majority in either group.

South Asians and Caribbeans thus share many socioeconomic characteristics. Data from the 1970s and 1980s, when most of the major disturbances took place, show that West Indians, Pakistanis, and Bangladeshis were predominantly employed in manual jobs. While a larger share of Indians held white-collar employment, this group is quite polarized and also contained substantial numbers of low-skilled manual workers (Smith 1977, 73; Brown 1984, 197). By the late 1970s, unemployment rates among Indian, Pakistani, Bangladeshi, and West Indian men were at approximately the same levels, and all well above the jobless rate among white Britons.[16]

I further analyzed employment and housing statistics to determine whether destination locales varied systematically by group. Significance tests confirm that it is not the case that local authorities in which Caribbeans settled in large numbers exhibited higher unemployment rates than local destinations of South Asians, or that these localities differed significantly in basic housing amenities.[17] Furthermore, both South Asian and West Indian enclaves were dominated by semiskilled or unskilled manual laborers, while higher-skilled individuals tended to reside in areas with relatively lower immigrant concentrations (Smith 1977, 78–79). In more recent years, however, a significant proportion of Indians has made substantial socioeconomic gains; compared with Caribbeans, Pakistanis, and Bangladeshis, Indians are more likely

[15] One exception is East African Asian migrants; see the subsequent text.

[16] In the early 1970s, unemployment rates were highest among Pakistanis and Bangladeshis and by the mid-1970s this was the case for West Indians. By 1978, unemployment among Indians, Pakistanis, Bangladeshis, and West Indians had reached very similar levels (at around 7 percent in 1978 and 9 percent in late 1979). These figures refer to the registered unemployment rate among men (Field, Mair, Rees, and Stevens 1981, 23).

[17] To arrive at these conclusions, I compared local authorities in which at least 3 percent of the population was born in the Caribbean or in South Asia, respectively, by 1981. Across destination authorities, statistical tests turn up no significant difference in unemployment rates; in households lacking both an inside bath and toilet; or in households just lacking an inside toilet. (Households in Caribbean destination authorities were slightly more likely to lack an inside bath, but the substantive difference, i.e., 1.4 percent of all households, was small.) Calculations are based on data available at www.nomisweb.co.uk.

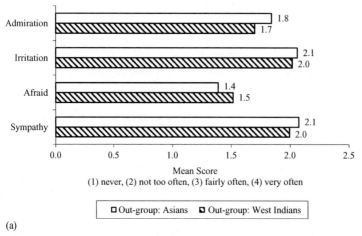

Mean Score
(1) never, (2) not too often, (3) fairly often, (4) very often

☐ Out-group: Asians   ◧ Out-group: West Indians

(a)

Now, I would like to ask whether you have ever felt the following ways about (out-group) and their families living here. For each feeling that I ask you about, please tell me whether you have felt that way very often, fairly often, not too often, or never.

Admiration   How often have you felt admiration for (out-group) living here?

Irritation   How often have you felt irritation at (out-group) living here?

Afraid   How often have you felt afraid of (out-group) living here?

Sympathy   How often have you felt sympathy for (out-group) living here?

FIGURE 3.1. Great Britain: (a) feelings toward the out-group; (b) reasons why immigrants don't do as well; (c) immigration policy opinion; (d) opinions about the outgroup. *Source:* Eurobarometer 30 (see Reif and Melich 1992).

to be employed and to live in middle-class neighborhoods (Modood, Berthoud, Lakey, Nazroo, Smith, Virdee, and Beishon 1997, 89; Office of the Deputy Prime Minister 2006). (Interestingly, none of the disturbances of the 1990s and 2000s have taken place in areas that are home to significant Indian minorities.)

We have already seen that native opinions about local immigrants do not necessarily correlate with outcomes of on-the-ground immigrant conflict. Similarly, differences in native prejudice across groups cannot account for the observed variation in conflict. Results from opinion surveys conducted in 1988 reveal that white Britons expressed similar levels of blatant and subtle prejudice against West Indians as they did against Asians living in Britain. Figures 3.1(a) through 3.1(d) depict the responses to a variety of questions about attitudes and feelings to the two groups as well as opinions about immigration policies and reasons why ethnic minorities "don't do as well as the British people." Respondents were randomly assigned to answer these questions based on one of two out-groups, that is, "West Indians" (513 respondents) or "Asians" (504 respondents). A cursory glance at these figures shows that there are no major differences in responses based on group assignment; for most questions, differences are indeed very small. If anything, levels of blatant racial prejudice are higher against West Indians; compared to opinions about Asians, a larger

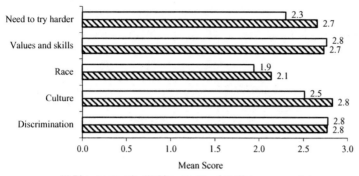

(1) Disagree strongly, (2) Disagree somewhat, (3) Agree somewhat,
(4) Agree strongly

□Out-group: Asians ◼Out-group: West Indians

(b)

Please tell me whether you agree strongly, agree somewhat, disagree somewhat, or disagree strongly with each of the following reasons why (out-group) living here may not do as well as the British people in Great Britain.

Need to try harder	It is just a matter of some people not trying hard enough; if (out-group) would only try harder they could be as well off as British people.
Values and skills	(Out-group) living here teach their children values and skills different from those required to be successful in Great Britain.
Race	(Out-group) come from less able races and this explains why they are not as well off as most British people.
Culture	The cultures of the home countries of (out-group) are less well developed than that of Great Britain.
Discrimination	There is a great deal of discrimination against (out-group) living here today that limits their chances to get ahead.

FIGURE 3.1 (*continued*)

share of respondents blamed West Indians' disadvantaged position in British society on their allegedly inferior cultural and racial backgrounds; see Figure 3.1(b). Finally, over-time survey data (from 1983 to 1996) also turn up "few differences in the levels and social distribution of white prejudice against black and against Asian Britons, suggesting the more distinctive cultural and religious practices of British Asian communities do not attract greater hostility from the white population" (Ford 2008, 610).

It is further unlikely that South Asians and West Indians held similar views about state institutions, but that blacks' disproportionate involvement in anti-state violence was due to some unobservable characteristics not present among South Asians (e.g., cultural predispositions) that would promote the engagement in this type of behavior. According to a 1982 survey, 64 percent of West Indians but only 30 percent of Asians thought that the police treated them "worse than white people." When it came to the courts and schools, 38 and 36 percent thought this was the case among West Indians, while 9 and 17 percent of Asians believed these state institutions to treat them worse than whites

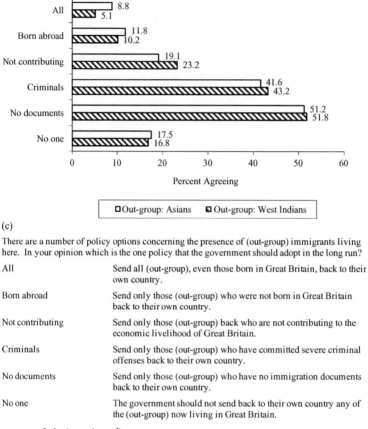

(c)

There are a number of policy options concerning the presence of (out-group) immigrants living here. In your opinion which is the one policy that the government should adopt in the long run?

All	Send all (out-group), even those born in Great Britain, back to their own country.
Born abroad	Send only those (out-group) who were not born in Great Britain back to their own country.
Not contributing	Send only those (out-group) back who are not contributing to the economic livelihood of Great Britain.
Criminals	Send only those (out-group) who have committed severe criminal offenses back to their own country.
No documents	Send only those (out-group) who have no immigration documents back to their own country.
No one	The government should not send back to their own country any of the (out-group) now living in Great Britain.

FIGURE 3.1. (*continued*)

(Brown 1984, 276; the survey did not include questions about local or central government).

There are, then, at least three questions that have to be answered: First, what explains the incidence of immigrant–native conflict? Second, what explains the incidence of immigrant–state conflict? Third, what explains the varied involvement in each across immigrant groups? The following sections provide answers to these three questions.

Explaining Immigrant Conflict

Since the early years of immigrant settlement, scores of journalists, academics, independent researchers, and policy makers have attempted to understand the causes of immigrant conflict in Britain. The case studies in Chapters 5 and 6 draw on these sources, which are very useful for tracing the chronologies and processes of such conflict (as well as its absence). This chapter aims to aggregate these accounts to provide a general explanation for the questions raised in the

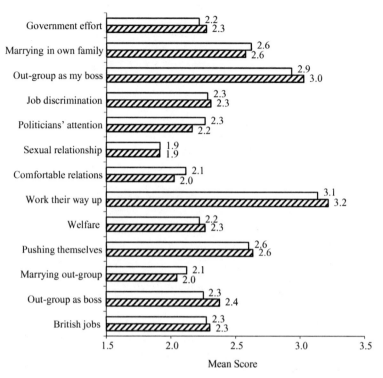

(1) Disagree strongly, (2) Disagree somewhat, (3) Agree somewhat,
(4) Agree strongly

□ Out-group: Asians ■ Out-group: West Indians

(d)

Now, I would like to ask you a few more questions about (out-group) and their families living here. Tell me as I read each of the following statements whether you agree strongly, agree somewhat, disagree somewhat, or disagree strongly.

Government effort	The government should make every effort to improve the social and economic position of (out-group) living in Great Britain.
Marrying in own family	I would not mind if an (out-group) person who had a similar family economic background as mine joined my close family by marriage.
Out-group as my boss	I would not mind if a suitably qualified (out-group) person was appointed as my boss.
Job discrimination	(Out-group) get the worst jobs and are underpaid in Great Britain largely because of discrimination.
Politicians' attention	Most politicians in Great Britain care too much about (out-group) and not enough about the average British person.
Sexual relationship	I would be willing to have sexual relationships with a (out-group) person.
Comfortable relations	British people and (out-group) can never be really comfortable with each other, even if they are close friends.

FIGURE 3.1 (*continued*)

Work their way up	Many other groups have come to Great Britain and overcome prejudice and worked their way up. (Out-group) should do the same without any special favor.
Welfare	Most (out-group) living here who receive support from welfare could get along without if they tried.
Pushing themselves	(Out-group) living here should not push themselves where they are not wanted.
Marrying out-group	Most British people would not mind if a (out-group) person with a similar family economic background as their own joined their close family by marriage.
Out-group as boss	Most British people would not mind if a suitably qualified (out-group) person was appointed as their boss.
British jobs	(Out-group) have jobs that the British should have.

FIGURE 3.1 (*continued*)

earlier text. I mainly consider source materials held at the National Archives as well as archives of the Labour and Conservative Parties. There are three advantages to using these data. First, the peaceful integration of the immigrant population was a high priority for policy makers and politicians alike. As a result, prime ministers and party officials collected information from many different sources throughout the country – local politicians, welfare and housing officers, town clerks, employers, and police chiefs, among others – that would help them understand the causes of immigrant conflict. I had access both to these local accounts and to correspondence at the elite level, which is informed by these local inquiries and is therefore useful in identifying the variables that underlie immigrant conflict.[18] Second, both the central government and politicians saw themselves as being hurt by immigrant conflict and consequently had a real stake in finding out the causes of such strife, leading them to assess its dimensions. Third, this correspondence between policy makers and politicians, most of which is labeled "top secret" or "confidential," has the added advantage of being relatively candid in nature, in contrast to public statements, which generally do not want to be seen as legitimizing native attacks on immigrants or immigrant opposition to the state.

Immigration without Immigration Policy

To appreciate variation in local immigrant integration patterns, it is helpful to first situate them in the broader institutional context in which they occur. Like many of its continental neighbors, including Germany, Great Britain has received continuous inflows of immigrants over the past half-century. Unlike Germany, however, these flows were not carefully planned by government technocrats, employers, and unions, but were a by-product of Britain's colonial past. Thanks to its imperial tradition, postcolonial Britain inherited a very

---

[18] A thirty-year closure rule applies to most records; most accessed files date back to the mid-1970s.

TABLE 3.2. *Net Immigration from Colonies and the New Commonwealth to Great Britain, January 11, 1948 to June 30, 1962*

Year	West Indies	India	Pakistan	Others	Total
1948–1953	14,000	2,500	1,500	10,000	28,000
1954	11,000	800	500	6,000	18,300
1955	27,550	5,800	1,850	7,500	42,700
1956	29,800	5,600	2,050	9,400	46,850
1957	23,000	6,600	5,200	7,600	42,400
1958	15,000	6,200	4,700	3,950	29,850
1959	16,400	2,950	850	1,400	21,600
1960	49,650	5,900	2,500	−350	57,700
1961	66,300	23,750	25,100	21,250	136,400
1962 (June 30)	27,037	19,245	23,837	13,652	83,771
TOTAL	279,737	79,345	68,087	80,402	507,571

Note: The 1962 Commonwealth Immigrants Act went into effect on July 1, 1962.
Source: Hiro 1991 (Appendix 2).

expansive nationality code that considered its "colonial subjects" British citizens who could move and settle freely in the mother country. In the immediate postwar period, both the Tories and the Labour Party reaffirmed Britain's commitment to the ideals of the Commonwealth with the passage of the 1948 Nationality Act. This piece of legislation created a citizenship regime under which Britons as well as colonial subjects were Citizens of the United Kingdom and Colonies. One assumption at the time was that cross-border mobility would mainly consist of Englishmen traveling and settling throughout the Commonwealth. Large-scale immigration from the so-called New Commonwealth (mainly from the West Indies and the Indian subcontinent) had not been conceived as a possibility – the Nationality Act's "aims were constitutional, not migratory, and it was never designed to sanction New Commonwealth migration" (Hansen 2000, 66). But such immigration became one of the legislation's major side effects. Although the 1949 Royal Commission on Population had explicitly favored pronatalist policies to address labor shortages and population declines and advised against significant inflows of immigrants, Britain's liberal nationality code as well as push factors in the sending regions soon turned England into a major destination for New Commonwealth migrants.[19]

The majority of these labor migrants hailed from the West Indies and the Indian subcontinent (see Tables 3.2–3.4). Initially, these immigrants filled labor shortages created by postwar reconstruction and economic expansion, taking

[19] For the ideological and political origins and unintended consequences of the 1948 Nationality Act and a historical-institutionalist analysis of the evolution of Britain's immigration and nationality laws from 1948 to 1981, see Hansen (2000). Paul (1997) refers to the racist notions underlying the policy prescriptions proposed by the Royal Population Commission and of Britain's immigration policies more generally.

TABLE 3.3. *Number of Citizens of Colonies and the New Commonwealth Allowed to Settle in Great Britain, July 1, 1962, to December 31, 1972*

Year	West Indies	India	Pakistan	East Africa	Others	Total
1962 (July–Dec.)	7,004	2,855	1,106	—	7,849	18,814
1963	7,928	17,498	16,336	—	15,287	57,049
1964	14,848	15,513	10,980	—	20,776	62,117
1965	14,828	17,086	9,401	—	12,336	53,651
1966	10,928	16,708	10,245	—	8,721	46,602
1967	12,424	19,067	18,644	—	7,513	57,648
1968	7,013	23,147	13,426	—	12,617	56,203
1969	4,531	10,958	12,658	6,249	5,795	40,191
1970	3,934	7,158	9,863	6,839	5,707	33,501
1971	2,774	6,874	6,957	11,564	5,006	33,175
1972	2,453	7,589	5,399	34,825[a]	9,584	59,850
TOTAL	88,665	144,453	115,015	59,477	111,191	518,801

Notes: The 1971 Immigration Act went into effect on July 1, 1973. The East Africa column refers to people who held a passport from the United Kingdom.
[a] This figure includes about 27,000 Ugandan Asians.
Source: Hiro 1991 (Appendix 2).

TABLE 3.4. *Number of Citizens of Colonies and the New Commonwealth Allowed to Settle in Great Britain, July 1, 1973, to December 31, 1988*

Year	West Indies	India	Pakistan	Bangladesh	East Africa	Others	Total
1973	2,685	6,240	3,638	1,753	10,443	7,488	32,247
1974	3,198	6,654	4,401	1,022	13,436	13,820	42,531
1975	3,698	10,195	7,724	3,276	13,792	14,580	53,265
1976	2,697	11,021	11,699	3,975	11,655	13,966	55,013
1977	2,237	7,339	13,331	3,306	6,401	11,541	44,155
1978	1,753	9,886	12,425	4,385	5,350	9,140	42,939
1979	1,282	9,268	10,945	3,915	4,038	7,599	37,047
1980	1,080	7,930	9,080	5,210	3,030[a]	7,290	33,620
1981	980	6,590	8,970	5,810	2,780	6,240	31,370
1982	770	5,410	7,750	7,020	2,720	6,710	30,380
1983	750	5,380	6,440	4,870	3,280	6,830	27,550
1984	680	5,140	5,510	4,180	2,690	6,600	24,800
1985	770	5,500	6,680	5,330	2,180	6,590	27,050
1986	830	4,210	5,580	4,760	1,680	5,600	22,660
1987	890	4,610	3,930	3,080	1,860	6,460	20,830
1988	1,030	5,020	4,280	2,890	1,910	7,670	22,800
TOTAL	25,330	110,393	122,383	64,782	84,215	138,124	548,257

Note: The East Africa column refers to people who held a passport from the United Kingdom.
[a] Here the classification was changed from people who held a passport from the United Kingdom to British overseas citizens.
Source: Hiro 1991 (Appendix 2).

jobs concentrated in less profitable and low-paying sectors (such as the textile industry and metal manufacturing) that were generally on the decline and less desirable to native workers. They predominantly settled in urban industrial areas such as Greater London, the West Midlands, and in northern conurbations such as Bradford and Manchester. The process of chain migration further intensified patterns of geographic concentration. As early as the mid-1960s, New Commonwealth migrants constituted between 5 and 15 percent of the resident populations in only 8 percent of Britain's parliamentary constituencies, but in more than half, these settlers made up less than 1 percent of the population (Patterson 1969, 194–196; Layton-Henry 1992, 14; Money 1997, 700–701).

When it became clear in the mid-1950s that immigration was indeed occurring at a fast pace, politicians took few steps to restrict, guide, or assist this inflow of labor. Indeed, archival records confirm that immigration was conceived of mostly as a political matter and illustrate just how uninvolved economic planners were in guiding postwar migration: In sharp contrast to Germany's immigration regime, the Minister of Labour was not even consulted in the British government's initial deliberations on the country's slowly developing immigration policy. When Conservative Prime Minister Eden convened a committee in 1955 to discuss the possibility of immigration legislation, it was not until the Minister of Labour requested "to be added to the Committee of Ministers to consider the problem of Colonial Immigrants, since he is much concerned departmentally with this question" that he was included in the talks.[20] In sum, early immigrant settlement occurred without much coordination or assistance from state authorities, and, as we will see in this and in later chapters, variation in local political and economic conditions greatly affected the ease of integration of the incoming migrant population.[21]

Over the course of the 1950s, labor migration into Britain continued unabated as political deadlock across and within parties on the issue paralyzed effective policy making. Within the Conservative and the Labour Parties, two factions – believers in free markets and open borders as well as adherents to traditional Commonwealth ideals – favored a liberal immigration regime. Restrictionist factions consisted of socially conservative Tories, who feared and opposed "mongrelization" of the British people, and Labour politicians, who contended that unchecked immigration would hurt their working-class constituents.[22] Similar divisions were also reflected in the British Cabinet, which had met for "the fifteenth time... [and had] considered the problem, without being able to reach a conclusion."[23] Given the lack of consensus on the issue,

---

[20] PREM 11/2920: Note to the Prime Minister (author unclear), December 3, 1955.

[21] See also Garbaye (2005) on the unplanned nature of British immigration and the ensuing focus on locally directed integration.

[22] See Foot (1965, 153–157, 189–190) and Messina (1989, 24–29) on these internal divisions.

[23] PREM 11/2920: Letter to the Prime Minister by Norman Brook, Secretary to the British Cabinet, November 10, 1955.

Prime Minister Eden thus thought it best if "further examination were first made of the problem which would have to be solved."[24] In other words, an assessment of the immigrant problem as it unfolded on the ground would have to break the ideological deadlock on immigration policy.

The measures that were eventually implemented to curb the inflow of foreign labor were taken partly in response to the local repercussions of unplanned immigration (Money 1997; Karapin 1999), but they also failed to guide migrant settlement in ways that would alleviate strains on public resources in the areas of concentration. The 1962 Immigration Act, for example, made immigration contingent on specific employment contracts in the case of unskilled labor, but it contained no procedures for registration or dispersal and no settlement assistance, even though many local authorities struggled with overcrowding and housing shortages, local social services tended to be overloaded in areas of concentration, and labor shortages were still acute in many sectors (Patterson 1969, 19–20).[25] The 1962 Immigration Act as well as later pieces of immigration legislation in fact probably exacerbated these problems. By restricting employment-based migration, successive governments inadvertently encouraged a disproportionate inflow of dependents; between 1963 and 1967, the number of dependents as a share of all New Commonwealth immigrants rose from 31.0 to 72.7 percent (Gish 1968, 26, 31; my calculations). Pressures on local services such as housing, education, and health care would thus only intensify, while immigrant taxpayers declined as a proportion of the total migrant population. As we will see later on, a similar pattern developed in Germany in the 1970s. Unlike the German immigration regime, though, which guided migrant settlement and provided accommodations but also restricted migrants' internal movement and coerced the departure of unemployed migrants, Britain's immigration regime contained neither supportive nor restrictive provisions that would have guided the arrival of newcomers and assisted in their local integration.

This lack of state intervention meant that local authorities themselves sometimes took the initiative. In the early years, this took the form of Voluntary Liaison Committees, which essentially consisted of groups of well-meaning native residents, often including members of the local clergy, who helped immigrants become familiar with their new environment and specifically with the provision of local services. The Labour government under Wilson later institutionalized these committees into community relations councils (CRCs) as part of its efforts to integrate the resident immigrant population while at the same time restricting new inflows.[26] These efforts included the enactment of antidiscrimination

---

[24] PREM 11/2920: Note by the Prime Minister to the Cabinet, November 10, 1955.

[25] Under the Immigration Act, the Ministry of Labour issued three types of labor vouchers: specific employment vouchers issued by employers to Commonwealth citizens (category A); vouchers for Commonwealth migrants with specific skills, especially in health care (category B); and a third type of voucher (category C) that covered all remaining applicants (Gish 1968, 25).

[26] The 1965 White Paper eliminated category C vouchers, restricted the number of employment-based vouchers, and put greater emphasis on skilled migration (Gish 1968, 29). Later legislation further tightened controls. The 1971 Immigration Act, enacted by the Conservative Heath

legislation in the form of several race relations acts.[27] While this legislation appears quite remarkable when viewed in European perspective, its remit was initially quite limited and many observers have dismissed the CRCs as well as the antidiscrimination laws as paternalistic attempts by the British establishment to maintain "racial buffers" between itself and immigrant newcomers, created to prevent the national politicization of immigration.[28] In the chapters that follow, these bodies do indeed barely come into play as independently significant in securing immigrants' successful access to scarce local state goods as local electoral incentives proved much more powerful.[29] When it came to financial assistance related to the settlement of immigrants, local authorities could apply for funds under the 1966 Local Government Act or could petition the center for monies under the Urban Programme (see subsequent paragraphs), though these programs were rather limited in scope.

The government's hands-off approach also characterized the settlement of East African Asian refugees. Though most of the migration from New Commonwealth countries consisted of labor migrants who would later be joined by their dependents, in the late 1960s and early 1970s Great Britain also experienced inflows of refugees. As Britain's African colonies gained independence, some expelled their non-African, mostly Indian-origin residents who had arrived decades earlier as part of the British Empire's efforts to build up local economies and act as middlemen between the indigenous population and the white colonial elite. African leaders, notably Kenya's Jomo Kenyatta and Uganda's Idi Amin, portrayed these Asians as dangerous fifth columns that threatened to undermine national unity and eventually forced them to leave. Amidst intense controversy about an impending refugee wave in the national and local press in the United Kingdom, both Labour and Conservative governments ultimately decided to accept these so-called East African

government, sought to limit (nonwhite) immigration from the New Commonwealth by distinguishing between "patrials," who had a parent or grandparent born in the United Kingdom and could enter, settle, and work without restrictions, and "non-patrials," all others without such a connection, who faced much stricter controls. The citizenship regime was not changed until 1981: Thatcher's British Nationality Act created three classes of citizenship and the right to enter without restrictions was reserved for British citizens (patrials). Moreover, children born in the United Kingdom had to have at least one parent born or legally settled in the country to automatically qualify for British citizenship (Coleman 1994, 59–60; Hansen 2000, 214; Hussain 2001, 24, 27).

[27] The 1965 Race Relation Act lacked enforcement mechanisms and was limited in scope: It sought to outlaw discrimination on racial or religious grounds but did not cover the areas where these occurred most frequently, i.e., employment and housing. The 1968 Race Relations Act did include these areas and also strengthened enforcement provisions. The 1976 Race Relations Act, also implemented under a Labour government, covered direct as well as indirect discrimination and established the Commission for Racial Equality to monitor and enforce the legislation's provisions (Ben-Tovim, Gabriel, Law, and Stredder 1986, 29–30).

[28] For this view, see Katznelson (1973, 179–181) and Messina (1989, 44–47). For a comprehensive account of CRCs, see Hill and Issacharoff (1971); for a discussion of British antidiscrimination laws in comparative perspective, see Bleich (2003) and Lieberman (2005).

[29] But note the antidiscrimination enforcement in the case of Deptford, Lewisham, given earlier.

Asians, following their conscience as well as their legal obligations toward former citizens of the British Commonwealth.[30]

From the perspective of local authorities, the arrival of these refugees presented challenges as well as opportunities. In contrast to primary labor migrants, East African refugees arrived as complete family units, including children, parents, and grandparents. The impact on schools, housing, social services, and municipal infrastructures more generally would thus be felt immediately. Moreover, limited to taking £50 per household out of Africa and forced to leave all their possessions behind, "Families arrived penniless in many cases" (Kuepper et al. 1975, 55). For most of the 1970s, finding work would also prove difficult for this population, and many had to accept employment that fell well below their qualifications. In the long run, the relatively highly skilled background of many East African Asians allowed this population to prosper, but in the short term, the initial arrival of East African Asians was associated with comparatively high demands on local public resources. As we see in Chapter 5, Leicester, which turned out to be one of the preferred destinations of Ugandan Asians, would confront important resource constraints.

Faced with a vocal backlash from local authorities,[31] central government attempted to alleviate local resource strains through a dispersal policy: The goal was to steer refugees away from "red" areas – authorities that experienced pressures in two out of the four areas of education, employment, housing, and social services – and instead guide newcomers towards "green" areas whose infrastructures were considered better equipped to absorb the impending population increase. In the end, however, close to two-thirds of the people settled in "red" areas, which generally consisted of those authorities that had already been home to a substantial preexisting Asian population. Central government did make additional funds available to local authorities whose budgets were affected by the inflow, but national public officials were also eager to keep expenditures low and out of the public eye.[32]

Immigrant Voters
What the British immigration regime lacked in economic concessions, it made up for in political rights. Most New Commonwealth migrants were entitled to participate in local and national elections and their settlement in concentrated

---

[30] The following brief discussion of East African Asian migration to Great Britain draws on Kuepper, Lackey, and Swinerton (1975), Bristow (1976), Robinson (1993 and 1995), and Hansen (1999 and 2000).

[31] For example, "when Peterborough had offered fifty homes to Ugandan Asians, such a local outcry resulted that the City Council explained its position in a special newspaper which was distributed to 30,000 people" (Kuepper et al. 1975, 77).

[32] In a note to the cabinet, it was suggested that "The least embarrassing arrangement might be to encourage the use for these purposes [of settling East African Asian refugees] of charitable funds, attracting in particular contributions from the existing Asian community in the United Kingdom and with the support of a Government contribution also." See CAB 129/164/16: "United Kingdom Passport Holders in Uganda," note by the Secretary of State for the Home Department and Lord President of the Council, September 6, 1972.

areas aroused the interest and concern of party strategists. While the newcomers represented considerable electoral potential, a sound party strategy would have to balance the votes delivered by this new constituency with the adverse native reactions it might provoke. A reporter covering constituency campaigns in the 1964 general election made this observation:

The politicians . . . will, with their customary side-step, evade the question of the Afro-Asian immigrant. An MP [Member of Parliament] holding a seat with a small majority and where constituents resent the 'influx' of non-whites, would commit political suicide were he to welcome them enthusiastically to the Motherland. In the light of this it is not surprising – though it seems hypocritical – that the local Labour parties not infrequently send 'secret delegations' to the immigrants on behalf of the candidate.[33]

Labour strategists were thus concerned with evaluating the dynamics of immigrant conflict, constantly calculating how they could gain "votes from coloured people to an extent equal to prospective losses from white Labour supporters due to this colour-clash."[34]

Candidates competing in local council elections faced similar trade-offs. In the West Midlands authority of Wolverhampton, where a sizable Indian Sikh population had settled, "both the major political parties were acutely aware of the appeal of anti-immigration policies . . . overt opposition to immigration control or support for the black cause came to be defined as a liability where votes were concerned" (Reeves 1989, 47). This assessment began to shift in the 1970s, coinciding with the election of the town's first Indian councilors.

By the mid-1970s, the Conservative Party's Research Department also declared that the party's "political posture, or 'image' towards the immigrant communities needs urgent attention," but it simultaneously warned that "community relations are a minefield. . . . In spite of extensive research already done, and the information circulated at the last Election, constituency by constituency, some M.P.s and candidates whose immigrant vote far exceeds their majority are known to be vague about immigrant communities they have in their constituencies."[35] This reluctance was in part due to fears about losing white support, especially if immigrants were incorporated into the party

---

[33] *The Guardian*, "Afraid to Vote," September 29, 1964.

[34] LAB: Letter from London District Organizer of the Labour Party, J. W. Raisin, to Mr. Morgan Phillips, Labour Party Secretary, September 11, 1958. Raisin made the following calculations for the North Kensington parliamentary constituency: "A Communist vote of 734 in the Borough Council Elections of 1956 might be raised to one of (say) 1,500 if sufficient hate were generated. Alternatively, the Liberal vote in the 1951 Parliamentary election of 1,583 might be developed against an alleged illiberal Member of Parliament. Either, or both, of these interventions could bring about our defeat." Raisin ultimately concluded that "At the moment and in the foreseeable future, the gaining of additional coloured votes could be secured *only* at the expense of many more white votes" (emphasis in the original). Even though Raisin suggested that the Labour Party should refrain from making overt appeals to the immigrant electorate nationwide, he also advised that "wherever there is a sizeable coloured community the Labour Party should take great pains to bring them as far as possible within their ambit."

[35] CON CRD 4/9/34: "Community Relations at the Constituency Level," confidential memorandum prepared by Brenda Hancock, July 5, 1974; emphasis omitted.

membership: "One of my major problems" wrote Tom Boardman, a Tory MP in Leicester, "is on the active recruiting of immigrants into existing branches which would immediately mean the dissolution of those branches, as the bulk of the indigenous members would resent it."[36] As we see in Chapter 6, Leicester's Labour Party at both the parliamentary constituency and local level did appeal to immigrant voters and candidates. A white backlash followed and initially cost Labour precious votes, but in future election cycles the Conservatives had to acknowledge that they had missed their opportunity to recruit the Asian vote.

But the Labour Party did not always reach out to the new voters and was also cautious about weighing immigrant supporters against potential losses among natives. An Indian-origin councilor in Ealing told me that members of local parties (who are in charge of selecting ward candidates) initially misinformed the Indian electorate that local ward parties were "full" and no longer accepted applications.[37] Growing the size of the local Labour Party was apparently not worth the risk of potentially losing white candidates and voters. Similarly, in the Labour Party Archives, a document that compares the size of the West Indian population at the parliamentary constituency level with the size of the electoral margin of these constituencies in the 1959 general election is followed by an assessment of anti-immigrant attitudes in Birmingham (mentioned earlier), which contained several hotly contested seats.[38] Nevertheless, as "whole streets which used to contain a solid Labour vote [had] now been repopulated with a coloured population,"[39] getting out the immigrant vote while reducing the "colour-clash" would become a top priority for Labour in some parliamentary constituencies and local wards. But a reduction in such intergroup tensions would first require an understanding of its causes.

The Economic Basis of Immigrant Conflict

Starting in the late 1950s, the Conservative government and the Labour Party began inquiring into the dynamics of immigrant–native conflict. According to government ministers and Labour officials, the central forces driving intergroup confrontations were of an economic nature. Competition was especially acute in the housing sector, which had been overburdened even before immigrants had arrived, thanks to a combination of poor planning and wartime bombings, which decimated 100,000 dwellings in London alone.[40] Central government planned to address the housing problem by expanding the public housing

---

[36] CON CRD 4/9/34: Letter by Tom Boardman to Brenda Hancock (Conservative Research Department), July 2, 1974.

[37] Interview held in Ealing, March 2005.

[38] LAB: Race Relations Box 1.

[39] LAB: Memorandum by David Ennals, Secretary of the Labour Party, International Department, July 2, 1963.

[40] See Senior (1957, 305). Senior further notes that newcomers to London would have to wait at least five years to even get on the city's waiting list for council housing. In Birmingham, over 60,000 residents had their names on the list (305–306).

supply while simultaneously embarking on major slum clearance projects that were to demolish unfit housing, thereby displacing millions of people. Local authorities had discretion over the implementation of these redevelopment projects, leading to differing clearance rates across cities. Furthermore, in the years to come it became clear that the completion rates for public housing fell short of initial expectations (Yelling 2000).

When the Labour Party sent out a circular in 1957 to establish "a more comprehensive and factual picture of the colour question in the United Kingdom," the responses of those districts that had experienced interethnic tensions (which were in the minority) all stressed the problems arising from battles over scarce housing, particularly in the Greater London area. In the working-class Vauxhall constituency, South London, for example, there had initially "never been any question of colour discrimination or prejudice... [but] there [had] undoubtedly been a change... due, among other things, to the appalling housing situation."[41]

Conservative politicians, who were generally less likely to fault economic conditions for racial conflict than their Labour counterparts, tended to agree: "The immigration problem is 10 per cent prejudice, 30 per cent schooling, and 60 per cent housing," proclaimed a Tory MP in 1964.[42] Correspondence between the Home Office and the Prime Minister's office as well as deliberations between Labour politicians and strategists further reveal that the 1958 Notting Hill riot (North Kensington, London) was also mostly blamed on the area's unsustainable housing situation. In a confidential letter to Morgan Phillips, General Secretary of the Labour Party, London District Organizer J.W. Raisin wrote the following:

The basis upon which racial tension in North Kensington (and other areas of London) rests is the shortage of housing. The large increase in the coloured population of this area creates in white people's minds the impression that their chances of securing adequate housing are lessened. This impression may or may not be correct (I think it is correct) but, politically, it is the impression which is important, rather than its accuracy.[43]

Housing was the main but not the only source of contention. Writing about the 1958 riots, "The information available to [the Home Secretary] indicated that the recent disturbances had not been deliberately instigated by an organized body. The clashes appeared to have arisen through competition for limited accommodations, a declining number of jobs, and women."[44]

---

[41] LAB: Letter from Elsie L. Boltz, Agent and Secretary of the Vauxhall Constituency, undated (this letter was most likely written in 1957, in response to the Labour Party's circular).

[42] Cited in Patterson (1969, 194). Patterson cites Sir Anthony Meyer, Conservative MP for Eton and Slough, in his statement to the *Slough Observer*, December 23, 1964.

[43] LAB: Letter from London District Organizer of the Labour Party, J. W. Raisin, to Mr. Morgan Phillips, Labour Party Secretary, September 11, 1958.

[44] PREM 11/2920: Note of a meeting held in the Home Secretary's room, September 8, 1958. Senior (1957, 304) also points to competition for "female companionship" as a source for interethnic antagonism.

The notion that white resentment toward nonwhite immigrants flared up only when newcomers were perceived to be advantaged in the distribution of resources informed much of the government's policy making. Under Wilson's Labour government, the Urban Programme was instituted to assist areas whose social services were overstretched as a result of large inflows of immigrants. Nonetheless, its design and implementation was very much shaped, and ultimately crippled, by political considerations, for officials were concerned that "It would be difficult to disguise the fact that the urban programme was really designed to help areas of immigration concentration rather than urban areas of social need" more generally.[45]

In the design stage of the program, policy makers deliberated at length how financial aid could be disbursed within the existing legal framework that guided fiscal relations between the center and the regions – for additional legislation would call unwelcome attention to the issue – while still delivering resources to the areas that needed it most.[46] In the end, only relatively small sums were freed up in an arrangement whereby community groups and voluntary organizations submitted grant proposals to their local councils, who then applied for matching funds under the program. Soon after its inception, it was generally agreed within the government itself that the Urban Programme was "really irrelevant to the problems of race relations,"[47] hamstrung by its designers' desire to keep the policy away from public scrutiny.[48]

In spite of this recognition, policy makers continued to follow the principle that "The aim of race relations policy should be to maximise the benefits given to the blacks [i.e., nonwhites] while minimising provocation to the whites."[49] This calculation not only was based on fears of a political backlash, but also intended to protect immigrants: Policy makers felt they had to "ensure that in the process they [immigrants] do not and are not popularly thought to get an unduly large share of the national cake (or any particular element in it), thus occasioning disaffection and political or physical protest among the remaining white population."[50] Officers working for the Conservative Party similarly advised their candidates to "avoid seeming to single out 'immigrant' voters for special care and attention. They would not respond, and the resentment this

---

[45] CAB 134/2906: Minutes of a meeting by the Official Committee on Immigration and Community Relations, May 24, 1968.

[46] Moreover, while targeting localized areas within local authorities would be most effective for dealing with the issues at hand, such as overcrowding of nurseries, schools, and housing, the existing laws only allowed central government to allocate resources at the local authority level. See CAB 134/2906: Memorandum ICR(0) (68) 6 by the Working Party on Immigration and Community Relations, May 22, 1968.

[47] CAB 184/139: "Draft Report: The Urban Programme," June 28, 1973.

[48] See Edwards and Batley (1978) and Kirp (1979) on the ineffectiveness of Britain's policies that were meant to target ethnic minorities but did so only indirectly.

[49] CAB 184/136: Letter by Mr. Plowden (Race Relations – Next Steps) to Central Policy Review Staff, April 24, 1973.

[50] CAB 184/136: Letter by Mr. Plowden, "CPRS Race Relations Study – Some Thoughts on Aims and Objectives," to Central Policy Review Staff, April 30, 1973.

might cause among whites should not be underestimated. We should start out on the premise that we are seeking the help and support of immigrant groups, not in this context to do things for them."[51]

In balancing immigrant and native needs, local politicians would thus have to walk a tightrope. By the late 1960s competition over housing had intensified since many immigrants had now fulfilled the minimum residency requirements that would allow them to apply for government-subsidized council housing. This type of housing comprised nearly one-third of the nation's residential dwellings in 1975 (Ravetz 2001, 2) and supplied more than 60 percent of the housing stock in several inner-city areas.[52] Having toured many areas with high concentrations of immigrants, a government-appointed Select Committee on Race Relations and Immigration concluded that "race relations in the places ... visited [were] reasonably good, in view of the conditions under which members of the community, both white and black, live; in some areas, surprisingly good." Nevertheless, they hastened to add that "It goes without saying that housing has a profound effect on race relations. Improvements in housing, both of indigenous people and of immigrants, [create] better race relations because they remove some deep causes of friction and resentment. Failure to cope with bad housing has the reverse effect."[53]

Two years later, a task force appointed by Conservative Prime Minister Heath to uncover the "causes of racial strife" conjectured that resource competition activated (latent) prejudice, and it struggled with the policy implications of this observation:

[W]e are thus faced with the need not only to cure irrational prejudice, but with the problem that relative improvements in black housing and jobs are likely to exacerbate the hostility felt by many whites. In short, an ideal solution might mean taking action against all ... factors simultaneously, so that whites prone to protest at blacks jumping the housing queue would suddenly themselves be whisked away to brand-new council semis. In practice, we may find ourselves faced with incompatible objectives.[54]

---

[51] CON CRD 4/9/34: "Community Relations at the Constituency Level," confidential memorandum prepared by Brenda Hancock, July 5, 1974; emphasis omitted.

[52] These figures are based on my calculations of council housing figures from the 1981 census (Table 15, "Tenure and Household Size"), available at www.nomisweb.co.uk. Throughout the twentieth century, and especially after the Second World War when much of Britain's housing stock had been damaged or destroyed, successive governments supported the expansion of housing that was owned and rented out by local authorities at subsidized rates. The quality of such council housing varied and included three-bedroom, semidetached, or terraced houses as well as flats in inner-city towers. The share of council housing declined under Thatcher, whose "Right-to-Buy" scheme aspired to turn council tenants into homeowners by selling these properties at highly discounted rates. See Ravetz (2001) for a comprehensive account of the history of council housing.

[53] HLG 118/1247: Select Committee on Race Relations and Immigration, Session 1970–71, "Housing" Volume 1, July 22, 1971.

[54] CAB 184/136: Note by W. J. L. Plowden to the members of the Central Policy Review Staff, February 2, 1973. Note that, until recently, the term "black" referred to all nonwhite immigrants, including South Asians.

This trade-off would become increasingly unacceptable in the 1970s, when the task force observed with rising alarm how continued neglect of the immigrant population and its economic needs could create mounting problems for the state and its representatives. The Home Office and London's Police Commissioner had informed the task force of increasing confrontations between primarily West Indian youth and the police, who, "for many coloured people... symbolize the social system" as a whole.[55] While immigrant–native clashes had been the focus in the past, public officials were now extremely concerned that a failure to integrate immigrants into the social and economic fabric of British society would create a "fifth column when the day of third world revolution comes, or, less dramatically, [cause]... riots of the Newark, New Jersey, type."[56] Moreover, policy makers were keenly aware that resentment against the state could rise and eventually boil over, as "Large-scale failure and disappointment by the second generation... [could be] exploited by a minority (white and black) ever-ready to attribute such difficulties to *our* failures."[57] Some ominously warned of parallels with Northern Ireland:

For 50 years British government condoned discrimination and deprivation in Ulster, and in the end Ulster blew up in their face. We believe that, not only for the reason of social justice, but for the more basic reasons of preserving social stability and order in the longer term, more should now be done to deal with the problems of race relations in this country... coloured communities... cannot be permanently denied what they see as their rights to equal treatment. They will, increasingly, press for these until they are satisfied.[58]

The Home Office and government ministers agreed with the task force's assessment that "the single most disturbing development in the race relations field [was] the growth of anti-social attitudes [of West Indians]... and second-generation West Indian militancy." They called for urgent action on the matter, but they also noted that they "were not aware that a similar problem [was] posed by young Asians."[59] Having reviewed the evidence from various cities and towns, policy makers thus recognized the multidimensional nature of immigrant conflict, as well as the difficulties involved in attempting to simultaneously reduce the likelihood of immigrant–native and immigrant–state conflict, as this quote illustrates:

[55] CAB 184/207: "Race Relations," by the Central Policy Review Staff, Volume 2 (paragraph 267), November 1973.
[56] CAB 184/136: Letter by Mr. Plowden, "CPRS Race Relations Study – Some thoughts on aims and objectives," to Central Policy Review Staff, April 30, 1973.
[57] CAB 184/137: Letter from Mr. Waldegrave to members of the Central Policy Review Staff, May 2, 1973; emphasis in the original (Waldegrave was a member of the staff).
[58] CAB 184/207: In "Race Relations," by the Central Policy Review Staff, Volume 1 (paragraph 2), November 1973.
[59] CAB 134/3778: Ministerial Committee on Community Relations and Immigration, July 16, 1974.

These examples... show how ambiguous is the idea of a "problem" in the race relations field. The term is sometimes used to describe the problems experienced by a coloured group – for example poverty or discrimination; sometimes the problems which they are said to cause – for example overcrowding; sometimes the second-order problems to which they give rise and with which governments must deal – for example 'Paki-bashing' or white demands that they be repatriated... we have recognised that the third kind of problem may greatly limit the freedom of governments to deal effectively with the first kind; attempts to do more for coloured people always risk exciting the "white backlash." A certain amount of good may have to be done by stealth.[60]

The most serious confrontations between West Indian youth and the police would not break out until the early 1980s. Even though policy makers and police chiefs had long appreciated the underlying economic grievances that would ultimately lead some immigrants to riot, many in the Thatcher administration tended to dismiss these outbreaks as nothing more than criminal behavior. In her autobiography, Thatcher concluded that missing "social constraints," rather than economic needs, had released young men's "high animal spirits... to wreak havoc" and further speculated that "What perhaps aggravated the 1981 riots into a virtual saturnalia... was the impression given by television that... rioters could enjoy a fiesta of crime, looting and rioting in the guise of social protest" (Thatcher 1993, 146–147).[61] This assessment contradicts Keith, who carefully dissects London's July 1981 disorders and finds that "knowledge of relations between Black people and the police remained structured much more by local lived experience than by higher-profile events which had received national media attention.... There was surprisingly little knowledge of events in other parts of London" (1993, 38). Archival sources also reveal that, almost a decade earlier, officials under a Conservative leadership seriously considered the threat of large-scale violence, which they understood to be part of a wider phenomenon of economic and sociopolitical exclusion. They argued that West Indian militancy would rise as attempts to break the "cycle of deprivation" would be "frustrated by discrimination" which prevented many "from getting [their] fair share of the public spending programmes aimed at the problems of cities."[62] In London, where "police dealing with West Indians" were "often mobbed and put at great personal risk,"[63] the Police Commissioner warned of "real danger of racial violence against the police" and policy makers decided that the threat of such violence

---

[60] CAB 184/140: Race Relations: Draft Report, Part 2, written by W. J. L. Plowden, July 5, 1973.

[61] Touring Toxteth, Liverpool, after several nights of rioting, Thatcher also dismissed the explanation, given by some, that unemployment left young men bored, with nothing else to do: "But you had only to look at the grounds around those houses [in Toxteth] with the grass untended, some of it almost waist high, and the litter, to see that this was a false analysis. They had plenty of constructive things to do if they wanted" (1993, 145).

[62] CAB 184/207: "Race Relations," by the Central Policy Review Staff, Volume 1 (paragraphs 71–72), November 1973.

[63] Ibid.

provided another reason for ensuring "that racial minorities get a fair deal out of society."[64]

The tense relationship between the police and West Indian youth in some localities had indeed been much discussed in government circles and officials noted certain flash points. The task force observed that "young West Indians, who are among the more deprived members of the urban working class, may well resent the police in principle as the authoritarian embodiment of a society which has failed to educate, house or employ them adequately," but it was also aware that "The problems are essentially *local* ones, and the details vary according to *local* circumstances."[65] Officials at the Home Office had pointed out that West Indian militancy was not a nationwide problem; it affected particular localities within towns and cities. A 1974 Home Office memorandum in fact accurately predicted the areas in London (e.g., Brixton) and elsewhere in the country (Birmingham and Manchester) in which West Indian youths would clash with the police years later, belying Thatcher's assessment of purely opportunistic rioting.[66]

However, policy makers were less discerning when it came to explaining the absence of South Asian involvement in confrontations with the police. They speculated that the groups' agricultural background, "certain introversion," and "respect for authority" were responsible for young Asians' apparent docility.[67] Only a few years later, South Asian youth movements and vigilante groups emerged to defend their members from racist attacks in several locations (Forman 1989).

In sum, relying on evidence produced by a variety of sources throughout the country, from the 1950s through the early 1970s, politicians, policy makers, and the police placed overwhelming emphasis on the primacy of economic competition and state-sanctioned economic discrimination as the respective drivers of immigrant–native and immigrant–state conflict. We have also seen that many of the violent disorders involving immigrants as victims and as perpetrators occurred during the economic recession of the 1980s and took place in areas that had been especially hard hit by the downturn. Moreover, years of lower-level confrontations between West Indian migrants and the forces of law and order in economically disadvantaged neighborhoods had preceded these major disturbances. Nevertheless, a focus on economic variables alone can only get us so far. Indeed, policy makers were at a loss when trying to account for South Asians' lack of antistate behavior in the face of West Indian militancy. Furthermore, what explains the disproportionate targeting of South

---

[64] CAB 184/207: "Race Relations," by the Central Policy Review Staff, Volume 2 (paragraph 254), November 1973.

[65] CAB 184/207: "Race Relations," by the Central Policy Review Staff, Volume 2 (paragraphs 249–250), November 1973; emphasis added.

[66] CAB 134/3772: "Disaffected West Indian Youth," Memorandum by the Home Office to the Official Committee on Immigration and Community Relations, May 6, 1974.

[67] CAB 184/207: "Race Relations," by the Central Policy Review Staff, Volume 2 (paragraph 251), November 1973.

Asians by native xenophobes? The next section provides the missing pieces to these puzzles.

The Political Basis of Immigrant Conflict

This study argues that an understanding of immigrant conflict must take immigrant groups seriously. This seems like an obvious point, yet it is generally not heeded. Until recently, studies of immigrant political behavior in Western Europe focused less on the characteristics of the groups themselves, and instead placed varying national institutions at the center of analysis.[68] In research that examines anti-immigrant attitudes, immigrants are often viewed from the native perspective – as monolithic out-groups. In contrast, this study obtains leverage by also exploring how differences in the social organization of immigrant groups crucially impact their potential capacity of and utility for mobilization, both from the perspective of the immigrant groups themselves and from the viewpoint of political entrepreneurs. While we have seen that South Asians and Caribbeans are predominantly economic migrants who share broadly similar immigration histories, these two groups are quite distinct in their social organization, which, when viewed from a political angle, translates into key differences that in turn bear on the incidence of immigrant conflict. As I will elaborate shortly, strong links of kin, caste, and clan among South Asian migrants have helped these settlers gain the local political power to effectively press for scarce state-controlled resources. The previous discussion has shown that competition over these goods has been the prime driving force of immigrant–native conflict. West Indians, however, have been less able to translate their presence into political leverage. As policy makers noted, West Indians' failure to get their fair share of state resources fostered a conflictual relationship between this immigrant group and the state.

The roots of electoral mobilization can be partly traced back to immigrants' social ties. The great majority of South Asian migrants hail from India, Pakistan, and Bangladesh, but, more specifically, they originate from a small set of regions and villages. Bradford's Pakistanis, for example, come from Mirpur, in Azad Kashmir; the East End's Bangladeshis call the Sylhet region home, and Southall's Sikh population originates from villages in East Punjab. Ties of kinship, caste, and tribe have both shaped the migration process and determined the destination areas in the new country. As a result, South Asian settlement in Britain is characterized by high concentrations of homogenous immigrant groups in specific locations.[69] Among West Indian immigrants, "family networks" were also central in "facilitating the passage of migration and settlement" (Chamberlain 2001, 38), but links with wider kinship networks have

---

[68] Scholars have also begun to investigate how social attributes correlate with the political behavior of migrants. See Fennema and Tillie (1999 and 2001) and contributions to the *Journal of Ethnic and Migration Studies*, Volume 30 (Issue 3), 2004.

[69] For essays about South Asian migration to and presence in Great Britain, see chapters in Ballard (1994).

been less extensive and settlement has been less concentrated.[70] Although we clearly observe authorities with a high overall concentration of West Indians, they tend to be more dispersed within these locations than their South Asian counterparts.

Census figures illustrate these differential patterns. When we examine the country's five local authorities with the highest share of West Indians (i.e., people who identify themselves as black British Caribbeans in the census) and South Asians (those who describe themselves as British Indian, Pakistani, and Bangladeshi, respectively), and when we take group share averages of the wards within these local authorities with the highest concentration of each group, we observe that, in 2001, the average proportion of black Caribbeans in wards with the highest share of black Caribbeans is 19.7 percent (see Table 3.5). In contrast, the corresponding figures for Indians, Pakistanis, and Bangladeshis are 51.0, 48.9, and 31.7 percent, respectively. Table 3.5 shows that we obtain similar differences when we take averages of the wards with the second- and third-highest group shares and when we examine figures from the 1991 census. In 1991, the highest share of Caribbeans in a single ward was 30.1 percent; by comparison, these shares for Indians, Pakistanis, and Bangladeshis were 67.0, 52.8, and 60.7 percent (data not shown).

In short, British South Asians are more likely to approach electoral majorities in wards than are West Indians, even in local authorities where both groups make up similar proportions of the total population. The political implications of this difference are straightforward: On the basis of purely geographic indicators, divergent settlement paths have served to enhance the potential for political influence among South Asians, but they have diluted such potential among Caribbeans.

Some observers stress that obligations, as well as opportunities, generated by the underlying clan and kin relationships greatly facilitate such mobilization, whereas "Failure to gain support within these traditional kin-based networks usually means the failure of a political enterprise" (Scott 1972–1973, 39). Political parties were all too aware of the importance of tapping into these networks, as indicated by the Conservative Party's Research Department: "There is still a strong sense of hierarchical respect for community leaders amongst Asians, and although one must be warned that assurances from self-styled leaders can turn out to be in the event disappointingly unrepresentative, it is nevertheless essential to pay personal respects to these leaders. . . . Many immigrant voters still tend to support the person they know more than the party or policy."[71] These dynamics have not necessarily vanished over the years; divisions of caste, clan, and kin can still provide the social glue for local political

---

[70] For instance, whereas 12 percent of West Indian households contained more than one family unit in the early 1980s, this was true for 22 percent of Asian households (Brown 1984, 46). Moreover, South Asians are more likely than Caribbeans (and whites) to be in regular contact with members of their extended families who live in Britain (Modood et al. 1997, 53).

[71] CON CRD 4/9/34: "Community Relations at the Constituency Level," confidential memorandum prepared by Brenda Hancock, July 5, 1974.

TABLE 3.5. *Five British Local Authorities with the Highest Share of Each Ethnic Group (%)*

Group	Black Caribbean	Indian	Pakistani	Bangladeshi
		1991		
Average group share at the local authority level	10.7	17.2	8.2	7.1
Average group share in wards with the				
Highest group concentration	21.8	48.7	35.3	27.1
Second-highest group concentration	19.9	44.9	27.9	15.6
Third-highest group concentration	18.7	41.8	25.4	12.6
As a share of the total British population	0.91	1.53	0.87	0.3
Total no. living in Great Britain	499,977	840,196	476,610	162,828
		2001		
Average group share at the local authority level	10.9	20.0	12.0	11.5
Average group share in wards with the				
Highest group concentration	19.7	51.0	48.9	31.7
Second-highest group concentration	18.2	46.9	39.5	22.1
Third-highest group concentration	15.8	44.9	36.6	18.3
As a share of the total British population	1.1	2.0	1.4	0.5
Total no. living in Great Britain	563,842	1,036,807	714,826	280,845

Note: The 2001 and 1991 figures are not directly comparable because the 2001 census also included categories for mixed ethnicity, which were not part of the 1991 survey.
Source: The 1991 figures are based on "Table S06 Ethnic Group: Residents," and 2001 data are derived from "T13 Theme Table on Ethnicity" (available at www.nomisweb.co.uk).

mobilization and can define lines of local political support (Solomos and Back 1995, 79–80). Far from being expressions of irrational, tribal loyalties, such behavior is quite rational when access to valued goods (in the political as well as in the social realm) depends on access to ethnic leaders. Nevertheless, ethnic mobilization can of course also cut the other way, if identity-based appeals replace more mainstream appeals and thus fail to deliver tangible goods in the economic realm, for example.[72] Interestingly, under this scenario, native opposition to immigrants should be much less likely. In short, strong social

---

[72] See Dickson and Scheve's (2006) analysis on the relationship between identity-based appeals and "policy slack."

networks among Britain's South Asian settlers have been conducive to both geographic concentration and mobilization, features that have endowed this group with considerable local political power.

The history of Caribbean political behavior in Britain has indeed been quite different. In addition to their less concentrated settlement, this group encountered difficulties when attempting to organize their fellow migrants locally. As one close observer of immigration and race relations in Britain noted, "The West Indians by and large vote Labour, if they vote at all – but their organizations are weak.... The Asians, on the other hand, both Indians and Pakistanis, are closely organized, and many of them look towards the leaders of the Indian Workers' Association for a guide to voting" (Foot, cited in John 1969, 2). Patterson's (1963, 59) early portrayal of the West Indian community in Brixton, South London, is emblematic of other characterizations:

The Brixton migrant settlement... lacks a potential élite or internal leadership. Taking this into account in conjunction with its relatively recent origin, with the individualistic attitude and high residential mobility of many of its members, and with the fact that the main areas of settlement do not lend themselves to the creation of a firmly delineated and isolated coloured quarter, it is not surprising to find that the Brixton migrant group has not as yet developed any notable feeling of community, nor any strong and durable organizational bond.

Similarly, Glass questions the potential for mobilization among London's West Indian newcomers on the grounds of the group's social heterogeneity and geographic dispersion, even within London, which prevented their associations from having a discernable local impact. West Indians were "on the whole not yet used to being 'organisation men'" (Glass 1961, 200–201). The Secretary of the West Hampstead (London) Labour Party also reported that "Quite a few Indians are members of the Party and attend Ward meetings... [but we] have met with less success with West Indians."[73] Examining the potential West Indian vote in the 1964 general election in Birmingham, a researcher concluded that the absence of community representatives made it "very difficult for anyone, whether West Indian or English, to try to speak to or influence the West Indian community as a whole. The canvassers were very disheartened by their attempts" (Shuttleworth 1965, 73).

In a survey of Nottingham's immigrant population, Lawrence (1974, 150–154) observes that West Indians not only lacked the organizational resources displayed by their South Asian counterparts; they were also less likely to approve of using ethnic membership for political purposes. Lawrence found that only 2 percent of West Indians in Nottingham were members of immigrant organizations and a full 90 percent were not aware of any such local associations. By contrast, 47 percent of Indians and 36 percent of Pakistanis were members of organizations catering to immigrants and only 37 and 18 percent

---

[73] LAB: Letter by Hon. Secretary Roy Shaw, West Hampstead, to Eric Whittle, Asst. Commonwealth Officer, February 5, 1957.

of Indians and Pakistanis, respectively, had not heard of any immigrant associations. Indians and Pakistanis were also more than twice as likely to agree with the idea of casting their ballots as a bloc vote to further the cause of their ethnic group in the political realm.[74] In addition to bringing to light groups' varied social and electoral behavior, these survey results show that differences in ethnic mobilization are not due to variation in the overall size of groups, since West Indians constituted the largest nonwhite migrant population in Nottingham at the time.

Others have also noted that West Indians in Britain are "ill-equipped by tradition and disposition to provide an exclusively 'ethnic' leadership. This is so because, whilst drawing much inspiration from the symbols and history of the ethnic group, West Indians are disinclined to base social and political action on ethnicity" (Goulbourne 1990, 297). Resistance to such calculated moves may have been less driven by objections to instrumental voting behavior than by divisions within their own ranks. Several accounts have stressed that the internal fissures among Britain's West Indian population routinely paralyzed concerted political action (cf. Heineman 1972, 76–77). While some have argued that class divisions have stunted collective action and deprived West Indians of group leaders (Patterson 1963, 378–379; Sharpe 1965, 29–30), others have pointed to rivalries that existed between immigrants from different islands, some of which were attributed to the divisive policies of their former colonial rulers.[75]

In addition to the ethnographic evidence that exists on the electoral mobilization of Caribbean and South Asian migrant communities in postwar Britain, quantitative data shed further light on these group differences. A recent survey carried out by the Home Office has sought to examine the social and political attitudes and behaviors of Britain's ethnic minority citizens (Home Office 2005). Containing high numbers of immigrant-origin respondents, this survey allows us to analyze the political behavior of different groups (for confidentiality reasons, the survey unfortunately does not contain local contextual variables that would allow us to correlate political behavior with economic conditions or conflict outcomes).[76] The drawback is, of course, that the survey was conducted two decades after the turbulent 1980s. Nevertheless, important

[74] The exact question wording is as follows: "Some people have suggested that it would help Indian immigrants (or Pakistani, etc., as appropriate) if they got together and decided to vote for the same party. What do you think of this view?" (Lawrence 1974, 150). Only 18 percent of West Indians agreed with this statement, compared with 37 percent of Indians and 45 percent of Pakistanis.

[75] Pilkington (1988, 141) writes, "Many of these rivalries were themselves a hangover from the Empire. For instance, the British used Barbadians to fill the ranks of the police forces across the West Indies, which meant that Barbadians were regarded with some suspicion by other islanders." See also Hiro (1991).

[76] Since some sampled areas contain only a few individuals of a given ethnic background, the inclusion of contextual variables and disclosure of the local authorities in which respondents reside could lead to the identification of respondents (email communication with Home Office Staff, January 2006).

group differences in turnout rates persist; among respondents of the Home Office survey, only 47.1 percent of black Caribbean immigrants, compared with 66.9 percent of South Asian settlers, reported having voted in recent local elections.[77]

Moreover, based on the previous discussion, the neighborhood presence of co-ethnics should further magnify these differences. We should expect ties of kinship and ethnicity to bind voters to local ethnic leaders, for most goods that can be obtained through such connections, such as assistance with council housing, area-based government grants, or planning permissions for small businesses, mosques, and churches, are disbursed locally. Additionally, the electoral arena – the ward – is several times smaller than the parliamentary constituency, providing for a more direct linkage between leaders and constituents during local elections than during general elections. This local neighborhood effect should be stronger among South Asian immigrants than among their black Caribbeans.

Figure 3.2 displays the effect of being a South Asian (Caribbean) immigrant on turnout at local elections at different levels of local concentration of co-ethnics, compared with the effect of being an immigrant hailing from the Caribbean (South Asia).[78] The concentration of co-ethnics measures the self-reported size of co-ethnics in the respondent's neighborhood, an area that most people interpret as their street or block (see Appendix B for regression results and variable codings).[79] The figure shows not only that South Asians are much more likely to cast votes in local elections than Caribbeans – the voting gap expands as the share of fellow South Asians increases. The share of Caribbeans in the neighborhood has no impact on turnout among this group.

Turning to general elections, we still observe a substantial gap between South Asian and Caribbean turnout rates. But Figure 3.3 also reveals that the neighborhood effect is much weaker among South Asians when the parliamentary constituency is the arena of political competition, compared to the impact of ethnic enclaves when elections are held at the ward level. The presence of co-ethnics, and presumably the ethnic networks that underlie them, thus appears to be much more important when councilors, rather than MPs, are up for election. Note that West Indians' lower propensity to vote and the nonexistent neighborhood effects when the arena of political competition is the larger parliamentary constituency suggest that this group's low turnout in

---

[77] The local turnout rate among Indian, Pakistani, and Bangladeshi immigrants is, respectively, 67.7, 67.0, and 63.6 percent. I restrict my analysis to Caribbeans and South Asians born outside of the United Kingdom, since much of the previous discussion is based on the political behavior of this group. The turnout rates among those born in the United Kingdom are lower for all groups, but Caribbeans again exhibit by far the lowest turnout rate.

[78] The solid line traces the estimated effect while the dashed line indicates the upper and lower bounds of the 95 percent confidence intervals associated with these estimates, based on probit regressions. In generating these figures, I follow Brambor, Clark, and Golder (2006).

[79] This understanding of the neighborhood is based on results from cognitive tests that were conducted in the pilot stage of the survey (Green and Farmer 2004, 63).

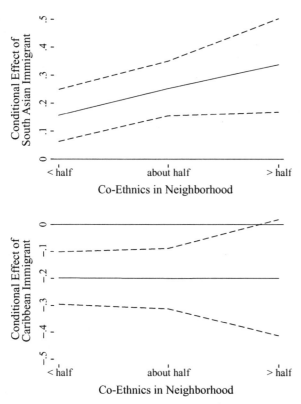

FIGURE 3.2. Turnout across groups: Local election.

local elections is not merely a response to lesser concentration at the ward level and associated diminished electoral impact, since ward-level concentration is much less important in the larger parliamentary constituency. Finally, these broad group differences remain once I control for age, gender, income, skill, and political interest (i.e., whether the respondent regularly reads the local or national newspaper).[80] Income and skill level – variables that usually impact turnout – have no purchase in explaining turnout among the immigrant electorate.

In sum, quantitative data on electoral behavior suggests that West Indian immigrants have not caught up with their South Asian counterparts when it comes to participating in local and national elections. The distinct effects of ethnic neighborhoods across groups and across elections are consistent with the qualitative accounts reviewed herein and suggest that the strategic functions of ethnic ties vary as the electoral arena changes, a finding that is in line

---

[80] With these controls in place, I find a small and statistically weak ethnic neighborhood effect on turnout among Caribbeans, but only in the general election. The main results also hold when I disaggregate South Asians into Indians, Bangladeshis, and Pakistanis (among Pakistanis and Bangladeshis, ethnic concentration has no effect on turnout during the general election).

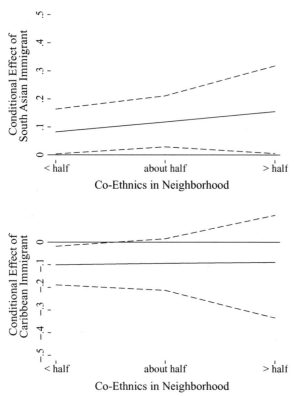

FIGURE 3.3. Turnout across groups: General election.

with evidence from other national contexts (e.g., Posner 2005). This mobilization of the ethnic vote at the local level has important distributional consequences in settings where local politicians allocate valued resources. As archival sources have revealed and empirical tests in later chapters confirm, scarcity of resources controlled by the state has resulted in immigrant conflict – but it is the political power of immigrant groups at the local level that decides whether natives will turn against immigrants or whether immigrants will turn against the state.

Summary and Conclusion

We are now in a position to answer the three questions posed earlier: First, what explains the incidence of immigrant–native conflict? Second, what explains the incidence of immigrant–state conflict? Third, what explains the varied involvement in each across immigrant groups?

The theoretical priors presented in Chapter 2 and the empirical evidence provided in the current chapter demonstrate that competition over scarce resources lies at the heart of immigrant–native conflict. True competition can only arise if two or more groups each have a realistic shot at obtaining goods that are desired by all. Furthermore, competition will be more likely to lead to sustained intergroup conflict if the supply of these goods is fixed in the short term. The aforementioned accounts have illustrated that conflicts over public housing allocations have been especially widespread. This should not come as a surprise, for such housing has not only been scarce but is also relatively finite in geographically circumscribed areas. The local council's housing queue is in fact a perfect illustration of zero-sum competition: Given fixed supply, if one household is added to or moved up on the list, another household must be dropped or moved down. In addition to being in short supply and subject to fierce competition, council housing is disbursed by the local government. Local government actors also wield significant control in the distribution of coveted – and finite – neighborhood redevelopment grants. Even if such grants originate from central government, local officials can exercise a great deal of discretion in allocating these resources to targeted local neighborhoods. Local councilors in Birmingham thus routinely bypassed minority neighborhoods whose inhabitants did not represent pivotal voting blocs (see Chapter 6).

Politicians' reluctance – or eagerness – to allocate goods to immigrant constituents is in turn a function of the perceived costs of such actions. I argued earlier that natives will engage in anti-immigrant behavior if such hostile actions are perceived to be effective in channeling resources away from immigrants and toward members of their own group. This assumption in turn implies that unless immigrants themselves are sufficiently victimized to refrain from demanding scarce goods, the actor who distributes resources is sensitive to the costs that anti-immigrant agitation produces. The Labour and Conservative Parties as well as national policy makers and politicians certainly calibrated their appeals to immigrants based on the costs associated with their assessment of native hostility. Chapters 5 and 6 will also show that local ward parties calculated whether immigrant turnout would trump the xenophobic vote, and would distribute resources accordingly.

Since it is immigrant political power that induces local parties to respond to immigrant needs in the first place, anti-immigrant voting may not always be enough to discourage parties from allocating resources to this new electorate. Under this scenario, physical violence directed against immigrants may have to supplement anti-immigrant electoral mobilization. For instance, when the Labour Party in Tower Hamlets had no choice but to rely on the immigrant vote for success, racist violence against immigrants was indeed stepped up, as voting for far-right parties did not act as a sufficient deterrent in wards where immigrants comprised the plurality of voters who turned out on election day (see Chapter 5).

The short-term trade-offs indeed seem unattractive. On one hand, poorly organized and politically weak immigrant groups will be less exposed to xenophobic vitriol by right-wing parties and racist violence by resentful whites than their better organized, politically active counterparts. On the other hand, the former might be systematically disadvantaged in the distribution of resources, while the latter use their political leverage to gain access to state-controlled goods. From the perspective of the state, this trade-off is further sharpened when continued neglect and deprivation at the hands of local state institutions engender growing resistance against the state and its representatives. For politically weak groups, access to the local political establishment is effectively blocked, for they cannot back up demands for highly valued goods with promises of highly valued votes.

Chapter 6 further illustrates how this exclusion from conventional political channels has led politically marginalized groups to articulate their discontent by engaging with the state on violent terms. Future chapters will also show that it is indeed substantive and not merely descriptive representation that matters in both delivering goods to minority groups and in potentially angering white natives in the process. Those familiar with the history of ethnic minority political incorporation will have noticed that several local authorities, such as Bradford or Haringey, had elected ethnic minority councilors when antistate violence occurred. But in Haringey, North London, where left-wing and West Indian councilors had promised to improve the delivery of services to the borough's predominantly West Indian immigrant population, the local political leadership did not deliver; it soon became "embroiled in conflicts between the various community representatives ... policy change was limited" (Solomos and Singh 1990, 106). In Bradford, the Pakistani-origin leadership had similarly failed to obtain economic goods for its constituents when antistate disturbances took place in 1995 (Dancygier 2007a).

The short-term trade-off between immigrant–native conflict and immigrant–state conflict during times of economic scarcity underlies the striking group differences that we observe in the incidence of immigrant conflict. As the previous discussion has shown, South Asians and West Indians have differed considerably in their electoral potential. It is this difference that accounts for South Asians' greater involvement in immigrant–native conflict and Caribbeans' increased propensity to be part of immigrant–state conflict. Even though policy makers understood the local economic sources of antistate behavior on the part of Britain's West Indian population, they could not account for Asians' relative absence in immigrant–state conflict, for they failed to appreciate that local electoral power was a necessary ingredient in the distribution of economic resources at the local level. Ironically, while policy makers did not recognize the political bases of immigrant conflict, the measures that they proposed to help West Indians acquire economic goods effectively substituted for this group's lacking political power at the local level. Specifically, the Cabinet urged the Home Office to give "sympathetic consideration" to applications for grant aid submitted under the Urban Programme[81]; "it was agreed that the highest priority should go to self-help groups aiming to reach disaffected West Indian youth" and the Home Office also acquiesced when asked "not [to] necessarily

---

[81] CAB 134/3772: "Disaffected Young West Indians," Memorandum by the Home Office to the Official Committee on Immigration and Community Race Relations, May 6, 1974.

insist on the same standards of accountability in these cases as in the general run of the Urban Programme."[82] After the 1981 riots, additional funds directed at "disaffected West Indians" were made available, and it had "become received wisdom that certain projects [had] been funded under the Urban Programme either because those who proposed them threatened that there would be riots if funding was not made available, or promised a reduction in local crime if it was" (Fitzgerald 1988, 393).

In this way, the government's approach mirrors Gurr's "strategy for incumbents" in the face of social instability and political violence: Gurr advises that "concessions [to the discontented] are most effective if they contribute to the capacity of the discontented to help themselves" (1970, 352). While the central government had to cajole local authorities to fund projects aimed at groups whose voting power fell short, subsequent chapters demonstrate how local councilors cooperated – sometimes reluctantly, other times keenly – with politically influential immigrant groups to ensure access to such government funds.

[82] HO 390/7: "Grant-aiding Projects which Benefit Ethnic Minorities," Draft submission for Mr. Howard-Drake's signature, February 7, 1977.

4

Dynamics of Racist Violence

In Chapter 3, we saw that the occurrence of large-scale violent clashes between immigrant-origin minorities and natives and immigrant-origin minorities and the state has varied across groups, cities, and over time. Intergroup and antistate confrontations on a smaller scale appear to track these patterns: South Asians often became targets of racist harassment, while low-level flare-ups involving state actors and ethnic minorities were particularly common among West Indians. Both faces of immigrant conflict became increasingly prevalent during the 1970s and 1980s, as economic conditions deteriorated, and they were also more likely to take place in Britain's most economically disadvantaged neighborhoods.

This chapter homes in on one of the aforementioned indicators of immigrant conflict: the incidence of everyday racist attacks, perpetuated by individuals acting alone or in small groups. I pursue two aims. First, I demonstrate that this type of violence correlates with another indicator of intergroup conflict, namely the presence of xenophobic political parties at the local level. Some have questioned the nature of this relationship, arguing, for example, that individuals are likely to resort to racist crime when no extremist parties are available to take up their grievances, or that such crime is guided by irrational impulses that do not follow political trends (see the subsequent text). Research on far-right parties in turn suggests that voters who support extremist organizations may do so in part to protest the political establishment, rather than to voice concerns about immigration or the ethnic diversity it brings about (cf. Mudde 2007, 226–229). By contrast, I have posited that the success of local far-right, anti-immigrant parties and the incidence of racist violence are both indicators of community-level conflict and should therefore go together. Employing racist incident data collected across British local authorities from 2003–2007, I illustrate that these events indeed correlate with the presence of the far-right, xenophobic British National Party. This finding increases our confidence that considering these two phenomena as signs of local-level conflict between immigrant-origin minorities and the indigenous population, as future chapters will do, is a valid approach.

The second goal of this chapter is to show that the variables that produce local-level immigrant–native conflict – immigrant political power and economic scarcity – shape the occurrence of racist attacks. I therefore take a closer look at the microlevel anatomy of intergroup clashes by investigating the determinants of racist crime. The evidence presented in this part of the chapter relies on racist incident data collected by the Metropolitan Police Service (MPS) in Greater London from April 1999 to March 2005.[1] Unlike the first data set, which simply records the overall racist incident rate, these data break down racist incidents by type and victim ethnicity.

With 28.8 percent of its 7.17 million residents considering themselves to be of an ethnic group other than white, London's population is very ethnically diverse.[2] Many observers thus think of London as a cosmopolitan modern capital where groups of all ethnic backgrounds live in peace and harmony (cf. Keith 2005). Public opinion polls indeed show Londoners to be more tolerant than other Britons: In 2000, 63 percent of respondents nationwide felt that "too much is done for immigrants," but only 39 percent of the capital's residents shared this sentiment. Since the Greater London area has witnessed very large inflows of immigrants and asylum-seekers, these more benign views are sometimes attributed to Londoners' increased personal contact with these newcomers (Saggar and Drean 2001, 15). Unfortunately, these assessments of a liberal, cosmopolitan London fit uneasily with ethnographic evidence that depicts the entrenched and often violent racism that prevails in various regions throughout Greater London.[3] The 2006 electoral victories of the British National Party (BNP) in several outer London boroughs also belie this favorable image. These successes should not be merely dismissed as a fluke. Opinion polls confirm that almost one-fourth of Londoners either have voted for the BNP or have contemplated doing so; these are higher shares than reported in the rest of the country (Joseph Rowntree Reform Trust 2005). Viewed in this light, the staggering number of racist incidents recorded in Greater London – a total of 105,875 were reported from April 1999 to March 2005 – may seem less surprising.

As I elaborate in greater detail below, in addition to being substantively interesting, the choice of Greater London for the study of racist crime offers several practical and theoretical advantages. On the practical level, studies have held up the United Kingdom as an example of good practice with respect to data-collection efforts in the area of racist crime (Oakley 2005; Goodey

---

[1] I thank Ross Gorman at the MPS for compiling these data for me.

[2] Author's calculations, based on "T13 Theme Table on Ethnicity" (available at www.nomisweb. co.uk). Unless otherwise noted, figures referring to ethnic group characteristics cited in this chapter are based on this source.

[3] See, e.g., Hewitt's (2005) study on white racism in Greenwich, South London and Bowling (1998) on the nature of racist violence in Newham, East London.

2007), giving us increased confidence in the reliability of the data used here. Focusing on a location within the United Kingdom that is covered by one police force that applies the same legal and operational standards to the identification, recording, and investigation of racist crime further reduces potential measurement distortions. On the theoretical front, Greater London's thirty-two boroughs provide important variation in both the dependent and independent variables, which allows us to undertake an effective comparative analysis. Economic conditions vary across locations and immigrant political power differs across groups. Yet, there are also drawbacks. Choosing London as our study site leaves us with just thirty-two observations. Moreover, the data span only six years. We therefore cannot test longer-term dynamics over time, as I do elsewhere in this book. More generally, the quantitative results presented here are based on indicators that imperfectly capture the political and economic dynamics that produce immigrant conflict. In contrast to the case studies that follow, they do not, for example, measure the nature of ethnic minority claims making or the specific economic goods that may or may not be the source of grievance in a given location.

In light of the practical limitations of accurate measurement as well as the many diverse theories that attempt to explain racist violence, the goal of this chapter is not to argue that such violence only spreads according to the local political and economic dynamics that produce immigrant–native conflict identified in the foregoing chapters. Rather, I demonstrate that patterns of individual-level violent xenophobia are consistent with the logic of community-level intergroup conflict; episodes of small-scale racist violence should not be understood as a series of unrelated events that arise from perpetrators' irrational impulses to act out their prejudice in violent, interpersonal ways. By differentiating between racist crime committed against members of politically powerful immigrant groups on the one hand and such violence committed against members of groups that wield relatively less electoral power on the other, the analysis finds that different dynamics are at work in the targeting of these groups with violent racism.

The chapter proceeds as follows. The next section situates this chapter's question and findings in the interdisciplinary literature by discussing some of the conceptual and empirical difficulties that scholars encounter when studying hate crime. The chapter goes on to provide a brief overview of different theoretical approaches that seek to account for the incidence of racist crime. I next present the correlation between the presence of the xenophobic BNP and the rate of racist incidents in British local authorities. The rest of the chapter discusses the data, empirical specification, and results of my analysis of the determinants of racist violence in London's thirty-two boroughs.

The Problem of Racist Violence

Racist violence is one of the most vicious and harmful phenomena commonly experienced in ethnically diverse societies today. Its forms are varied, encompassing verbal slurs, graffiti, vandalism, harassment, arson, physical assault, and murder. Its effects are deeply felt by its immediate targets[4] as well as by the groups to whom the victims belong, as community-wide fear and a sense of vulnerability may follow these heinous acts.[5] Despite the prevalence and severity of racist crime, scholars are only beginning to gain an understanding of the nature and causes of this problem. This shortcoming is due in part to data limitations. In most countries, efforts to collect systematic information on hate crime more generally, and racist crime in particular, if undertaken at all, are relatively recent phenomena. In the United States, for example, the concept of hate crime did not enter the public consciousness until the late 1980s and only since the passage of the 1990 Hate Crime Statistics Act has the recording of hate crimes based on race, religion, sexual orientation, or ethnicity been a federal requirement.[6] In Great Britain, the escalation of racially motivated attacks, including a series of murders, compelled the government to respond to the issue of racist violence in the early 1980s (Bowling 1998, 58–100; Bleich 2007, 150–153). Since then, government agencies and law enforcement have formulated various policies to guide the recording of hate crime, and several recent pieces of legislation enhance penalties for "racially aggravated" unlawful conduct (cf. Mason 2005, 841–842).

While legal definitions and data-collection methods have evolved over time within the United States and Great Britain and still vary across localities, these differences seem minor when viewed from a cross-national perspective. Within Europe, countries differ sharply in how they conceptualize and hence record racist violence. The collection of hate crime data in Germany, for example, has focused on extreme-right-wing violence, propaganda, and speech, reflecting the country's historical experience with Nazism (Watts 2001; Falk and Zweimüller 2005). This category therefore does not just cover crimes against immigrants but also includes attacks against Jews and Jewish institutions, homosexuals, the disabled, the homeless, and left-wing extremists.[7] In France and the Netherlands, law enforcement has tended to concentrate on organized or political forms of racist violence and pays less attention to hate crimes in which extremist political organizations seemingly play no role (Witte 1995, 491). A comprehensive report on racist violence commissioned by the European Union concluded

---

[4] Studies have found that victims of hate crime suffer from a higher degree of posttraumatic stress than victims of crimes that do not exhibit a bias motivation. See, e.g., Herek, Cogan, and Gillis (2002) and McDevitt, Balboni, Garcia, and Gu (2001), as well as results from the 2000 British Crime Survey (Home Office 2001a, 37–38).

[5] The potential community-wide repercussions of hate crimes committed against individual victims ("secondary victimization") has indeed been one of the main arguments put forth by those in favor of hate crime legislation, including the United States Supreme Court in *Wisconsin v. Mitchell* (1993); see also Iganski (2001).

[6] At the state level, however, there remains great variation in the legal definition of hate crime (specifically which target groups are covered), and only a few states mandate the collection of hate crime data (Jenness and Grattet 2001; Shively 2005).

[7] In 2001, Germany departed from this conception and since then records "politically motivated" acts independent of their categorization as extremist (Oakley 2005, 13).

that many member states do not in fact define racially motivated violence, and, in the ones that do, data collection is often patchy or nonexistent, making it very difficult to assess accurately the actual extent and nature of violent racism. What does seem certain is that the countries with the best-developed recording mechanisms (e.g., Finland, Great Britain, and Sweden) also exhibit the highest crime rates, suggesting that differences in collection methods may significantly distort actual levels of racist crime (European Monitoring Centre on Racism and Xenophobia 2005, 158).

Divergent conceptions of racially motivated crime are also associated with varying notions of the underlying causes of such violence. In Germany, efforts to combat racist violence usually address the structural conditions that are thought conducive to the dissemination of Nazi ideology, focusing less on the impact of victimization at the level of the minority group. Conversely, British authorities have tended to view racist crime as an indicator of the quality of intergroup relations. Policies aimed at reducing the incidence of racially motivated crime (which can consequently also be committed by members of minority groups against members of the majority white population) go hand in hand with improving intergroup relations more generally (Witte 1995, 491). The empirical evidence presented in this chapter puts this notion to the test by investigating whether the determinants that foster peaceful intergroup relations are also associated with lower levels of racist crime. Before moving on to the statistical analysis, I briefly turn to the diverse theoretical approaches that have been formulated to explain the incidence of hate crime.

Explaining Racist Crime: Existing Theoretical Approaches

Individual-Level Explanations

Explanations of the phenomenon of hate crime have emerged in a range of scholarly disciplines using various empirical methods. Psychological studies have focused their attention on the behavioral and psychological traits that distinguish perpetrators of racist violence from the population at large. This body of research assumes that the same processes that lead individuals to hold prejudiced attitudes will propel them to commit crimes of hate (cf. Green et al. 2001, 485; Dancygier and Green 2010). However, a focus on bigoted beliefs would greatly overpredict the incidence of hate crime, for not all bigots commit bigoted crimes (Green, Abelson, and Garnett 1999). Scholars have also tried to establish whether the biographical profiles of hate criminals set them apart from nonoffenders. Studies of perpetrators in Germany and Great Britain have found that offenders are overwhelmingly young white men (between the ages of 15 and 24 years), who, compared to nonoffenders, tend to have relatively low levels of educational achievement and are more likely to be unemployed, to come from disadvantaged social backgrounds, and to have a history of aggressive behavior starting in early childhood. Their affiliation with racist political groupings is highly variable (Willems 1995; Wahl 2003; Commission for Racial Equality 2005). This variation suggests that racist violence may occur in the absence of political mobilization against ethnic minorities; an increase in the supply of young white jobless men would translate into a rise in hate crime, regardless of the political context.

An alternative approach concentrates less on perpetrators' backgrounds and more on the motivations behind their attacks. Psychologists have found it useful to apply the concepts of reactive and instrumental aggression to the study of hate crime. Perpetrators who commit reactive hate crimes act defensively and often spontaneously in response to a perceived threat by a social outgroup; their aggression is driven less by feelings of racial superiority and more by a desire to protect members of their group against this encroachment by unwelcome intruders. Instrumental hate criminals, by contrast, commit bigoted violence as a means to establish the social dominance of their group. Their crimes, and the selection of their targets, are premeditated and purposeful and motivated by a strong ideological resolve to demonstrate their perceived superiority (Dunbar 2003, 204; Sullaway 2004, 263).

This broad distinction maps onto more fine-grained perpetrator typologies. Willems' study of German hate criminals, for example (Willems, Eckert, Würtz, and Steinmetz 1993, 200–207; Willems 1995), distinguishes between the right-wing activist, the ethnocentrist youth, the criminal youth, and the fellow traveler. Ethnocentrist youths use racist violence to register their discontent with the economic disadvantages and competition perceived to be brought on by immigration, while right-wing activists commit racist violence to underscore their ideological commitment to racism. Hate criminals may not necessarily embrace ethnocentric attitudes, but a general propensity to violence among criminal youth or the pressures of peer dynamics in the case of fellow travelers may lead to their commission of hate crimes. The typology of McDevitt and colleagues (McDevitt, Levin, and Bennett 2002) yields some analytical overlap. Relying on Boston police files of recorded hate crimes, the authors claim that most hate criminals are simply thrill-seekers in search of excitement. The second most common type are defensive perpetrators, who employ bigoted violence to protect their neighborhood from intrusion by outsiders, followed by retaliatory offenders, who want to avenge a preceding hate attack, and the very rare mission offenders, who are solely driven by bigotry.

Applied to the conflicts investigated in this book, the heterogeneity of perpetrator motives and types suggests that the spread of racist violence might not necessarily mirror the logic of immigrant–native conflict. At the same time, elite-engineered collective expressions of intergroup conflict, such as anti-immigrant rallies or recruitment drives, and electoral victories of far-right parties might focus attention on particular victim groups or inspire various types of potential perpetrators to commit crimes of hate. In this way, strategic elite actions might increase opportunities for expressive and rational violence on the part of individuals.

Contextual Explanations

As the possible interplay between elite-level behavior and individual-level behavior suggests, psychological accounts can also be placed within larger social contexts. Some sociological accounts stress the importance of macrovariables such as modernization and economic transformation and the social dislocations that these forces unleash (e.g., Heitmeyer 1993). Ray and Smith (2001) thus situate their study of racist violence in Greater Manchester in the context of social transformations that have occurred over the past 200 years, such as increased pluralism, general feelings of disenchantment, economic globalization, and the development of transnational identities. Focusing on one confined geographical area over a brief period of time, the present study holds these larger phenomena constant but still finds considerable variation in the production of racist violence. This result does not, of course, invalidate the theoretical merits of these macrostructural accounts, but it remains difficult to subject them to empirical scrutiny.

Economic approaches do question the validity of these cultural explanations and instead argue that a rise in the occurrence of bigoted violence is generally accompanied by deteriorating economic conditions, which may increase both frustration and intergroup competition. Falk and Zweimüller (2005) thus dismiss the argument that East Germany's different historical trajectory and socialization processes are to blame for the region's higher prevalence of hate crime compared to the country's western states. Their state-level analysis of officially recorded right-wing extremist crimes shows that higher levels of unemployment in the East are the main driver of this difference. These findings stand in stark contrast to Krueger and Pischke's (1997) analysis, which turns up no relationship between unemployment and right-wing violence in Germany's eastern or western states. It is difficult to adjudicate between these two studies, since they employ different data, operate at different levels of aggregation, and apply to different time periods.[8] Ethnographic studies, however, have also stressed the links between economic recession, the frustration and resentment these downturns may engender, and the commission of hate crimes (e.g., Pinderhughes 1993; Ray and Smith 2004).

The importance of macroeconomic variables has been challenged by Green, Strolovitch, and Wong (1998).[9] In their study of racially motivated violence in fifty-two New York City community districts, Green and colleagues show that demographic dynamics, rather than economic conditions, explain the incidence of such violence: In-migration of nonwhite minorities into areas with more homogenously white populations tends to be associated with higher

---

[8] Falk and Zweimüller's analysis operates at the state level, relies on official data recorded by the Federal Criminal Police Office (*Bundeskriminalamt*), and covers the years 1996–1999; Krueger and Pischke's study uses the county as the unit of analysis and is based on newspaper reports from January 1991 to June 1993. See also Chapter 7.

[9] See also Green, Glaser, and Rich (1998), who question the purported relationship between economic conditions and antiblack lynching in the United States.

racist crime rates compared with that into areas that are more ethnically mixed. Consistent with the reactive or defensive perpetrator type just discussed, the authors' Defended Neighborhood Model contends that residents living in white strongholds may be more likely to react violently to a sudden influx of newcomers because they perceive control over their turf and their way of life to be under threat. Ethnographic studies of racially motivated violence in Great Britain have also underscored the importance of the relationship between "white territorialism" (Hesse, Dhawant, Bennett, and McGilchrist 1992, 171–173), or "neighbourhood nationalism" (Back and Nayak 1999, 277), and racist violence.[10] Male youths who live in predominantly white, run-down areas that have been hit hard by economic downturns are seen as most likely to turn to violent racism to protect their turf, suggesting that neighborhood defense is conditional on economic conditions.

The study of Tower Hamlets will also illustrate that violence and hostility against Bangladeshi in-migration was especially pernicious in predominantly white areas that experienced rapid Bangladeshi in-migration. But this demographic change was closely linked to the contested distribution of scarce and highly valued council housing, pointing to interactive effects of economic scarcity, patterns of in-migration, and demographic balance on racist crime, as well as on a community's sanctioning of this type of violence. Case studies of two London boroughs in which racial harassment is a daily occurrence reveal that equally important to understanding individual characteristics of perpetrators is an appreciation of the communities that produce hate crime offenders and that may legitimize their violent bigotry with tacit or explicit support.[11]

Racist Violence and Racist Voting

The contextual accounts just given here underline that racist violence does not occur in a social vacuum. As Bowling (1993) points out, racist crimes are best understood if put in the context of the specific relationships between social and political actors at the neighborhood and community level.[12] Communities that harbor resentments against their ethnic minority neighbors may thus foster racist attacks as well as support for xenophobic political parties.

Observers of race relations in Great Britain have noted that areas where anti-immigrant parties compete for elected office also tend to be sites of hostile native attacks against immigrants. Writing about Britain in the 1970s and early 1980s, Benyon concludes that "It was evident that the National Front was actively encouraging racial hostility in many of the areas where attacks were

[10] See also Bowling (1998, 188–89) and Hewitt (1996).
[11] See Sibbit (1997). See also Fearon and Laitin (1996), who provide an explanation of inter-ethnic peace that stresses the importance of intra-community dynamics, such as the ability to police and sanction co-ethnics who target members of an ethnic out-group.
[12] See also Karapin (2002) for an explanation of racially motivated riots that privileges local political opportunities.

occurring, even if its *direct* involvement in them was hard to prove" (1986, 250; emphasis in the original). In Tower Hamlets, resentment against Bangladeshis escalated into violent racism in the 1980s and delivered BNP victories in the early 1990s (Chapter 5). In Bradford, the xenophobic party also gained at the polls as relations between the Pakistani and the white community deteriorated (Dancygier 2007a). Similarly, in Oldham, a northern town that, like Bradford, experienced large-scale rioting between whites and South Asians in 2001, the BNP issued leaflets proclaiming "Community self-defence is no offence!," a call for the use of violence to protect whites from "gangs of Muslim thugs" (quoted in Ray and Smith 2004, 694).

But racist violence clearly also takes place in the absence of campaigns by far-right parties. Given limited financial and personnel resources, the BNP and other extremist political parties select a subset of localities for electoral competition. Nevertheless, *all else equal*, the record tends to show, and this book has stipulated, that the presence of xenophobic political parties and the incidence of racist crime at the local level are both indicators of community-wide conflicts between ethnic minorities and the indigenous population.

Others have challenged this relationship. Koopmans (1996) argues that individuals are more likely to commit bigoted crimes against ethnic minorities when less costly channels for the expression of xenophobia – such as voting for racist parties – are unavailable. Comparing cross-national extreme right and racist violence data aggregated at the country level, Koopmans maintains that the existence of well-organized parties of the extreme right effectively substitutes for racist violence. As the author admits, comparing these figures across countries is problematic. To illustrate this point, Witte (1995, 492) presents data that show France to have had 188 recorded incidents of racist violence in 1993 compared with Britain's 9,762 in the same year. Furthermore, focusing on national data may obscure correlations between violence and voting at the subnational level.

Nevertheless, the theoretical claim that violence and voting may substitute for one another should be taken seriously. If the inverse relationship holds true, problems of inference would arise. Reliable data of small-scale racist crime are unavailable for most local authorities and for most years, not only in Great Britain but also in most other European countries. Nevertheless, we can more easily observe whether a xenophobic party competed at the polls and, if so, how well it performed. In the absence of hate crime data, the success and failures of such parties can thus serve as an indicator of local immigrant–native conflict. Unless, of course, engaging in racist violence – a behavior that often goes unrecorded – substitutes for voting for xenophobic parties. For local election years in which data on racist crime are available, however, the quantitative results I present here bear out the positive correlation between racist violence and the presence of xenophobic parties that has been suggested by qualitative accounts: The two move in tandem.

The quantitative data I employ in this section cover the years 2003 to 2007. In light of data limitations, it is unfortunately not possible to track the occurrence of small-scale racist violence over the span of several decades, the time frame adopted in most of the book's chapters. Most local authorities or police force areas simply have no record of racist crime that goes back even to the 1980s. Any quantitative cross-sectional analysis of racially motivated violence in Great Britain must therefore start in the late 1990s, when British law enforcement began to record racist incidents more systematically. British legislation does not explicitly address or define hate crime as a general offense, but since 1998 it provides for enhanced penalties if an offense can be shown to be racially aggravated. This common legal definition of racially motivated crime is a necessity for a meaningful comparative analysis of these offenses. But equally important as a shared legal framework is a common law enforcement approach to the identification and recording of such violence. British police departments and statutory agencies follow the wide definition recommended by the Stephen Lawrence Inquiry: "A racist incident is any incident, which is perceived to be racist by the victim or any other person."[13]

Since the early 2000s, the Audit Commission (an independent organization monitoring local service delivery and a range of social and economic developments) has published the rate of racist incidents (the number of racist incidents per 100,000 residents) in English local authorities.[14] In the analysis that follows, I test whether the racist incident rate in authorities in which the BNP runs for office exceeds the rate in authorities where the BNP does not contest elections. The analysis is meant to be correlational, not causal; throughout the book, I have assumed that a set of factors – the electoral clout wielded by immigrant-origin minorities and the scarcity of economic resources – drives both racist crime and racist voting. Here, I am simply interested in finding out whether racist crime and the presence of xenophobic parties go together.

Table 4.1 shows the results that I obtain when I regress the racist incident rate on a variable indicating whether BNP candidates competed in local elections as well as on two additional variables, the share and number of votes cast for the BNP in 2004.[15] I display bivariate regressions as well as results controlling

---

[13] Macpherson (1999, 328). Stephen Lawrence, a Briton of Jamaican descent, was stabbed to death by a group of white boys in London in 1993. His murder and the following unsuccessful criminal investigation received wide publicity, leading to a public inquiry. This investigation, conducted by Sir William Macpherson, widely condemned the Metropolitan Police Service's handling of the case, starting from the police's failure to provide first aid at the scene to errors during the investigation. The report considered the police's incompetence, as well as the nationwide failure by the police to address racial incidents, signs of institutional racism and made dozens of recommendations for reform (Macpherson 1999).

[14] These data are available at http://www.audit-commission.gov.uk.

[15] Since, at the time of data analysis, I only had access to ward-level data and therefore had to compile votes and vote shares at the level of the local authority manually, I restrict my investigation of these two variables – the share and number of votes collected by the BNP – to the 2004 election. I thank Brian Cheal from the Local Government Chronicle Election Centre (University of Plymouth) for providing me with the 2004–2007 local election data. I use

TABLE 4.1. *Racist Incidents and the British National Party*

	Racist Incidents													
	All Years		2003–2004		2004–2005		2005–2006		2006–2007		2003–2004		2003–2004	
BNP candidates – dummy	37.096 (5.758)	31.445 (5.327)	44.239 (8.213)	38.078 (7.665)	13.665 (4.368)	11.316 (4.347)	35.538 (11.087)	37.793 (10.060)	28.292 (5.517)	22.716 (4.996)				
BNP – vote share											6.139 (1.411)	4.648 (1.359)		
BNP – number of votes													0.009 (0.001)	0.007 (0.001)
Percent nonwhite		3.235 (0.426)		2.862 (0.608)		1.372 (0.432)		2.651 (0.428)		4.207 (0.486)		2.814 (0.650)		1.911 (0.620)
R^2	0.11	0.31	0.20	0.33	0.04	0.08	0.06	0.23	0.08	0.26	0.14	0.26	0.34	0.39
N	833		118		231		175		311		118		118	
Number of local elections where BNP competed	296		57		22		76		141		57		57	
Mean share of nonwhites in local authorities holding elections	5.10		5.53		2.90		9.68		4.03		5.53		5.53	

Notes: Ordinary least squares coefficients with standard errors are given in parentheses. A constant term is included but not shown. The model pooling all years clusters observations on local authority. All coefficients are significant at the $p \le .01$ level. All models (except model 2004–2005) exclude the outlying observation of Portsmouth. Model 2004–2005 excludes the outlier Bristol. Observations that were collected in ways that caused the Audit Commission to express doubt about their quality were dropped from the analysis (amounting to twenty-six observations in the pooled model; eighteen in 2003–2004; eight in 2004–2005; and none in 2005–2006 and 2006–2007).

for the percentage of nonwhites living in a local authority, to ensure that the association between racist crime and BNP candidacies is not simply due to the fact that both occur in ethnically diverse areas (all results that follow are robust to replacing the share of nonwhites with the percentage of Muslims).[16] The first set of regressions, pooling all election years, reveals that local elections in which BNP candidates compete are associated with a 31- to 37-point increase in the racist incident rate ($p = .000$; the mean racist incident rate is 27.3, with a standard deviation of SD = 52.6). Breaking down the analysis by election, we see that this positive and statistically significant relationship remains, but differs in magnitude, reflecting varying levels of ethnic diversity in the local authorities holding elections in a given year (see Table 4.1 for the average shares of nonwhites). Moreover, as BNP performance improves (measured in terms of the number of votes and the vote share received), the recorded racist incident rate rises as well.

Synthesizing this information, we can conclude that there is indeed a positive association between the presence and success of the xenophobic British National Party and the rate of racist incidents at the local level. Existing qualitative evidence and these quantitative results paint a consistent picture that racist violence and racist voting constitute strategies that communities who are hostile to ethnic out-groups may use jointly.

But we also know that it does not necessarily take racist elites to stoke such hateful crime. In the late 1990s and early 2000s, the period covered by the Greater London racist crime data set, racist incidents tended to occur in the absence of BNP candidacies. The party had made a strategic choice to contest local elections in other parts of the country, but decided to run candidates in several London boroughs in the 2006 elections. Explaining what shapes patterns of racist violence in London's thirty-two boroughs is the purpose of the next section.

The Determinants of Racist Violence

My rather cursory review of the literature on hate crime conveys the great range of diverse methodological and theoretical approaches that have attempted to explain this phenomenon. Perpetrator studies document a variety of motives at the individual level that should make us wary of any parsimonious, macrostructural theory of racist crime. Given the multifaceted nature of hate crime, studies

---

racist incident data from 2003–2004 onward; in previous years, more than 10 percent of local authorities did not report racist incident rates.

[16] In Table 4.1 I regress the racist incident rate as recorded from April to March, spanning two years, on the presence (and votes) of the BNP in the election held in May or June in the second of those two years. Doing so is meant to take into account BNP campaigning – and associated racist crime – in the months prior to elections. Very similar results obtain when regressing the racist incident rate on BNP presence and votes in elections held in the first of the two years in which these racist incident data are collected.

that test the relationship between specific ecological parameters and the incidence of racist violence – including the present one – are likely to pick up a lot of noise. A statistical analysis that shows a robust link between economic variables and the incidence of racist violence at the level of the locality, for example, will capture individual acts of hate crime that are committed by thrill-seekers or mission offenders whose aggression is not driven by material concerns. Nevertheless, to the extent that adverse economic circumstances increase the pool of potential hate criminals or compel potential hate criminals to action by producing neighbors and elites that highlight the linkage between economic grievances and immigration, such a test will still be informative. The intention of this chapter is thus not to propose a universal theory of racist crime; such a theory is bound to fail. Rather, the goal is to examine whether the dynamics that are at the core of immigrant–native conflict at the level of the locality are also evident in patterns of racially motivated crime committed by individuals.

This book has highlighted the interaction between political and economic variables in the production of intergroup conflict between immigrants and natives at the local level. Does the incidence of racially motivated crime occurring on a small scale travel along the same trajectory? If so, I would expect that the effect of in-migration of a *politically powerful* ethnic group on the incidence of racially motivated crime increases as levels of local prosperity decrease. Conversely, in-migration of a *politically weak* ethnic group should have much smaller effects on the incidence of racially motivated crime directed against this group, regardless of levels of local prosperity. The next section discusses the empirical data and model that evaluate these, as well as alternative, hypotheses.

Data and Variables

Since the racist incident data used in the previous section do not provide any details about victims, I turn to a different source here. The following analysis employs data that have been collected by the Metropolitan Police Service from April 1999 to March 2005, which covers Greater London's thirty-two boroughs. On the practical side, the fact that this data set distinguishes between South Asian and black (African and Caribbean) victims allows us to examine whether these two groups, who also differ in their electoral power, are subject to different dynamics of racist victimization. Furthermore, relying on racist crime data that have been collected in London boroughs has the advantage that the study covers a large, densely populated area that is administered by only one police force that applies one common set of standards in pursuing such crime (MPS 2000). The data gathered in London since the late 1990s are also of higher quality than previous information on criminal racist incidents. During the time period under study, the MPS launched a major initiative, the Racial and Violent Crimes Task Force, to recognize, investigate, and combat racial, homophobic, and domestic violence (Ray and Smith

2001, 212). It established Community Safety Units across all areas of Greater London, where staff members have been specially trained in intergroup relations, as well as in local cultural issues, to encourage the reporting of racially motivated incidents, ensure victim confidentiality, provide support for victims, and investigate individual incidents. These units liaise with local law enforcement and local government agencies to further improve their data-collection efforts and victim support services (MPS, n.d.). In sum, law enforcement's uniform approach across boroughs as well as its increased efforts greatly reduce reporting biases across locations and enhance the quality of the data.

Notwithstanding these administrative advantages, the data also have drawbacks. First, we are left with only thirty-two borough-level observations. Moreover, the six-year time span is rather short, especially when compared to the long-term dynamics studied in the rest of this book. The data therefore cannot capture important trends, such as the marked improvement in economic conditions beginning in the mid-1990s. Additional complications are linked to the behavior of perpetrators and victims. A limitation of the present data is the lack of information on perpetrator ethnicity. Newspaper reports, case studies, and perpetrator and victim surveys indicate that young whites are the most common offenders in hate crimes committed against ethnic minorities. The 2000 British Crime Survey, which asks respondents about their victimization experiences in the previous year, found that, in cases in which victims identified the perpetrator's ethnicity, 74 and 67 percent of all black and Asian victims of racially motivated crime, respectively, reported having been attacked by white perpetrators. Only 2 percent of black victims reported Asian offenders, while only 13 percent of Asian victims reported crimes by black perpetrators (Home Office 2001a, 35).

Another common shortcoming of hate crime studies more generally is the serious issue of underreporting by victims. This problem is particularly vexing if such underreporting is not random, but is more likely among certain groups or localities. Researchers have observed, for example, that individuals may vary in their willingness to engage in counterattacks and this variation has been tied to racial group membership (Craig 1999). In his study of racist crime in New York City, Garofalo (1991) also finds reciprocity in the occurrence of hate crimes between blacks and whites, but not between Hispanics and either of these two groups. The present study has no way of assessing these potential distortions. The Community Safety Units' emphasis on confidentiality and its efforts to limit the exposure of victim details even in cases that go to court (MPS, n.d.) will reduce bias induced as a result of varying fears of retribution. Nevertheless, different victim groups may vary in their propensity to report racist incidents to the police for a host of other reasons. The empirical analysis below does not compare the frequency of incidents across groups, so unless underreporting also systematically varies along economic or demographic characteristics of localities, which is less likely given the MPS's shared set of uniform standards, these potential differences should not bias the results. Restricting the analysis to racist crime that results in serious injury or murder and excluding, for example, verbal insults (see below) will also increase the likelihood of reporting and hence reduce measurement error.

The main empirical strategy of the analysis is to test whether the determinants of racist crime vary across victim groups that share a host of demographic features, but that differ in their local political power. I thus estimate two sets of regressions with two dependent variables, anti–South Asian and antiblack racist incidents. Furthermore, for both sets of regressions, I restrict my analysis to *violent and harmful* racist crime (summed up over six years by borough). The main dependent variable of interest includes racist incidents that have resulted in actual or grievous bodily harm or murder, but it excludes offenses such as common assault, harassment, robbery, burglary, theft and handling, and criminal damage. Between April 1999 and March 2005, these incidents numbered 12,207, or 11.5 percent of all recorded racist incidents.

This operationalization does not intend to minimize the harm that these excluded bigoted offenses may cause to the immediate victim or to the victimized community at large. Indeed, studies have found that the cumulative effects of repeated racially motivated verbal abuse or graffiti can be associated with great fear and psychological trauma (Bowling 1998, 201). Limiting the analysis to attacks that cause physical injury is instead meant to increase the reliability of the analysis. Moreover, the analysis excludes attacks that can be motivated by financial gain to draw a clear distinction between racial animus and other types of motivations that may go along with bigotry. Critics may, of course, claim that this operationalization undermines the very notion of most hate crime legislation, which insists that to be considered bias crimes, offenses may only be *partly* driven by racial animus. I thus also estimate models that contain all remaining types of racist incidents in the robustness checks to empirically test how the determinants of racist crime may change depending on our definition of these offenses.

As I mentioned, using data collected in Greater London has some theoretical advantages. First, the two victim communities under study exhibit many similarities in terms of their size, their geographical spread, and their migration patterns across boroughs. In 2001, London was home to 733,635 residents who considered themselves to be of Indian, Pakistani, or Bangladeshi origin while 782,849 Londoners identified themselves as black British (this category includes Africans and Caribbeans; see below). Their concentration across boroughs is very similar, both in terms of the two groups' absolute population shares and with regard to their spread (see Table 4.2). Finally, between 1991 and 2001, South Asian and black minorities also displayed comparable migration patterns, with a mean percentage point increase of 2.45 and 2.64, respectively, and similar standard deviations. Socioeconomic profiles are also alike. In 2001, 27.3 percent of South Asians and 28.7 percent of blacks were employed in routine or semiroutine occupations. London residents of South Asian origin

TABLE 4.2. *Summary Statistics: Racist Violence*

Variable	Mean	SD	Min.	Max.	Source
Racist crime against South Asians	87.19	39.48	29	186	MPS data set
Racist crime against blacks	81.00	30.01	30	164	MPS data set
South Asian in-migration	2.352	2.615	−0.63	11.12	www.nomisweb.co.uk
Black in-migration	2.640	2.309	−1.07	8.20	www.nomisweb.co.uk
Population 1991					
South Asian %	7.597	6.839	1.4	24.6	www.nomisweb.co.uk
Black %	7.872	6.315	0.7	22.0	www.nomisweb.co.uk
Local prosperity	14.00	5.011	5.628	23.58	DCLG (2004)
Male youth unemployment 2001	11.52	3.228	5.730	19.44	www.nomisweb.co.uk
Log of total population 2001	12.30	0.210	11.90	12.71	www.nomisweb.co.uk

Source: 1991 census figures are based on "Table S06 Ethnic Group: Residents." Figures on in-migration and total population use 2001 data from "T13 Theme Table on Ethnicity." Data on male youth unemployment are based on "Table S32 Sex and Age and Level of Qualifications by Economic Activity."

do, however, fare better in the labor market, with an unemployment rate of 8.0 percent, compared with a jobless rate for blacks of 12.9 percent.[17]

There are also important distinctions between these two groups that provide us with significant analytical leverage. With regard to migration, the destination boroughs have varied (the correlation of South Asian and black in-migration is −.02), which isolates the effects associated with in-migration of a given group. Further, there are significant differences in the political capital of South Asians and blacks. One way to measure local political power is by counting the number of ethnic minority councilors in a borough. Though minority groups can flex their electoral muscle in the absence of having "one of their own" represented in local government and can also be marginalized even when co-ethnics hold elected office, the existence of councilors with an immigrant background is one of the most visible signs of potential minority political power. London borough Web sites contain photographs of councilors; based on their physical appearance and their names, I classified councilors as South Asian, black, or other in February 2006. Unless elected in by-elections (scheduled as a result of the resignation or death of a sitting councilor), these candidates were elected in May 2002. Despite the slightly larger number of black residents than South Asian residents in the Greater London area, by early 2006 there were 199

[17] Note that South Asians' self-employment rate (10.8 percent) is twice that of blacks (5.3 percent). The disparity in unemployment rates may thus be a somewhat inaccurate reflection of the groups' relative labor market performance.

candidates of South Asian descent who had been elected but only 84 black candidates who had secured council seats. As one would expect in a political setting with ward-level elections, there is a high correlation between the percentage of ethnic minorities in a borough and the number of councilors these groups field ($r = .94$ among South Asians and $r = .79$ among blacks). Among blacks, though, the number of councilors tends to hover around the low single digits (with a mean of 2.6), with only two boroughs claiming ten and eleven councilors, respectively. By contrast, ten or more candidates of South Asian descent have been elected in seven boroughs and the mean number of South Asian councilors is 6.2.

Unlike previous chapters, the relative underrepresentation of blacks discussed here not only refers to blacks of West Indian descent but also includes those who consider themselves black African.[18] Over the course of the 1990s, the size of Britain's black African community nearly doubled and now reaches close to half a million, many of whom live in the London area. For the purposes of the data analysis, I have to group black Africans and black Caribbeans together, since the Metropolitan Police data do not differentiate between these two victim groups. From a theoretical standpoint, this aggregation should not compromise the main analysis but may in fact strengthen it, because black Africans are more residentially concentrated – but not more likely to vote – than black Caribbeans. In thirteen London wards, black Africans constituted at least 20 percent of the population, but this was true for only six wards among black Caribbeans. Turnout rates, however, are low for both groups: In 2003, 39.1 percent of black Africans and 39.8 percent of black Caribbeans living in London reported having voted in the last local election (among South Asians, this figure stood at 60.0 percent).[19] Moreover, one in five black Africans identified themselves as Muslim, whereas less than 1 percent of black Caribbeans did so.[20] In short, though these two groups differ in their level of residential concentration and in their religious backgrounds, they are similar in their electoral behavior. If, net of electoral power, ward-level residential concentration or Islam provoke racist violence, such a backlash should show up in the subsequent statistical analysis.

Summing up, we see that the presence of black minorities translates into only modest gains in terms of black political representation. By contrast, the presence of residents with South Asian backgrounds tends to lead to much higher numbers of co-ethnic representatives on the local council. In-migration of residents with an Indian, Pakistani, or Bangladeshi background is thus associated with a rise in the local political power of these groups, while increases

[18] The census category black British also includes "black other." This group constitutes 7.7 percent of all blacks in London.
[19] These figures are derived from analysis of the 2003 Home Office Citizenship Survey; see Chapter 3.
[20] Author's calculations, based on "Table S104 Ethnic Group by Religion," available at www.nomisweb.co.uk.

in the share of the black population do not boost black political influence on the local council to the same extent. In the statistical analysis, the key independent variable of in-migration – the percentage-point population change of South Asians or blacks between 1991 and 2001 – should thus have a positive effect on racist crime committed against South Asians (especially if economic conditions worsen), but it should be correlated more weakly, if at all, with the victimization of blacks.

Ideally, I would provide a direct measure that tracks changes in South Asian and black political representation. My count of ethnic minority councilors relied on current Web site information, and election data broken down by the candidates' ethnic background are unfortunately not available for earlier years. As an alternative strategy, I identified councilors' South Asian background by reference to their names and created a variable comparing South Asian political representation in 1998 and 2002 in the robustness checks that follow (West Indian names are not easily distinguishable from English names).

Turning to economic variables, we see that London contains some of the poorest but also some of the richest areas of the country, which allows us to test explanations that focus on economic determinants of racist violence, including the theory of immigrant–native conflict proposed in this study. The important caveat is, however, the missing time trend, especially in the face of economic improvements in the late 1990s and early 2000s. My measure of economic prosperity is drawn from the 2004 *English Indices of Deprivation.* These indices compile information on seven dimensions – income, employment, health deprivation and disability, education skills and training, barriers to housing and services, crime, and lastly, living environment – covering small geographic areas below the ward level (known as super output areas, or SOAs). These data are then ranked nationwide and aggregated to the local authority level. Nationwide, this measure ranges from 1 (most deprived) to 354 (least deprived) and Greater London displays almost the complete range, from values of 4 to 301. I created a new variable that draws on these indices but extracts the crime indicator, since our dependent variable represents a subset of all occurring crime. I first created a boroughwide score for each deprivation dimension (excluding crime) by summing population-weighted scores at the SOA level to one borough-level score. I next assigned weights for each dimension that correspond to the indices' weights with the crime dimension included[21]; the sum of these population-weighted scores (divided by 1,000 to avoid infinitesimal coefficients) produces the prosperity variable, with increasing values indicating increasing prosperity.

Compared to the qualitative evidence provided in the case studies, this variable is a rather blunt measure (the sensitivity analysis will also employ

---

[21] The weighting is as follows (weights excluding crime/weights including crime): income (25%/22.5%), employment (25%/22.5%), health and disability (15%/13.5%), education, skills and training (15%/13.5%), barriers to housing and services (10%/9.3%), and living environment (10%/9.3%); the crime score accounts for 9.3% in the original indices.

alternative indicators of economic scarcity). It provides us with a general idea of local deprivation and resource scarcity, but it does not allow us to make inferences about which components, if any, have been most politicized locally. This limitation is a significant drawback compared to the more detailed analysis of local resource shortages that the case studies will provide. Nevertheless, the measure does contain elements that take into account both the supply of and demand for economic resources. The statistical model further controls for the level of unemployment among young men (aged 16–24 years). As I already mentioned, studies of perpetrators have consistently found that offenders are overwhelmingly male, fall in this age range, and tend to have lower socioeconomic profiles than nonoffenders.

Statistical Model and Results

The following statistical analyses evaluate whether the in-migration of an electorally powerful group – in this case, South Asians – is associated with an increase in racist attacks committed against this group, and, furthermore, whether this effect is magnified as economic resources decline. Moreover, in line with this book's main theoretical argument, I expect to find that the in-migration of a politically weaker group – that is, blacks – should not provoke the same levels of racist victimization, regardless of economic conditions.

The analyses will also test economic hypotheses suggested by the literature. According to these accounts, as economic conditions deteriorate (i.e., a decline in prosperity and a rise in the number of young men without jobs), the incidence of racist attacks against both victim groups should increase. Finally, I test the Defended Neighborhood Model according to which the effect of in-migration of an ethnic group on the incidence of racially motivated crime increases as the preexisting population share of the in-migrating group decreases. Note that results supporting the defended neighborhood thesis might not be inconsistent with the book's central argument, so long as they hold among politically powerful groups but not politically weak groups. Specifically, in settings where South Asians already make up a large share of the population, and, by implication, already possess local political power, a further increase in the South Asian population may translate into a less pronounced change in this group's political power when compared with areas where South Asians are just beginning to make their presence felt politically.

To test these hypotheses, I estimate negative binomial regression models, which are suitable for event count data and estimate the excess variability, or overdispersion, around the expected number of events (King 1989, 49–50; Long 1997, 230–238). For example, two boroughs may share many characteristics leading to otherwise similar levels of racist crime, but the initial incidence of such a crime in one borough may spawn a cycle of reprisals, thus increasing the probability of observing more such events compared to the London borough that did not witness an initial incident. The negative binomial model allows for the possibility of such contagion, or overdispersion.

I estimate the incidence of racially motivated crime as follows:

$$\lambda_i = \exp(\alpha + \beta_1 \text{IM}_i + \beta_2 P_i + \beta_3 \text{IM}_i \times P_i + \beta_4 \text{PEG91}_i + \beta_5 \text{IM}_i \\ \times \text{PEG91}_i + \beta_6 \text{MYU01}_i + \beta_7 \text{POP01}_i),$$

where i indexes the borough, λ_i is the expected number of racist crimes, α is the constant, IM measures group in-migration, P indicates local prosperity, PEG91 stands for the preexisting (i.e., 1991) percentage of an ethnic group (South Asians or blacks), MYU01 measures the male youth unemployment rate in 2001, and POP01 is the log of the borough population in 2001 (included to control for the possibility that boroughs with more residents might witness more racist crimes). If the incidence of racist crime unfolds according to the logic put forth in this book, we would expect a negative estimate of the interaction between in-migration and prosperity ($\text{IM}_i \times P_i$) in the regression predicting crimes against South Asians; as areas become richer, the effect of an increase in politically powerful South Asians on racist crime decreases. Note, however, that the negative binomial model already imposes an interactive relationship on variables. The nonlinear functional form assumes that the effect of one variable will differ at varying levels of other independent variables. For example, the estimate of in-migration by itself (β_1) may respond to changes in prosperity.

Models 1a and 1b in Table 4.3 present estimates based on racist crimes directed against South Asians and blacks, respectively. The results appear to show support for the book's central theory. Among South Asians, in-migration has a large positive and statistically significant effect on racially motivated crime when prosperity and percent ethnic group 1991 (the variables that in-migration is interacted with) equal zero, while the corresponding effect in Model 1b, predicting antiblack racist crime, is insignificant. The sign of the interaction term In-Migration × Prosperity is negative in Model 1a, suggesting that as areas become more prosperous, the effect of in-migration on racist crime decreases. But the coefficient is not significant. According to likelihood ratio tests comparing the unrestricted models, Models 1a and 1b, with the restricted models, Models 2a and 2b, that drop the interaction term, I cannot reject the null hypothesis that excluding In-Migration × Prosperity is valid. As I mentioned, the functional form of the model already assumes a nonlinear relationship between variables. I will thus continue the analysis by examining the marginal effects of in-migration at different levels of prosperity in Models 2a and 2b.

Let us first examine the effect of in-migration on the incidence of racist attacks across groups. The coefficients on in-migration indicate a strong positive relationship when it comes to South Asian in-migration, but increases in black population shares are associated with a weaker and statistically insignificant effect (when preexisting group shares are held at zero). Figure 4.1 presents the predicted number of racist crimes at different values of in-migration across groups, holding all other variables at their means. There is a considerable

TABLE 4.3. *Determinants of Racist Violence*

Variable	Racist Crime Directed Against South Asians		Racist Crime Directed Against Blacks	
	Model 1a	Model 2a	Model 1b	Model 2b
In-migration	.218* (.120)	.213*** (.059)	−.009 (.059)	.058 (.061)
Prosperity	−.094*** (.019)	−.095** (.019)	−.085*** (.021)	−.078*** (.022)
In-Migration × Prosperity	−.0003 (.005)		.005 (.005)	
Percent ethnic group 1991	.039*** (.012)	.039*** (.011)	.016 (.018)	.020 (.016)
In-Migration × % Ethnic Group 1991	−.009** (.004)	−.009*** (.003)	−.001 (.005)	−.003 (.004)
Male youth unemployment 2001	−.134*** (.026)	−.134*** (.027)	−.071* (.035)	−.073** (.035)
Log of population 2001	.062 (.202)	.063 (.201)	−.013 (.225)	.046 (.250)
Constant	5.966** (2.873)	5.975** (2.892)	6.307* (2.957)	5.509 (3.309)
Overdispersion parameter	.049** (.021)	.049** (.021)	.054*** (.024)	0.54** (.024)
Log-pseudo-likelihood	−140.754	−140.755	−140.844	−141.066
N	32	32	32	32

Notes: Negative binomial coefficients are given with robust standard errors in parentheses. The source of the information is the same as in Table 4.2.
*p < .10; **p < .05; ***p < .01.

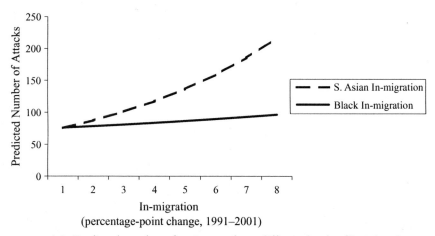

FIGURE 4.1. Predicted number of racist attacks at different levels of in-migration.

difference in the effect of in-migration on racist violence across South Asian and black victims.

Moreover, the marginal effect of in-migration varies as levels of prosperity change. Figure 4.2 plots this effect for both groups across the observed range of prosperity (with all other variables again set at their means). As areas become more prosperous, the marginal effect of South Asian in-migration on the observed number of racist attacks directed against this group declines and remains statistically significant at all levels of prosperity. Among black victims, the effect is much less pronounced and statistically insignificant. Figure 4.3 presents the effect on racist incidents of a one-standard-deviation increase in South Asian and black in-migration, respectively. The upper and lower bars of

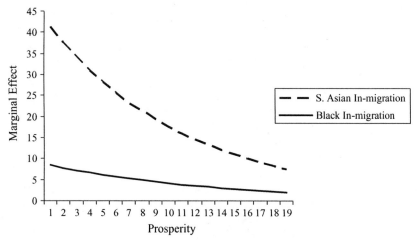

FIGURE 4.2. Marginal effect of in-migration on racist violence at different levels of prosperity.

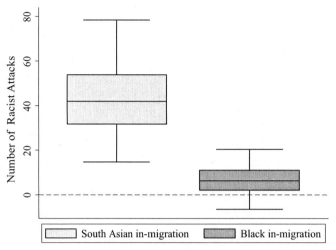

FIGURE 4.3. Effect of in-migration on racist violence.

the box plots represent the boundaries of the 95 percent confidence intervals
of the estimates. A one-standard-deviation increase in the share of a borough's
South Asian population raises crime against South Asians by around forty-three
attacks. This impact is much lower and statistically insignificant (the confidence
interval includes negative values) with regard to black in-migration.

To assess the defended neighborhood hypothesis, it is necessary to estimate
the marginal effects of in-migration at changing levels of percent South Asian
1991 and percent black 1991, respectively. While in-migration of South Asians
leads to a rise in the number of bigoted attacks directed against this group
in areas with few South Asian residents, simulations reveal that this effect
approaches zero (and becomes insignificant) in areas with larger preexisting
shares of South Asians (data not shown). I find no evidence of such a violent
defense of territory when the victim group is black. As discussed, this result
among South Asians is consistent with qualitative studies about white territorialism in various areas in Great Britain. Nonetheless, the fact that neighbors
apparently find it important to defend their territory only against the encroachment of a group that is likely to make political inroads also serves to underline
the significance of the wider sociopolitical context.

Turning again to the economic variables, we have already seen that economic accounts receive some support. All else equal, increases in prosperity
decrease the incidence of racist attacks against South Asians and blacks. This
effect also partly explains why the overall number of racist attacks against
blacks is only somewhat lower than attacks targeted at South Asians; in London, blacks are somewhat more likely to live in economically disadvantaged
boroughs than are South Asians. A surprising finding relates to the effect of the
unemployment rate among male youths on the incidence of racist violence. I
had hypothesized that an increase in the share of young jobless men would also

raise the share of potential hate criminals, but in both models, increases in male youth unemployment significantly *decrease* the incidence of racially motivated crime. The negative effect of male youth unemployment is puzzling, but it also likely indicates the limitations of relying on cross-sectional observations, in turn a result of lacking time-series data. The British economy expanded considerably during the 1990s. As a result, the areas that registered relatively high levels of unemployment in 2001 have at the same time witnessed the biggest *drop* in unemployment over the course of the previous decade (the correlation between 2001 unemployment rates and percentage-point changes in unemployment rates between 1991 and 2001 is $r = .90$). In this context, high rates of youth unemployment among men also capture improving economic trends over time (note that in the case of prosperity, this problem does not arise, for the variable represents a relative ranking of boroughs). Dynamics such as these may in fact underlie the inconclusive results found in the literature surrounding the relationship between unemployment and racist violence.

Robustness Checks and Extensions

This section tests the robustness of the results reported in Models 2a and 2b. I first replaced preexisting population shares and in-migration of South Asians with the share of councilors this group elected in 1998 and the change in this share between 1998 and 2002, identifying councilors' ethnic background by their first and last names. The change in the percentage of councilors correlates with the change in population shares between 1991 and 2001 at $r = .62$. An increase in the share of South Asian councilors is also associated with a statistically significant rise in racist attacks directed against this group, though the magnitude of the effects are smaller compared with the effects of in-migration. This is partly due to the fact that I compare changes during a shorter time frame, as it is very difficult to obtain first names of councilors going back to the early 1990s.

I also replaced other independent variables. Ethnographic studies of racist crime in Great Britain have emphasized the highly localized nature of such violence (Hesse et al. 1992; Bowling 1998; Back and Nayak 1999). Hesse and colleagues (1992, 127–157), for example, forcefully argue that an analysis of racist violence and harassment that addresses both the systematic spatial entrenchment of these offenses in particular areas as well as their spread across locales helps refute the impression that these crimes are random, unrelated incidents. Patterns of racist violence in Tower Hamlets (see Chapter 5) also show that the incidence of racist violence varied *within* the borough, rising sharply in wards where competition over council housing was fiercest. These studies thus suggest measuring local prosperity in ways that take the local concentration of deprivation below the borough level into account. I created such a measure by calculating levels of prosperity (as done earlier) at the SOA level, an area that comprises, on average, 1,533 residents in our sample. For each borough, I retained the SOAs with the lowest prosperity scores that together constitute approximately 10 percent of a borough's population and then calculated a population-weighted average. Substituting this concentration of deprivation variable for the original prosperity variable does not alter the results in substantively meaningful ways. The results are also robust to replacing prosperity with a variable that aligns less closely with the standard index of deprivation, but that includes only deprivation in two domains, barriers to housing and services and income deprivation. The housing and services domain has been highlighted in Chapters 2 and 3 and also figures prominently in the case studies, while income deprivation proxies for the level of need for these resources.

I further reestimated the regressions excluding the male youth unemployment variable, for this measure is partly captured in our prosperity variable. In the estimation predicting racist violence against South Asians, this exclusion causes the magnitude of prosperity to drop considerably, and the effect of in-migration, while still positive and strongly significant and similar in magnitude, responds to changes in prosperity to a much lesser degree. Leaving out male youth unemployment does not affect the main results in the regression estimating antiblack attacks. I also wanted to exclude the possibility that the violent response to South Asian in-migration is due to the events of September 11 and the rise in Islamophobia associated with them. I therefore ran the main model on data that covered the collection periods of 1999–2000 and 2000–2001 (from April 1999 to March 2001). Results for this time period are not substantively different than results covering all available years.

The sensitivity analysis also addresses demographic variables. As I stated earlier, a glance at migration patterns in Greater London over the past fifteen years shows that areas of South Asian in-migration do not overlap a great deal with areas where the black population has increased in size. To ensure, however, that the effects in our model predicting anti-South Asian (antiblack) racist crime are not confounded by the in-migration of blacks (South Asians), I controlled for the percentage-point increase in the size of the black (South Asian) population in a borough from 1991 to 2001 as well as their preexisting (1991) share of the population in the estimation explaining anti-South Asian (antiblack) racist crimes. These demographic variables are not statistically significant and do not affect our results.

I also expanded the dependent variable to test whether the dynamics that produce racist violence resulting in serious injury or murder are similar to the logic that produces all types of racist crime, ranging from verbal abuse and graffiti to homicide. These events obviously vary in their severity, but they each may nevertheless represent manifestations of similar underlying social, political, and economic forces. In the data, the incidence of racist crimes resulting in actual or grievous bodily harm or murder is correlated at $r = .76$ and $r = .81$ with the occurrence of racist crimes of all remaining forms directed against South Asian and black victims, respectively. These correlations suggest that various forms of racist violence do represent interconnected phenomena. Indeed, among both victim groups, the results remain largely unchanged in models predicting all remaining crime types. While the confidence intervals associated with in-migration are wider (which is most likely due to the reduced reliability of the recording of less violent crimes, such as verbal harassment), it appears that the dynamics producing less violent forms of hate crime correspond to the forces that drive the commission of racially motivated bodily harm and murder.

The results given here are also not driven by particular observations. Dropping local authorities that experienced the highest or lowest rates of in-migration, or the highest or lowest number of attacks, does not change the main effects. In a final sensitivity check, I modified the estimations' calculation of the overdispersion parameter. The results are based on an overdispersion parameter that is a function of $X\beta$, assuming that excess variability increases along with the expected number of racist crimes. This parameterization makes sense if, for example, victims who live in low-crime areas are more likely to report crimes to the police because they represent a rarity, resulting in a more accurate crime count in these areas than in high-crime areas. I reestimated the analysis with a parameterization that holds overdispersion constant across observations. This modification does not alter the substantive results.

Conclusion and Discussion

The statistical results presented in this chapter suggest that the forces that compel some individuals to commit racist violence track the dynamics of intergroup conflict at the level of the locality. First, areas in which xenophobic candidates compete for office also witness higher rates of racist crime. Moreover, when xenophobes do well at the polls, racist incidents rise as well. In the next part of this book, where I trace and explain the presence – and absence – of immigrant-native conflict in four localities in depth and over time, I also observe that casting votes for anti-immigrant candidates and harassing immigrant neighbors are phenomena that tend to coincide. Together, these findings rule out the notion that these two behaviors are substitutes. They also give us confidence that voting for local candidates that espouse xenophobic views and policies is not simply a form of protest behavior that is unrelated to immigration-related grievances. Though some voters certainly opt for extremist parties without themselves embracing an extremist agenda, the fact that voting and violence move in tandem suggests that anti-immigrant mobilization can comprise both phenomena.

Second, this chapter has shown that the in-migration of an ethnic group that makes its presence felt politically will be met with violent resistance by segments of the local population. Moreover, the effect of such in-migration on the incidence of hate crime is magnified as economic deprivation increases. This latter effect is, however, less robust than the differential effects on racist violence of patterns of in-migration across groups that vary in their electoral clout. As more data become available that allow us to introduce economic trends over time, we will gain a better understanding of the impact of economic conditions on bigoted violence.

Ethnographic studies of hate crime in Great Britain support this chapter's overall findings. In their study of racist violence in deprived areas in Greater Manchester, Ray, Smith, and Wastell document the resentment that perpetrators and the communities that harbor them express at the "special deals" that South Asians receive from local government, be it to regenerate their neighborhoods, to start their businesses, or to buy their houses from the city council (2004, 352). Corresponding to the theory of immigrant–native conflict proposed here, the authors also found attacks against South Asians to be more widespread than violence directed against blacks, for the former were perceived to possess "power, privileges and success [as well as] a special link with the providers of public funds" (357). Moreover, the fact that a bundle of less violent hate crimes, consisting, for example, of verbal harassment or criminal damage, follow the same dynamics as crimes resulting in serious physical injury suggests that hate crime, broadly understood, represents a phenomenon that is sensitive to changing local sociopolitical and economic conditions. This finding further implies that apparently less severe forms of racist crimes, such as hateful graffiti, should not be dismissed but may instead constitute warning sings of more dire things to come.

Notwithstanding these parallels between microlevel violence and macrolevel conflicts, important differences also emerge. Regardless of demographic variables or group characteristics, racially motivated violence increases as local economic conditions decline. I also find a defended neighborhood effect, but only in the case of South Asian in-migration, which provokes more anti-South Asian hate crimes as the preexisting share of this group in a borough declines. Neighborhood defense does not follow a purely demographic logic, but instead operates only with regard to an incoming group that makes its presence felt in the neighborhood *and* in city hall.

Nevertheless, the statistical analysis presented in this chapter can only indirectly link immigrant political power to racist violence. Specifically, it may be variables that lead to minority political power in the first place that provoke racist violence. Since the group that is more powerful politically is also the group that is more tightly concentrated at the neighborhood or ward level (see Chapter 3), the evidence presented in this chapter is also consistent with an argument that stresses the importance of perceived demographic invasion. Nevertheless, it should be noted that black Africans, who constitute about half of all black Britons in London, display patterns of residential clustering that exceed the concentration observed among black Caribbeans. That this clustering does not coincide with high turnout and political clout serves to disentangle geographic concentration and electoral leverage. The case comparisons that follow in the next part of this book deploy more detailed, over-time data that allow us to better isolate the effect of political power in the production of immigrant conflict.

INTRODUCTION TO PART III

Chapters 3 and 4 have demonstrated that immigrant conflict varies system-atically across groups, place, and time. Immigrant groups that are influential local political actors are more likely to be greeted with violent anti-immigrant mobilization than groups that wield no such electoral clout. The latter, by con-trast, have been shown to be involved in clashes with state actors. Both types of conflict have occurred more frequently where local economic resources are under pressure. These patterns are consistent with the main argument pro-posed in this book: Natives protest resource allocation to electorally pivotal immigrants, leading to immigrant–native conflict, while politically powerless immigrant minorities, who will not be able to induce local politicians to dis-burse scarce goods to them, will register their discontent with an unresponsive state, leading to immigrant–state conflict.

The evidence presented thus far corresponds to this logic, but some questions are still left unanswered. First, do groups that are residentially concentrated invite a xenophobic backlash? Given that local electoral clout tends to require geographic concentration (at least in the context of British council elections), correlations between immigrants' electoral power and immigrant–native con-flict might in fact be due to residential patterns – though with these patterns' effects being mediated by economic conditions – rather than political muscle. Second, the investigations have thus far not explicitly addressed the timing of events. Is it indeed true that natives mobilize against immigrants who have attained political power, or is it instead the case that immigrants, once victim-ized, respond to native xenophobia by mobilizing politically? Similarly, does the allocation of economic goods to immigrant-origin minorities – as well as local government's failure to do so – precede rather than follow the occurrence of the two types of immigrant conflict? Finally, the correlation between eco-nomic conditions and immigrant conflict does not tell us whether economic goods are actually at the center of immigrant conflict. Do immigrant groups whose economic needs are neglected by the state and who engage in antistate behavior in fact ask for economic goods from the state? Likewise, do natives who drum up opposition against their immigrant neighbors do so because these newcomers make effective demands for economic resources, rather than for cultural, religious, or other types of goods?

Chapters 5 and 6 address these questions by examining the development of immigrant conflict in four locations over time. Tracing the political processes, economic conditions, and conflict trajectories across similar locations, but also within locations over time, establishes the sequence of events and also helps identify the connections that tie immigrant political behavior and economic scarcity to immigrant conflict. Before delving into the in-depth study of conflict determinants and outcomes in the four locations, I introduce the cases and also address alternative explanations here.

Previewing the Cases

Immigrant conflict in Ealing and Tower Hamlets (in Greater London) and Leicester and Birmingham (in the Midlands) reflect the varied patterns of conflict and calm suggested in the previous chapters. Immigrant political power and economic scarcity – and hence conflict patterns – have varied significantly across cases and over the years, despite similar levels of ethnic diversity. When Indian migrants first settled in the Southall area of Ealing, a borough in outer London, white British residents greeted them with racist vitriol and physical attacks. Over the course of the 1960s, the area became a stronghold of anti-immigrant parties who lobbied for migrants' repatriation and witnessed serious racist violence. In the decades to come, however, the situation changed and intergroup relations eased considerably. Less than fifteen miles away, Tower Hamlets, an inner London borough, has not fared as well. Here, Bangladeshi migrants battled skinheads on the streets and xenophobic parties at the ballot box in the 1970s and continued to confront mobilized racism throughout the 1980s and 1990s.

In Birmingham, large inflows of migrants from the Indian subcontinent and the West Indies failed to provoke a significant electoral backlash. In spite of numerous attempts, the xenophobic National Front repeatedly foundered at the polls. Major instances of intergroup violence also did not occur. Notwithstanding these circumstances, immigrant integration did not proceed peacefully. Low-level as well as larger-scale confrontations between immigrant-origin youths and the police were part of the inner-city landscape of the 1970s and 1980s. Yet, these developments did not reflect events in nearby Leicester. Leicester's local white population collectively resisted the inflow of Indian migrants initially and allowed the NF to thrive. Today, though, the British Home Office has extolled the city for its exemplary record of intercultural harmony, community pride, and "positive approach to diversity" (Home Office 2001b, 15).

In sum, clashes between immigrants and natives occurred in Ealing and Leicester, but intergroup relations had improved by the 1990s. In Tower Hamlets, confrontations between the Bangladeshi-origin minority and the native population remained hostile for decades, while such battles did not characterize the city of Birmingham where confrontations between ethnic minorities and state actors gained salience during the 1970s and 1980s. Table III.1 previews how changing values of the relevant variables – immigrant political power and economic scarcity – produce such varied conflict outcomes.[1] The case-selection method thus chooses from a set of diverse cases that vary in the key independent variables, both across and within cases, but that hold constant a range of other variables.[2]

Comparing Tower Hamlets and Ealing, we observe similarly high levels of immigrant political power. Beginning in the first years of settlement, immigrant candidates contested competitive elections and challenged mainstream parties by mounting successful campaigns as independents. Likewise, the case studies will show that Bangladeshis in Tower Hamlets and Indians in Ealing were able to use their electoral clout to acquire valued and scarce economic goods, specifically housing. This constellation produced immigrant–native conflict in both towns. Over time, though, intergroup tensions in Ealing eased for two economically grounded reasons. First, since most of Ealing's housing stock has been privately owned, native demands to limit selling and renting exclusively to natives did not prove effective as real estate brokers benefited from the rising house prices that Indian immigration helped bring about. In Tower Hamlets, by contrast, the government has controlled most of the residential housing supply. Employing racist voting and racist violence, natives warned ruling parties and Bangladeshis that disbursing undersupplied and highly desired council flats to immigrant households would be costly. Politicians proved receptive, making anti-immigrant behavior a strategy that paid off. Second, overall levels of economic need, and ethnic minority needs in particular, decreased considerably in Ealing but remained much higher in Tower Hamlets (see Table III.1).

Conflict outcomes in Leicester and Birmingham vary because immigrant political power differs across cities. Ethnic minority political incorporation turned out to be a long and arduous process in Birmingham, especially when compared with that in Leicester, where immigrants found a place in city hall soon after their arrival. As a result of their political powerlessness, immigrant groups in Birmingham were in no position to make credible claims for scarce economic goods. While this marginalization meant that natives did not feel the need to engage in sustained anti-immigrant mobilization, state neglect led immigrant-origin minorities to confront the state during economically hard times. In Leicester, however, Indian migrants used their strong electoral

---

[1] To put these values into nationwide perspective (referring to local authorities where the share of New Commonwealth immigrants – nonwhites beginning in 1991 – exceeded the national average), the average percent of households in council housing in 1981 was 32; the unemployment rate was 4 (1971), 10 (1981), 11 (1991), and 7 (2001) percent, respectively; and the nonwhite unemployment rate was 20 (1991) and 11 (2001) percent, respectively (see Table III.1 for sources). National figures on ethnic minority political representation are unfortunately less readily available.

[2] See Seawright and Gerring (2008, 300–301) on the claims to representativeness of the diverse case method.

TABLE III.1. *Incidence of Immigrant Conflict in Four British Localities: Overview of Variables and Argument*

	Immigrant Political Power						Economic Scarcity										Immigrant Conflict
	Election of Immigrant-Origin Independent Candidate (prior to 1990s)	Share of City Councilors of Immigrant Background (%)				Overall Assessment	% in Public Council Housing (1981)	1991 Index of Local Conditions (higher = less deprived)	Unemployment Rate (%)						Overall Assessment	
		1973–74	1982–83	1990–91	1998–99				Total				Dominant Immigrant Group(s)			
									1971	1981	1991	2001	1991	2001		
Tower Hamlets	yes	0	8	20	44	High	82	7	5	14	22	11	47	24	High	I-N conflict
Ealing	yes	2	11	20	27	High	22	38	3	8	11	6	14	6	High to Lower	I-N conflict to no conflict
Birmingham	no	0	4	15	18	Low	35	5	5	14	14	9	25	15	High	I-S conflict
Leicester	no	2	17	23	25	High	36	37	4	12	14	8	16	8	High to Lower	I-N conflict to no conflict

Notes: The 1991 Index of Local Conditions includes indicators of both individual-level and area-based deprivation. I-N = immigrant-native; I-S = immigrant-state.

Source: Immigrant political power is derived from electoral returns held at local authority archives and from data in Phillips (2000), Rallings, Thrasher, and Ware (2006), and Solomos and Back (1995). Public housing and unemployment rates are derived from the national census, various years (available at www.nomisweb.co.uk and from Rees, Martin, and Williamson 2002). See Lee (1999) for data on 1991 local conditions.

position to extract material concessions from local government, prompting immigrant–native conflict. In developments that mirror events in Ealing, the lessening of pressures on state resources over time, as well as an improvement of Indians' employment situation, diminished intergroup conflict.

Figure III.1 presents an illustration of minority political representation and unemployment patterns over time. (Note that to capture the second generation, these figures, as well as the chapters that follow, use "ethnic group" rather than "country of birth" statistics beginning in 1991, when the census first asked respondents about their ethnicity.) The figure shows Birmingham to be a laggard with regard to the descriptive political representation of its immigrant-origin minorities when compared with the other three cases, while Tower Hamlets stands out for the rapid rise with which its Bangladeshi population gained access to city hall.

Turning to economic conditions, we see that Figure III.1 shows the distribution of economic disadvantage within localities by displaying unemployment rates at the ward level. Unemployment had risen overall and particularly in immigrant areas over the course of the 1970s and 1980s. By 1991, Tower Hamlets and Birmingham registered especially high joblessness rates – up to 33 percent – in wards with high concentrations of the localities' dominant ethnic groups. In Ealing, by comparison, they remained at a much lower level while in Leicester the dominant minority lived in both high- and low-unemployment areas. Figure III.2 reveals the stark differences in unemployment rates among minorities (unavailable before the 1990s). Bangladeshi unemployment in Tower Hamlets is uniformly high across wards, whereas Indian unemployment in Ealing tends to be uniformly low. In Birmingham, minority joblessness rises along with ethnic minority concentration while this relationship is much less pronounced in Leicester. Together, these figures show that the correlation between economic disadvantage and ethnic minority concentration has waned over the years in Ealing and Leicester; in these two localities, immigrant enclaves' reliance on economic assistance from local government has declined along with immigrant–native conflict. In Birmingham and Tower Hamlets, by contrast, immigrant-origin minorities have been less able to escape economic deprivation, as well as immigrant conflict.

While variation in unemployment rates conveys a sense of differences in economic need, the case studies will provide more details about the supply of local economic goods. To measure the key economic and political variables as well as the ways in which they link up to one another, I draw on a number of sources, including archived local newspapers (I visited the British Library Newspapers Archive in Colindale – London – and the Record Office for Leicestershire, Leicester, and Rutland); national newspapers available electronically; census statistics; electoral returns; secondary sources; and elite interviews. These diverse sources allow me to assemble a comprehensive and vivid account of the ways in which immigrant conflict unfolded across localities over time. Before turning to these accounts, let me address important alternative explanations.

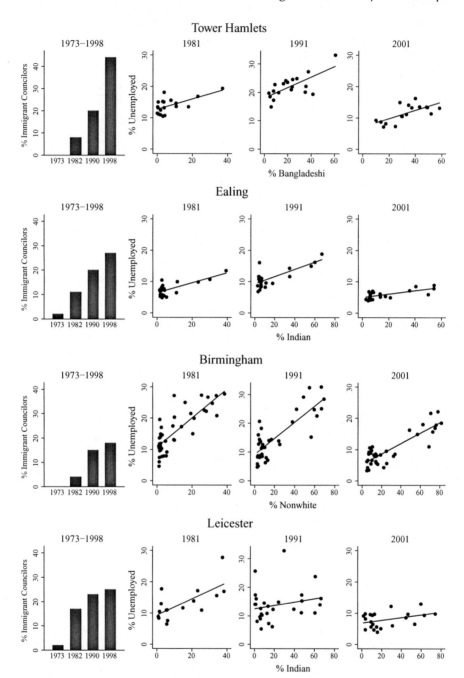

FIGURE III.1. Immigrant political power and unemployment in four locations. (Note: For each locality, scatterplots depict the share of a given immigrant group and unemployment rates at the ward level. *Sources:* see Table III.1.)

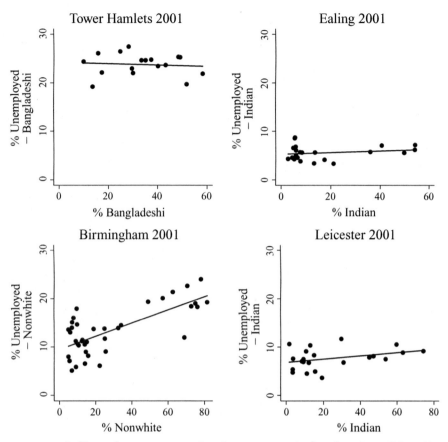

FIGURE III.2. Unemployment among immigrant groups in four locations. (Note: For each locality, scatterplots depict the share of a given immigrant group and unemployment rates among that group at the ward level. *Sources:* see Table III.1.)

Addressing Competing Explanations

In Chapter 3, we have seen that native Britons' attitudes toward the racial or cultural features of Asians and West Indians do not help us explain broad conflict patterns across groups. Similarly, if minorities' racial, cultural, or religious backgrounds were responsible for conflict outcomes, we would not observe the conflict dynamics that took shape in Ealing, Tower Hamlets, Birmingham, and Leicester. By 1971, immigrants from New Commonwealth countries constituted 6 percent of the population in Birmingham, 7 percent in Tower Hamlets, 8 percent in Leicester, and 11 percent in Ealing. Twenty years later, approximately one-third of all residents in Ealing and Tower Hamlets were of nonwhite origin, while in Birmingham and Leicester these shares had risen to 22 and 28 percent, respectively. Residents of Indian origin represent the dominant ethnic minority group in Ealing and Leicester. In both towns, but particularly in Leicester, some of these migrants had arrived as political refugees via Africa. Bangladeshis constitute the largest share of nonwhites in Tower Hamlets. Birmingham's ethnic minority population has been more evenly balanced between first- and later-generation immigrants of West Indian, Pakistani, and Indian origin.

Native opposition targeted migrants that were predominantly of Indian origin in Ealing and Leicester, but the same groups coexisted in relative calm with their white neighbors in the 1990s. Birmingham and Tower Hamlets are both home to sizable Muslim minorities, but the East London borough was the site of sustained intergroup clashes, while collective anti-immigrant mobilization consistently failed in the West Midlands city. This outcome is particularly relevant in light of the fact that the public face of Islam had been more visible in Birmingham, where, according to a 1984 survey of local authorities, the provision of religious services for Muslims was much more extensive when compared with that of Tower Hamlets. Muslims had been allocated burial areas; schools took religious needs into account (e.g., in the areas of meals, sex education, and religious dress); and one purpose-built mosque had been built, and local planning provided for several more. None of these policies were in effect in Tower Hamlets (Nielsen 1986). Furthermore, public reactions against the publication of Salman Rushdie's *Satanic Verses* were "low-key affairs" in Tower Hamlets, especially when compared to mobilizations in other British cities (Begum and Eade 2005, 183). These stark differences in the public salience of Islam manifested themselves at a time when Tower Hamlets experienced vicious immigrant–native strife, while Birmingham witnessed serious immigrant–state conflict.

Aspects of demography or segregation are also unlikely to lead to differences in immigrant conflict. "White flight" cannot explain reduced levels of antagonism against immigrants. In all four cases, the indigenous population (i.e., residents born in the United Kingdom) decreased over the course of the 1970s, as did the total number of residents. During the 1990s, the number and share of the white population fell once again in all four localities.[3]

Nor is it the case that patterns of spatial segregation and social cohesiveness drive conflict. Birmingham's ethnic minority population is highly concentrated within certain wards, but xenophobic movements failed here. In 1991, three-fourths of the city's Pakistani-origin residents and two-thirds of the city's Indian-origin residents lived in one-sixth of Birmingham's wards, but, for reasons spelled out in Chapter 6, this concentration – and the tight community networks underlying it – did not produce electoral clout during the 1970s and

---

[3] Between 1971 and 1981, the population born in the United Kingdom shrank by 13.3 percent in Ealing and by 19.0 percent in Tower Hamlets; figures for Birmingham and Leicester are 9.5 and 8.0 percent, respectively. Between 1991 and 2001, the number of white residents also fell in all four localities: by 4.1 percent in Ealing, 2.7 percent in Tower Hamlets, 8.7 percent in Birmingham, and 8.9 percent in Leicester. Calculations are derived from census statistics in Rees et al. (2002) and also from statistics available at www.nomisweb.co.uk.

1980s. Absent immigrant political influence, strong social ties and residential concentration proved insufficient to provoke immigrant–native conflict in Birmingham. Two cases of eventual intergroup peace – Leicester and Ealing – are also marked by high levels of segregation and social cohesiveness. In 1991, three-fourths of Ealing's and two-thirds of Leicester's Indian-origin population lived in one-fourth of each town's wards. This spatial insulation is also said to be matched by social "self-segregation" and the avoidance of contacts with other ethnic groups on the part of Leicester's Indian-origin population (Seliga 1998, 233). Thus, if it is true that groups "hunker down" in the face of ethnic diversity, as argued by Putnam (2007), it is also true that such separation does not have to produce open conflict.

Finally, demographic balance fails to account for conflict patterns. The fact that Birmingham is home to more than one large immigrant group is unlikely to be related to conflict outcomes once immigrant political power is controlled for. Other British local authorities whose populations comprised one major immigrant group (but who did not produce effective political leaders), such as Lambeth or Haringey (in London), witnessed large-scale immigrant–state conflict in the 1980s. Looking beyond Great Britain to Germany and France, it will also become apparent that there is no simple correlation between a group's local demographic dominance and local conflict outcomes.

5

Immigrant–Native Conflict in Two London Boroughs

This chapter compares two London boroughs: Tower Hamlets, located in the East End, and Ealing, located on the western edge of the capital city. Only fourteen miles apart, the two boroughs' South Asian communities have fared very differently over the past several decades. While white residents in both areas reacted to nonwhite immigration with hostility and violence in the initial decades of settlement, Ealing turned itself around in the 1980s and now serves as a model of good community relations. Immigrant–native confrontations in Tower Hamlets, by contrast, only escalated over the same time period. Moreover, in Tower Hamlets interethnic conflict spread unevenly throughout the borough; by the late 1980s, the incidence of violent racism and the success of fiercely anti-immigrant parties concentrated in particular areas of the borough. What accounts for these strikingly different developments?

This chapter argues that the ways in which local economies collide with electoral contests are key to understanding intergroup relations. The starting points in both boroughs were very similar: Immigration coincided with chronic, preexisting housing shortages and immigrant demands for accommodation could not be easily sidelined by the local political leadership, for the dominant ethnic minorities in both boroughs have had considerable local electoral clout. In the context of highly competitive electoral environments, the local Labour parties were compelled, albeit reluctantly, to address the concerns of this new constituency. In both boroughs, substantial segments of the native population therefore initially retaliated against this encroachment by voting for anti-immigrant candidates, and a smaller share of the population engaged in racist violence to deter Asian immigrants from making further demands. By the 1980s, however, the two boroughs' paths diverged. In Ealing, anti-immigrant agitation had no staying power, whereas such campaigns, and the violence associated with them, intensified in the East London borough. Moreover, a checkered pattern of xenophobic violence emerged within Tower Hamlets, with escalating racist attacks concentrated in certain neighborhoods.

Differences in pressures on state-provided resources, I argue, explain this variation. In Tower Hamlets, the pervasive shortage of affordable housing provoked increased anti-immigrant agitation. Such campaigns were widespread and sustained as a result of the borough's economically deprived population. They proved effective, since most of the area's housing stock has been controlled by the local council, which in turn was painfully susceptible to anti-immigrant demands. Further, when, due to a decentralization experiment, electoral incentives led to different housing-allocation rules within the borough, the areas that operated a needs-based housing policy – effectively benefiting Bangladeshi residents – witnessed a spike in racist violence and far-right party success, compared with areas where distribution guidelines favored white natives.

In Ealing, by comparison, the local council has not been in charge of most of the borough's housing stock. Furthermore, pressures on existing public sector housing as well as on other state resources were not as acute as a result of the more heterogeneous socioeconomic profile of the borough's white and Indian-origin residents. Anti-immigrant activities did not pay off in preventing immigrants from purchasing private homes; economic shortages affected the borough's more affluent population to a lesser degree; and Ealing's Indian population gradually gained a more secure economic footing. As a result of these economic conditions, intergroup relations took a turn for the better, even as the political power of the borough's Indian-origin residents expanded.

In other words, economic scarcity was intense in Tower Hamlets because of the shortages in the dominant state-owned housing sector and high levels of demand among the borough's economically disadvantaged population. In Ealing, high levels of scarcity in the predominantly privately owned housing stock coincided with lower levels of need among the town's residents. In Tower Hamlets, conflict between electorally pivotal Bangladeshis and whites thus became deeply entrenched, while in Ealing the confrontations between politically powerful Indians and whites dissipated over the years. Put simply, the comparison of Tower Hamlets and Ealing holds constant immigrant political power, but varies economic scarcity.

The chapter proceeds by discussing developments in Tower Hamlets and Ealing in turn. For both cases, I first provide a brief overview of postwar immigrant settlement and the local political economy. I then chart the boroughs' political histories, provide evidence on immigrants' rising political power as well as their pursuit of valued economic resources, and finally show how these demands interacted with the areas' economic conditions to produce varying patterns of immigrant–native conflict over time within boroughs and across the two boroughs as well as across Tower Hamlets' neighborhoods.

Tower Hamlets

Tower Hamlets, part of London's East End, has long been a destination for the world's most desperate immigrants. Before the arrival of Bangladeshi migrants, there were French Huguenots, Irish migrants, and Polish and Russian Jews who fled persecution and poverty to settle in this chronically poor, run-down area. The London Great Mosque (Jamme Masjid) on Brick Lane in Spitalfields ward, the heart of the Bangladeshi community, perhaps best exemplifies these migration waves. Built by Huguenots as a place of worship in 1742, it later functioned as a Methodist chapel, then turned into a Jewish orthodox synagogue, and finally was bought by Bangladeshi businessmen in the 1970s and converted into a mosque (Eade 1996, 218–219).[1]

Early and limited Bangladeshi migration started in the late nineteenth century and was initially made up of steady streams of Bengali seamen (*lascars*), who had been employed on British merchant navy ships but were drawn to London for its higher wages. In typical chain-migration fashion, this migrant population hailed from a cluster of *Londoni* villages in a confined rural area (Sylhet) whose residents were connected by tight social and kin networks, which facilitated the migration and settlement process. East London's Bangladeshi settlement expanded rapidly in the 1960s, when predominantly male migrants responded to the area's need for unskilled labor, and further increased in the 1970s, when wives and children joined their husbands and fathers, fearing that increasingly restrictive immigration laws would eventually prevent family reunification (Gardner and Shukur 1994). By 2001, Bangladeshis constituted the largest share of Tower Hamlets' ethnic minority communities, numbering close to 70,000, or 33.4 percent of the borough's total population and making up close to or more than 50 percent of residents in several electoral wards (see Table 5.1; see Figure 5.1 for a ward map).[2]

During the 1960 and 1970s, the local garment industry employed many Bangladeshi migrants in its small factories and workshops. When these jobs vanished in the 1980s, unemployment skyrocketed among this population. Since the beginning of the late 1990s, though, a general economic upswing and the entrepreneurial skills of some Bangladeshis have contributed to an improvement in their economic conditions. Nevertheless, Bangladeshis in Tower Hamlets, as well as elsewhere in the country, belong to Britain's most disadvantaged ethnic minority groups (Modood et al. 1997).

In the twentieth century, the area was still among the country's poorest regions. Official rankings routinely singled out Tower Hamlets for its high

---

[1] Observers have indeed noted the similarities between the Polish and Russian Jewish settlement and that of the Bangladeshi Muslim population and "the way one ethnic group slots neatly into the hole left by the previous one ... they too find work in the rag trade and other low-grade occupations; they too have their own language, their shops, eating habits and religion. They even echo the Jewish passion for gambling" (Burney 1967, 84–85). See also Phillips (1988).

[2] According to the 2001 census, Tower Hamlets is 51 percent white. The second- and third-largest ethnic groups are black Africans (3.4 percent) and black Caribbeans (2.7 percent; see "T13 Theme Table on Ethnicity," available at www.nomisweb.co.uk). The present study tracks intergroup relations between Bangladeshis and whites from the late 1960s until the late 1990s, but rapid demographic change has shifted intergroup dynamics in the twenty-first century. In relation to the most recent newcomers, Bangladeshis comprise the "indigenous" population and, depending on the location, the dominant majority.

TABLE 5.1. *Concentration of the Bangladeshi Population in Tower Hamlets, 1981–2001*

Tower Hamlets	All Residents 1981	All Residents 1991	Bangladeshis (%) 1981	Bangladeshis (%) 1991		All Residents 2001	Bangladeshis (%) 2001
TOTAL	140,002	161,042	7.0	22.9		196,106	33.4
Spitalfields	6,416	8,861	37.1	60.7	Spitalfields & Banglatown	8,383	58.1
St. Mary's	5,771	5,659	23.1	41.5	Whitechapel	12,046	51.8
St. Katharine's	9,631	13,807	17.8	34.9	Shadwell	12,078	49.0
Weavers	8,674	9,771	10.7	27.8	Bethnal Green South	13,675	48.3
Shadwell	7,908	10,038	10.6	35.5	St. Dunstan's & Stepney Green	12,679	43.2
St. Dunstan's	7,720	10,015	7.8	37.5	Bromley-by-Bow	11,581	40.1
Redcoat	6,460	6,571	4.2	23.7	Weavers	11,685	37.3
St. Peter's	9,303	10,360	3.9	23.0	Mile End East	11,139	35.0
Blackwall	5,490	4,780	3.8	18.3	Bethnal Green North	11,765	33.3
Bromley	8,195	9,632	3.7	16.3	Mile End and Globe Town	11,801	30.0
Holy Trinity	7,600	9,410	3.3	24.1	Limehouse	12,484	29.5
Limehouse	8,562	8,476	3.1	19.9	East India and Lansbury	11,496	28.2
Grove	4,713	5,182	1.9	5.7	St. Katharine's & Wapping	11,245	24.7
St. James'	6,173	5,940	1.9	12.1	Blackwall & Cubitt Town	11,939	17.3
Bow	7,450	8,203	0.7	4.8	Millwall	12,892	15.7
Millwall	9,986	13,771	0.5	7.9	Bow West	10,421	13.7
Lansbury	7,495	8,383	0.4	9.0	Bow East	8,797	10.0
East India	6,512	6,881	0.2	7.9			
Park	5,943	5,302	0.1	3.8			

Notes: Tower Hamlets underwent boundary changes that are reflected in the 2001 census figures. Until 1981, entries refer to country of birth. As of 1991, entries are based on ethnic origin and thus also include children born in the United Kingdom to parents of Bangladeshi descent.

Source: The 1981 data are based on "Table 4 Country of Birth All Residents." The 1991 figures are based on "Table S06 Ethnic Group: Residents," and 2001 data are derived from "T13 Theme Table on Ethnicity" (available at www.nomisweb.co.uk).

141

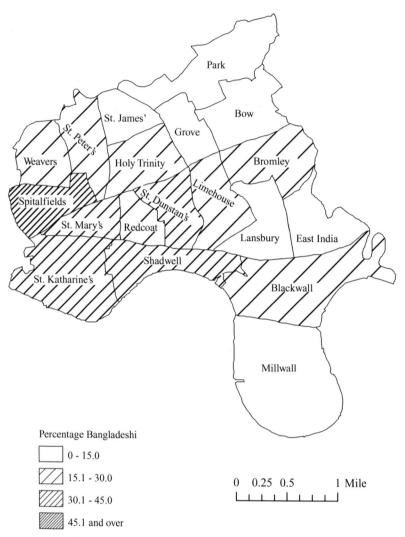

Percentage Bangladeshi

0 - 15.0

15.1 - 30.0

30.1 - 45.0

45.1 and over

0   0.25 0.5   1 Mile

FIGURE 5.1. Tower Hamlets 1991 ward map. (© Crown copyright. All rights reserved. License number 100049655.)

unemployment, low incomes, and general economic deprivation (Thompson 1972; Department for Communities and Local Government 2004), but it is the area's deplorable housing conditions and acute overcrowding that have been the most intractable source of crisis. Severely depleted as a result of wartime bombings, housing was still scarce by the 1980s, with over 9,000 people on the waiting list for council accommodation. The existing private dwellings were in such poor conditions that authorities deemed 42 percent of them "unfit" for habitation (Phillips 1988, 362). According to an examination of the area's housing stock in the 1960s, "The horror stories which lie behind these statistics paint a picture of rottenness, filth, and unhealthiness which can scarcely be exaggerated. (A man who had been chief city planner for Chicago... could not believe his eyes)" (Burney 1967, 88). During the 1980s and 1990s, the situation did not improve much because of low budgets, insufficient help from the center, and continued underinvestment in the borough's housing stock. With at one point over 80 percent of the local authority's population living in public accommodation, housing has been a highly contested resource that has dominated local politics for decades.

A portrayal of the East End's history would not be complete without brief mention of its tradition of racist exclusion. The area is no stranger to far-right mobilization. The British Brothers' League agitated against Jewish immigrants at the turn of the twentieth century, a campaign followed up by the British Union of Fascists and National Socialists in the 1930s. The postwar Union Movement and the National Front in the 1970s and 1980s attracted voters with openly anti-Semitic and anti-immigrant slogans. This long history of xenophobic agitation has led observers to conclude that the East End's tradition of racist exclusionism reflects a deeply embedded culture of racism that is directed against newcomers whose social insulation and ethnic distinctiveness present a threat to the East End way of life (Husbands 1982; Phillips 1988, 366). The ferocity of resentment that greeted Bangladeshi migrants in Tower Hamlets indeed suggests that this area of London has a well-functioning racist infrastructure that facilitates xenophobic mobilization – but when and where are anti-immigrant sentiments activated? Such mobilization has varied over time and also across space within the borough. The following pages will demonstrate that anti-immigrant mobilization and violence occur when electoral dynamics and competition for state-owned resources coalesce.

Tower Hamlets' Political Landscape

Electoral History
Like other boroughs in London's East End, the area covering Tower Hamlets had been a Labour stronghold since the 1930s. For decades, local Labour, dominated by traditional trade-union leaders, was the only party in town. Even into the 1960s and 1970s, the party controlled local politics, running unopposed in several wards. In 1968, Labour lost only one seat to a Communist candidate, and in 1971 and 1974, Labour candidates won twenty out of twenty wards in low-turnout elections (see Table 5.2).

But by the late 1970s, similar to many areas in the country, the Liberal Party[3] entered local politics and mounted a serious challenge to Labour's Old Guard. Having failed to deliver basic services to many of the borough's residents, the

---

[3] The Liberal Party was a forerunner of the Liberal Democrats. The latter came into existence in 1988, as a merger between the Liberal Party and the Social Democratic Party (SDP), a breakaway party founded by Labour MPs to the right of many Labour positions. In previous elections, the Liberals ran on their own or in alliance with the SDP.

TABLE 5.2. *Local Election Results for Tower Hamlets, 1964–2002*

Year	% Share of the Vote			Wards Won			Council Control
	CON	LAB	LD	CON	LAB	LD	
1964	5.3	72.9	6.7	0	18	0	LAB
1968	9.9	63.6	5.4	0	19	0	LAB
1971	7.0	83.0	0.7	0	20	0	LAB
1974	3.0	77.0	8.1	0	20	0	LAB
1978	16.0	58.8	11.2	0	16	3	LAB
1982	8.6	44.4	37.6	0	11	7	LD
1986	7.3	44.2	42.4	0	9	10	LD
1990	5.4	43.5	43.8	0	7	12	LAB
1994	3.9	52.0	27.7	0	16	3	LAB
1998	13.8	49.6	25.2	0	15	4	LAB
2002	15.4	43.1	30.0	0	12	5	LAB

Notes: The Liberal Democrats were founded in 1988; until then, the Liberal Party had formed an alliance with the Social Democratic Party. Results prior to 1988 refer to the performance of this alliance or when the Liberals ran on their own. CON = Conservatives; LD = Liberal Democrats; LAB = Labour Party.
Source: Rallings and Thrasher (2003, 30).

Labour Party's decades-old machine-style politics was under serious threat by a new party eager to point out Labour's shortcomings. By 1978 the Liberals had made some headway, winning three out of nineteen wards, and narrowing the margin in many more. The Liberals further improved their performance four years later when they captured seven wards, compared to the incumbent party's record of eleven, and won 37.6 of the overall vote, closing in on Labour, which scored 44.4 percent (see Table 5.2).

The entrenched Labour leadership ultimately had to relinquish its control of the council to the Liberals in 1986 and would not get it back until 1994. During this time, Tower Hamlets had gained nationwide notoriety as the first local authority in the country to elect a British National Party candidate to its council, and the borough also became infamous for its despicable record of extreme racist violence. While observers blamed severe poverty for the outbreaks and persistence of such crime, the connection between electoral and economic competition on the one hand and violent racism on the other has not been made. As council elections became more hotly contested, the size of the Bangladeshi community grew steadily. Was this latest group of immigrants able to translate its numerical strength into political capital during this time?

Electoral Competition and Bangladeshi Votes
Bangladeshi East Londoners started participating in local politics early on. By the 1970s, the new settlers had formed various pressure groups that frequently clashed with representatives of white interest groups, who accused the council of giving special treatment to their South Asian neighbors (Eade

1989, 30–31). In 1976, a section of the Bangladeshi community came together in the Bengali Housing Action Group (BHAG, translating to "tiger" in Bengali), which endorsed and organized its members' squatting of vacant council properties. Other pressure groups focused on the population's educational, employment, and health care needs (Forman 1989, 51). Importantly, active participation in the borough's electoral politics bolstered these demands.

As early as 1964, when Bangladeshis made up less than 1 percent of the population,[4] "there were some polling districts in Stepney where Muslim and Sikh names accounted for over 10 per cent of the totals. In one polling district [around Brick Lane in Spitalfields] the figure was nearly 20 per cent" (Burney 1967, 85). Examining ward-level election results over the next decades provides us with further clues. In the 1978 election, Labour's majorities were still generally secure boroughwide and in the wards containing the highest number of Bangladeshi electors, but the party's hold on power nevertheless showed signs of considerable weakening. In several wards with high Bangladeshi concentrations, Labour's vote share had fallen by close to 30 percent, as various parties on the extreme right and left splintered the once-solid Labour vote (see Table 5.3). In light of the strong showing of the National Front in Tower Hamlets as a whole – the party contested all wards in 1978 and scored over 10 percent in eleven out of nineteen wards – Labour leaders were at pains not to publicize their links with the Bangladeshi electorate. In spite of the rapid influx of Bangladeshi migrants into Spitalfields in the late 1960s and 1970s, the ward's Labour Party made no reference to this population in its electoral addresses in the run-up to the 1978 and 1982 elections. There was a general reluctance on the part of the party leadership to establish formal links with this new electorate and a hope that informal relationships would suffice in delivering the Bangladeshi vote to the Labour Party (Eade 1989, 55). With over one-third of Spitalfields' residents having been born in present-day Bangladesh, however, obtaining the immigrant vote should have been a key priority for the ward Labour Party. In the 1982 election, Bangladeshis indeed showed Labour that their vote was not to be taken for granted. They ran as Independent candidates in Spitalfields and won first and fourth place, respectively, beating Labour into second. By 1986, the Labour ward party fielded Bangladeshi candidates and won back its seats (see Table 5.3).

Similar dynamics unfolded in other wards. In Weavers ward, Labour lost to the Liberals, who had fielded Bangladeshi candidates, in three consecutive crucial elections; its lowest poll came in 1990, when the Liberals had put up two Bangladeshi candidates.[5] In St. Mary's ward, the intervention of

---

[4] Bangladesh did not come into existence until 1971. This figure refers to the number of residents, recorded in the 1961 census, born in Pakistan – the majority of whom originated from present-day Bangladesh – living in the Metropolitan boroughs of Stepney, Bethnal Green, and Poplar, which were amalgamated in 1965 to form the borough of Tower Hamlets (Burney 1967, 83).

[5] The Labour Party also fielded a Bangladeshi candidate who received 1,158 fewer votes than that of the Liberals, an indication of the internal heterogeneity within the Bangladeshi community itself (see subsequent text).

TABLE 5.3. *Electoral Results in Tower Hamlets Wards with the Highest Bangladeshi Concentration, 1968–1998*

	% of Vote				South Asian Candidate			No. of South Asian Councilors	% of Vote: Additional South Asian Candidates
Election Year	LAB	CON	LD	NF/BNP	LAB	CON	LD		
Spitalfields									
1968	57.9	24.7	—	—	no	no	—	0	—
1971	89.2	10.8	—	—	no	no	—	0	—
1974	74.2	—	25.8	—	no	—	no	0	—
1978	46.4	8.0	—	4.3	no	no	—	0	—
1982	26.1	—	19.4	—	no	—	yes	1	54.5
1986	43.1	7.4	20.4	—	yes	no	yes	2	29.0
1990	56.6	14.0	—	2.6	yes	yes	—	2	9.2
1994	59.6	—	31.6	—	yes	—	yes	3	9.1
1998	70.1	29.9	—	—	yes	yes	—	3	29.6
St. Mary's									
1968	43.1	—	—	—	no	—	—	0	—
1971	60.8	11.0	—	—	no	no	—	0	—
1974	63.8	11.6	—	—	no	no	—	0	—
1978	59.2	20.7	—	3.1	no	no	—	0	—
1982	60.9	10.5	16.7	—	no	yes	yes	0	—
1986	64.0	14.7	21.3	—	no	yes	yes	0	—
1990	34.1	3.3	34.8	—	no	yes	no	0	17.8
1994	67.1	4.3	5.8	—	yes	yes	yes	1	—
1998	69.8	30.2	—	—	yes	yes	—	2	—
St. Katharine's									
1968	76.4	—	—	—	no	—	—	0	—
1971	87.6	—	—	—	no	—	—	0	—
1974	79.0	—	—	—	no	—	—	0	—
1978	52.7	12.8	—	5.7	no	no	—	0	—
1982	41.5	10.7	27.4	—	yes	no	no	2	6.8
1986	56.7	15.8	24.5	—	yes	no	yes	2	—
1990	52.5	22.0	—	—	yes	yes	—	3	7.8
1994	46.9	8.4	26.3	—	yes	no	yes	2	11.8
1998	46.6	35.5	18.0	—	yes	yes	yes	2	—
Weavers									
1978	42.3	13.1	32.4	12.2	no	no	no	0	—
1982	27.3	9.7	54.1	—	no	no	yes	1	8.9
1986	42.2	5.8	52.0	—	no	no	yes	1	—
1990	30.8	1.7	65.5	—	yes	yes	yes	2	2.0
1994	41.3	—	25.5	—	yes	—	yes	1	25.1
1998	41.9	5.4	26.5	—	yes	yes	yes	1	—
Shadwell									
1968	63.4	—	—	—	no	—	—	0	—
1971	86.6	—	—	—	no	—	—	0	—
1974	81.6	—	—	—	no	—	—	0	—
1978	53.7	13.0	—	7.7	no	no	—	0	—
1982	51.6	—	48.4	—	no	—	no	0	—
1986	51.0	9.0	40.0	—	no	no	no	0	—
1990	74.5	25.5	—	—	yes	no	—	1	—
1994	47.8	9.4	22.7	—	yes	no	yes	2	13.4
1998	50.0	21.9	—	—	yes	no	—	2	28.1

(*Continued from page 146*)

Election Year	% of Vote				South Asian Candidate			No. of South Asian Councilors	% of Vote: Additional South Asian Candidates
	LAB	CON	LD	NF/BNP	LAB	CON	LD		
St. Dunstan's									
1968	78.9	—	—	—	no	—	—	0	—
1971					no	—	—	0	—
1974	86.8	—	—	—	no	—	—	0	—
1978	58.4	19.3	—	10.7	no	no	—	0	—
1982	53.6	23.4	—	—	no	no	—	0	—
1986	44.1	8.7	38.0	9.2	yes	no	no	1	—
1990	59.9	5.6	27.9	—	yes	no	no	1	—
1994	72.5	—	19.7	—	yes	—	yes	1	7.8
1998	70.1	29.9	—	—	yes	no	—	2	—

Notes: All wards return three councilors, except for St. Mary's (two starting in 1978) and Spitalfields and St. Katharine's (four until 1974). Candidates who receive the highest number of votes are elected. Additional South Asian candidates are candidates that did not run for Labour, the Conservatives, or the Liberal Party/Liberal Democrats Alliance. In 1971 in St. Dustan's, Labour ran unopposed. Weavers first held elections in 1978. The 2002 elections were held under new ward boundaries. CON = Conservatives; LD = Liberal Democrats; LAB = Labour Party; NF/BNP = National Front/British National Party.
Source: Rallings et al. (2006); author's calculations.

several Bangladeshi candidates as Independents, Conservatives, and "Community Campaign" candidates was partly responsible for Labour's massive, 30-percentage-point drop in votes in 1990; Labour lost the ward by twelve votes. Finally, in wards with a high Bangladeshi concentration where Labour did not lose seats, local Bangladeshi community leaders tended to run as Labour candidates. Whereas Britain's ethnic minorities had lent their support to the Labour Party in overwhelming numbers in national elections and in many other local authorities,[6] local politics in Tower Hamlets were much more volatile.

In sum, shortly after their arrival in Tower Hamlets, Bangladeshi migrants took active part in the borough's politics. Aware of their potential electoral muscle, the newcomers ensured that they would not be taken for granted by the political leadership and instead offered their vote to the highest bidder. Electoral statistics show that, by the 1980s, no party that hoped to gain control of the council, let alone of the wards where Bangladeshis had settled in great numbers, could afford to alienate this crucial voting bloc. But did Bangladeshis parlay their electoral clout into valued goods for their constituents? If so, how did white East Enders react?

Bangladeshi Demands

Notwithstanding the common material concerns of the Bangladeshi community, it would be false to characterize this group as a homogeneous electoral

---

[6] In each general election between 1974 (October) and 1997, over 80 percent of ethnic minority voters supported Labour, except in 1987, when their vote share fell to 72 percent (Saggar 2000, 122). For the determinants of ethnic minority support for the Labour Party, see Dancygier and Saunders (2006).

bloc whose constituents shared the same policy preferences or the same ideas on how to convert their sheer numbers into political power. Indeed, the internal rivalries and disputes over how to best represent community interests seemed at times to overshadow their unity (Eade 1989). An investigation of local election statistics is again useful, for it illustrates that Bangladeshi candidates often competed against one another in ward elections. In 1982, for example, four Bangladeshi candidates ran as Independents in Spitalfields and one stood for the Social Democrats/Liberal Alliance, divvying up the immigrant vote between them. In St. Mary's ward, the Alliance and the Conservative Party fielded one Bangladeshi candidate each. Similar patterns obtain in other wards with a high concentration of immigrants (see Table 5.3, right-most column, for an indication of the competition over the community franchise by co-ethnics outside of the established parties).

This type of detailed election data provides us with an indication of the growing electoral leverage as well as the internal divisions of the Bangladeshi electorate in Tower Hamlets. Ethnographic work by John Eade nicely complements and confirms the patterns gleaned from these data and also portrays how internal fissures ultimately gave way to a consensus that privileged the provision of resources as the major policy concern of the Bangladeshi population in the 1970s and 1980s. Eade (1990, 1989), who chronicled the Bangladeshi community's forays into local politics, vividly illustrates the relationship between this new electorate and the local political establishment as well as its internal deliberations regarding political representation. Despite the rapidly growing size of this electorate, senior Labour councilors initially resented the "Strident public demands for more resources and attacks on . . . [Labour] policies by Spitalfields activists . . . as unhelpful and insensitive to the constraints within which they were operating" (Eade 1989, 41). These constraints not only were financial in nature but referred primarily to the racist backlash at the ballot box that these demands induced.

While Labour politicians sometimes spoke out against racism, many immigrants viewed these pronouncements as a cheap way to buy off and silence the Asian electorate. In an open letter to Labour leader Paul Beasley, the Bengali Housing Action Group condemned Labour's stated opposition to racism as "a cynical exercise in Asian vote catching" by a party that was merely "concerned about the increasing defection of Labour votes to the Tories and the National Front" rather than with the actual well-being of a population that was suffering from racist attacks and unfair housing allocation practices.[7] Even within the Bangladeshi community, though, some argued that activists "shouldn't press the council too hard and to publicly declare for our demands. The reasons being that if the Labour council was seen to be capitulating to blacks, it would lose votes to the National Front."[8]

---

[7] The open letter is printed in *Race Today*; see Dhondy (1977, 66).
[8] See *Race Today* (1978a, 109).

Nevertheless, defection by Bangladeshis turned out to be even more damaging for the Labour Party. It was indeed the growing dissatisfaction with local Labour, which was failing to deliver vital services and to take Bangladeshi needs seriously, that led many to turn to other parties or to try their luck as Independent candidates. In the words of one Bangladeshi activist, putting up their own candidates would make "every political party... realise that we have no faith in them, so they will begin to take up what we are looking for" (Eade 1989, 48). As is apparent from the electoral data, this move had its intended effect. After Labour had lost the 1982 election in Spitalfields ward, left-wing Labour activists in several wards (Spitalfields, St. Dunstan's, and St. Katharine's) allied with Bangladeshi community organizers in a mutually beneficial partnership. Similar to ethnic minority communities elsewhere, Bangladeshis in Tower Hamlets were initially suspicious of white left-wing motivations, fearing that they were seen as useful pawns in the fight for a working-class revolution that Bangladeshi immigrants were less interested in pursuing. Notwithstanding these ideological differences, the two groups "concentrated on the provision of public funds and resources in the areas of housing, education, employment, welfare rights and amenities" as their main priorities (Eade 1990, 495). Moreover, access to the Labour Party "enabled [Bangladeshis] to gain public funding from Labour controlled agencies [while the] success of the five Bangladeshi Labour candidates and the defeat of the Independent... in the 1986 council election suggested that the alliance with white left-wingers was not a major liability in certain wards in the borough" (Eade 1990, 500).

In short, having established its electoral muscle and credibly demonstrated its ability to withdraw political support if resources were not forthcoming, the Bangladeshi community successfully allied with the Labour Party to acquire highly valued and scarce material goods.[9] Tower Hamlets' white residents did not react kindly to Bangladeshis' rising political and economic strength.

White Backlash

The political ascendancy of the Bangladeshi community and its effective mobilization around scarce resources was met with fierce resistance on the part of white East Enders who felt increasingly threatened by this community's political and economic gains. Having fielded not a single candidate in the 1974 council elections, the National Front (NF) earned over 10 percent of the overall vote share in 1978, with much higher totals in several wards. These electoral gains went hand in hand with increased racist attacks against Bangladeshis. The NF made racist violence part of its recruitment strategy, while the perpetrators of racist violence in turn employed physical intimidation to deter immigrants from

---

[9] See also Forman (1989, 50–67) for a more detailed account of the proliferation of Bangladeshi pressure groups lobbying for improved service delivery by the local council.

moving into their areas and taking "their" homes.[10] Asian community leaders had called for an increased police presence as individualized racist attacks, seen to be connected to the operations of the NF in the area, steadily grew in the late 1970s.[11] The first racist murder was only waiting to happen; it occurred *on election night* in 1978 when a young Bangladeshi man was stabbed to death on his way home from work in Brick Lane, in the heart of the Bangladeshi settlement.

This tragic event had immediate repercussions. The murder galvanized the Bangladeshi community into forming an Action Committee Against Racist Attacks (ACARA), which organized an 8,000-strong march to Downing Street to protest the homicide and to petition the Home Office to commission an official inquiry into racist violence.[12] The violence continued when, in June 1978, a mob of 150 to 200 skinheads went on the attack in Brick Lane, hurling bottles, shouting insults and threats, and causing property damage and physical injury.[13] Several weeks later, "2,000 protesters, led by Bengalis, demonstrated . . . to counter National Front activity in their area."[14] This event was followed by a sit-down, in which nearly 2,000 Bangladeshis occupied the middle of a busy road.[15] Using protest tactics, Bangladeshis, along with white antiracist organizations, also took steps to drive out dozens of National Front paper-sellers who disseminated the party's racist propaganda.[16] This hateful rhetoric had contributed to the escalation of what an official report called "an appalling catalogue of violent crime – hammer attacks, stabbings, slashed faces, punctured lungs, clubbings, gun shot wounds, people beaten with bricks, sticks, umbrellas or kicked unconscious even in broad daylight."[17]

The 1970s had been a difficult decade for Bangladeshis in Tower Hamlets, but the situation hardly improved during the 1980s. Even without the prodding of the National Front, which had collapsed all around the country as a result of the internal infighting of its members and subsequent organizational splits (Husbands 1983, 14–20), racist violence escalated to unprecedented levels.

---

[10] This rational calculus, of course, may not have been at the forefront of all perpetrators; see Chapter 4 for additional objectives that may motivate such offenders. As I will elaborate subsequently, the specific threats and attacks committed by whites in Tower Hamlets, and the community support that these enjoyed in some quarters, do indeed strongly suggest that perpetrators used racist violence as a deliberate tactic in the battle over scarce resources.

[11] Starting in the second half of 1970s, various issues of *Race Today* chronicle the rise of racist violence and Asian self-defense groups in Tower Hamlets.

[12] This display of organized resistance was apparently not a completely voluntary response for some. In the days leading up to the demonstration, Bangladeshi activists visited all "Asian-owned business [and] . . . their owners [were] politely requested to close their shops, cafes and cinemas on the day of the demonstration. At the same time a strong rumour was spread that anyone ignoring this request would find his premises vandalized" (*Race Today* 1978b, 76).

[13] *The Times*, "Mob of Youths Attack Bangladeshi Area in East End of London," June 12, 1978.

[14] *The Guardian*, "13 Arrests in Brick Lane Race Demo," July 17, 1978.

[15] *The Guardian*, "An 80-Minute Protest Heralds New Era of East End Struggle," July 24, 1978.

[16] *The Guardian*, "Brick Lane March Shows the Flag," August 21, 1978.

[17] Cited in *The Guardian*, "No Racial Overtones in Asian Murder," September 28, 1978.

Racially motivated attacks in the borough soared to such an extent that it made regular headlines even in national newspapers. As police were unable or unwilling to protect the borough's Bangladeshi residents, local activists formed the Community Alliance for Police Accountability, which started tracking racist incidents and the police response to them (Forman 1989, 204).

The escalation of the violent expression of racism has been linked to the severity of economic deprivation in the borough. Tower Hamlets was ranked the third-poorest local authority in Great Britain, suffering from chronic unemployment, endemic poverty, and the most acute housing shortage in the country.[18] In the face of a severe housing crisis, the council, now led by the Liberal Party, lacked the funds to even make its over 3,000 vacant homes habitable and instead considered housing families aboard a passenger ship, a scheme that Labour councilors denounced as "a floating ghetto for a new race of boat people."[19] While this plan never materialized, housing supply was further squeezed by expansive Canary Wharf business developments in the eastern part of the borough. As the private housing sector was also extremely limited, many Tower Hamlets residents were "forced to compete for the scarce and often unpopular public resources" (Phillips 1988, 362). The economic recession, which by 1993 had left over 30 percent of the borough's male residents unemployed (Keith 1995, 553), increased demand for affordable housing, while the Conservative government's drastic spending cuts deepened the sense of economic and social crisis. By 1986, a House of Commons Select Committee issued a warning to the Thatcher government that Tower Hamlets would suffer deteriorating race relations if no additional monies for housing were made available. But no significant spending increases were forthcoming (Burns et al. 1994, 216–217). Instead, in 1983–1984 the central government's spending on housing in Tower Hamlets was cut to a third of its 1975–1976 level, corresponding to trends in the rest of the country (Phillips 1988, 363).

The Local Entrenchment of Racist Violence

While there certainly seemed to be a connection between the grievances created by poverty on the one hand and the entrenchment of violent racism on the other, a focus on economic conditions alone cannot account for the ways in which bigoted attacks unfolded in Tower Hamlets during this period of brutal xenophobia. Newspaper reports started emphasizing the spread of racist incidents in particular areas of the borough and on particular council-owned housing estates. The Millwall and Blackwall wards in the southeastern Isle of Dogs neighborhood, for example, experienced a massive rise in racist attacks over the decade. In 1983, five racist incidents were recorded there; by 1993, the same year that the country's first BNP councilor was elected in a by-election in Millwall, this number had shot up to 141 (see Figure 5.2). While the incidence of racist violence had exploded boroughwide, these two wards, which in 1983

[18] *The Guardian*, "Council's Welfare Outlay 'Too Low,'" October 28, 1989.
[19] *The Guardian* "Council May Put Homeless Aboard Ship," July 19, 1986.

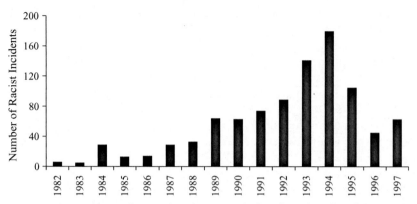

FIGURE 5.2. Racist incidents, Isle of Dogs (Blackwall and Millwall wards), Tower Hamlets. (*Source: Foster 1999, 270.*)

only accounted for 1.6 percent of all racist attacks in Tower Hamlets, produced 37.6 percent of all such incidents occurring in the borough by 1993. Meanwhile, the share of Tower Hamlets' Bangladeshis living in this area had only increased from 2.7 to 5.3 percent between 1981 and 1991 (see Figure 5.3).[20] The two wards did experience a rapid increase in their Bangladeshi population, but so did a lot of other wards during this time (see Table 5.1); demographic change alone cannot explain the disproportionate upsurge in racist attacks.

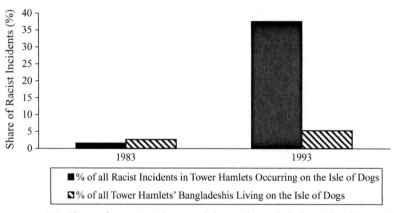

FIGURE 5.3. Share of racist incidents and share of Bangladeshis, Isle of Dogs (Blackwall and Millwall wards), Tower Hamlets, 1983 and 1993. (*Sources: The Economist, The Independent,* Foster 1999, and Table 5.1; see footnote 20 for more information.)

[20] For racist incident data for Tower Hamlets as a whole, see *The Economist,* "Racial Harassment; Nasty Neighbours," February 2, 1985 for 1983 data and *The Independent,* "Racist Attacks 'Every Day' in East End," July 4, 1994 for 1993 data. These figures are based on police data. For Isle of Dogs data on racist incidents, see Foster 1999, 270; based on Home Office data. Population figures for 1983 and 1993 are based on the 1981 and 1991 census, respectively; see Table 5.1 for sources.

In addition to these disturbing trends, several large housing estates became infamous sites of violent racism. A council inquiry singled out the area of Stepney (encompassing St. Mary's, St. Dunstan's and Redcoat wards) as producing the highest rate of increase in racist attacks.[21] Many of these attacks occurred in and around Stepney's large Ocean Estate, which became a notorious site of endemic, routine racist aggression inflicted on its Bangladeshi tenants. Bangladeshi residents, having waited to be allocated housing space for years, commonly requested transfers to escape the daily dose of harassment. Adding insult to injury, Bangladeshis had long been accused of using allegations of racist attacks as a pretense in order to be moved to better housing (Forman 1989, 193). The streets surrounding the Ocean Estate turned into "no-go" areas for Bangladeshis, as children stopped attending school because they feared having to walk through "hostile territory" on their way to get there.[22] Eventually, the education authorities were forced to bus these children to schools less than a mile away from their homes to escape racist harassment and violence, while the Ocean Estate Tenants' Association protested that this was just another example that "Too much [was] being done for them."[23]

Institutional Change and the Escalation of Immigrant–Native Conflict

What accounts for these patterns? Why did white East Enders target Bangladeshis in particular areas of the borough? To understand the overall rise in racist violence in Tower Hamlets, as well as its entrenchment in specific areas of the borough, we have to take into account how institutional changes of the 1980s coincided with further increases in Bangladeshi political power and economic scarcity to make Bangladeshis a pivotal voting bloc whose demands politicians ignored at their peril. To preview, first, the abolition of the Greater London Council (GLC) meant that an increased number of local councilors – many of whom relied on the Bangladeshi vote for reelection – were now in charge of housing allocation. Second, a decentralization experiment whereby councilors could essentially decide whether to allot housing to Bangladeshis or to whites produced variation in allocation outcomes *within* the borough. Crucially, in those neighborhoods where politicians depended on the immigrant constituency, Bangladeshis were more likely to secure council flats and anti-immigration mobilization ensued as a result.

The system of housing-allocation rules was altered throughout London as Margaret Thatcher dismantled the GLC. This Londonwide body had controlled over half of the public housing stock, but after its abolishment in 1986, local borough councils were given full authority over the distribution of this highly

---

[21] *The Docklands Recorder*, "Probe Finds Racial Abuse Soaring," November 12, 1987.
[22] *The Guardian*, "Education Guardian: East End Crisis – When Can I Go To School?," June 27, 1989.
[23] *The Guardian*, "Asian Children in Tower Hamlets Are Taken to School by Bus due to Racial Attacks," September 12, 1989.

valued resource (Forman 1989, 37). An independent research inquiry established that the GLC had operated institutionally racist housing procedures that only allocated Bangladeshis to estates within a confined area in and around Spitalfields, the center of Bangladeshi settlement. Moreover, within these estates, Bangladeshis were generally assigned worse-quality flats (Phillips 1987). Given that all of Tower Hamlets had only elected two councilors to the GLC, whose single-member districts coincided with the borough's two large parliamentary seats (containing 11.7 and 2.6 percent of Bangladeshi-born residents in 1981, respectively[24]), it is not surprising that housing officers felt no pressure to take into account Bangladeshi demands at the expense of the needs of the white majority. Nevertheless, once Thatcher transferred control over all housing allocations to local authorities, made up of many ethnically diverse multimember wards containing much larger shares of Bangladeshi voters, incentives changed.

The Liberals further decentralized decision making over the distribution of economic resources. The party had run on a populist platform, claiming that Labour's bureaucratic and detached leadership had failed its people and pledging to return local politics back to the grass roots. The Liberals promised to "rescue the old neighbourhoods, neighbourhood loyalties and ethnic identities from obscurity, provide them with a new political autonomy and model local government around them" (Burns et al. 1994, 69). In a borough whose population was spatially segregated along ethnic lines, such a philosophy also coincided with pandering to white racism, a charge that Liberals defused by asserting that their approach simply empowered the ethnic groups that were dominant in particular neighborhoods (Burns et al. 1994, 70). Indeed, Bangladeshis were to be found among Liberal candidates and councilors.

The Liberals' communitarian notions had tangible institutional consequences. Once elected, the party translated their ideas of neighborhood revitalization into action by instituting a revolutionary decentralization experiment, whereby the borough was divided into seven neighborhoods, each composed of two to four wards. These neighborhoods were responsible for service delivery in their areas and received an annual budget that they were authorized to spend according to their own priorities (Stoker et al. 1991). Moreover, true to their pledge to empower the grass roots, the Liberals allowed the Labour Party to run the neighborhoods whose wards had elected a majority of Labour councilors, even though the Liberals had won control of the overall council.[25]

After the 1986 election, three out of the seven neighborhoods were indeed controlled by Labour councilors whose adopted policies differed from those of their Liberal counterparts. In the realm of housing, this difference was

---

[24] These figures, pertaining to the 1983 boundaries of Bethnal Green and Stepney and Bow and Poplar, are derived from "Table 4 Country of Birth," author's calculations (available at www. nomisweb.co.uk).

[25] Specifically, voters still elected councilors from individual wards, but the party that garnered the most seats within a neighborhood won control of the neighborhood.

particularly stark. The Liberal-controlled neighborhoods would reinstate the traditional "sons-and-daughters" policy, commonly practiced in other London boroughs as well (Hewitt 2005, 41–42), whereby residents who had long-standing family ties in the borough – that is, not immigrants – would be given preferential treatment. The Labour Party, however, was in no position to alienate its Bangladeshi base. As we have seen in the previous text, Bangladeshi voters were not easily co-opted by local Labour leaders and several Bangladeshi candidates also campaigned as Liberals. Having seen its once unassailable majority dwindle over the course of a decade, the Labour Party had to shore up the Bangladeshi vote by allocating housing based on objective need – a policy that would effectively advantage Bangladeshis, who by 1987 constituted 90 percent of the borough's homeless population (Forman 1989, 231). As a result, Bangladeshis who lived in Labour neighborhoods were allocated council flats at much higher rates than Bangladeshis who lived in areas under Liberal control. These Labour areas included the aforementioned Stepney and Isle of Dogs neighborhoods – the two areas that had witnessed a surge in racist violence.

This variation in allocation procedures explains the varied incidence of racist violence in particular areas of the borough. White residents who felt they had lost out in the fight over scarce resources retaliated with an unprecedented use of violent force as "more people used racism as a weapon in holding onto what they had got" (Forman 1989, 209). Whites had for years employed racist violence to turn housing estates into "unofficially recognised but very effective 'no-go' areas" for Bangladeshis (Phillips 1988, 365–366) and this tactic was taken to an extreme once Labour allocation rules took Bangladeshi needs into account. The aforementioned escalation of racist violence in the Blackwall and Millwall wards, which together made up the Labour-controlled Isle of Dogs neighborhood, was a direct result of the interplay between Bangladeshi political power and resource competition, which in turn intensified as a result of increased electoral competitiveness. Whites who resented having to share the already scarce housing supply at a time when unemployment rose and affordable housing was in higher demand than ever – not a single home for private rental use had been built in almost a decade of rapidly expanding business development on the Isle of Dogs – consciously targeted the council flats that had been allocated to Bangladeshi newcomers. One of the first families to be transferred to the Isle of Dogs neighborhood was welcomed by a pig's head left at the front door; others had their telephone lines cut and their mailboxes set on fire. Council flats assigned to Bangladeshis were vandalized or even the target of arsonists. In some cases, local resistance achieved its intended results, as allocation decisions were reversed (Foster 1999, 258, 266–270, 280).

Ethnographic research conducted on the Isle of Dogs illustrates how white residents objected specifically to Bangladeshis being housed in valued council flats, rather than to the in-migration of these newcomers per se. According to one local white resident, "Ten years ago when the Asians... moved in... they were put in dumps. No one ever cared." But when Bangladeshis were moved to homes that white families wanted, local resistance was fierce. A Labour councilor explained the spread of violent resistance in these terms: "The feeling on the Isle of Dogs is that you can move as many 'Pakis' as you like on to – [estate] cos they don't want [that] for their sons and daughters anyway. They don't want to live there...but if you move a 'Paki' family onto – [estate] that's where they want to live" (Foster 1999, 265; estate names deleted in the original).

Similar to other communities ridden with ethnic conflict, not only in Great Britain, but around the world, local rumors greatly exaggerated the threat that the in-migrating ethnic group represented.[26] In the case of the Isle of Dogs, exaggerations about alleged preferential treatment of Bangladeshis in the allocation of public housing prompted the creation of a local pressure group (the Isle of Dogs Action Group for Equality), whose agenda not only included barring ethnic minorities from housing but that also sought a complete ban on immigration and the withdrawal of all welfare benefits to nonwhites. While housing was the most politicized issue, perceived preferential backing of Bangladeshis at the expense of whites in the funding of community groups and other government initiatives was also contentious among members of the white community.[27] Perpetrators of racist violence in turn often draw encouragement from members of their communities, who legitimize these heinous crimes with tacit or overt support (Pinderhughes 1993; Sibbit 1997). This was certainly the case on the Isle of Dogs, where local pressure groups provided cover for racist attackers. As one local tenant professed, "Some of 'em actually know that it's their sons that are out and doing it...and try to defend what their sons are doing, that's the horrific part of it" (Foster 1999, 266).

Campaign tactics further intensified hostilities. In the 1990 local election campaign, the Liberal Democrats issued a fake leaflet, designed to look like it had been produced by the Labour Party, suggesting that the latter would privilege Bangladeshis in the provision of council housing and other social services (Keith 1995, 556). Liberal Democrats on the Isle of Dogs contested the election with the slogan "Island homes for Island people."[28] When a by-election was called in the Millwall ward after the resignation of a Labour councilor in 1993, the BNP saw an opportunity to exploit the soaring ethnic tensions for electoral gain. It stepped up its vicious anti-immigrant campaign, which in turn provided further fuel for the perpetrators of racist crime. As already

[26] On the role of rumors in the context of ethnic riots, see Brass (1997) and Horowitz (2001, 74–88).

[27] See Foster (1999, 279–281). According to an Island resident in her study, "The Bangladeshi people are getting thousands of pounds in grants and this is what creates the tension when people have worked for what they've got and they can see it all being taken away from them and being given over to ethnic groups. It's not because people are racist, it's because they're having what they worked for taken away from them." See also Back and Keith's (1999, 143–145) discussion about white youths' perception that they are losing out to Bangladeshis in the provision of youth services on the Isle of Dogs.

[28] *The Guardian*, "Ashdown Warned in 1991 of Tower Hamlets Racial Tactics," September 20, 1993.

mentioned, the number of racist attacks in the Millwall and Blackwall wards skyrocketed to unprecedented levels (see Figure 5.2). Bangladeshi youths had started responding with violent reprisals themselves, but they were increasingly portrayed as the criminal instigators of interethnic clashes by the national and local media (Keith 1995, 558–560).[29] The BNP seized on these attacks by organizing protest marches through Tower Hamlets, which escalated into "scuffles and fights between young whites and local Asians."[30] Meanwhile, white boys continued to engage in "local ethnic cleansing," stabbing a Bangladeshi boy on his way home to a predominantly white estate in broad daylight.[31] In the Stepney neighborhood, home of the Ocean Estate, an attack by a group of whites left a Bangladeshi boy in a coma. This assault was followed by a vigil that turned violent as BNP supporters and white and Asian antiracist and antifascist groups clashed with each other as well as with the police.[32] Soon afterward, skinheads went on a violent rampage through Brick Lane, reminiscent of events in 1978. The BNP secured its first council seat in Millwall a few days later.

National media attention and staged anti-BNP demonstrations helped to reduce, but not eliminate, the racist party's electoral popularity in the borough.[33] Racist violence persisted and became an institutionalized feature of some neighborhoods, as no-go areas not only continued to exist for Bangladeshis but also emerged for whites (Back and Keith 1999). Baroness Uddin, a former Labour councilor and the first female Muslim member of the House of Lords, who grew up in the borough, declared that "in Tower Hamlets... the social apartheid is clear for all to see. Everyone there will tell you very little has changed. They will tell you that racism is as grave now as it was 20 years ago."[34]

Summing up, conflicts between Bangladeshi migrants and white natives began in the 1970s and escalated in the 1980s and 1990s because Bangladeshi migrants' electoral clout increased as economic conditions declined. Labour councilors had to rely on the Bangladeshi vote and implemented allocation procedures that would benefit immigrant households in the provision of economic resources, specifically public housing. When the disbursement of goods came at the expense of white natives – which was especially likely to occur in neighborhoods controlled by Labour – natives retaliated by employing racist violence and racist voting.

---

[29] In 1990, a gang of Bangladeshi youths stabbed a white boy, perforating his lung, an incident that set off reporting of Bangladeshi-on-white violence; see *The Guardian*, "Stabbing Protest Fuels Racial Tension," February 23, 1990. The BNP quickly took advantage of the situation and leafleted the area. In its campaign literature, the party continued to claim that whites were the main victims of racist attacks (Back and Keith 1999, 145).

[30] *The Guardian*, "Outrage at BNP Meeting in School," April 18, 1990.

[31] *The Guardian*, "When Ethnic Cleansing Came to the East End," June 2, 1993.

[32] *The Independent*, "Police Hope To Prevent BNP Election Backlash," September 14, 1993.

[33] In 1994, the BNP ran in four wards where it collected between 19.1 and 28.5 percent of the vote. In 1998, the party contested three seats, with vote shares ranging from 4.7 to 17.3 percent but its overall vote fell to 2.2 (the NF scored 10.1 percent in the one ward where it competed).

[34] *The Independent*, "Stranded in the Slipstream of Multiculturalism," April 6, 2004.

Fortunately, developments elsewhere have not been as bleak. Similar to that in Tower Hamlets, Ealing's South Asian community also flexed its political muscle early on, demanding access to housing at a time when housing was in short supply. Just as occurred in East London, this constellation of immigrant political power and economic scarcity provoked a native backlash. In contrast to events in Tower Hamlets, however, intergroup relations relaxed because pressures on state-provided economic resources proved less acute, the borough's population has been more affluent, and Indians' economic position improved. While the logic that connects minority political power to economic resource allocation and therefore to intergroup conflict produced spatial variation in the incidence of immigrant–native conflict in Tower Hamlets, the case of Ealing provides us with a case in which a decrease in economic scarcity causes intergroup tensions to wane over time. Comparing across the two boroughs, we see that South Asian immigrants have possessed electoral leverage in both, but it is only in Ealing, where economic scarcity lessened, that immigrant–native conflict declined.

Ealing

Ealing and Tower Hamlets share a host of similarities with respect to post-war migration trends. Like its neighbor to the east, Ealing received a large influx of South Asian immigrants that settled in a tightly concentrated area in the borough's southwestern wards. The process of chain migration set in when labor shortages prompted local factories to recruit workers from abroad to perform manual, low-skilled jobs that were increasingly shunned by the native workforce. Throughout the 1950s and 1960s, a steady stream of Indian Sikhs left their farms in East Punjab and came to work in Ealing's industrial plants. Like their counterparts in Tower Hamlets, most of the initial arrivals were thus of peasant background, had received little or no education, and were unfamiliar with the English language; initially, "no more than one per cent . . . belong[ed] to the skilled category" (Marsh 1967, 14). Nevertheless, there was also a "steady trickle of the Punjab's intelligentsia (clerks, teachers and petty officials)," who would soon represent their fellow Sikhs in local matters (Campaign Against Racism and Fascism [CARF] 1981, 7).

Ealing's Indian population grew steadily as men had their families come join them from abroad. In the late 1960s and early 1970s, Ealing received new waves of Indian-origin immigrants from East Africa that had been expelled from some of the continent's newly independent nations. Reflecting their clerical and commercial status in Africa, these so-called twice migrants brought with them valuable portable skills (Bhachu 1985, 6–7) and as a result also diversified the skill profile of Ealing's Indian-origin population. This influx of refugees, together with labor migration, family reunification, and high birth rates, led to a rapid rise in Ealing's Indian-origin population. The newcomers numbered 8,700 in 1966 (Hill and Issacharoff 1971, 38); by 1981 they had increased to over 30,000 (over 10 percent of the population); and the 2001 census counted almost 50,000 Indian-origin residents in Ealing (see Table 5.4; see Figure 5.4

TABLE 5.4. *Concentration of the Indian Population in Ealing, 1981–2001*

Ealing	All Residents		% Indian		Ealing	All Residents	% Indian
	1981	1991	1981	1991		2001	2001
TOTAL	278,675	275,228	10.7	16.1		300,948	16.5
Northcote	13,382	11,177	46.9	67.0	Southall Broadway	13,049	54.2
Glebe	14,249	12,858	38.5	59.9	Southall Green	12,895	54.1
Mount Pleasant	13,316	12,550	32.7	56.2	Lady Margaret	12,806	49.9
Waxlow	12,013	11,936	17.8	34.9	Dormers Wells	13,073	40.6
Dormers Wells	13,527	12,642	16.2	34.7	Norwood Green	12,647	35.9
Perivale	12,485	12,371	10.3	17.9	North Greenford	13,089	21.1
Costons	10,455	10,495	7.0	11.1	Perivale	13,441	17.4
Walpole	12,695	12,337	6.6	6.4	Greenford Green	12,466	13.6
Elthorne	11,390	11,787	5.6	6.0	Greenford Broadway	13,297	13.3
Wood End	11,213	10,805	5.5	10.3	Northolt Mandeville	12,888	8.3
Vale	6,889	7,113	4.8	4.1	Hanger Hill	14,010	7.7
Hanger Lane	11,549	11,631	4.4	5.8	Northolt West End	13,420	7.6
Northfield	12,162	11,993	4.3	4.8	East Acton	14,448	6.5
Ravenor	11,691	11,479	4.2	6.7	Walpole	12,688	6.0
Victoria	7,235	7,695	4.0	5.0	Hobbayne	13,068	6.0
Heathfield	12,724	12,425	3.9	4.5	Elthorne	12,328	5.9
Springfield	11,316	12,081	3.7	3.7	Cleveland	14,179	5.9
Mandeville	11,402	10,715	3.5	5.9	Acton Central	13,442	5.7
Hobbayne	11,296	10,965	3.5	5.6	Ealing Broadway	12,634	5.5
Argyle	12,181	12,960	3.3	4.6	Ealing Common	12,804	5.3
Pitshanger	12,104	12,614	2.8	3.1	South Acton	13,318	4.9
West End	11,414	11,767	2.8	6.6	Northfield	12,477	4.4
Southfield	10,624	10,256	2.7	2.6	Southfield	12,481	2.7
Ealing Common	11,363	12,576	2.7	3.8			

Notes: Ealing underwent boundary changes that are reflected in the 2001 census figures. Until 1981, entries refer to country of birth. As of 1991, entries are based on ethnic origin and thus also include children born in the United Kingdom to parents of Indian descent.
Source: See Table 5.1.

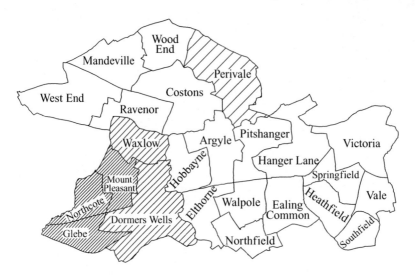

Percentage Indian

0 - 15.0

15.1 - 30.0

30.1 - 45.0

45.1 - 100.0

0   0.5   1   2 Miles

FIGURE 5.4. Ealing 1991 ward map. (© Crown copyright. All rights reserved. License number 100049655.)

for a ward map). Table 5.4 also reveals that the settlement of this population was highly concentrated; by 1991, Indians formed the majority ethnic group in three wards and over one-third of residents in two others.

While the steady increase of the town's immigrant population mirrors demographic developments in Tower Hamlets, there are important differences between these two boroughs. Unlike Tower Hamlets, Ealing cannot, on the whole, be described as a deprived area and is home to a population that is socioeconomically diverse. The central wards have been solidly middle class, but there are also pockets of poverty, especially in Southall in the southwest as well as in the eastern part of the borough.[35] Tower Hamlets and Ealing experienced the same macroeconomic swings, but as a result of its more diversified workforce – both native and immigrant – the recession did not hit Ealing as

---

[35] Even back in 1976, only 10 percent of the total economically active population in the borough's central wards consisted of unskilled manual laborers. In the western (comprising Southall) and eastern parts of the borough, these shares rose to 23 percent and 17 percent, respectively (Messina 1989, 89).

TABLE 5.5. *Local Election Results for Ealing, 1964–2002*

Year	% Share of Vote			Wards Won			Council Control
	CON	LAB	LD	CON	LAB	LD	
1964	42.8	47.0	7.1	9	11	0	LAB
1968	62.2	27.0	4.0	17	2	0	CON
1971	41.1	50.5	2.0	7	13	0	LAB
1974	41.6	45.4	9.3	8	12	0	LAB
1978	48.8	42.5	4.9	14	9	0	CON
1982	39.9	34.3	21.1	13	10	1	CON
1986	34.7	46.2	16.9	6	17	1	LAB
1990	43.2	42.6	9.7	12	12	0	CON
1994	38.1	47.7	10.5	6	18	1	LAB
1998	30.0	48.1	13.8	4	20	1	LAB
2002	29.5	44.8	16.3	6	16	1	LAB

Notes: The Liberal Democrats were founded in 1988; until then, the Liberal Party had formed an alliance with the Social Democratic Party. Results prior to 1988 refer to the performance of this alliance or when the Liberals ran on their own. Labour's massive losses in 1968 were part of a regionwide swing against the unpopular Labour government, led by Wilson. CON = Conservatives; LD = Liberal Democrats; LAB = Labour Party.
Source: Rallings and Thrasher (2003, 9).

hard. Ealing's heterogeneous class structure has also had important political consequences. For most of its existence, Ealing's city council has continuously changed hands between the two main parties. In this politically competitive setting, securing the Indian vote soon became crucial.

Ealing's Political Landscape

Electoral History

At the time of Indian arrival in Ealing in the 1950s, the main area of settlement, Southall, was an independent municipality that was later merged with Ealing and Acton to form the London borough of Ealing in 1965. This amalgamation brought together a socioeconomically stratified population whose political allegiances were split. While the district's working-class electorate could be counted on to turn out for the Labour Party, Ealing's middle class tended to support the Tories. Between 1966 and 1992, the four (by 1974, three) parliamentary constituencies covering Ealing were never controlled by the same party.[36] Unlike in Tower Hamlets, where an entrenched Labour machine did not confront serious opposition until the late 1970s, control over Ealing's city hall has been contested since the borough's inception. Within thirty years, the council switched partisan control five times (see Table 5.5). Local politicians thus keenly eyed the growing size of the Indian electorate. But in light of

[36] In 1997, all three constituencies were captured by Labour (Kimber and Outlaw 2004).

the tight electoral margins confronting them, local party strategists were also acutely aware of the potential damage that a white electoral backlash could produce. Local councilors thus walked a political tightrope, trying to covertly appeal to the town's dominant ethnic minority while holding on to their white supporters. The increasing organizational prowess and impressive turnout rates of the Indian-origin electorate made this electorate too costly to ignore.

Electoral Competition and Indian Votes

The history of chain migration produced tight social networks that easily lent themselves to political mobilization. Within this migrant community,

[M]utual reliance and help were both essential and natural – essential because 45 per cent of the men were unable to speak any English, and natural because the men all came from a fairly small area, often from the same village, and knew each other; many were blood relations. Thus an informal network of mutual aid was established. The 20 per cent who spoke fluent English became the interpreters and leaders ... The educated or experienced people helped in interpreting or filling in forms, the influential in arranging employment or education for the newcomers ... Out of these informal groupings of friends and relatives the first community organisations emerged. The Indian Workers' Association [IWA] was formed in Southall on 3 March, 1957, by some of the younger, more radical elements of the Punjabi community. (CARF 1981, 9–10)

The IWA soon became an influential political broker that represented the Sikh community, reliably delivering the votes of its members to the candidates it had endorsed.

While the IWA usually endorsed the Labour Party and encouraged its constituents to cast their ballots for the party's councilors and MPs, it also advised them to refrain from doing so if candidates were seen to be hostile to immigrant interests (John 1969, 160). Additionally, the once unassailable position of the IWA as the sole representative of the Indian community waned as the number of organizations representing immigrant interests rose. The link between Labour and Southall's immigrants, while still tight, thus weakened in the late 1960s, when some community representatives, and prospective councilors, allied with the Conservatives, who had also developed an interest in the borough's new electorate. In the 1968 local election, a Conservative Indian candidate only fell eight votes short of winning a seat in the Northcote ward while his Labour opponent turned out to become Ealing's first Sikh councilor.[37] His impressive get-out-the-vote efforts relied on his access to the Sikh community's dense social networks; as the victor proudly noted, "On the eve of the election,

---

[37] Note that the vote shares listed in Table 5.6 always refer to a party's top vote getter. The eight-vote difference is based on the Labour candidate who came in third, and the Conservative candidate who came in fifth. Unless otherwise noted, all ward-level election data are based on election results supplied to me by the London borough of Ealing. I thank Paul Willman for providing me with these data.

TABLE 5.6. *Electoral Results in Ealing Wards with the Highest Indian Concentration, 1968–1998*

Election Year	% of Vote				South Asian Candidate			No. of South Asian Councilors	% of Vote: Additional South Asian Candidates
	LAB	CON	LD	SRA/NDP/NF	LAB	CON	LD		
Northcote									
1968	30.6	26.1	—	29.4	yes	yes	—	1	9.5
1971	43.8	8.3	5.0	17.5	yes	yes	yes	1	25.4
1974	34.7	8.6	—	—	yes	yes	—	1	56.7
1978	43.0	7.5	—	—	yes	yes	—	2	48.3
1982	42.4	4.3	14.5	—	yes	yes	yes	1	38.8
1986	83.7	8.6	7.7	—	yes	yes	yes	2	—
1990	91.7	8.3	—	—	yes	yes	—	3	—
1994	84.9	15.1	—	—	yes	yes	—	3	—
1998	62.2	8.1	4.9	—	yes	no	no	3	24.8
Glebe									—
1968	20.0	36.5	—	38.6	no	no	—	0	—
1971	45.7	19.6	—	18.5	no	no	—	0	13.9
1974	55.6	20.8	14.7	—	no	yes	yes	0	9.0
1978	69.0	19.1	11.9	—	yes	yes	yes	2	—
1982	55.2	15.7	13.6	—	yes	yes	yes	2	13.3
1986	66.0	8.0	10.8	—	yes	yes	yes	2	15.3
1990	85.6	14.4	—	—	yes	yes	—	3	—
1994	72.6	17.1	—	—	yes	yes	—	3	—
1998	69.8	8.3	4.8	—	yes	no	no	3	10.7
Mount Pleasant									
1978	63.4	36.6	—	—	no	yes	—	0	—
1982	41.1	13.9	16.2	—	yes	yes	yes	1	28.7
1986	65.8	12.8	21.3	—	yes	yes	yes	2	—
1990	71.6	21.3	7.2	—	yes	yes	yes	2	—
1994	77.7	22.3	—	—	yes	yes	—	2	—
1998	65.1	13.7	7.7	—	yes	yes	no	3	13.5
Waxlow									
1968	34.7	53.5	5.4	6.4	no	no	no	0	—
1971	64.7	35.3	—	—	no	no	—	0	—
1974	56.1	32.9	11.0	—	no	no	no	0	—
1978	55.8	44.2	—	—	no	yes	—	0	—
1982	41.3	30.0	19.5	—	yes	yes	yes	1	9.2
1986	55.9	31.8	12.3	—	yes	yes	no	1	—
1990	54.5	45.5	—	—	yes	no	—	1	—
1994	62.7	37.3		—	yes	no	—	2	—
1998	58.2	27.5	14.2	—	yes	no	no	2	—
Dormers Wells									
1968	18.7	65.0	8.4	7.9	no	no	no	0	—
1971	55.4	44.6	—	—	no	no	—	0	—
1974	56.2	43.8	—	—	no	no	—	0	—
1978	54.8	45.2	—	—	no	no	—	0	—
1982	42.3	36.0	21.7	—	yes	no	yes	2	—
1986	56.8	26.1	10.7	—	yes	yes	yes	2	9.0
1990	52.8	30.0	7.2	—	yes	yes	no	2	—
1994	57.7	32.8	9.5	—	yes	yes	yes	1	—
1998	59.5	17.9	12.3	—	yes	no	no	2	—

Notes: All wards return three councilors. Additional South Asian candidates are candidates that did not run for Labour, the Conservatives, or the Liberal Party/Liberal Democrats Alliance. The 2002 elections were held under new ward boundaries. Mount Pleasant first held elections in 1978. CON = Conservatives; LD = Liberal Democrats; LAB = Labour Party; SRA/NDP/NF =Southall Residents' Association/National Democratic Party/National Front.

Source: Data supplied by Ealing Borough Council and Rallings et al. (2006); author's calculations.

120 people with 50 cars volunteered to work for me. On the evening of election day this soared to 200 with 100 cars. It was like a military operation."[38]

The mobilizational capacity of Ealing's Indian electorate was, however, not always a boon for the local Labour Party. In 1978, for example, an Indian candidate protested the council's neglect of Southall and ran as an Independent, promising to "promote healthier and more attractive living conditions."[39] This platform gained him the highest vote share in the Northcote ward and a seat on the city council in an election that Labour lost to the Tories (see Table 5.6). In short, by the 1970s, there had been "a noticeable shift in local politics . . . towards a more plural form of party competition on race issues" (Saggar 1991, 54) and the mobilization of the Indian vote for the Labour Party could no longer be taken for granted.

By the 1980s, the Indian electorate had made sure that, to be successful, any reelection strategy on the part of the Labour Party had to take Indian interests into account. Ealing's Indian-origin voters turned out at almost twice the rate as their white counterparts (Anwar 1986, 58) and they increasingly filled more than just one token seat in the borough's multimember wards. Starting in the 1982 election, when Labour was hoping to win back control of the council, the party reluctantly opened its ranks and leadership positions to members of Ealing's Indian minority population and the number of Indian councilors rose as a result (see Table 5.6). While Labour suffered a narrow loss in the 1982 contest, it had nevertheless improved its performance compared to its 1978 result and thus continued to recruit the Indian vote, even beyond Southall's wards.

Commitments for increased ethnic representation were also made at the parliamentary constituency level. In December 1982, party archives show that the Ealing North Labour Party (which does not cover Southall wards) submitted a resolution promoting "racial equality" within the Labour Party to "ensure that a multi-racial Parliamentary Labour Party forms the next government" (Labour Party (Great Britain), 1990).

At the local level, in the run-up to the 1986 election, prospective Indian councilors carried out relentless recruitment drives to boost the Party's ward membership with fellow Indians who in turn voted to field co-ethnics in ward elections. In time for the 1986 election, when Labour regained control of the council, local branch membership had increased from 32 to 436 in Northcote and from 105 to 865 in Glebe, and it had risen to 552 in Mount Pleasant.[40]

Indian candidacies outside of Southall also proliferated over the years; overall, the wards where Indian-origin candidates contested elections increased from three in 1974 to six in 1978 to eight in 1982 and to eleven in 1986.

---

[38] *The Times*, "Ealing's First Sikh Councilor," May 14, 1968.

[39] *The Times*, "Campaigner Gets the Street Swept," January 21, 1978.

[40] *The Guardian*, "Asian Divisions May Conquer Veteran Labour MP," February 11, 1985. These membership drives were also meant to threaten Southall's long-standing (white) Labour MP, Sydney Bidwell, whose position was weakened as a result.

Finally, looking only at the skin color of representatives fails to acknowledge that white councilors had also espoused minority-friendly positions. One long-time Southall white councilor recalled that he "got a lot of abuse in the early years from some whites. They called me "Indian-lover", traitor, and all sorts... [But South Asian electors] have never seen me as a white Englishman.... I've campaigned with them... I've got 11,000 friends around here, since I've got well-known and become part of the new community here, they look upon me as a Punjabi, just like them."[41]

In sum, by the 1980s the position of Ealing's Indian-origin electorate within and outside the Labour Party ensured that Indian concerns would be heard.

Indian Demands

The concerns that were at the heart of Indian political mobilization in Southall were consistently of a material nature and most often involved housing and education.[42] To be sure, the settlement of a community with cultural and religious traditions that were distinct from the indigenous white population also meant that specifically ethnic goods, such as the building of Gurdwaras (Sikh temples) or, later on, the opening of a Sikh school, were in high demand. But cultural and religious groups by and large stayed outside of party politics. Intervention by Sikh religious groups "into local politics still remained the exception rather than the rule" and tended to concentrate on such mundane issues as a road-widening proposal outside Gurdwara premises (Saggar, 1991, 54–55).

In the first decades of settlement, when the IWA was the Indian minority's main voice, the organization consistently campaigned on mainstream issues. The decision to emphasize material concerns that were shared by white voters had not been reached without some infighting. Similar to developments in Tower Hamlets, some immigrants would have favored striking out on their own and addressing issues that were unique to the immigrant and minority experience (John 1969, 150–58). The IWA leadership nonetheless ultimately concluded that espousing an ethnically based course of action would prove self-defeating.[43] It assuaged its militant critics by arguing that it would be counterproductive to have "their militancy... directed towards friendly whites" (John

---

[41] Cited in Baumann (1996, 142). Baumann draws on fieldwork conducted by Hawkes (1990).

[42] For reasons of space, the following will focus on housing issues, which have engendered the fiercest backlash among Ealing's white population. Initial resentment against "overcrowding" in schools that was due to the rapid increase of Indian-origin schoolchildren in Southall was defused when Ealing council followed central government guidelines and bussed these children to schools throughout the borough. This dispersal scheme was first supported by the Indian community as an integrationist measure, but it had become very unpopular by the 1970s. Years of lobbying ended the policy in the early 1980s. See Saggar (1991, 81–111) for a detailed discussion.

[43] John (1969, 159) provides an overview of the IWA in the 1960s when the leaderships of the Indian (specifically the Punjabi) communities in Britain led intense discussions about two

1969, 164) and convinced its rank and file that operating within the institutional framework of mainstream politics would be the optimal strategy to advance its members' interests. Yet, focusing on the delivery of material goods would also soon risk antagonizing Ealing's white voters, who feared threats to their economic position.

The IWA's pronouncements in the local newspaper illustrate the organization's position. In 1964, the IWA president announced that the group was "recommending the Labour party because it is the party of the working class, and because it stands for the Commonwealth rather than the Common Market, and because of its general policies, particularly in housing" (cited in Woolcott 1965, 37). Throughout the 1970s and 1980s, housing and education continued to feature heavily in local political debates (CARF 1981; Saggar 1991, 81–111).

To summarize, Ealing's Indian-origin population was very adept at getting out the community vote. In the context of competitive elections, this electoral leverage compelled the political establishment to take Indian votes and demands seriously. Immigrant voters' emphasis on economic goods furthermore meant that responding to this new constituency would have material consequences that could impinge on the economic interests of long-settled white residents. As we will see next, immigrant–native conflict thus ensued, but it did not persist. The small share of state-provided goods, the relative affluence of Ealing's residents, and the growing economic security of the borough's Indian population diffused pressures on economic goods and caused intergroup conflict to fade.

From Conflict to Coexistence

In the early years of immigrant settlement there was an abundance of jobs for both immigrants and English natives in Southall, but the town's housing market had been characterized by a chronic shortage since the end of the war. Problems of overcrowding had been so acute in the town that, even prior to the arrival of immigrants, local officials had to devise an official policy to resettle residents and industries into neighboring areas (Kirwan 1965, 49). These measures eased housing pressures to some extent but were not conceived with the impending immigration wave in mind. Immigrant families tended to buy old and run-down properties that they were only able to afford by renting out rooms to fellow migrants, leading to crowded homes: "Southall [was] the only place in London which parallel[ed] Spitalfields' levels of overcrowding" (Forman 1989, 120).

Pressures on council housing were also intense. By the mid-1960s, 2,000 families were on the waiting list. Unprepared for the large influx of new residents – between 1959 and 1964 the houses occupied by Indian-headed households nearly quadrupled – the city council and local MPs soon came under

questions: "(1) who are the enemies of the immigrants? (2) what role should the IWAs play in the process of acceptance?"

increasingly sharp attacks for accommodating Indian immigrants at the expense of the town's long-settled white residents and were pressured to serve eviction notices for those living in overcrowded conditions. Many recent homebuyers feared that the value of their properties would decline along with the area's increasing immigrant concentration (Woolcott 1965, 33–34).

These native fears and accusations were most vocally expressed by the Southall Residents' Association (SRA). Founded in 1963, the express purpose of the SRA was to keep immigrants from buying or renting properties in Southall.[44] The organization, whose members "were almost wholly lower-middle class and respectable working class, tasting postwar prosperity for the first time and now finding it threatened" (Walker 1977, 52), started playing a crucial role in local politics and provided an institutional channel for the expression of anti-immigrant sentiment. Unable to stop immigrants from buying private properties, the organization turned to the Labour Council and presented it with a petition, signed by "625 white residents urging them to buy vacant properties in Dormers Wells Ward to prevent the silent invasion of immigrants" (Hill and Issacharoff 1971, 40). By putting pressure on the local council to purchase private housing, the SRA thus apparently recognized one of the claims made in this book: Elected officials would be far more cautious in allocating scarce goods – in this case housing – to immigrants than market actors would be, especially if politicians anticipated that such allocations would invite an electoral backlash.

In addition to urging the council to buy up housing, the SRA endorsed the British National Party, which most likely contributed to the BNP's success in local and general elections. In the 1963 local contest, the BNP ran in the two wards with the highest concentration of immigrants and indeed managed to push the Tories into third place, taking an average of 28 percent of the vote (Saggar 1991, 75). In the 1964 general election, the BNP secured 9.1 percent of the vote, "the highest percentage yet won by a blatantly racialist candidate in a British parliamentary election" (Walker 1977, 53).

Galvanized by their electoral successes, the xenophobic lobby continued to press the local council for anti-immigrant measures. Thanks to the relentless agitation by the SRA, in 1965 Conservative councilors proposed an amendment effectively barring immigrants from applying for council housing by stipulating a fifteen-year residency requirement for immigrants only, while allowing natives to put their names on the housing list after five years of residency in the borough (Saggar 1991, 75). This proposal put the Labour Party in a difficult position. In the most recent election, Labour had narrowly defeated the Conservatives, winning eleven against the Tories' nine wards. Accepting the divisive housing proposal would infuriate the immigrant electorate that

---

[44] Some of the founding members had hoped that the SRA would cooperate with the IWA to help solve local problems and in fact work for the integration of Indian immigrants. These members resigned when it became clear that the organization was actively discriminating against Indian migrants (Walker 1977, 52).

had helped deliver electoral victory and that had made its interest in housing clear, as the aforementioned statement by the IWA illustrates. Rejecting the initiative would, however, alienate its white working-class support base. Labour had already felt increasingly vulnerable as a result of its alliance with Southall's Indian electorate, which their opponents never tired of pointing out. One Conservative councilor made this remark at a party meeting in 1964:

We have always felt that the Labour Council in Southall has been too easy with the Indians on the question of overcrowding. Anyone who has watched the contortions of the Labour Party in Southall as they have angled, twisted and turned in order to secure both the support of the Indians and at the same time keep the support of their white supporters must have a nasty taste in their mouths. (cited in Hill and Issacharoff 1971, 218)

In the end, the vote on council housing allocations split the Labour Party. The governing Labour council rejected the discriminatory amendment but had to expel six Labour rebels who did not vote along party lines on this controversial issue.[45] In a development that would transpire twenty years later in Tower Hamlets, the Labour Party had decided to allocate housing based on need, rather than ethnicity – a move that must be seen in light of the electoral muscle of the Indian electorate in a highly competitive electoral setting. The decision had political repercussions. In the 1968 local elections, the nascent NF, which only fielded fourteen candidates throughout Greater London, put up seven contenders in Ealing, while two of the ousted Labour councilors ran and won on the SRA ticket in the Northcote and Glebe wards (Hill and Issacharoff 1971, 39–42; Walker 1977, 51–58; Husbands 1983, 9). As mentioned earlier, 1968 also marked the first election in which a Sikh immigrant had gained a seat in one of these two wards (Northcote); it was "almost as profitable to bid for the anti-immigrant vote in the ward as to bid for the immigrant vote" (Hill and Issacharoff 1971, 243).

As the prominence of anti-immigrant parties rose, so did the escalation of racist attacks directed against the newcomers. Community leaders had alerted the police as early as 1966 of an alarming rate of attacks committed by right-wing extremist groups (CARF 1981, 35). In late 1969 and in the run-up to the 1970 general election, Southall "saw an epidemic of racial violence – lightheartedly referred to as 'Paki-bashing' – further encouraged by literature put out by the NF, the SRA and the RPS [Racial Preservation Society]," which was an offshoot of the SRA (CARF 1981, 41–42).

But the 1970s and 1980s saw a host of contradictory developments. Homegrown racism seemed to falter, despite continued outside interventions by racist parties and groups that kept the issues of race and immigration in the headlines. In the 1970 general election the NF received a disappointing 4.35 percent of the vote in Southall (Kimber and Outlaw 2004), less than half of the votes secured by the BNP six years earlier, and it did not even field candidates in

---

[45] *The Times*, "Labour Group Expels Six Councillors," July 3, 1965.

the general elections of 1974, a time when its support rose in other parts of London, in particular in the East End (Husbands 1983, 10). Moreover, the two SRA councilors did not retain their seats in 1971 and, unlike in Tower Hamlets and in other ethnically diverse British towns at the time, in Ealing, far-right parties did not even put up any candidates in local elections in 1974, 1978, and beyond.

Data on the spread of racist violence in Ealing throughout the 1970s are unfortunately not available, and existing accounts do not paint a clear picture. According to the same source, racist attacks only continued sporadically in the peripheral, mostly white, areas of the borough throughout the 1970s, rose again in the late 1970s, but were reported to have declined according to the police (CARF 1981, 43, 62). Even when an Indian youth was killed in front of an IWA-owned cinema in Southall in 1976 – an event that clearly sent shockwaves throughout the community – reports do not suggest that this killing further polarized intergroup relations, as is often the case after such ethnically motivated murders.[46] Some even suggested that the killing, and the demonstrations that ensued, "brought the white and coloured population closer together."[47] The attack did have political consequences, spawning the Southall Youth Movement. Spurred into action by racist attacks and the police's apparent failure to prevent them, this movement soon became less preoccupied with fighting racist violence and turned to concerns such as youth unemployment and social work (Peggie 1979).

Outsiders nevertheless tried to foment intergroup tensions. The major racist confrontations that Southall came to be known for were instigated by racist groups that did not enjoy much popular support within the borough. In the spring of 1979, the NF petitioned the Conservative council to permit a party meeting in the parliamentary constituency of Southall. After initially turning down the proposal, the council allowed the gathering to go forward on the grounds of free speech. A wide cross-section of Ealing's population, including the borough's "most prominent citizens ... [as well as] diverse political, religious, and social groups" (Messina 1989, 83) organized a 5,000-strong protest march the day before the NF rally (in Tower Hamlets such interethnic events were marked by their absence). The day of the meeting, however, a peaceful sit-down strike escalated into a violent confrontation between Southall's ethnic minority population and white members of the Anti-Nazi League on the one hand, and the NF and the police on the other. Hundreds of demonstrators were arrested and injured and a white Anti-Nazi League protestor received a fatal head blow by the police (Messina 1989, 83).

In 1981, similar events transpired when a group of white skinheads were bussed into Southall from East London to attend a rock concert in a pub in the heart of Southall. A heavy police presence was ordered to prevent riotous outbreaks and members of Southall's Indian-origin youth demonstrated against the

---

[46] On this point, see Fearon and Laitin's (2000) discussion of the literature.

[47] *The Times*, "Death of Southall Asian 'Brought People Together'," July 20, 1976.

invasion of hostile whites: "At the height of the riot, some 500 Asian youths and about 300 white skinheads... were throwing bricks, Molotov cocktails and masonry at each other" and the pub in which the rock band was scheduled to perform was set on fire.[48] Asians were also critical of the police, who many felt were "present purely to protect those [skinheads] marching and are therefore in agreement with their political beliefs" (Scarman 1982, 31). While one Indian-origin resident told me that the arson was planned by racist outsiders in a move to polarize the population,[49] members of the rock band proclaimed that they had involuntarily become the focal point for right-wing agitators who infiltrated their audiences and used their concerts to stoke racist violence.[50]

It is impossible to verify at this point where the truth lies. What is established, though, is that the 1981 disturbances were the last major confrontation between racist groups and the borough's ethnic minority population to date and that racist groups did not represent neighbors, but outsiders, apparently trying – without success – to poison intergroup relations. Indeed, days after the riot had occurred, Southall was portrayed as "one of the most encouraging examples of racial integration in Britain. It has a heavy concentration of Asian immigrants and their British-born children. But Friday night's fighting was watched by many of the older generation, white and brown, and they remained on friendly terms throughout a long ordeal... routine day-by-day contact between ethnic groups has been amicable."[51]

Newspaper coverage further distinguished between the antistate confrontations that had shaken up Brixton (South London) from events in Ealing where "poverty and petty crime is not the issue.... White youngsters from outside, egged on by fascist groups, have vented their own aggressions on Southall, often travelling there to do so."[52]

While racist violence in Tower Hamlets proliferated throughout the 1980s and the BNP gained shocking popularity in the 1990s, interethnic tensions

---

[48] *The Observer*, "Police in Riot Mix-up," July 5, 1981.

[49] Interview with an Indian-origin Ealing councilor who was present during the demonstration, Ealing, England, March 2005. The interviewee gave this explanation: "We still believe that Hambrough pub was burned down by the outsiders [but the] Asian youth was accused [for it].... How can you tell me that there's 200 people sitting in the hall; they very peacefully left the building, walked away from the burning building, and nobody was injured.... There were individuals who very proudly claim, that 'look at the Asian youth who could not tolerate all that and will not accept it, look ... the Asian youth are quite willing to go to that extent' – that was one view. My view is, and at that time was, that no, it was an inside job, they burned the pub down themselves." When asked to clarify, the councilor said he thought the National Front had been behind the fire.

[50] The band bemoaned the fact that the NF would send members to its gigs and that its audience was constantly targeted by political extremist groups of the right as well as of the left: "We try to stop them distributing NF literature. But then you've got to stop the SWP [Socialist Workers' Party] from distributing their stuff. And then you're called a Nazi. You can't win." *The Guardian*, "We Weren't Looking for Trouble...," July 10, 1981.

[51] *The Observer*, "Portrait of an Urban Village," July 5, 1981.

[52] *The Guardian*, "The Fight-back Begins," July 6, 1981.

have steadily declined over the same time period in Ealing. A social anthropologist who had studied Southall for several years in the mid- to late 1980s indeed observed that "one cannot say that 'the Southall riots' have left a deep imprint in most Southallians' collective consciousness. While outsiders may still associate 'Southall' with 'riots', local people rarely mentioned them without prompting... they seemed to be... battles of a distant past, overtaken by local concerns" (Baumann 1996, 59). The absence of major intergroup confrontations or of the severe manifestations of more individualized forms of racist crime most likely contributed to the riot's negligible place in the locals' collective memory. In stark contrast to Tower Hamlets, major newspapers made no mention of large- or small-scale instances of racist violence over the course of the 1980s.[53] Following a series of riots involving youths of South Asian origin in three northern towns in 2001, the Home Office sent a review team to Ealing to learn from the town's successful experience with diversity (Home Office 2001). A local report, commissioned by a Sikh organization, concurred: "Southall is a very good example of an area where different distinct cultural communities co-exist... in harmony" (Sikh Human Rights Group 2002, 6). How is it that initially serious immigrant–native conflict slowly subsided and became replaced by such "harmony"? Moreover, why was Ealing able to reverse course, while nearby Tower Hamlets spiraled deeper into conflict during the same time period?

Explaining Interethnic Peace

The source of the greatest interethnic acrimony in Tower Hamlets and Ealing has been the struggle over scarce economic resources, and housing in particular. This fight started in the early years of immigrant settlement in both boroughs, but it continued in Tower Hamlets throughout the 1980s and 1990s. In Ealing, by comparison, the competition over housing had less staying power and was only briefly pursued with ferocity and racist vitriol. This rather short-lived agitation, I maintain, did not last for two economically focused reasons. First, racist campaigning around housing did not prove effective in Ealing because the private market, rather than the local council, has controlled most of the housing stock in the borough. As I have argued, market actors will be much less sensitive than state actors to anti-immigrant voting and violence, especially if they stand to gain from increased prices. In the context of competition over market goods, xenophobia is thus not likely to be a strategy that pays off. Second, Ealing's population is more socioeconomically diverse than that of London's East End, diffusing pressures on economic goods in general and on housing in particular. Although the political power of South Asian immigrants rose in both Tower Hamlets and Ealing, varying pressures on state-provided economic goods explain varying patterns of immigrant–native conflict across the two boroughs.

---

[53] I searched *The Guardian, The Observer,* and *The Times* for such instances, using only the general search criteria of "Ealing" or "Southall" (pertaining to the entire document text). After the events of 1981, no article mentioned such confrontations.

Table 5.7 presents the size of the public housing stock in Tower Hamlets and Ealing as a share of the boroughs' total housing supply (left-most column). The differences are quite striking and have not narrowed much over the years, despite privatization of council housing. With less than 16 percent of housing in the hands of Ealing's local council, local politicians have not been an adequate target for residents who tried to prevent immigrants from taking up scarce housing. Moreover, the wards with the highest concentration of immigrants were largely devoid of council housing. Notably, the Southall Residents' Association attempted to bring more private housing under local authority control – presumably because it had much less leverage with real estate brokers than it did with elected officials. The local council rejected the petition and the organization tried to pressure local real estate agents into banning sales of properties to Indians (Hill and Issacharoff 1971, 40–41). In light of the rapid rise of the Indian population in Southall, however, these exclusionist measures apparently did not bear much fruit. Indeed, the large influx of new homebuyers into the Southall housing market was a boon for property agents, as the price for housing, most of which was reported to be run down and in need of serious repair, quadrupled in the span of only a few years.[54]

The scarcity of housing has in fact prompted many residents, white and Indian, to leave Southall wards during the 1980s (Baumann 1996, 43). Note that it is unlikely that the departure of whites is responsible for a decline in Ealing's interethnic tensions, for whites also left Tower Hamlets during this decade. Even though Tower Hamlets' overall population increased between 1981 and 1991, this rise is due to the fast expansion of its Bangladeshi-origin residents, which exceeded the drop in its white residents. Several Tower Hamlets wards actually saw their populations decline (St. Mary's, Blackwall, Limehouse, St. James, and Park) even as the absolute number of Bangladeshis rose.[55] In contrast to developments in Tower Hamlets, Indians in Ealing settled largely into private homes, following both their preference for homeownership[56] and the structure of the local housing market.

---

[54] In the early 1970s, "the price of a modest family house soared from £3,000–£5,000 to as much as £15,000 over about a period of about three years" (CARF 1981, 27).

[55] Calculations are based on figures from Table 5.1. Unfortunately these calculations are estimates only, because the 1981 figures (based on country of birth) and the 1991 figures (based on ethnicity) are not directly comparable. But even when we multiply the population born in Bangladesh in 1981 by 1.5, for a rough adjustment of Bangladeshi-origin children who were born in the United Kingdom, the absolute increase in the Bangladeshi population exceeds the absolute increase in the total population in ten out of nineteen wards. Moreover, these calculations do not take into account the growth of other minority populations, suggesting a further decrease of the white population during a time when intergroup tensions escalated.

[56] Many studies emphasize the predilection for homeownership among immigrants, especially among Asian settlers. By the late 1970s, however, demographers detected a shift toward council tenancy, for council homes were often in better condition than the private homes that immigrant families could afford to buy (cf. Robinson 1981, 154–155, 161–162). While this transition marked assimilation to British practices, some – rightly – feared that "Under such circumstances, increased competition for scarce resources by an active Asian population could well herald the escalation of latent hostility" (Robinson 1981, 155).

TABLE 5.7. Council Housing Allocations: Tower Hamlets and Ealing (%)

Year and Location	Households in Council Housing (1)	Share of Council Housing Occupied by Bangladeshis/Indians (2)	Bangladeshis/Indians Living in Council Housing (3)	Overall Share of Bangladeshi/Indian Households (4)	Representation (Under or Over) of Bangladeshis/Indians in Council Housing (2 – 4)
1981 Tower Hamlets	82.0	—	—	—	—
1981 Ealing	21.6	—	—	—	—
1991 Tower Hamlets	58.3	13.5	76.6	10.3	3.2
1991 Ealing	15.8	6.5	9.6	10.7	–4.2

Notes: The percentage of households with Bangladeshi or Indian residents is substantially lower than the shares of these groups' residents in Tower Hamlets and Ealing. This is due to larger family sizes and fewer single-person households among the boroughs' ethnic minority populations. In the country as a whole, the representation of nonwhites in council housing is relatively proportionate to their household shares, with a 1991 representation score of 0.47. In authorities where the share of nonwhites exceeds the national average, this score falls to 0.30.

Source: Entries are derived from "Table 15 Private Households with Residents" for 1981 data and "Table L49 Ethnic Group: Housing" for 1991 data (available at www.nomisweb.co.uk). The 1981 census did not break down housing statistics based on ethnicity.

As a result of these circumstances, when the political power of the Indian minority expanded in the 1980s, the allocation of council housing was not nearly as politicized as it had been in Tower Hamlets and an Indian councilor even occupied the chair of the Housing Department (Candappa and Joly 1994, 109). In Tower Hamlets, by contrast, Bangladeshis had no choice but to seek accommodation in council housing, which, even in 1991, after a decade of Thatcher's "right-to-buy" scheme, supplied almost 60 percent of the local housing stock. As this analysis has demonstrated, Bangladeshis' rising political clout in the 1980s compelled the Labour Party to disburse housing in ways that would benefit the borough's more disadvantaged Bangladeshi residents. By 1991, Bangladeshis did occupy a disproportionate share of local authority housing, while Indians in Ealing were underrepresented in the public housing sector, not only in absolute terms but also when placed in the context of nationwide trends (see Table 5.7, right-most column and notes section; note that these figures do not adjust for housing need).

An additional advantage concerns Ealing's socioeconomically diverse population. Unlike its poorer neighbor to the east, much of the borough's white population has been employed in professional occupations. Residents are relatively affluent as a result, affecting the demand side of local economic scarcity. Moreover, while Ealing's Indian workforce is quite heterogeneous, by 1991 the majority of the economically active Indian-origin population also worked in skilled occupations (see Table 5.8), representing a significant change from the skill profiles of Indian settlers in the 1950s and 1960s mentioned previously (Marsh 1967). These figures also diverge sharply from patterns in Tower Hamlets, where 47 percent of Bangladeshis worked in jobs that required little or no skills. Between 1981 and 1991 the skill profile of Tower Hamlets' population improved (presumably as a result of the twin forces of deindustrialization and gentrification), but it still lags behind that of Ealing. The recession was therefore especially severely felt in the East London borough, where unemployment rates were almost twice as high and close to 50 percent of economically active Bangladeshis were unemployed in 1991, compared with only 14 percent of Ealing's Indian-origin labor force. By 2001, only 6 percent of British Indians in Ealing were without jobs. As already discussed, Tower Hamlets' poverty put enormous pressures on the borough's public housing stock. In Ealing, Indian residents had progressively fewer economic needs than their Bangladeshi counterparts, defusing pressures on economic goods over time, including demands for the council's limited housing supply.

In sum, the low share of state-controlled resources in Ealing reduced the effectiveness of anti-immigrant agitation, while the population's relative affluence has meant that no particular area of contestation has emerged on which such exclusionary campaigns could converge. This is not to say that the local white population has never voiced complaints over the distribution of government monies that it perceives to be benefiting ethnic minorities. Nor do I mean to suggest that local politicians have never been responsive to anti-immigrant appeals. Indeed, Messina (1989, 92–100) and others (CARF 1981

TABLE 5.8. *Skill Levels and Unemployment Rates, Tower Hamlets and Ealing, 1981–1991 (%)*

	1981		1991	
	Tower Hamlets	Ealing	Tower Hamlets	Ealing
Skill levels				
Professional and skilled occupations: entire pop. of Tower Hamlets/Ealing	20.9	44.6	44.4	60.7
Partly skilled and unskilled occupations: entire pop. of Tower Hamlets/Ealing	37.5	21.9	25.2	17.2
Professional and skilled occupations: Bangladeshis/Indian	—	—	25.9	51.7
Partly skilled and unskilled occupations: Bangladeshi/Indian	—	—	47.3	28.5
Unemployment rates				
All Residents	13.9	7.6	21.8	11.0
Bangladeshi/Indian residents	—	—	47.2	13.7

Source: 1981 skill figures: "Table 52: Social Class of Households (10% Sample)." 1991 skill figures: "Table L91 Social Class and Economic Position (10% Sample)." 1981 and 1991 figures take all economically active residents as their base. 1991 skill figures for Bangladeshis and Indians: "Table L93 SEG, Social Class and Ethnic Group (10% Sample)." These figures are based on residents, aged sixteen years and older, that are employees or self-employed. 1991 unemployment figures: "Table L09 Economic Position and Ethnic Group 16 and over." 1981 unemployment figures: "Table 5 Economic Position" (all data are available at www.nomisweb.co.uk).

28–29; Saggar 1991, 47–79) illustrate Labour's strained efforts to keep the local political discussion a color-blind one. Despite the persistent housing shortage, which caused greatest hardship among Ealing's Indian-origin residents, the Labour council refused to raise local taxes in the late 1970s, effectively arguing that the improved housing conditions that a rate increase would facilitate would not be worth the deterioration in race relations that such a tax raise, seen to benefit the Asian minority, was assumed to bring about.[57]

Nevertheless, the costs that the white population has directly attributed to immigrant needs have been rather low and diffuse in Ealing – especially when compared to Tower Hamlets – and have declined as Indians have become more prosperous. As a result, after the initial protests over housing proved

[57] Messina (1989, 98) cites Labour's former housing spokesperson: "[We] consider[ed] the impact of the rate increases on ... matters like race relations and how the citizenry as a whole ... [would] have reacted to a large rate increase confined merely to dealing with a severe problem in housing. These are matters which one would have had to consider very carefully and I think on balance we would not necessarily have served the best interests of the community in Southall by adopting an extreme view."

ineffective, local white opposition has not been concentrated or organized and did not become so when the political clout of the borough's Indian-origin residents rose throughout the 1980s. In the late 1980s, when the country had experienced years of economic hardship, Ealing was still characterized as "A classic middle-class suburb in every respect – solid and unyielding." Even neighborhoods that used to be undesirable were "now rising fast."[58] It is Ealing's political economy – its low share of contested public resources and the mixed class structure of its white and Indian population – that has prevented these various resentments from merging into a continued and effective anti-immigrant movement.

Conclusion

This chapter has demonstrated that differences in economic scarcity explain variation in immigrant–native conflict in areas where immigrant groups are politically powerful. In Tower Hamlets, persistent high demand for economic resources among whites and Bangladeshis and sustained shortages of state-provided goods coincided with minority electoral clout. I have shown that Bangladeshis successfully used their political muscle to demand scarce housing from local government and that a change in allocation patterns favoring Bangladeshis in turn provoked a white backlash. In Ealing, South Asian migrants also constituted a pivotal voting bloc early on, leading to immigrant–native conflict in a setting where housing was limited. But in contrast to Tower Hamlets, such conflict did not persist because large shares of Ealing's white and increasing shares of the borough's Indian population belonged to the middle class, exhibiting much lower levels of economic need when compared to Tower Hamlets' residents. Moreover, anti-immigrant lobbying did not prove effective in Ealing, where private actors – rather than politicians – controlled most of the housing stock.

Explaining variation in conflict patterns *within* Tower Hamlets and *over time* in Ealing, the analysis further increases our confidence that the conflict outcomes are not due to potential town-level differences not captured here. A decentralization experiment in Tower Hamlets produced housing-allocation patterns favoring Bangladeshis, but this change in the distribution of council flats only took place in neighborhoods controlled by Labour. It is precisely in these neighborhoods that racist violence escalated and that the BNP scored important victories at the polls. In Ealing, white residents were initially hostile to Indian neighbors, ruling out the notion that whites were more acceptant of Indian Sikhs and Hindus than they were of Bangladeshi Muslims. Hostility faded in Ealing because economic conditions made collective resistance against immigrants both ineffective and, from the perspective of whites, much less necessary.

---

[58] *The Observer*, "Queen of the Suburbs," November 20, 1988.

In the next chapter, we will see that the story of immigrant–native conflict in Leicester shares similarities with Ealing's trajectory. Immigrant conflict in Birmingham, however, took a different path: Politically powerless immigrant communities provoked little organized resistance on the part of natives but instead voiced their dissatisfaction with the state.

6

Two Faces of Immigrant Conflict in Two Midlands Cities

As the histories of Tower Hamlets and Ealing have demonstrated, violent intergroup strife and organized resistance against migrant newcomers are the likely outcomes when immigrant groups use their electoral clout to claim their share of scarce state resources. But what happens when immigrant groups are in no position to make politically credible demands? This chapter contrasts two cities in the British Midlands, Birmingham and Leicester, to show how variation in immigrants' local political capital – holding available economic resources relatively constant – leads to profoundly different relations between immigrants and natives on the one hand, and immigrants and the state on the other.

Both cities reacted to the large inflow of ethnically distinct postcolonial immigrants with hostility. In Birmingham, however, this hostility proved insufficient to engender support for collective resistance. Despite repeated efforts, xenophobic parties did not make significant electoral inroads, local anti-immigrant pressure groups failed to gain momentum, and riots or organized street violence between immigrants and natives did not characterize intergroup relations. The resistance and violence that did occur in Birmingham was of a different kind: Politically excluded immigrant-origin minorities found themselves in conflict with the local state and its institutions. Leicester, by contrast, responded to the large inflows of predominantly Indian immigrants – who were soon incorporated politically – with fierce and organized resentment. The city became a National Front stronghold and defenders of the newcomers' presence and physical safety engaged in antiracist campaigns as well as street battles with their racist opponents. By the 1990s, though, Leicester had managed to leave its fractious past behind and was considered a model of "best practice" in the area of intercommunal relations.

Birmingham and Leicester share a host of similarities. They are located in the British Midlands, roughly forty miles apart. For most of the twentieth century, the cities' economies relied on manufacturing. The industrial restructuring and economic downturns of the 1970s and 1980s therefore seriously affected both cities, with unemployment rates rising to the double digits. Shortages also characterized the housing market in both cities, where thousands of residents had applied for council accommodation by the time immigrants had arrived, and the city councils were engaged in comprehensive slum clearance programs to demolish dilapidated housing. Moreover, public housing represented just over one-third of the housing stock in both cities. Pressures on social services and education were also intensely felt. Because the ethnic minority populations in both Leicester and Birmingham were more likely to be unemployed than their white British counterparts, these nonwhite residents were more likely to be in need of these scarce resources. In short, up to the 1980s, economic conditions were similar in the two cities. Finally, there were also parallels in the political arena: In both Birmingham and Leicester, control of city hall was contested between the Tories and Labour until the early 1980s, when the Labour Party started its two decades of electoral domination.

The main difference is to be found in the ways in which the two cities' immigrant populations participated in electoral politics. In Birmingham, the ethnic minority electorate was marginalized, while in Leicester, immigrant-origin voters became pivotal players in city politics. Birmingham's ethnic minority population, while sizable, is composed of various ethnic groups who were not able to translate their considerable numbers into pivotal votes. Fragmentation within and across groups along regional, national, religious, and ideological lines – a circumstance that was encouraged by Birmingham's Labour leaders – helped to push aside immigrant concerns. In Leicester, by contrast, a more unified and well-organized Indian-origin electorate soon delivered important votes to a Labour Party that was eager to snatch council control from the Tories. Although this left Leicester's main immigrant group in a better position to claim scarce resources than their counterparts in Birmingham, it is this position that invited a fierce backlash against the city's newcomers. In Birmingham, then, immigrants' political exclusion and high levels of economic scarcity contributed to immigrant–state conflict, while in Leicester, which initially faced similar economic conditions, immigrants' political incorporation provoked immigrant–native conflict.

The case comparison thus holds constant economic scarcity while varying immigrant political power. The analysis then proceeds by examining how improvements in the socioeconomic position of Leicester's Indian population and an increase in the supply of previously scarce resources influenced immigrant–native conflict. In a development that shares parallels with events in Ealing, the ensuing reduction in economic scarcity in Leicester contributed to an improvement in intergroup relations.

This chapter relates events in Birmingham and Leicester in turn. For each case, as in the previous chapter, I first outline the nature of postwar immigrant settlement and the local economy. I next discuss the party political landscape and identify the position of ethnic minorities in both cities' electoral environment. I then show how the political behavior of immigrants interacted with local economic shortages to bring about contrasting conflict outcomes.

TABLE 6.1. *Concentration of the Nonwhite Population in Birmingham, 1981–2001*

Birmingham	All Residents			Indian (%)			Pakistani (%)			Black Caribbean (%)		
	1981	1991	2001	1981	1991	2001	1981	1991	2001	1981	1991	2001
TOTAL	996,363	960,970	977,088	2.98	5.3	5.7	2.5	6.9	10.6	2.3	4.7	4.9
Soho	19,759	28,096	25,634	23.9	31.3	26.8	3.5	8.9	14.0	8.9	17.0	18.1
Handsworth	23,926	24,783	25,912	12.5	20.2	18.7	5.8	16.9	25.2	10.8	17.7	15.3
Sparkbrook	17,368	25,896	28,311	7.8	7.6	5.7	17.3	30.6	40.5	4.0	10.6	7.4
Sparkhill	25,426	26,251	30,011	16.7	14.5	10.4	12.9	34.8	45.4	3.2	5.0	3.9
Small Heath	21,886	31,617	35,102	5.9	5.8	4.1	16.2	37.2	50.6	4.1	5.2	3.8
Rotton Park	11,613			11.6			6.0			7.8		
Nechells	11,744	22,846	27,390		1.1	3.2		32.1	37.2		7.3	7.7
Aston		26,817	26,972	4.7	4.8	4.2	10.7	15.2	21.0	8.5	16.6	17.6
Deritend				5.4			9.2			8.3		
Saltley				1.3			16.2			2.3		
Sandwell	28,182	27,206	27,614	11.8	33.9	36.8	1.0	3.3	6.7	6.2	12.5	13.2
All Saints'	9,332			9.6			2.3			6.4		
Washwood Heath	25,056	28,213	27,822	1.0	1.5	1.7	9.7	27.0	41.5	2.5	4.0	4.1
Newtown	12,387			2.9			2.8			7.1		
Ladywood	10,926	24,706	23,789	1.1	12.9	11.7	0.3	7.5	10.6	7.5	13.6	13.2
Duddeston	9,508			0.8			0.8			6.4		
Gravelly Hill	22,603			1.6			1.5			5.1		
Moseley	23,392	22,081	22,447	3.1	6.2	6.3	3.3	10.7	13.9	2.2	3.1	3.0
Edgbaston	21,698	20,512	23,527	3.2	6.0	8.9	1.3	3.3	5.6	3.1	6.4	6.0
Harborne	22,089	21,651	21,868	3.1	2.5	4.2	0.4	0.5	1.2	1.2	1.8	2.2
Acock's Green	24,032	26,095	26,271	1.6	2.7	4.1	1.3	2.3	5.4	1.2	2.6	3.8
Selly Oak	22,748	21,334	25,792	2.3	3.3	3.5	0.6	2.2	2.6	0.8	1.5	1.4
Hall Green	27,033	24,856	25,921	2.1	7.3	11.2	0.6	3.4	8.3	0.6	0.9	1.4
Perry Barr	22,138	21,878	23,123	0.9	3.7	7.4	0.1	0.4	2.1	1.5	5.1	7.1
Fox Hollies	22,296	23,345	24,083	1.1	5.9	7.0	0.4	3.1	8.5	1.0	2.6	3.1
Stechford	23,280			0.4			0.4			1.3		

Stockland Green	25,832	24,212	23,060	0.7	2.7	3.3	0.2	3.0	5.5	1.2	7.5	8.6
Brandwood	35,253	26,413	24,530	1.0	2.1	2.8	0.3	0.8	2.5	0.8	2.6	2.9
Erdington	35,289	24,382	23,853	0.5	1.7	2.1	0.2	1.1	2.6	1.1	2.8	4.3
Quinton	26,845	20,318	19,798	0.8	3.2	5.8	0.1	0.3	0.9	0.7	2.1	2.8
King's Norton	36,204	22,662	20,729	0.6	0.4	0.5	0.1	0.2	0.3	0.8	2.2	2.0
Kingstanding	22,841	27,659	25,702	0.5	1.3	1.7	0.1	0.2	0.9	0.8	3.0	3.7
Shard End	33,535	23,644	23,154	0.2	0.2	0.6	0.1	0.2	0.7	1.0	1.9	2.8
Longbridge	29,308	23,362	30,964	0.4	0.5	0.7	0.1	0.1	0.4	0.9	1.5	1.8
Sutton New Hall		31,040	32,363		1.0	1.7		0.2	0.5		0.6	1.1
Sutton Four Oaks		30,201	28,613		1.3	2.1		0.1	0.7		0.2	0.5
Weoley	41,875	21,750	21,623	0.5	0.5	1.1	0.1	0.2	0.4	0.8	1.5	2.0
Billesley	26,215	27,029	26,974	0.7	2.3	3.4	0.1	1.0	2.5	0.7	1.6	2.3
Northfield	32,501	24,202	23,042	0.3	0.4	0.6	0.1	0.1	0.2	0.7	1.1	1.2
Oscott	21,868	21,926	21,660	0.5	2.1	2.8	0.0	0.1	0.3	0.6	2.0	3.4
Hodge Hill		25,164	24,825		0.8	1.4		0.8	4.5		2.6	3.5
Bournville		24,277	24,412		1.2	1.8		0.5	1.3		1.8	1.9
Bartley Green		22,116	21,793		0.7	1.2		0.2	0.6		2.2	3.1
Kingsbury		19,419	16,480		0.3	1.1		0.2	0.9		2.5	2.8
Yardley	25,618	23,179	22,976	0.6	1.8	2.3	0.1	1.9	5.2	0.5	2.7	3.3
Sheldon	22,993	20,770	20,130	0.3	1.1	1.4	0.1	0.4	0.9	0.4	1.0	1.2
Sutton Vesey		29,062	28,818		1.5	2.5		0.3	0.7		0.6	1.2
Sutton Coldfield No. 3	27,325			0.6			0.1			0.2		
Sutton Coldfield No. 1	28,743			0.5			0.1			0.2		
Sutton Coldfield No. 2	30,074			0.6			0.1			0.1		

Notes: Birmingham underwent boundary changes that are reflected in these census figures. Until 1981, entries refer to country of birth. As of 1991, entries are based on ethnic origin and thus also include children born in the United Kingdom to parents of Indian, Pakistani, and Black Caribbean descent.

Source: The 1981 data are based on "Table 4 Country of Birth All Residents," 1991 figures are based on "Table S06 Ethnic Group: Residents," and 2001 data are derived from "T13 Theme Table on Ethnicity" (all data are available at www.nomisweb.co.uk).

Birmingham

With just under 1 million residents, Birmingham has long been known as Britain's "second city" and represents the country's largest local authority. Having experienced decades of postwar immigration, the city is also one of Britain's most ethnically diverse, with nearly 30 percent of its residents identifying themselves as ethnically nonwhite in 2001. Large-scale immigration from the West Indies and the Indian subcontinent dates back to the 1950s and 1960s, when Birmingham's then-thriving industries attracted large shares of economic migrants. Birmingham is home to several sizable ethnic minority communities. Until the recent numerical rise of the city's Pakistani community, roughly equal shares of residents of Indian, Pakistani, and Caribbean descent have called Birmingham home (see Table 6.1). Of Birmingham's South Asian population, about two-thirds are Muslim, 10 percent are Hindu, and 15 percent are Sikh, while the majority of black Caribbeans are of Christian faith.[1]

Part urban, part provincial, the city's population is not only ethnically diverse but also socioeconomically mixed. In a pattern that would repeat itself in many British cities and beyond, the first waves of immigrants tended to take low-paid manual jobs in the industrial sector that were left behind by an increasingly suburban middle class and deemed undesirable by those aspiring to climb up the class ladder. In another parallel development, immigrant settlement coincided with a severe, preexisting housing shortage. In the 1950s, the council's housing list was over 60,000 persons long with a wait time of five years (Senior 1957, 306), and many newcomers hoped to improve their often deplorable housing conditions by applying for state-owned accommodations. In the 1960s, immigrant enclaves that had "not yet reached the night of slumdom" but were "aptly called twilight zones" (Rex and Moore 1967, v) thus existed alongside the city's modernization and rising affluence. In the coming decades, these disparities would grow more pronounced. With the decline of manufacturing in the 1970s and the steep economic downturn of the 1980s, many immigrants and their descendents found themselves without jobs and with few skills to fall back on, living in neighborhoods that lacked employment opportunities and also provided inadequate health, social, and recreational services. As the following pages show, these economic circumstances shaped the integration of Birmingham's ethnic minorities. But unlike developments elsewhere, these material shortages did not give rise to systematic violence and sustained campaigns of opposition against immigrants. Rather, conflictual relations between the city's ethnic minority population and state institutions ensued. It is only in conjunction with Birmingham's political landscape and the position of ethnic minorities in the city's electoral geography that we can understand this divergence.

---

[1] Over 90 percent of Pakistanis and Bangladeshis are Muslim; among Indians, 47.9 percent are Sikh, 32.7 percent are Hindu, and 8.9 percent are Muslim. These figures are based on the 2001 census table "S104 Ethnic Group by Religion" (available at www.nomisweb.co.uk).

Birmingham's Political Landscape

Electoral History

For most of the twentieth century, Birmingham's electoral politics were a two-party affair, reflecting local as well as national class politics. In the postwar decades, Conservatives and Labour alternated in controlling the council in competitive elections that left no wards uncontested. Starting in the 1980s, the Liberal Party made a credible showing as the third party in town, but thanks to first-past-the-post ward elections, the party did not break the pattern of two-party competition until much later. In 1984, Birmingham departed from national electoral politics and voted in the Labour Party, which was to reign over the city for nearly two decades (see Table 6.2 and Phillips 2000, xxii–xxv). In light of the citywide competitiveness of elections, capturing the immigrant vote in the 1960s and 1970s could have well been a priority for Labour and Tories alike.

Looking at the distribution of the immigrant electorate, as well as at the electoral contests at the ward level, however, we see how different incentives dominated.

Electoral Competition and the Immigrant Vote

Before we turn to the literature on immigrant political behavior, it is instructive to first consult census figures and electoral data. Table 6.1 indicates that Indians, Pakistanis, and black Caribbeans were roughly equal in number across the city. Moreover, many ethnically diverse wards were not dominated by one ethnic group. In 1981, for example, Sparkhill was home to similar shares of residents born in India and Pakistan; Handsworth and Rotton Park contained comparable proportions of Indians and black Caribbeans; and in Aston, Pakistanis and black Caribbeans constituted approximately equal shares of the ward's population (note that 1991 figures reflect extensive boundary changes; see Figure 6.1 for a ward map). In short, while several wards clearly stand out for having a high concentration of immigrant residents, based on population shares, it appears that initially no single ethnic group acting alone would have been in a position to decisively influence ward-level politics.

Population shares of course tell only part of the story, for what matters in turning numbers into pivotal votes is the size of a given group relative to electoral margins. I therefore measured the electoral competitiveness in several wards with the highest concentration of ethnic minority residents.[2] From 1973 to 1983, the period that was marked by intense two-party competition at the city level, seats in these wards were not very hotly contested. Indeed, out of a total of fifty-six ward elections, only three produced a margin of 5 points or less; for each ward, the average margin during this time is at least 22

---

[2] I chose to include the seven wards that had the highest ethnic minority concentration in 1991. Other wards with a high number of ethnic minority residents experienced electoral dynamics similar to the ones discussed here.

TABLE 6.2. *Local Election Results in Birmingham, 1968–2003*

Election Year	% Share of Vote			Wards Won			Council Control
	CON	LAB	LD	CON	LAB	LD	
1968	64.7	26.3	8.0	36	3	0	CON
1969	60.3	30.1	7.5	32	4	2	CON
1970	47.7	45.3	5.9	21	16	2	CON
1971	57.0	37.7	4.3	9	33	1	LAB
1972	43.3	50.9	5.1	13	25	3	LAB
1973	41.8	42.9	13.0	16	23	3	LAB
1975	49.7	32.2	16.4	25	14	3	No Control
1976	53.8	34.7	9.7	25	15	2	CON
1978	49.9	41.1	5.5	20	19	3	CON
1979	48.2	43.7	5.9	20	20	2	No Control
1980	40.8	49.4	7.8	13	27	2	LAB
1982	38.1	34.6	24.9	20	17	2	CON
1983	42.2	42.3	14.4	19	20	0	CON
1984	37.7	46.3	14.7	13	24	2	LAB
1986	33.4	43.2	21.3	11	26	2	LAB
1987	42.4	34.9	21.0	22	15	2	LAB
1988	37.9	47.0	9.7	10	26	2	LAB
1990	30.7	49.0	11.6	6	28	5	LAB
1991	39.2	38.6	17.7	16	18	5	LAB
1992	49.6	35.6	13.0	21	15	3	LAB
1994	29.0	48.2	20.3	4	29	6	LAB
1995	25.7	53.4	18.2	3	31	5	LAB
1996	29.3	47.3	18.7	6	27	6	LAB
1998	31.6	43.7	18.1	7	26	5	LAB
1999	31.2	42.1	18.6	7	25	5	LAB
2000	35.5	34.7	19.6	14	16	7	LAB
2002	30.2	39.8	21.7	11	23	5	LAB
2003	28.7	34.0	29.2	11	15	12	No Control

Notes: The Liberal Democrats were founded in 1988; until then, the Liberal Party had formed an alliance with the Social Democratic Party; results prior to 1988 refer to the performance of this alliance or when the Liberals ran on their own. Labour's massive losses in 1968 and 1969 were part of a regionwide swing against the unpopular Labour government, led by Wilson. CON = Conservatives; LAB = Labour Party; LD = Liberal Democrats.
Source: Phillips (2000), Rallings and Thrasher (2003, 66), and Rallings et al. (2006).

points, if not well above that (the two highest average margins are 44.7 and 53.7 points).

These sizable margins might to a large extent be due to the votes of immigrant electors and therefore could simply signal that immigrants controlled election outcomes, rather than being powerless to put pressure on the dominant party. One indication of a group's potential electoral clout can be gleaned from the group's ability to field and support its own independent candidates. As we observed in Chapter 5, the South Asian electorate's capacity to credibly

Percentage Indian, Pakistani and Black Caribbean

☐	0 - 15.0
▨	15.1 - 30.0
▨	30.1 - 45.0
▨	45.1 - 100.0

FIGURE 6.1. Birmingham 1991 ward map (© Crown copyright. All rights reserved. License number 100049655.)

threaten to take its votes elsewhere certainly contributed to the incorporation of Bangladeshi and Indian candidates and demands in Tower Hamlets and Ealing. As we can see in Figure 6.2, developments in Birmingham were quite different.[3] Here, it is not until the mid- to late 1990s that minority candidates ran campaigns outside the established party framework that seriously upset the electoral balance (in Ealing's Northcote ward, by comparison, independent candidates scored over 50 percent of the vote in 1974). Starting in the 1980s, ward Labour Parties did begin selecting nonwhite candidates and the number of ethnic minority councilors began to rise considerably by the late 1980s – when Labour dominated city politics (Solomos and Back 1995, 218–221; see Figure 6.2).[4]

These electoral data, while certainly insightful, do not yet provide us with a complete picture of immigrants' potential political muscle, for we need to know to what extent immigrant electoral support for the ruling ward party could be taken for granted or whether such support was indeed conditional on party behavior. The relative absence of successful independent candidates up to the 1990s suggests that, until then, Birmingham's ethnic minority electorate did not constitute organized blocs whose votes could be deployed in ways to maximize pressure on ruling parties. A number of local accounts confirm this notion. Writing about Birmingham's West Indian population, observers have tended to emphasize this group's low turnout rates and lack of organization. Remarking upon the groups' class and island divisions, Rex and Moore (1967, 99) state that "More than any other group . . . the West Indians display a heterogeneity that defies simple categorization," internal divisions that might have also stunted their political engagement in this area and led to the failure to "produce leaders capable of speaking on their behalf" (158). Reporting on the 1964 Sparkbrook[5] general election campaign, Shuttleworth (1965, 73) comes to a similar conclusion, noting that West Indians' fragmentation made it difficult to find an interlocutor and to canvass the population effectively. In nearby Handsworth,[6] survey results from the mid-1970s indeed indicate

---

[3] I collected similar data on candidacies and election results as I did for the case studies of Tower Hamlets and Ealing, but since elections in Birmingham and Leicester take place more frequently than in London boroughs, election results and candidacies are too numerous to display effectively in tabular form. In Birmingham, all wards return one councilor in single-member, first-past-the post elections, except in 1973 and 1982, when the entire council was up for reelection and all wards elected three councilors. Each ward elects a total of three councilors in consecutive elections. Additional nonwhite candidates are those who did not run for Labour, the Conservatives, or the Liberals/Liberal Democrats. This number might be slightly lower than the true number because the names of black Caribbean candidates do not reveal their ethnicity. The ethnic origin of elected councilors is based on information provided by Solomos and Back (1995) and on photographs contained in newspaper articles for later years.

[4] In the Aston ward, where in the 1970s Labour had been on a losing streak, the party started running ethnic minority candidates in 1975.

[5] The Sparkbrook parliamentary constituency comprised three wards, Sparkbrook, Sparkhill, and Fox Hollies, in addition to small sections of neighboring wards (Shuttleworth 1965, 55).

[6] The survey area covers not just the Handsworth ward but also sections of the surrounding areas.

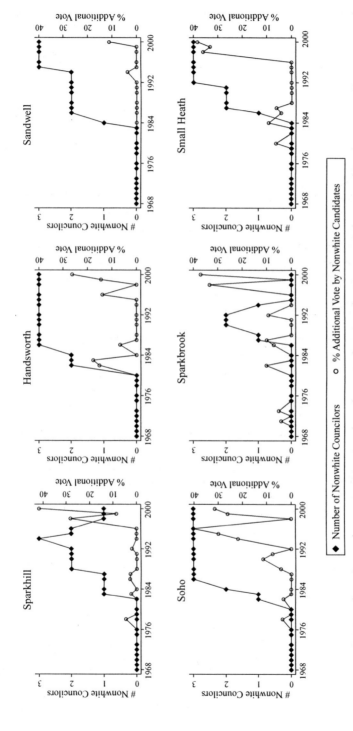

FIGURE 6.2. Nonwhite electoral representation in selected Birmingham wards. (*Sources*: Solomos and Back 1995; Phillips 2000; and Rallings et al. 2006, author's calculations. See footnote 3 for more information.)

that well over half of eligible West Indian voters failed to cast ballots in local elections (Ratcliffe 1981, 277).

Such apathy was not matched by all newcomers. In the same survey, three quarters of Asians in Handsworth reported to have voted in local elections (Ratcliffe 1981, 277). But similar to their West Indian counterparts, Birmingham's Asian electorate was internally divided within and across nationality groups. In the 1960s, Sparkbrook's various Pakistani elites had not "crystallized into a single leadership," as there were "a number of competing leaders, most of them with some kind of organizational base and able to call on regional loyalties" (Shuttleworth 1965, 71). Factionalism based around "village, political or religious" lines proved divisive enough such that "effective action at the community level [could] be, and mostly [was], blocked" (Rex and Moore 1967, 117). In the early years, the city's Indian population also did not act in unison. Early attempts to found associations that would unite and represent Birmingham's growing Indian population failed, falling prey to "schisms within the local community" (Desai 1963, 92). The Birmingham branch of the Indian Workers' Association further managed to alienate many Punjabis who did not agree with its program, which was considerably more militant and skeptical of the white political establishment than its sister organization in Southall (John 1969, 160–163).

Given that heterogeneity within these groups existed alongside the numerical fragmentation across groups even at the level of the electoral ward, it is hardly surprising that the city's ethnic minority communities were not able to coalesce around a coherent organizational or electoral strategy. Unlike in many other British towns, in Birmingham, Asian voters did not represent a pivotal voting bloc. As a result, during the first decades of immigrant settlement, "immigrant grievances" did "not register in the City Hall" (Rex and Moore 1967, 162) and few immigrants saw "fit to use the formal party-political machinery to voice grievances" (Ratcliffe 1981, 281). In his study of Birmingham city politics, Newton (1976, 214–215) portrays the situation as follows:

[R]ace relations have not been much of an issue in local elections in the city, and most council members seem to feel that they can get by quite adequately without making any special appeal to immigrant groups. For their part, the immigrant communities in the city are too internally divided to present a solid election front.... So far as it exists at all, the coloured vote seems to have had remarkably little effect on election results.... Their inability to deliver an appreciable vote may partially account for the lack of interest which council members display when it comes to making any special election appeals.

In sum, during a time when the competitiveness of city politics could have provided an opening for immigrant voters to dispense pivotal votes, organizational fragmentation and internal disunity prevented them from doing so. Lacking electoral leverage, immigrant needs were largely ignored by the political establishment.

Judging from the rise in nonwhite councilors in the 1980s (see Figure 6.2), it appears that at least sections of Birmingham's ethnic minority population were able to overcome organizational hurdles, if not their divisions across groups. It would seem, then, that minority representatives were in a better position to successfully lobby the council to deliver valuable goods to their constituents. At the same time, however, a glance at city-level election results (see Table 6.2) indicates that the ascendance of ethnic minority councilors coincided with the rise of Labour's hegemony. On the one hand, the party's more comfortable margins could have allowed it to risk a drop-off in white support that might have ensued if the party had decided to consider immigrant needs. On the other hand, such appeals might have seemed unnecessary, given the solid position of the Labour Party within ethnic minority wards, which was due to the hitherto unbroken electoral support the party enjoyed among nonwhite voters.[7] Furthermore, Labour's capture of the council had not been brought about by the ability of nonwhite candidates to rally their co-ethnics, but was rather due to inroads by white Labour candidates in wards previously held by Tories (Garbaye 2005, 110).

In light of this electoral map, ethnic minority councilors did not have the leverage that their rising numbers might suggest. Moreover, once elected, these councilors were once again fragmented along several lines, a development that Labour's Old Guard encouraged actively in its struggle for leadership. During the 1970s and 1980s, the Birmingham Labour Party was itself divided along ideological lines, with the entrenched leadership, representing the right-wing of the party, trying to curb the influence of a rising number of left-wing councilors. The right-wing side feared that the agenda of the "loony left" would spell electoral defeat and thus fiercely resisted the left-wing side's embrace of more progressive policies toward immigrants and other minorities. The recruitment of ethnic minority candidates by Labour's Old Guard was thus intended to bolster the position of the latter vis-à-vis the new generation of more leftist Labour politicians. Exchanging posts and other sources of patronage in return for selecting vetted minority candidates and voting with the old leadership, this strategy not only weakened progressive policies but also prevented a united ethnic minority caucus from emerging.[8]

Additionally, internal rivalries and disagreements among ethnic minority councilors contributed to this lack in cohesiveness. Tensions between South Asian and black Caribbean communities and their political representatives have

---

[7] Writing about Birmingham's Muslim population, Joly argues that the link between immigrants and the Labour Party was due to class position as well as to interests arising from the group's immigrant status (1995, 93). Until the late 1990s, all nonwhite councilors in Birmingham belonged to the Labour Party.

[8] For reasons of space, this section does not do justice to the nuances and complexities that Solomos and Back (1995) and Garbaye (2005) discuss in their excellent work on ethnic minority political incorporation in Birmingham. During the 1980s, there was considerable controversy at the local and national levels over the formation of a united ethnic minority caucus ("Black Sections") within the Labour Party. See Solomos and Back (1995, 85–91) for a discussion of the fate of the movement in Birmingham; see Howe (1985) for a collection of articles in favor of Black Sections.

at times been salient (but have also been overplayed[9]), and, within the South Asian category, regional and religious fissures continued to prevent collective action. On the basis of research conducted in the late 1980s and early 1990s, Joly also points to the national and regional differences that have divided Birmingham's Muslim councilors, distinctions that map onto ideological left–right cleavages and splits in opinion regarding the formation of a separate ethnic minority caucus (Joly 1995, 90). More generally, disagreements over the very role that nonwhite councilors could and should play in local politics – ranging from communal patrons, to working-class advocates, to activists who placed the incorporation of ethnic minority interests at the forefront of left-wing politics – meant that the increase in descriptive representation was not matched by substantive empowerment.[10]

Thus, from the first years of immigrant settlement throughout the 1980s, the distribution of the nonwhite vote across Birmingham's electoral map, the internal fragmentation of this electorate, and the Labour Party's skillful manipulation of ethnic minority representatives came together to thwart the effective articulation of immigrant interests in the city. This marginalization had tangible consequences.

Immigrant Needs and Demands

Upon initial settlement, the most immediate consequence of this neglect was felt in the field of housing. As mentioned earlier, when Birmingham's first post-war immigrants arrived in the city, they confronted a tight housing market and thousands of households were on waiting lists for accommodation by the council. Similar to their counterparts in Ealing, council members in Birmingham operated policies that effectively kept immigrants off, or at least at the bottom, of these queues. In contrast to Ealing, however, where the contentious housing issue split the Labour Party, there was little resistance on the part of councilors to the operation of such schemes.[11] When the Birmingham Community Relations Council published a document that detailed the city council's

---

[9] Solomos and Back (1995) and others (see, e.g., West Midlands County Council [WMCC] 1986) make the case that the media and other actors greatly exaggerated the conflicts between these two groups.

[10] Solomos and Back point out that these three categories are ideal types that do not exhaust the various routes into politics taken by ethnic minorities (1995, 136). Their interviews revealed that "With one exception, all of the councillors ... expressed dissatisfaction with the degree of influence they had in the political process, often claiming that if they could act as a united caucus they would be able to apply much greater pressure for change" (154).

[11] For a detailed account of the multiple ways in which Birmingham's housing department discriminated against West Indian and Asian residents, see Henderson and Karn (1984 and 1987). Among other things, the authors argue that discrimination on the basis of race was intertwined and amplified by discrimination on the basis of social class and gender as features that disproportionately characterized ethnic minority households (e.g., large-sized families in the case of Asians and single-parent households in the case of West Indians) coincided with negative conceptions of lower-class households.

discriminatory housing policies (including a five-year residency requirement for eligibility, a points system that prioritized waiting time over housing need, and the systematic allocation of worse-quality housing to immigrants) and proposed actions that would remedy the situation, "it was summarily rejected by the chairman of the Birmingham City Housing Committee on the grounds that it favoured immigrants and was discrimination in reverse" (Hill and Issacharoff 1971, 234).

Much of the city's existing housing stock was also of poor quality; 80,000 houses, or one-fourth of the total housing stock, had been built before 1900, much of it concentrated in areas of immigrant settlement (Ratcliffe 1981, 139; Flett 1982, 47). As a result, the city council embarked on a comprehensive slum clearance and redevelopment initiative in the 1960s and 1970s. Yet, officials decided against including many areas of immigrant concentration in this program, despite the fact that many of these neighborhoods were in need of redevelopment.[12] This exclusion not only ensured the further deterioration of immigrant areas, but also meant that a large share of immigrants were disadvantaged in the allocation of council housing, for those tenants that lived in buildings that were due to be demolished were moved up on the waiting list.

A further restriction – the banning of current or former owner-occupiers from council housing applications – considerably discriminated against immigrant households, many of whom had purchased cheap, run-down houses precisely because the rented sector had been closed off to them.[13] By the late 1960s, severe decay, chronic overcrowding, and lack of basic facilities[14] produced often appalling housing conditions that were the source of great grievance among Birmingham's immigrants. While tenants of "slum council property" in Soho voiced similar complaints as their counterparts elsewhere in the city, "the neglect of Soho in comparison with other city wards [was] an oddity indeed" (Holman 1970, 39). Officials insisted that efforts were being undertaken to ease the deplorable situation, but "the opinion of local people" held that "although something is being done, compared to the need that exists and the length of

---

[12] Henderson and Karn (1987, 6) note that "there was speculation at that time . . . as to whether local authorities were excluding areas of black residents from clearance programmes specifically because they wished to avoid rehousing black families. Another explanation offered was that authorities avoided multi-occupied areas, whether white or black, because of the size of the rehousing responsibility incurred."

[13] See Rex and Moore (1967, 260–265), Rex and Tomlinson (1979, 130), and Henderson and Karn (1987, 48–59). According to one survey, no West Indian or Asian owner-occupier household was allocated council housing, while housing officials made exceptions for 10 percent of white owner-occupiers (Henderson and Karn 1987, 51).

[14] According to the 1966 census of the Soho ward in the heart of Handsworth, 11.5 percent of dwellings housed over 1.5 persons per room, compared to 3 and 1.2 percent in Birmingham and England and Wales, respectively. About one-third of the dwellings did not have use of hot tap water, had no use of a fixed bath, and had an outside toilet only. Figures for the city and country as a whole are considerably lower (Holman 1970, 37).

time that this situation has been known to authorities, what is being done is in fact extremely little" (John 1970, 21).

Residents also judged the authority's handling of other service areas as wholly inadequate. When economic conditions began to decline in the 1970s, immigrant enclaves, already considered "twilight zones" during the booming 1960s, further deteriorated. The city's substandard provision in the area of education, recreational facilities, and social services were cause of constant complaint (Holman 1970; John 1970). With unemployment on the rise, these shortages were experienced by increasing numbers of the city's ethnic minority population. In the larger Handsworth area the number of unemployed nearly tripled between 1974 and 1977 while the number of nonwhites as a share of the total unemployed rose from 25.5 to 43.4 percent (Rex and Tomlinson 1979, 110); by 1981, male unemployment rates neared or exceeded 30 percent in many wards with a high concentration of nonwhites (see also Figure III.1 in Part III). To make matters worse, central government programs that were designed to improve conditions in urban areas faced with decay and deprivation (referred to in Chapter 3) generally bypassed Birmingham's nonwhite residents. One survey found that while voluntary groups headed by ethnic minorities had secured a slight increase in funding, these resources constituted a mere 10 percent of the entire budget; "90% of funds hardly affected ethnic minorities."[15]

This consistent neglect of immigrant needs had, of course, a political basis. As Newton recognized in the mid-1970s, "coloured people in the city are not in a sufficiently strong political position to fight unfavourable policies.... The fact is that coloured people have few political resources, and few friends among those who do" (1976, 221). By the 1980s, continued political weakness coincided with ever-increasing levels of material deprivation. The countrywide recession was severely felt in Birmingham and put further pressures on local services that the city council felt few incentives to provide. This systematic marginalization of ethnic minority needs crucially shaped intergroup relations in Birmingham.

Native Reaction

For most of the 1950s and 1960s, observers paint a somewhat puzzling picture of the city's intergroup relations. Rex and Moore (1967) note, for example, that "there was widespread disquiet amongst Birmingham people at the presence in their midst of over 50,000 coloured immigrants" (19–20), but the authors nevertheless believed the prospect of "race riots...to be slight" (191)

---

[15] See B. Jacobs (1986, 159). Interestingly, a disproportionate amount of voluntary group funding was allocated to Afro-Caribbean groups, which was partly due to the funding of the "Birmingham Rastafarian Association" (B. Jacobs 1986, 160). This outcome is consistent with the government's directive to discreetly channel resources to disaffected West Indians, as discussed in Chapter 3.

and indeed characterized the situation in Sparkbrook as one of "segregated and peaceful coexistence" (149).[16] In a similar vein, Rose (1969, 251) points out that protest against continued immigration never crystallized into "a genuinely popular movement," but "tapped real resentments." Hill and Issacharoff (1971, 49) speak of "Sporadic racialist activity" occurring in the 1950s, but they also show that efforts to organize against immigrants were mainly based on the initiatives of only one Conservative councilor. Reports of the 1964 general election campaign noted that even though anti-immigrant agitation had been feared in Sparkbrook, in the end there was "barely a hint of racialism" to be detected (Shuttleworth 1965, 58).[17] By the mid-1970s, only 16 percent of West Indians and 8 percent of Asians living in Handsworth thought that the area was marked by "racial problems" (Ratcliffe 1981, 110). It appears, then, that the sizable inflow of immigrants evoked hostile sentiments among Birmingham's white population, but that such hostility proved insufficient to generate sustained organized opposition or violent confrontations.

Election results reflect this state of affairs. Anti-immigrant candidates scored only in the low single digits in wards with a high concentration of immigrants. Moreover, these parties did not fare well across the city, in spite of numerous attempts. A variety of explicitly anti-immigrant parties – the Union Movement, the British National Democratic Party, the National Front, the British Movement, the British Democratic Party, and the British National Party – contested a total of 114 ward elections between 1962, when the Union Movement first appeared in Birmingham, and 1990. During this time, these parties' average vote share in wards where they competed (rather than in the city as a whole) was a mere 2.98 percent; anti-immigrant parties only once managed to gain over 10 percent of a ward's vote.[18] Racist parties were also unsuccessful in parliamentary elections, even when such contests were accompanied by propaganda and local coverage. The 1977 by-election in the Ladywood constituency, for example, attracted a lot of attention as members of the leftist and anti-fascist

---

[16] In the 1950s, a newspaper portrayed intergroup relations in Sparkbrook with this headline: "It's Live and Let Live in Birmingham's Harlem" (*Daily Herald*, November 4, 1955; cited in Solomos and Back 1995, 47).

[17] In addition to examining official campaign literature, Shuttleworth notes that canvassers did not appeal to anti-immigrant sentiments: "There is no evidence at all of a different position being put on the doorsteps" than had been put forth in the parties' manifestos (1965, 61), even though housing was an issue of central importance during the election in Sparkbrook. Solomos and Back (1995, 54) note the exception of the anti-immigrant campaign in the Perry Barr constituency (in the city's northwest) and attribute the relative absence of anti-immigration rhetoric during the 1964 campaign in part to an agreement among Conservative politicians, which had been enforced by the national leadership (see Messina 1989 on the bipartisan efforts to keep issues of race and immigration outside of mainstream two-party politics).

[18] The National Front gained 10.8 percent of the poll in the Saltley ward in 1976. In part as a result of internal infighting, the NF declined nationwide in the 1980s, but the average vote share of these parties between 1962 and 1980 (in wards that they contested) is only slightly higher (3.38 percent); author's calculation, derived from Phillips (2000).

Socialist Workers' Party attacked National Front members verbally and physically. In the end, the NF improved its result by only 127 votes in an area where Labour had felt that "race relations appeared to be good" (Layton-Henry 1977, 133). Observers interpreted even this modest gain not to a show of support of the NF, but as a protest vote against the violent tactics employed by far-left extremists who stood "accused of needing to dramatise the 'fascist threat' to win support among coloured people" (Taylor 1978, 62).

It is important to underscore that I do not argue that organized and sustained immigrant–native conflict failed as a result of the tolerant nature of Birmingham's population. Indeed, the opinion poll cited in Chapter 3 refutes this notion. Rather, despite the resonance of the issues of race and immigration, large-scale confrontations between immigrants and natives – violent or nonviolent – simply did not characterize intergroup relations because natives did not need to resort to such measures: Politically excluded immigrants did not constitute threatening competitors in the fight over economic goods. Electoral calculations did not compel ruling parties to allocate resources away from natives and toward immigrants.[19] Needless to say, this systematic and deliberate marginalization of immigrant needs, while appeasing white disquiet, left sections of the city's minority population with few resources and increasingly alienated from the state.

Immigrant Backlash against the State

Persistent state neglect of immigrant needs forestalled the organization of anti-immigrant movements, but it also left a lasting impact on Birmingham's ethnic minorities. With local politicians proving inaccessible to the city's growing ethnic minority population, some minority residents pursued alternative strategies that fell outside of the orthodox party political machinery.

During the 1970s a large number of immigrant-led self-help organizations emerged in Birmingham. The specific goals of these associations were varied, but their overarching theme was to help immigrants in the social and economic realm. They offered advice and assistance in the housing field, provided educational, recreational, and cultural resources, and, more generally, tried to help immigrants navigate the local bureaucracy (John 1970, 28; Rex and Tomlinson 1979). Officially independent of state institutions, these groups often liaised with the local state if such connections promised to deliver government resources released by the center. As we have seen, however, the allocation of these funds to such voluntary groups via these channels was quite modest indeed. Moreover, sections of the ethnic minority population had become so disenchanted with the state and its representatives that they considered any

---

[19] For a discussion of the various attempts to politicize immigration and race relations and instigate clashes (most prominently by Enoch Powell's xenophobic Rivers of Blood speech, delivered in Birmingham in 1968), see Solomos and Back (1995, 43–62).

type of liaison with public officials to be "selling out" to a state whose interests were not aligned with those of ethnic minorities.[20]

A second reaction to the state's systematic neglect of immigrant needs was thus one of withdrawal from the political establishment. In their study of Handsworth in the mid-1970s, Rex and Tomlinson noted that segments of the area's ethnic minority communities had become increasingly suspicious of the local state and as a result rejected as accommodationist the efforts, by social workers or their elders, that aimed to integrate them into the social and political sphere. The authors considered the proliferation of groups that had embraced an oppositional stance toward the state a significant departure from the early years of immigrant settlement in Birmingham, when attempts to engage with the political establishment had been the norm (Rex and Tomlinson 1979, 242).

Conflictual relations between ethnic minorities and the police came to encapsulate these larger themes as low-level clashes between the immigrant-origin population and these state actors became entrenched. By the late 1960s, tensions between the city's ethnic minority youth and police officers were said to be symptomatic of "the sheer deterioration in the quality of life, the perennial lack of basic resources and amenities, the sense of being de facto second-class citizens, [and] the sense of hopelessness" that was to be found among immigrant youth in Birmingham (John 1970, 29; emphasis omitted). Many argued that friction between the forces of law and order on the one hand and nonwhite youths on the other was, therefore, not merely to be resolved by a change in police tactics:

[O]ne of the root causes of bad police-community relations is the fact that, as a failure of social agencies and the absence of relevant social policies, the police are called upon to salvage a basic situation not of their own making... the police forces... cannot be expected to pick up the pieces in the absence of a more serious attack on the basic social problems by Government and local authorities. (Nandy 1970, 53)

This assessment of local affairs in Birmingham coincides with the government's (confidential) interpretation of police–immigrant relations, recounted in Chapter 3. By the early 1970s, before the eruption of larger unrest, the Home Office had thought it "reasonable to suggest that the black disaffected constitute a real problem... in Birmingham."[21]

After a decade of small-scale clashes between the police and immigrant-origin youths, Birmingham witnessed two events of large-scale violence involving ethnic minorities and the forces of law and order. The first such event occurred in the summer of 1981 in Handsworth, when groups of predominantly male youths attacked police vehicles and local shops, leaving behind

---

[20] There were accusations, e.g., that money coming from the center (through Inner City Partnership Funds) was "used by the local police to fund a layer of community organisation which would not only be supportive of police initiatives but literally in their debt" (WMCC 1986, 64). This interpretation is in line with the intentions of the Home Office, referred to in Chapter 3.

[21] CAB 134/3772: "Disaffected West Indian Youth," Memorandum by the Home Office to the Official Committee on Immigration and Community Relations, May 6, 1974.

over £100,000 worth in damages and forty injured police offers. This first outbreak of violence, which involved West Indians, Asians, and whites, was rather
limited.[22] When Lord Scarman visited the area shortly afterward, the police
spoke of relations with Asian and black Caribbean youths that had in fact
improved, mainly owing to the direct involvement of permanent beat officers
in local communities. While representatives of the police, the county council,
and the city council all agreed that efforts at community policing should be
developed further, the official view also emphasized that the disorders were
"the product of unemployment and alienation from authority, rather than
anti-police" per se (Scarman 1982, 221).

Birmingham's turn to community policing may thus have provided a fleeting
veneer of calm, but ultimately it did not prove adequate to prevent the disorders
that shook the city as the 1980s unfolded. Sociopolitical and economic realities
loomed much larger. Ethnic minority leaders "stressed that the recent disturbances had been neither racial nor directed against the police ... the underlying
reasons for the disturbances were considered to be essentially social and economic," an interpretation that was followed by a call for increased government
funds (Scarman 1982, 228). As had been recognized by policy makers in the
early 1970s, the police stood in as a representative of a distant, inaccessible
state. Local opinion seemed to reflect these views. In a survey conducted by
the Home Office, 43 percent of Handsworth residents blamed the outbreak of
violence on unemployment, while only 9 percent believed police harassment to
have caused the riot.[23]

In light of these analyses, the Conservative-led city council was compelled to
announce initiatives that aimed to take ethnic minority interests into account. It
declared its commitment to multicultural education and proclaimed its goal to
promote equal access to public employment opportunities. The Labour regime
took these initiatives further; it established a race relations and equal opportunities committee and created a Race Relations Unit, which was charged with
promoting interracial harmony and monitoring racial discrimination in the
council's areas of service delivery. Promising on paper, the progressive policy agenda was soon denounced for its wanting implementation in practice
(Garbaye 2005, 106–107). Without the pressure of a credible electoral threat,
minorities' protests only yielded limited concessions from the state.

When urban violence broke out again in September 1985, the failure to
regenerate immigrant neighborhoods and the council's continued marginalization of ethnic minority needs were important reasons cited by community
representatives for the continued hostile relationship between sections of the
ethnic minority population and the local state (WMCC 1986). The alleged

---

[22] *The Times*, "Copy-cat Mobs in Petrol Bomb Attacks on Police," July 13, 1981. Solomos and
Back (1995, 91) note that "Civil conflict in Birmingham was fairly limited [in 1981], particularly
when compared with London or Liverpool."
[23] *The Financial Times*, "A Fuse Just Waiting to be Lit...; Britain's Inner Cities," September 12,
1985.

trigger that set off two nights of rioting was a confrontation between a police officer and a West Indian man on the basis of a traffic violation. A few hours after the incident had occurred, firemen, called in to put out a fire at an abandoned bingo hall, were pelted with bricks and attacked with petrol bombs. Several hundred youths also hurled bricks and fire bombs at police and turned burning cars into barricades. The violence was much more serious than the events of 1981; the unrest caused £2.5 million in property damage and injuries to sixty firefighters and police. Two Asian postal workers died, trapped in a burning post office. Of those arrested, 221 were identified as Afro-Caribbean, 129 as whites, and 49 as Asians; over 80 percent of these offenders lived within a five-mile radius of the disturbances (Layton-Henry 1986; Mullins 1986).

The riot provoked a diverse set of responses. The media attempted to construct the unrest as a violent instance of West Indian–Asian antipathy, but West Indian and Asian activists denied these claims forcefully (Solomos and Back 1995, 84). The police leadership, as well as much of the political establishment (including Handsworth's Labour MP Rooker and Home Secretary Douglas Hurd) attributed the outbreak of violence to West Indian criminality and drug dealing, which in turn was seen to have fostered confrontations with the police. Disagreeing with this assessment, a report commissioned by the Labour-led city council instead drew attention to the multiethnic character of the riot and pointed to unemployment and discrimination, as well as police harassment, as the main causes behind the riots (Layton-Henry 1986).

Finally, a group of Asian and West Indians headed an inquiry that consulted sixty-seven local organizations in an effort to gather the views of Birmingham's ethnic minority community that had been thus far neglected. The report rejected the ideas that West Indian criminality or tensions between Asians and West Indians were to blame; instead, it focused on economic and social inequalities. In addition to relating residents' grievances in the areas of social services, housing, education, and training schemes, the report laid bare how institutional racism and discrimination had systematically prevented ethnic minorities from receiving government funds that had originally been destined to reach immigrant neighborhoods. While Labour leader Dick Knowles had pointed out that over £20 million had been poured into Handsworth as part of the Urban Programme, the report cited research indicating that a mere 3 percent of these funds had actually been spent on projects headed by ethnic minorities. Moreover, big contractors and outside labor, rather than the local workforce, tended to be the main beneficiaries of urban renewal initiatives (WMCC 1986, 17, 54–57). Dismissing the council's Race Relations Unit as a "joke" (88), the report also attributed the continued neglect of ethnic minority needs to their "exclusion from the decision making arena" (84).

The various post hoc analyses of the riot should not be divorced from the intentions of their authors, who themselves were directly or indirectly implicated in the conflict. An examination of the political and economic conditions that prevailed during the first several decades of postwar immigrant settlement and that affected the position of ethnic minorities in Birmingham's political economy nevertheless elucidates the context in which conflictual relations between ethnic minorities and state institutions occurred. I concur with Solomos and Back, who maintain that the disturbances "exposed the stark inequalities that had emerged in the aftermath of de-industrialisation . . . [and] also signified an important failure on the part of the political system to satisfy the aspirations of large sections of the city's youth" (1995, 67). Aware of the "less than objective" attempts to interpret the 1985 riots, Rex and Samad similarly conclude that "What does seem to be the case . . . was that large numbers of Black people were alienated from both the Council and the police, and, in the subsequent years, these disturbances were the reference point of debates about ethnic minority policy and constituted an important source of pressure for a stronger commitment to equal opportunity, anti-racism and multi-culturalism" (1996, 17).

In 1987, the Labour Party did indeed encourage the formation of an umbrella group that would represent over 300 ethnic minority organizations and facilitate communication between the city's ethnic groups and the council. On the whole, however, Labour politicians with ambitious inclusive goals faced an electoral geography – and a strong right-wing caucus within the ruling Labour group – that still militated against the implementation of policies that would be seen to benefit ethnic minorities at the expense of whites. As Joly (1995, 96) notes, "ethnic questions became caught in the tension between the moderate right wing of the Labour Party and its active left wing. Another potential tension existed between the traditional 'white' working class electorate and the ethnic electorate competing for the provision of services," a tension that the Conservative Party was generally eager to exploit. It should not come as a surprise, then, that most of the council's progressive policy agenda that was implemented in the 1980s was considered a failure.

To review, from the 1960s to the 1990s, the political sidelining of Birmingham's ethnic minority population coincided with economic disadvantage. Resource shortages in employment, education, housing, and social services disproportionately affected the nonwhite population whose unemployment rates and economic needs surpassed those of the city's white residents. Unable to induce the city council to distribute government resources to areas of minority concentration, politically powerless ethnic minorities did not become targets of collective xenophobic organization, but instead engaged in antistate actions. In Leicester, by contrast, initially similar economic conditions interacted with a politically powerful immigrant population, leading to different conflict outcomes.

Leicester

Similar to its Midlands neighbor, Leicester is a city that is both urban and provincial; its population is socioeconomically mixed and ethnically diverse.

The city boundaries encompass an inner-city core, middle-class suburbs, and an outer ring of working-class council estates. Leicester has experienced New Commonwealth immigration since the 1950s, when labor shortages attracted small numbers of West Indian migrants who were soon followed by settlers from the Indian subcontinent. During the late 1960s and early 1970s, the city received a further wave of migrants of Indian descent, who arrived in Leicester via Africa, having been expelled by the Africanization policies of newly independent nations, such as Kenya and Uganda. This group of migrants, most of them Gujarati Hindus, has most decisively shaped Leicester's multicultural character. In 1981, over 13 percent of the city's residents had been born in India or East Africa, and by 2001, over 25% of the city's population identified themselves as being ethnically Indian (see Table 6.3).

During the twentieth century, Leicester developed a reputation for prosperity, innovativeness, and entrepreneurial spirit. Small firms and family-owned companies were considered the engines of the city's growing economy, and labor shortages in the hosiery and footwear industries drew in migrants as well as a large female workforce. While the "epithet 'prosperous' is widely applied to the city by its historians, at all periods" (Lomas 1975, 15) and the "image of Leicester as a prosperous city has been especially potent" despite periodic downturns (Nash and Reeder 1993, xi), the nationwide economic decline that began in the 1970s did not spare the city. In the mid-1970s, Leicester was thus faced with absorbing large shares of immigrants while experiencing its first economic contraction in decades. The fact that the arrivals constituted refugee families, including children and an elderly population, meant that pressures on education and social services would be more immediately felt when compared to the migration of single workers. The electoral environment of the time ensured that this challenge would not be met gracefully.

Leicester's Political Landscape

Electoral History

In the postwar period, Labour and Tories alternated in their control of city hall and traditional class issues dominated the local political debate. The local Labour Party contained a strong trade union contingent and focused its attention on the politics of municipal service provision, while the local Conservative group was made up largely of small businessmen and shopkeepers (as well as housewives) who countered Labour's call for improved service delivery with a focus on keeping the local tax rate low (Nash and Reeder 1993, 102–106). Similar to developments in Birmingham, the 1980s witnessed the ascendancy of the Labour Party while the Liberals disrupted the pattern of two-party competition in the late 1980s (see Table 6.4). In a clear departure from Birmingham politics, however, Leicester's Labour Party secured electoral advantage by openly courting the city's nonwhite voters.

TABLE 6.3. *Concentration of the Indian Population in Leicester, 1981–2001*

	1981			1991			2001	
	All Residents	Indian (%)		All Residents	Indian (%)		All Residents	Indian (%)
Leicester	276,244	13.3	Leicester	270,629	22.3	Leicester	279,917	25.7
Spinney Hill	17,234	38.3	Latimer	7,952	66.7	Latimer	11,581	74.1
Wycliffe	14,130	37.5	Crown Hills	9,585	65.6	Belgrave	10,297	63.2
Latimer	14,072	34.3	Spinney Hill	10,035	60.9	Spinney Hills	21,249	59.7
Belgrave	22,398	25.6	Rushey Mead	11,479	60.5	Rushey Mead	15,134	53.6
Charnwood	15,863	23.4	Belgrave	10,661	47.5	Coleman	12,099	46.9
St. Margaret's	13,950	21.0	Charnwood	9,290	47.2	Stoneygate	17,068	44.8
Westcotes	13,361	14.9	Abbey	8,537	47.1	Evington	9,788	31.0
Evington	19,599	6.1	Stoneygate	9,239	39.5	Charnwood	10,664	29.7
The Castle	10,149	5.9	Wycliffe	11,504	29.8	Humberstone & Hamilton	11,893	19.1
Knighton	15,797	5.6	Coleman	8,985	24.3	Knighton	16,265	15.6
The Abbey	27,597	5.4	Westcotes	8,855	18.9	Westcotes	8,653	14.9
North Braunstone	17,644	2.8	Evington	8,513	18.1	Abbey	12,713	12.8
de Montford	16,983	2.5	West Knighton	8,595	14.4	Western Park	9,892	12.2
Newton	20,438	1.5	West Humberstone	9,883	13.9	Thurncourt	9,937	11.1

Ward	Total	%
Rowley Fields	9,740	12.6
Beaumont Leys	15,637	9.9
Western Park	11,199	7.6
St. Augustine's	9,618	6.9
East Knighton	7,823	6.8
Castle	8,423	6.3
Thurncourt	9,996	5.9
Humberstone	8,713	5.5
Aylestone	9,900	2.7
Saffron	11,287	1.7
New Parks	10,315	1.2
Mowmacre	7,029	0.9
North Braunstone	8,723	0.7
Eyres Monsell	9,113	0.4

Ward	Total	%
Beaumont Leys	13,838	10.6
Castle	13,465	9.2
Fosse	10,733	9.2
Braun. Park & Rowley Fields	16,614	8.5
Freemen	9,983	3.7
New Parks	16,020	3.5
Aylestone	10,801	3.5
Eyres Monsell	11,230	1.6
Humberstone	18,415	1.1
Aylestone	18,614	0.8

Notes: Leicester underwent boundary changes that are reflected in the census figures for each year. Until 1981, entries refer to country of birth. In 1981, all those born in East Africa are coded as Indians, which is due to the large inflows of East African Asians during the late 1960s and early 1970s. As of 1991, entries are based on ethnic origin and thus also include children born in the United Kingdom to parents of Indian descent.

Source: The 1981 data are based on "Table 4 Country of Birth All Residents," 1991 figures are based on "Table S06 Ethnic Group: Residents," and 2001 data are derived from "T13 Theme Table on Ethnicity" (all data are available at www.nomisweb.co.uk).

TABLE 6.4. *Local Election Results in Leicester, 1968–2003*

Election Year	% Share of Vote			Wards Won			Council Control
	CON	LAB	LD	CON	LAB	LD	
1968	65.2	25.1	8.0	16	0	0	CON
1969	62.8	29.0	6.2	16	0	0	CON
1970	51.3	42.9	5.2	9	7	0	CON
1971	39.2	57.8	2.3	3	13	0	CON
1972	42.1	50.9	2.6	4	12	0	LAB
1973	37.5	46.2	5.0	3	13	0	LAB
1976	42.5	35.2	4.0	9	7	0	CON
1979	40.1	47.5	6.9	6	10	0	LAB
1983	37.5	48.2	12.3	8	20	0	LAB
1984	36.5	55.9	6.8	4	15	0	LAB
1986	34.1	43.4	21.4	5	13	1	LAB
1987	37.9	41.7	19.7	8	16	4	LAB
1991	30.5	47.9	17.3	6	19	3	LAB
1995	18.6	56.1	19.0	2	22	4	LAB
1996	20.9	55.1	19.3	3	21	4	LAB
1999	22	47.3	27.1	5	15	8	LAB
2003	22.2	35.5	31.0	4	9	9	No Control

Notes: The Liberal Democrats were founded in 1988; until then, the Liberal Party had formed an alliance with the Social Democratic Party. Results prior to 1988 refer to the performance of this alliance or when the Liberals ran on their own. Labour's massive losses in 1968 and 1969 were part of a regionwide swing against the unpopular Labour government, led by Wilson. CON = Conservatives; LAB = Labour Party; LD = Liberal Democrats.

Source: Leicester Mercury (various issues), "Declaration of Poll Results" (Leicester City Council), Rallings and Thrasher (2003, 283, 423), and Rallings et al. (2006).

Electoral Competition and the Indian Vote

As Table 6.4 shows, between 1971 and 1979, Leicester's city hall switched hands three times. Electoral contests were fought against the backdrop of a rapidly rising nonwhite population. While 3.9 percent of Leicester's residents were born in New Commonwealth countries in 1966, this figure rose to 8.2 percent in 1971 and reached 15.1 percent in 1981. The majority of these migrants (88.9 percent, or 13.3 percent of the total population) was of Indian descent and had either come straight from the subcontinent or via East Africa.[24] These East African Asians were often linked through ties of kinship or friendship with immigrants from the subcontinent and initially found accommodation in the same streets and neighborhoods, or, depending on financial circumstances, even in the same houses as family and friends. As the numbers in Table 6.3 convey, migration to Leicester had given rise to a large, highly concentrated

---

[24] For 1966 and 1971 figures, see Marrett (1989, 2, author's calculation); for 1981 figures, see Table 6.3. The vast majority of migrants from East Africa were of Indian background and I count them as such.

Indian settlement; by 1981, six out of the city's sixteen wards (or 38 percent) contained an Indian population exceeding 20 percent.

Leicester's Indian population exhibits strong social networks and dense organizational links. By the early 1970s, forty different associations catered to the social and welfare needs of Asian settlers. When East African Asian refugees arrived in Leicester, a group of self-styled leaders founded the British Asian Welfare Society to help settle the new arrivals and act as a liaison with the city council as well as with central government agencies overseeing refugee resettlement. A branch of the Indian Workers' Association was also active in the city, as were the Gujarati Hindu Association, and its offshoot, the Gujarati Welfare Society. At times, these groups vied for the representation of Leicester's Indian residents and their leaders made claims to speak for all, or for specific sections, of this growing population. As their names suggest, regional divisions also mapped onto these and other associations. Gujarati leaders would periodically denounce the communist leanings of the Punjabi-dominated IWA, who in turn accused the former of being self-appointed opportunists.[25] Notwithstanding these rivalries, these groups shared a common interest in participating in local politics. The IWA was "most adept at getting its voters out" (Nash and Reeder 1993, 108), and a member of the Gujarati Welfare Society, a Kenyan Asian, became Leicester's first Asian councilor in the Charnwood ward in 1973.

An examination of the ward map (Figure 6.3) and ward-level electoral results (Figure 6.4)[26] reveals why capturing the immigrant vote would soon become indispensable for the Labour Party. In the close election of 1970, when Labour won seven seats against the Conservatives' record of nine, three out of the five wards with the highest concentration of Indian migrants came under Labour's control. In 1976, when the electoral contest was equally tight and Labour again narrowly lost to the Conservatives, four out of these wards had returned Labour councilors; in Belgrave ward, where Conservatives won, the winning margin (7.6 points) was much smaller than the vote produced by the National Front and the English National Party (26.8 percent), suggesting both the benefits and the costs of appealing to this new voting bloc. By 1979, all five wards had voted in Labour candidates, three Asian councilors had been elected (see Figure 6.4), and it was widely acknowledged that Labour's reliance on the Indian vote delivered the party's victory. In the run-up to the election (which

---

[25] Marrett (1989, 83–104) portrays these rivalries nicely and concludes with a rather critical assessment of the British Asian Welfare Society and its efforts to integrate the East African refugees.

[26] Single-member elections were held until 1972. Latimer, Spinney Hill, and Belgrave held three-member elections from 1973 to 1979. Between 1983 and 1999, two candidates were elected in all wards – except in 1984, when only one candidate was elected in Latimer, Spinney Hill, Rushey Mead, and Charnwood, and in 1986, when only one candidate was elected in Belgrave and Crown Hills. There were no elections in 1984 in Belgrave and Crowns Hills and in 1986 in Latimer, Spinney Hill, and Charnwood. Additional South Asian candidates are those who did not run for Labour, the Conservatives, or the Liberal Democrats.

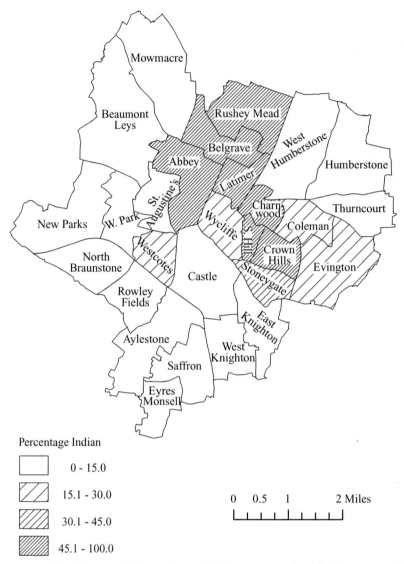

FIGURE 6.3. Leicester 1991 ward map. (© Crown copyright. All rights reserved. License number 100049655.)

coincided with a general election), Jim Marshall, Labour MP for South Leicester, even called for an increase in the number of Asian representatives on the city council.[27] When Marshall was reelected in "a spectacular victory with a swing to Labour of 0.75 percent against the national swing to the Conservatives of

---

[27] *Leicester Mercury*, "City MP Wants To See More Asian Members in Local Government," March 19, 1979.

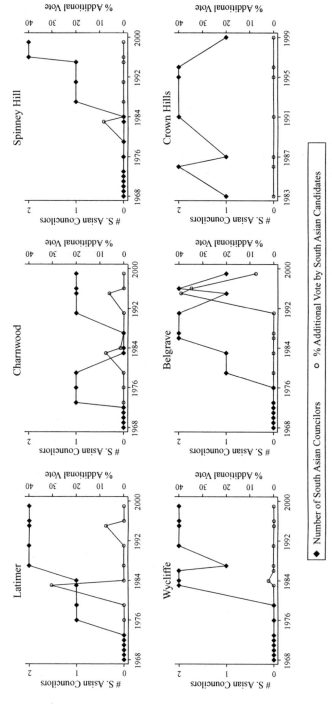

FIGURE 6.4. South Asian electoral representation in selected Leicester wards. (*Sources: Leicester Mercury*, up to 1987; "Declaration of Poll Results," Leicester City Council, for results starting in 1991, and Rallings et al. 2006, author's calculations. See footnote 26 for more information.)

5.2 per cent... Conservatives admit[ted] that they [had] missed the boat over the immigrant vote in Leicester."[28] After their 1979 defeat, Leicester's Tories ran an increased number of South Asian candidates.

These developments show that Labour counted on the immigrant vote for its return to city hall – but to what extent were these votes rewarded? Figure 6.4 does not suggest that Labour's position among Leicester's immigrant electorate was seriously challenged by community representatives running as Independent candidates, perhaps implying that Labour did not need to exchange valued goods for valued votes. In the case of Leicester, however, the lack of these interventions does not signal political apathy or missing sophistication on the part of the city's Indian electorate, but rather reflects that immigrant interests were in fact represented in the Labour Party since the 1970s. Similar to developments in Ealing, where the issue of immigration and ensuing battles over housing split the Labour Party into two camps, nine Labour councilors in Leicester rebelled against their party's call for local immigration restrictions in the wake of the Ugandan Asian influx.[29] One of these rebels (Jim Marshall) became the new party leader in 1973 and the following election campaigns witnessed a shift in the party's stance to the city's newcomers as Labour's emergent left-wing caucus persuaded more pragmatically oriented councilors of the Old Guard that seizing the immigrant vote would be a winning strategy at the ballot box. By 1974 the party "was among the first of the Labour branches to print electoral messages in Asian languages" (Marrett 1989, 168), and by 1976 the Labour Party included three Asian councilors.

A younger and growing section of Leicester's Labour Party was indeed ideologically committed to fighting racism and incorporating ethnic minority interests into the Party's platform; but for those "councilors who didn't really like what [the left-wing] was saying," the decision to openly link up with the immigrant electorate was also "based on a shrewd understanding" of electoral politics.[30] Unlike in Birmingham, then, the voting power and mobilizational strength of the minority community broke the tie between the Old and the New Guard in favor of the latter. In the interviews that I conducted in Leicester, some have emphasized Labour's ideological convictions, while others have espoused a more cynical interpretation of the party's policy shift as being driven by a mutually beneficial alliance between the Labour machine and community vote brokers. The crucial point, echoed by the Conservatives' assessment of their 1979 defeat, is that an immigrant-friendly policy was also to become good politics. In Birmingham, where the electoral landscape put a lower premium on the immigrant vote, we have seen that progressive left-wingers were

---

[28] *Leicester Mercury*, "Variations on the Immigrant Vote Enigma," May 17, 1979.

[29] In August of 1972, an all-party delegation visited the Home Office, declaring, "We told the minister that Leicester is full up." *Leicester Mercury*, "Whitehall Told – Leicester Is Full Up," August 31, 1972. See also Marrett (1989, 54).

[30] Interview with a council official and longtime Leicester resident, Leicester, England, March 2005.

unable to sway the Old Guard to openly and actively embrace their nonwhite constituents.

Labour's position vis-à-vis the city's ethnic minorities does not suggest that Indian leaders did not find it necessary to remind the party of their pivotal electoral position. In the 1979 council elections, for example, the Indian Workers' Association asked Labour to stay true to its pledge to develop a multiethnic Leicester and to refrain from running candidates in the wards that the IWA planned on contesting.[31] This move was of course strongly resisted by Labour councilors, who argued that "it would be far better from [the IWA's] point of view to work with the existing political parties."[32] In the end, no IWA candidates ran in 1979, and, commenting on Labour's success in the 1979 elections, immigrant leaders mentioned the "local Labour Party's efforts in trying to involve the ethnic minority groups in political activities" as one of the main reasons behind their vote.[33] By the 1980s, Labour was still the party of choice among most immigrants, but the Tories and the Liberals had made inroads among this electorate and had also begun fielding ethnic minority candidates.

In summary, Indian voters played an important role in Leicester's elections soon after they had arrived in the city and their support was crucial to Labour's electoral strategy. This pivotal position would ensure that Asian needs would be addressed.

Immigrant Needs and Demands

Links with local government were important in helping Asian immigrants establish themselves in the city, and the issues that were at the forefront of their concerns were education and housing. Given that the period of rapid and large immigration inflows coincided with preexisting shortages in school places and a deteriorating and limited housing stock, the Labour Party, still dominated by the entrenched trade union leadership, tried to initially distance itself from being seen as a provider for immigrant needs. The Labour-led council was the only one in Britain to take out a full-page ad in the *Ugandan Argus*, a Kampala newspaper, urging prospective refugees to avoid the city of Leicester where

---

[31] *Leicester Mercury,* "Indians Seek 'Deal' with Labour," March 20, 1979. Mohinder Farma, the president of Leicester's IWA branch, was quoted as saying that "We would like to get support from the local Labour Party. If they want to see more coloured people on the council we feel they should not put their candidates in wards we shall be contesting. We shall be asking them to do this. This would give a lead to the development of a multi-racial society in Leicester. We are similar to the Labour Party politically because we are a workers' organisation, but we have our own aims and, although siding with Labour, we would put forward our own views."

[32] *Leicester Mercury,* "Indian Workers' Move Won't Worry Us, Say Councillors," March 22, 1979. This quotation cites Peter Soulsby, then Labour councilor in Spinney Hill. Soulsby, who became Labour's leader in 1981, has been credited for promoting an inclusive policy agenda and building bridges across the city's ethnic groups. He was knighted by the Queen in 1999 to honor his service to Leicester and elected MP for Leicester South in 2005.

[33] *Leicester Mercury,* "Variations on the Immigrant Vote Enigma," May 17, 1979.

education, housing, and social and health services were said to be "already stretched to the limit."[34]

The shortage in education was especially acute, and the arrival of a large number of refugee children exacerbated the situation. In order to accommodate the newcomers, the city provided two emergency schools, housed in a previously closed down building, and it also decided to put up schoolchildren in makeshift, mobile units, a move that some Conservative councilors resisted vociferously. The voluntary sectors also stepped in and offered part-time education to fill staff shortages. Between 1967 and 1974, the number of schoolchildren had indeed increased by 20 percent. In 1973, several hundred children had not been allocated school places, prompting calls from inner-city Labour councilors that authorities were neglecting their moral and legal duties toward both Asian and white children (Marrett 1989, 119–126).

Housing was another problem area that affected Indians and longtime residents alike. The settlement of immigrants in densely populated areas with substandard housing facilities led to conditions of severe overcrowding and housing decline.[35] While council housing was more accessible to immigrants in Leicester than it had been in Birmingham – the council operated a one-year residency rule compared to Birmingham's five-year restriction – the waiting list counted 14,000 applications in 1975. Pressures on more affordable public housing also grew more intense as the rapid population increase had helped to raise house prices during a time when economic conditions and incomes declined. During 1974 and 1976 the number of jobless individuals increased fourfold, the city's unemployment rate surpassed the national rate for the first time in decades, and long-standing businesses that had been mainstays of the local economy had to close their doors – developments that seriously dented Leicester's image as a prosperous city (Marrett 1989, 143; Nash and Reeder 1993, 75).

---

[34] The full page ad, dated September 17, 1972, is reprinted in Martin and Singh (2002, 26) and reads, "The City Council of Leicester, England, believes that many families in Uganda are considering moving to Leicester. If YOU are thinking of doing so it is very important you should know that PRESENT CONDITIONS IN THE CITY ARE VERY DIFFERENT FROM THOSE MET BY EARLIER SETTLERS. They are: HOUSING – several thousands of families are already on the Council's waiting list. EDUCATION – hundreds of children are awaiting places in schools. SOCIAL AND HEALTH SERVICES – already stretched to the limit. IN YOUR OWN INTERESTS AND THOSE OF YOUR FAMILY YOU SHOULD ACCEPT THE ADVICE OF THE UGANDA RESETTLEMENT BOARD AND NOT COME TO LEICESTER" (emphasis in the original).

[35] Relying on data from the 1971 census (which predates the arrival of the majority of Ugandan Asians and thus understates the extent of overcrowding), Lomas finds that no wards with a New Commonwealth immigrant population exceeding 10 percent was found in the top housing class; three were in the middle category (Latimer, St. Margaret's, and Belgrave) and three were in the bottom category (Spinney Hill, Charnwood, and Wycliffe). In terms of overcrowding, 17.7 percent of "coloured" households lived at or over 1.5 persons per room, compared with 1.3 percent of "non-coloured" households (Lomas 1975, 33, 27). In 1975, the Spinney Hill Conservative Association publicized figures showing that 67 percent of Asians violated housing statutes by living in illegal multioccupation (Marrett 1989, 143).

White Backlash

Shortages in education and housing, a declining economic environment that compounded the effects of such scarcity, and a growing immigrant population whose needs received increased attention from the city's political establishment proved to be a toxic combination for intercommunal relations in Leicester. The National Front eagerly calculated the tax burden associated with integrating Ugandan Asians (allegedly £124 per refugee), white parents registered their discontent with inadequate education facilities, the housing shortage was feared to cause "racial trouble," and the first Ugandan Asian family who was offered council housing was not only greeted with a lot of media attention but also with verbal and physical attacks from fellow council tenants.[36] A host of anti-immigrant organizations emerged locally, including the Anti-Immigration Society and the Enoch Powell Support Group, and several xenophobic parties, such as the National Democratic Party, the English National Party, and most notably, the National Front, began contesting elections in the city. Soon the NF boasted the fastest-growing branch in all of Britain, with election results to prove it. Running on the themes of housing, education, and unemployment, the NF made its first real electoral gains in 1973, when its average vote share in the ten wards it contested reached 16.0 percent.[37] It achieved its best result in the inner-city Latimer ward (27.1 percent), followed by a poll of 21.4 percent in Charnwood, where Labour had run a candidate of Kenyan Asian origin. In 1976, when the Labour group had become more firmly committed to its Indian electorate and employment and housing shortages had intensified, the NF scored spectacular victories. It contested all of the city's sixteen wards, attained an overall average of 18.2 percent, scored over 29 percent in two wards, and fell only 61 votes short of attaining a council seat in the Abbey ward.[38]

The success of the extreme right in Leicester also prompted a grass-roots response from groups that were opposed to racism. The first such group was the Inter-Racial Solidarity Campaign (IRSC). Its aim was to counter the emerging anti-immigrant agitation with nonviolent forms of resistance. Members organized marches, sometimes several-thousand strong, to protest the Front

---

[36] Marrett cites the President of the Leicester and County Estates Agents Association, who spoke of the city's "nightmare housing problem" and "a threat of racial trouble of a kind which has already occurred elsewhere" (1989, 138; see also 59, 117, and 144).

[37] It has to be noted that from 1973 until 1983, Leicester held multimember elections, with each ward returning two to three councilors, while councilors in Birmingham were most often elected in single-member districts. Electors in Leicester could thus split their votes. Direct comparisons between the two cities are possible for 1973 and 1983, when all of Birmingham's council seats were up for election in multimember contests. In 1973, the Front did not even field candidates in Birmingham (a decision that might have been prompted by a poor 3.28 percent result in a 1972 by-election in Sandwell ward). In 1982, the NF received 1.85 and 2.17 percent of the vote, respectively, in the two wards it contested.

[38] National Front results are based on my calculations; see Figure 6.4 for sources. This section also relies on Husbands (1983, 89–92), and Marrett (1989, 58–60).

and its supporters and distributed leaflets that aimed to discredit the anti-immigrant party by exposing the anti-Semitic and extreme roots of National Front activists. One leaflet, given to me by a former IRSC member turned Labour councilor, read as follows:

The National Front tries to make cheap gains from the frustrations of the British people. Their answer is to blame immigrants. *The housing shortage, overcrowded schools* and *unemployment were problems long before immigration began.* Hitler could not solve Germany's problems by picking on Jews and we will not solve ours by picking on immigrants. The solution lies with working people, black and white, uniting to resist racism and to demand a massive increase in social spending.[39]

The nonpartisan ecumenical organization, Unity Against Racism, also organized peaceful processions to demonstrate against prejudice and took out a full page in the *Leicester Mercury* denouncing racism, which was signed by 500 signatories, including by many of the city's key figures.[40]

For some who opposed racism, these tactics did not go far enough. Hoping that a violent polarization between the National Front and leftist groups would bring the NF in disrepute locally – which in Leicester had tried to avoid or hide the use of violence in an attempt to preserve an air of respectability among the city's middle class – the Anti-fascist Action group (AFA) pursued a strategy of violent confrontation. According to one former member, the group

formed a telephone tree that if any left-wing group or black group encountered the NF in any way, they only had to phone around and we could mobilize a hundred people in half an hour to go to that meeting and defend it basically from fascists smashing it up. So our strategy...was to use physical force against the fascists. Because we had nothing to lose, because we didn't have an electoral base. But they did. And every time there was a punch up at one of their meetings a few of them, all middle-class members, didn't turn up again. Because they didn't want to be associated with this rough stuff. They wanted to be nice, respectable racists.... We felt the only way to deal with them was physically.[41]

AFA members also made it their job to paint over the racist graffiti that began to cover the city's buildings, an activity that routinely got them arrested (as well as publicity) because they were accused of damaging private property in broad daylight.

In contrast to events in Birmingham, then, where politically shut-out ethnic minorities clashed with the state but a collective native reaction against immigrants did not materialize, Leicester's politically influential Indian-origin minority population did not turn against state actors but had to confront

---

[39] Emphasis in the original. The leaflet advertised a demonstration against racism, which was to take place in Leicester in April, 1973.

[40] Among the signatories were members of the football team, the Indian-born singer and Leicester resident Engelbert Humperdinck, the bishop, and former Labour leader Marston, who had once campaigned against the arrival of immigrants.

[41] Interview with a former member of the Anti-Fascist Action, Leicester, England, March 2005.

organized racism. We do, however, observe parallels with developments in Birmingham when we turn our attention to the city's small West Indian population. Though the experience of Leicester's sizable Indian-origin community has tended to dominate accounts of the city's postwar immigration, Leicester is also home to a black Caribbean community that constituted 1.5 percent of the population in 1991. Because of their low numbers, black Caribbeans have been much less visible and more easily ignored by the local political leadership. Just as in Birmingham, in the 1970s and 1980s this neglect in the face of economic hardship left some West Indians in Leicester hostile to the state: "Opposition to the State was important and to many people the power of the state was most heavily felt through interaction with the police. The threat form the far right NF was less a focus of attention."[42]

That the West Indian experience with white racism in Leicester should have been different from that of the Indian population demonstrates that whites' racist targeting followed the logic of immigrant–native conflict proposed in this book. Whites' racist reaction was not an undifferentiated expression of prejudice; it was directed at a group that represented a threat to natives' economic welfare, and it was much less concerned with West Indians who did not constitute such a threat. Furthermore, that West Indians' relationship with the state was different from that of the city's Indian population supports the notion that it is an immigrant group's political behavior – rather than unobserved city-level variables – that drives variation in the two types of conflict in the context of economic scarcity, even within one city.

Turnaround

Campaigns to eradicate the racism that Indian immigration evoked continued throughout the 1970s. The IRSC and AFA remained active in distributing leaflets and the Anti-Nazi League started carrying out activities in Leicester in the late 1970s, countering NF rallies with their own demonstrations and attacking Front marchers. But as in other cities across the country, the Front's electoral performance in the late 1970s was harmed by the fact the party had overstretched itself nationally. In the 1979 council elections, the party's average vote share had dropped to 5 percent with no ward producing results in the double digits. This decline was not just due to strategic miscalculations. While some mocked Prime Minister Heath's praise of Leicester as a "model of how to build

---

[42] See Chessum (2000, 222–223). The disturbances that took place in many inner cities in the summer of 1981 also spread to Leicester, but they received little attention here, including from Chessum, whose book only devotes one paragraph to them. Other local histories in fact state that "Leicester has been free from the riots and racial disturbances which have plagued other British cities" (Seliga 1998, 233). None of the people I interviewed mentioned the disturbances, unless I prompted them. One former local Labour Party councilor who lived in the affected area dismissed them as resulting from the start of the summer vacation, while a local (white) official, who had participated in the events, considered them to be "anti-Thatcher" riots; interviews with the author, March 2005.

and maintain race relations,"[43] by 1980 the local paper also commented on the city's "improving community relations picture."[44] One year later, this view was echoed by the superintendent of Leicestershire's county's police community relations office, who stated that "We are not aware of any racialist attacks by extremist groups in Leicestershire and we are rightly proud of our good community relations for which many people have worked extremely hard."[45] This assessment paints a picture that many might have found too rosy. Nevertheless, it was clear that the 1980s was a period of easing tensions. But how did this turnaround come about?

Reductions in Economic Scarcity

Immigrant–native conflict started to decline as resource pressures began to ease. Increases in the supply of previously scarce goods along with an improved socioeconomic position of the city's major immigrant group – and hence decreased demand for state resources – brought about a reduction in economic scarcity.

In education, the school system had recovered from the large increase in schoolchildren and was able to absorb the new settlers and their children with relative ease by the early 1980s. In 1982, the school building that had been reopened to take in many of the refugees' children was shut down and the school that had consisted of mobile classrooms had merged with existing schools years earlier (Marrett 1989, 123–124). Many of the costs associated with education provision for refugees were covered by central government grants and thus did not place a burden on local taxpayers (Marrett 1993, 254), thereby preempting possible local fights over financing that would be in part directed toward ethnic others. Whereas in the late 1960s, Leicester's per student expenditures on education fell just below Birmingham's levels, several years later, they were more than twice as high.[46]

As a result of a variety of developments, housing pressures eased as well. First, beginning in the mid-1970s, large numbers of Leicester's white residents vacated houses in the Belgrave area because this section was scheduled for redevelopment. While these residents moved to adjacent neighborhoods in the city into recently completed housing estates, many Asian households filled the vacuum. However, the redevelopment did not end up taking place, ensuring long-term housing space for the immigrant population (Phillips 1981, 108; Nash and Reeder 1993, 27). Second, rather than demolishing substandard housing and thereby squeezing the housing supply further, the city council used central government monies to renew and renovate existing housing in

---

[43] Quoted in Troyna and Ward (1982, 455). The authors question this image of the city and present survey results (based on responses recorded in the fall of 1978) that show both the salience of immigration and race and the negative attitudes toward immigrants expressed by the majority of respondents in Leicester.

[44] *Leicester Mercury*, "Not Good Relations," April 16, 1980.

[45] *Leicester Mercury*, "Racial Attacks To Be Probed," May 7, 1982.

[46] HO 390/7: Urban Deprivation Unit, January 30, 1976.

an effort that included 14,000 homes. As a result, "Completed grant work indicates a rate of housing improvement better than that achieved nationally; the modest degree of housing disrepair continues to be the envy of most other English councils." Finally, additional residential dwellings were made available through the conversion of office space (whereas in Tower Hamlets, the reverse had taken place: Commercial buildings opened up at the expense of residential homes).[47]

These developments expanded the supply of adequate private housing and meant that Leicester's Asian population would not compete over council housing, as had been feared by many in the 1970s. In 1971 the share of Indian households in state-owned housing amounted to less than 4 percent, and by 1991 this figure had increased to only 8.8 percent.[48] Singh (2003, 45–46) also identifies the lack of competition for public housing as one important factor in helping to alleviate intergroup tensions. Large numbers of Indian settlers decided to remain in private, inner-city housing, while those with sufficient means moved to the suburbs.

Changes on the supply side that makes up local economic scarcity were also matched by changes on the demand side. Though many refugees from East Africa had professional, skilled backgrounds, upon arrival in Leicester they were disproportionately employed in menial jobs. Moreover, many had been forced to leave their financial assets behind in Africa. Initially, this population – whose demographic composition already made it more reliant on state services compared to primary labor migrants – was thus more likely to be in need of government assistance and less likely to contribute to the local tax base, putting pressures on local resources. Notwithstanding these initial setbacks, beginning in the mid-1970s the share of jobless Asians actually declined steadily, in spite of a generally unfavorable employment picture (Marrett 1993, 251). The occupational status and economic performance of Leicester's Indian population improved as young Asians continued to stay in higher education rather than take low-paying jobs during a recession and their parents' entrepreneurial background paid off in the private sector. In 1981, 13 percent of Leicester's Asians were unemployed, compared with 10 percent of the city's white population (Sills, Tarpey, and Golding 1983, 35–37). This gap is quite small, when compared with national trends: In the early 1980s, ethnic minority unemployment rates tended to be twice as high as overall rates (see Chapter 7). Over the years, this difference narrowed further and ultimately disappeared, in a development that is quite distinct from patterns in Birmingham, where the ethnic minority

---

[47] See Nash and Reeder (1993, 28–29). Government-financed home improvement grants were first started in the late 1940s to encourage landlords to modernize run-down housing stock. As the rate of low-income homeownership rose in the following decades, these grants were increasingly allocated to owner-occupiers who could not afford to repair and update their poor-quality housing. These policies were scaled down in the 1990s; see Leather (2000).

[48] Lomas (1975, 26) states that 3.9 percent of "coloured" households rented accommodations from the council. The 1991 figures are derived from "Table L49 Ethnic Group: Housing" (available at www.nomisweb.co.uk).

workforce continued to be much more likely to be unemployed than its white counterpart (see Table III.1 in Part III).

Most observers have linked this economic rise to Indians' commercial background and trading skills, especially in evidence among Indians who had come from East Africa. Indeed, 59 percent of shops on Belgrave Road (the main street running through the Gujarati Hindu settlement) were Asian owned in 1976; two decades later, there were thousands of Asian-owned businesses in Leicester (Seliga 1998, 234; Martin and Singh 2002, 13). Though not all of these businesses have been successful, a survey carried out between the economically difficult years from 1978 to 1984 showed that the survival rates of Leicester's Asian businesses far exceeded those of white businesses.[49]

The relative economic prosperity of the city's Indian population in turn allowed the city council to divide government funds more equitably across immigrant and nonimmigrant areas, further quelling sources of immigrant–native conflict. Beginning in the late 1970s, Leicester, like Birmingham, was on the receiving end of central government funds directed at inner-city wards experiencing urban decay and economic deprivation. Some of these funds came with few strings attached and thus afforded councilors "a degree of political largesse . . . making [them] at once both a politically attractive and powerful mechanisms."[50] Unlike in Birmingham, though, where the majority of funds ended up in white hands, Leicester's city council allocated these resources across white and nonwhite areas. For instance, in addition to targeting four inner-city areas containing high shares of ethnic minorities with resources from the Inner Area Program, the council included three almost exclusively white council estate areas located at the outskirts of the city in the priority zones that benefited from such funds (Sills et al. 1988, 68). Such actions were duly noted by the local paper, which in the run-up to the 1983 elections praised the ruling Labour group for having "worked ceaselessly to earn the affection and trust of both the vast army of council house tenants and ethnic minorities."[51] Since Labour's continued electoral success relied both on the ethnic and on the white working-class vote, equitable spending policies made political sense. But it is the relatively favorable economic position of Leicester's dominant ethnic

---

[49] During this time, 38 percent of white-owned businesses survived compared with 58 percent of Asian-owned businesses (McEvoy and Aldrich 1986, 35).

[50] Sills, Taylor, and Golding (1988, 68). The authors refer to the Inner Area Programme (IAP), which between 1979 and 1986 amounted to close to £11 million (153), and supported "a very considerable investment in employment and economic projects" (124). They note that though these funds were insufficient to bring about major improvements, they were "large enough to have made a significant difference to local groups in Leicester" (152).

[51] *Leicester Mercury*, "Labour To Keep Control," May 4, 1983. The editorial goes on to say, "True, Labour recently received a setback when the Indian Workers' Association Independent Labour Movement decided to contest Charnwood and Spinney Hill and they must be unhappy that the other two main parties also have Asian candidates. But even so, I believe that they have the majority of the ethnic voters sewn up – and that the Tories have allowed them to do this with very little opposition."

minority that has allowed politicians to distribute these finite resources across both groups in the first place.

In light of such reduced resource claims coming from the Indian community, attempts to maintain the racist backlash collapsed. When the BNP ran candidates in two wards with high shares of council tenants, they only attracted sixty-one votes (Rowley Fields in 1987) and fifty-four votes (New Parks in 1991), respectively. This failure is particularly striking when we consider that the Indian population had increased to more than 12 percent in Rowley Fields (see Table 6.3), providing further evidence that significant and rapid in-migration of a culturally distinct group in the context of few resource pressures does not provoke neighborhood xenophobia. As we saw in Chapter 5, in Tower Hamlets' Millwall ward, where the Bangladeshi population had increased to 8 percent and such demographic change *was* associated with the capture of scarce resources by a politically potent ethnic group, an entirely different native response ensued. Leicester's turnaround in intergroup relations is thus a direct result of "the limited claims that ethnic minorities [have] made on collective goods" in the city (Singh 2003, 51).

In sum, the settlement of Indian migrants, who had arrived as complete family units after having been expelled from East Africa, put strains on Leicester's resources, especially in the areas of education and housing. Since the Indian newcomers were able to use their electoral clout to secure a share of these scarce goods, a racist backlash followed. Over time, however, a reduction in economic scarcity – which was due to increased supply and decreased demand by an economically rising minority – caused intergroup tensions to subside. During a time of overall economic contraction and hardship, declining pressures in education, a relative absence of interethnic competition for state-allocated housing, and lessening ethnic minority demands for public resources transformed interethnic relations in Leicester.

Conclusion

This chapter has demonstrated that the electoral position of immigrant communities crucially shapes local parties' responses to them and, in turn, the potential for each type of immigrant conflict. The comparison has contrasted two cases that both experienced economic resource shortages, but that differed in the electoral strength of their immigrant populations. The chapter further showed that the alleviation of resource pressures over time caused a gradual decline in immigrant–native conflict.

In Birmingham, the fragmentation of large but ethnically diverse and internally divided immigrant groups deprived the newcomers of electoral leverage, even during electorally competitive times. When city politics came under Labour hegemony, the party's Old Guard was more concerned with maintaining white support and actively played on the cleavages dividing Birmingham's ethnic minorities. The lack of political pull among the city's immigrant groups and the ensuing marginalization of their economic needs helped to keep the anti-immigrant movement in check, but it ensured that Birmingham's South Asian and West Indian population developed grievances against a state that many considered to be opposed to their interests and needs.

In Leicester, agitation from the xenophobic right *was* a key concern for the city's Indian population. The degree of electoral mobilization of this group convinced even reluctant factions within the Labour Party to incorporate the needs of Leicester's Indians, even if this meant antagonizing white support-ers. Since Indians' political incorporation occurred during a time of shortages in education and housing, satisfying immigrant demands posed a threat to white economic interests. Moreover, the nature of Indian refugee immigra-tion, which consisted of large family units rather than single workers, further compounded pressures on municipal resources. As a result of this combina-tion of economic scarcity and immigrant political power, conflict between immigrants and natives was severe. Over the course of the 1980s, however, economic scarcity grew less intense and intergroup confrontations dissipated accordingly.

In the case of Leicester, then, changes in one of the two key variables driving immigrant conflict brought about changes in intergroup relations. By the same token, we can expect changes in political power – the other central variable determining immigrant conflict – to also cause shifts in conflict outcomes. In Birmingham, such a shift did indeed occur. Though the case studies have traced developments through the 1990s, it is instructive to briefly relate developments in the early 2000s. A notable development starting in the late 1990s has been the gradual increase of successful ethnic minority candidates that have run outside the established political parties (see Figure 6.2). Disgruntled with Labour's longtime neglect, Ali Kahn, former Labour member in the inner city, left Labour to become leader of the People's Justice Party (PJP):

We saw the Labour party running this city for decades and yet we saw little change in our own area. The high unemployment and poor housing continues. We thought we could make ourselves heard by campaigning from within the Labour party, to improve the inner city, but they weren't listening.... They've only listened [now] because we've taken their votes. If we finish tomorrow, they'll go back to their old ways.[52]

In 2000, when Labour only secured two more seats than the Conserva-tives, the new PJP came out on top in two wards and nearly stole a third seat from Labour. These victories, occurring against the backdrop of Labour's citywide decline, meant that the latter had to at times rely on the PJP to pass important pieces of legislation, such as the city budget and local tax rates.[53] As a result of the newly pivotal role of immigrant-origin candidates (which prompted "the council's Labour cabinet itself [to recognize] ... that the policies

[52] *The Guardian*, "Tough Justice," June 19, 2002.
[53] *Birmingham Evening Mail*, "Labour Vote Cuts It Fine for Tax Rise Budget Boost," February 4, 2004. In February 2004, The PJP had two councilors, both in Small Heath; the budget and corporate plan passed by two votes.

of the last two decades were a failure" (Garbaye 2005, 108)), Labour spear-headed new initiatives aimed at increasing the size of the ethnic minority public workforce.

Compared with their counterparts in Leicester, it has taken ethnic minorities in Birmingham much longer to secure an influential position in their city's electoral landscape. Yet, such a position, especially when harnessed to garner economic goods, has not been without costs. In the 2006 and 2007 local elections, the BNP contested all of the city's wards, averaging close to or over 10 percent of the vote[54] – results that had eluded the National Front from the 1960s onward.

[54] Author's calculations, based on electoral data available at http://www.birmingham.gov.uk/.

INTRODUCTION TO PART IV

The accounts of Tower Hamlets and Ealing and of Birmingham and Leicester have illuminated the specific developments and mechanisms that connect immigrants to electoral power; tie electoral power to access to scarce economic goods; and link up immigrants' access to such goods to conflict outcomes. Moreover, they have shown that conflict outcomes can vary within the immigration and citizenship frameworks of one country, variation which is in turn a function of immigrant electoral behavior and local political economies.

The remainder of this book brings the significance of national institutions and their interplay with local political economies into sharper relief. Chapters 7 and 8 investigate the implications of immigration and citizenship regimes for the economic and electoral variables that shape local-level immigrant–native and immigrant–state conflict. Chapter 7 explains immigrant conflict outcomes in Germany where guest-worker migration took place within the confines of a coordinated immigration regime and a closed citizenship framework. These institutions thus diverge from Britain's relatively uncoordinated arrival of migrants and its more liberal nationality code. Chapter 8 then turns to France, whose national postwar immigration regime and citizenship laws more closely resemble those of Britain, but whose local electoral institutions have been more difficult to penetrate by immigrant-origin newcomers, especially when set against the comparatively open ward-level system in which Britain's immigrant minorities have competed. Put differently, when juxtaposing Britain and France, the analysis reveals that similar national immigration and citizenship institutions meet differences in the parameters that shape local immigrant political power across countries.

To preview, Chapter 7 addresses the following question: Why has the incidence of both types of local immigrant conflict involving Germany's guest-worker population been low, particularly when contrasted with conflict patterns in Great Britain? The answer, I show, lies in the immigration regime that guided the recruitment and settlement of these labor migrants. Guest workers obtained employment, housing, and social services when economic times were good. Once economic conditions deteriorated and local resources came under pressure, rules and regulations guaranteed that natives would retain privileged access over these resources; compelled economically nonintegrated migrants to leave the country; and targeted the remaining immigrant population with integration measures that ensured a minimum standard of economic welfare. In short, local economic scarcity remained comparatively low, preventing both intergroup and antistate conflict from gaining momentum at the local level, even as political power eluded the guest-worker population. Yet, several decades after the inception of the guest-worker regime, its rules no longer apply and new economic and political realities shape the occurrence of immigrant conflict in Germany in the twenty-first century.

The chief goals of Chapter 7 are to explain conflict patterns involving the guest-worker population and its descendents, and to contrast these patterns with developments involving postwar migrants in Great Britain. But the chapter also shows how a radically different immigration regime – the unexpected inflows of ethnic German *Aussiedler* and asylum-seekers – resulted in dramatically different conflict patterns. In essence, by law these two groups were entitled to economic resources, even if such access disadvantaged the indigenous population. The law – rather than local electoral power – thus endowed these groups with the capacity to claim scarce goods and anti-immigrant mobilization ensued as a result. However, the law proved to be a less reliant vehicle for the acquisition of economic resources than electoral leverage. Facing native protests on the one hand and electorally nonpivotal immigrant groups on the other, politicians enacted legal reforms that scaled down migrants' opportunities to claim local economic goods. The incidence of immigrant–native conflict diminished as a result.

Chapter 8 begins by analyzing developments in France, where both types of local immigrant conflict have manifested themselves. I discuss France's postwar immigration regime, focusing primarily on how it provided for the employment and housing of its migrants, and address how the country's local political system has integrated the newcomers. Having established this broader context, the chapter then seeks to show that local economic resource shortages and immigrants' electoral leverage – or lack thereof – can help explain the varied conflict patterns we observe across French municipalities.

The rest of the chapter outlines the broad changes in immigration regimes, citizenship acquisitions, and local economic developments that have occurred across Western European countries beginning in the 1990s. In doing so, it sketches the institutional contours in which immigrants and natives face one another, as well as the state, in European cities in the early twenty-first century. The discussion thus departs from the in-depth, microlevel investigations offered in previous chapters and instead draws the reader's attention to the macro institutions that influence local economic scarcity, immigrant political power, and, hence, overall conflict levels.

7

Economic Integration, Political Exclusion, and Immigrant Conflict in Germany

In the early 1980s, when Great Britain had witnessed violent confrontations between ethnic minorities and the police and a host of cities had seen their share of anti-immigrant mobilization, policy makers and academics in Germany grew concerned about the future integration of the country's immigrant population. By 1980, the country was home to 4.5 million non-Germans, mostly guest workers and their dependents, and it had now become apparent that the majority of these economic migrants would remain in Germany. As rising numbers of immigrants coincided with rising numbers of unemployed, the topic of immigration and immigrant integration began to gain national salience. Nevertheless, contemporary observers who compared developments in the two countries noted that the settlement of immigrants had proceeded much more peacefully in Germany. In comparison to Britain, one author points out, there had been no violent or nonviolent "open conflict on a larger scale" between immigrants and natives in Germany (Koch-Arzberger 1985, 3). A government-commissioned report on youth violence also concluded that "immigrant youth in Germany, in contrast to Great Britain, have not participated in . . . violent confrontations" with the police.[1] Local anti-immigrant parties did not garner German voters' support either. Indeed, especially when placed in comparative perspective, the first decades of guest-worker settlement in Germany appear relatively peaceful; organized responses at the local level against the significant immigrant presence largely failed to gain momentum.

This contrast presents a puzzle. Germany and Great Britain share many similarities with respect to their postwar immigration histories. By the early 1980s, mass immigration had been taking place in both countries for nearly three decades. Most arrivals were economic migrants who had hoped to return to their homelands as economic success stories, but who ended up staying in the host countries. The majority of immigrants in Germany and Britain settled in urban centers, performed labor that had been left behind by the native

---

[1] BT Drs 9/2390, January 17, 1983, p. 29.

workforce, and was generally of a lower socioeconomic status than the average native worker. Immigration also brought ethnic and religious diversity to these traditionally Christian societies. Turks, the majority of whom are Muslim, constitute the largest single nationality group among Germany's immigrant population and Islam has become the second-largest religion in both countries. What, then, explains the varying patterns of immigrant conflict in Germany and Great Britain?

I argue that crucial differences in the two countries' immigration regimes and the ways in which these mapped onto each country's political economies account for these differential outcomes. In Great Britain, the legacy of the country's colonial past, rather than detailed economic plans, facilitated the settlement of millions. While these settlers had access to full political rights, few steps were taken to guide their economic integration. As the previous chapters have demonstrated, the inadequate supply of economic resources has been the root cause of immigrant conflict here, with variation in on-the-ground political power and claims making accounting for the type of immigrant conflict we observe when resources are scarce. In Germany, the pattern is reversed. Here, the state, employers, and organized labor were actively involved in fashioning the immigration regime. Economic considerations dictated the nature of postwar guest-worker immigration, and economic integration of immigrants into the country's labor market institutions occurred by design. Economically active, employed guest workers were incorporated into Germany's social market economy, while those who could not hold on to jobs were coerced or induced to leave the country. Political exclusion of labor migrants was the norm.

Furthermore, an economically based immigration regime was embedded in a more coordinated economic system and welfare state to contain competition between immigrants and natives and to reduce levels of economic dissatisfaction among immigrants. As the following pages will show, politicians and policy makers devised the rules and regulations of the guest-worker scheme not only with labor market and fiscal considerations in mind, but also to prevent both types of immigrant conflict from occurring. Immigrants were not to gain access to economic goods at the expense of natives, but policy makers also sought to forestall the emergence of an entrenched migrant underclass. The fear of social unrest – both between natives and immigrants and between immigrants and the state – became one of the guiding motives of immigrant policy in the 1970s and 1980s.

Rather than tracing local histories over time, this chapter focuses on the main features of a national immigration framework and how these shape the incidence of immigrant conflict in the places where newcomers settle. There are both practical and theoretical reasons for this approach. In contrast to the study of local-level immigration in Great Britain, fine-grained, longitudinal data on early postwar immigrant settlement and conflict are largely missing in the German case (perhaps reflecting the notion that the guest workers' stay was perceived to be temporary). While there is sufficient data to measure the existence or absence of immigrant conflict (i.e., anti-immigrant mobilization in the form of demonstrations, riots, and electoral success, and small-scale or major violent and nonviolent confrontations between immigrants and the state), descriptive studies of the sociopolitical effects of immigrant settlement over time in particular locations remain rare. Moreover, with regard to racist violence, German authorities do not publish data on right-wing extremist acts at the city level, but only at the highly aggregated level of the country's sixteen federal states (*Länder*).[2] On the theoretical side, the analysis seeks to demonstrate how an understanding of national immigration regimes and immigrant integration policies can help us make predictions about the ways in which immigrant conflict unfolds on the ground. For this reason, I focus on the area of the former West Germany, unless otherwise noted.[3]

The primary goal of this chapter is thus to demonstrate how differences in national immigration regimes and political economies explain variation in broad patterns of on-the-ground immigrant conflict across countries. But this chapter also addresses a second puzzle: Why was the relative absence of open conflict replaced by brief but fierce local-level anti-immigrant mobilization in some places in the late 1980s and early 1990s, over thirty years after initial guest-worker settlement? I argue that the different nature of immigration – unforeseen and unplanned by the state – and the type of immigrants who arrived – ethnic German *Aussiedler* and asylum-seekers with privileged access to state resources – account for the anti-immigrant activity. By law, *Aussiedler* and asylum-seekers were given priority over the allocation of resources, particularly housing, giving them and edge over the indigenous population. These legal stipulations thus effectively substituted for political clout, but they would soon be trimmed down, causing confrontations to decline.

The evidence presented in this chapter relies on primary and secondary sources. Government archival materials (e.g., policy memoranda, administrative guidelines, minutes of meetings and conferences, and correspondence between various government ministries; accessed until 1977) illuminate official motivations for the design and implementation of immigration and integration policies and their intended effects on immigrant conflict. I further consult archived parliamentary documents that shed light on the major concerns and policy initiatives as they relate to immigrant integration and conflict from the 1970s through the 1990s. The secondary literature provides further evidence on immigration and immigrant conflict, especially covering more recent years.

This chapter proceeds as follows. The first section spells out the rationale and design of the guest-worker regime and how its institutions helped reduce the probability of immigrant conflict. The second section demonstrates how these

---

[2] Other institutions sometimes publish statistics below the state level, but these data are subject to aggregation problems of a different kind. See Koopmans and Olzak for a discussion (2004, 208–209).

[3] Political and economic institutions as well as immigration regimes were obviously different in the German Democratic Republic. In the early 2000s, about 200,000 non-Germans (about 1.5 percent of the population) lived in the states of the former East Germany and the distribution of origin countries is quite different from that in the western *Länder* (many non-Germans hail from countries of the former Soviet bloc as well as Vietnam; only 12,000 Turks reside in the former East; see Statistisches Bundesamt 2007).

rules operated during times of economic recession and scarcity to restrict competition between immigrants and natives for employment, housing, and public
resources, thereby limiting the incidence of immigrant–native conflict. I then
show how policy makers simultaneously reduced the likelihood of immigrant–
state conflict by forcing or inducing economically unsuccessful migrants to leave
the country while implementing integration measures for those who stayed
behind. Next, I illustrate how the guest-worker regime on the one hand and
Britain's postwar immigration regime on the other are associated with differences in the economic position of migrants, make reference to cross-national
variations in local scarcity related to differences in social spending, and discuss
the economic implications of the demise of the guest-worker scheme at the end
of the twentieth century. The chapter then turns to a discussion of immigrant–
native conflict involving ethnic German *Aussiedler* and asylum-seekers in the
late 1980s and early 1990s and argues that it is these groups' entitlements to
state resources that explain the xenophobic mobilization. The conclusion syn-
thesizes the main argument and charts some of the principal features of contemporary immigrant integration and their implications for immigrant conflict
in Germany.

The Economic Logic of Guest-Worker Immigration
and the Prevention of Resource Competition

In the postwar years, the economic reconstruction of Germany was the dominant theme guiding national politics. When developments on the German labor
market pointed to future bottlenecks in key regions and industries, the guest-
worker program presented a seemingly convenient solution that would promote
the continued revitalization of the country's economy. Employers, unions, and
the state designed the temporary worker program in ways that would benefit
each of their constituencies. Employers faced tight labor markets and regional
labor imbalances that threatened to push up wages and impede production.
Unions, although initially skeptical, were not averse to immigration either. In
exchange for the inflow of low-skilled labor, German workers received a shorter
work week, more extensive education and training, and upward mobility. In
addition to facilitating the smooth functioning of the German economy, the
state valued the employment of immigrant labor for its anticipated beneficial
fiscal impact. Guest workers, especially if they were young and living without
dependents, were expected to contribute more to unemployment, pension, and
health insurance systems than they would take out, would put little pressure on
public resources such as schools and social services, and offered the additional
benefit of helping to stave off inflationary pressures, because of their tendency
to save and send money home.[4]

---

[4] These are just some of the economic considerations that shaped decision making on immigration
in the 1950s and 1960s. See Steinert (1995), Herbert (2001), and Schönwälder (2001) for more
detailed accounts.

TABLE 7.1. *Number of Selected Foreign Nationals in Germany According to Nationality, 1989 and 2003*

Nationality	1989		2003	
	No. of Foreign Nationals	Share of All Foreign Nationals (%)	No. of Foreign Nationals	Share of All Foreign Nationals (%)
Turkey	1,612,623	33.3	1,877,661	25.6
Former Yugoslavia[a]	610,499	12.6	1,054,705	14.3
Italy	519,548	10.7	601,258	8.2
Greece	293,649	6.1	354,630	4.8
Poland	220,443	4.6	326,882	4.5
Russian Federation	—	—	173,480	2.4
Portugal	74,890	1.6	130,623	1.8
Spain	126,963	2.6	125,977	1.7
Romania	21,101	0.4	89,104	1.2
Morocco	61,848	1.3	79,794	1.1

Notes: Note that as a result of reforms in Germany's citizenship laws, many foreign nationals have naturalized in the period between 1989 and 2003. Ethnic Germans or *Aussiedler* are generally not included here, because they obtain German citizenship.

[a] Includes Serbia and Montenegro, Croatia, Bosnia and Herzegovina, Macedonia, and Slovenia.

Source: Beauftragte (2005, 578, 581) and BT Drs 12/6960, March 11, 1994 (53).

With interests aligned in this fashion, Germany signed its first recruitment treaty with Italy in 1955. Treaties with Spain and Greece (1960), Turkey (1961), Portugal (1964), Tunisia and Morocco (1965), and Yugoslavia (1968) followed (see Table 7.1 for a population breakdown). The planning and execution of guest-worker migration was quite extensive. The Federal Employment Office (*Bundesanstalt für Arbeit*) and employers set up recruitment centers in the sending countries, offered language and job training, and arranged for the trip to Germany. In contrast to Great Britain, where several pieces of legislation aimed to curb large waves of initially unexpected postcolonial immigration by successively imposing economic guidelines, labor migration to Germany was only possible within the confines of a tightly governed system of rules and regulations. Even though their time in Germany was always meant to be temporary, during their stay guest workers would be fully integrated into the country's social market economy. Recruitment of individual workers was thus contingent upon the allocation of specific jobs that were subject to social insurance contributions (*sozialversicherungspflichtig*). Migrants who had been granted work permits were legally required to receive treatment in the employment and welfare fields that was equal to their German counterparts (*sozialrechtliche Gleichstellung*) and thus were employed under the same labor laws and collective bargaining agreements.[5] In 1971, the Federation of German Trade Unions

---

[5] See, e.g., Huber and Unger (1982, 131) and Kühne (2000, 45).

(DGB) also officially committed itself to representing the interests of Germans and guest workers on an equal basis. The latter joined labor unions and works councils in increasing numbers and, in later years, local and national union leaders welcomed their participation in collective activities and strikes (Kühne 2000, 54–58).

During the early years of recruitment, economic integration of immigrants thus occurred by design. Equality of treatment not only provided guest workers with a guaranteed level of compensation and benefits, it also reassured natives that the importation of low-skilled foreign labor would not negatively impact working conditions and would reduce downward wage pressures.

While guest workers were embedded in an already existing set of economic and social welfare laws, additional measures had to be taken to find accommodation for the hundreds of thousands of incoming workers. The recruitment treaties specified from the very beginning that employers would have to provide housing for the workers they had brought in from abroad, and the Federal Employment Office only placed foreign workers in a job once it could be verified that they could be housed. The Federal Employment Office also subsidized employer-provided housing and had spent DM 450 million on its construction by 1973. Housing types varied, but purpose-built hostels that housed migrants close to the factories that employed them were most common. Living conditions were quite modest, as employers were only asked to comply with housing laws dating back to the 1930s. Over the course of the 1960s, however, pressure from sending countries, the Federal Employment Office, as well as guest workers themselves led to successive improvements in these facilities. Moreover, in 1971, partly in reaction to the growing publicity that the poor-quality housing arrangements had provoked, the Ministry of Labor spelled out the minimum standards that these lodgings would have to meet in order to ensure "adequate and humane" accommodation.[6] Legislation made these guidelines binding in 1973 and required that they apply equally to German and foreign workers. In reality, guest workers who were housed in employer-provided hostels did generally not enjoy the same standards as their German counterparts. Government planners and employers justified this discrepancy by referring to the temporary nature of guest workers' stay, their intention to save and ensuing preference for cheap housing, and the lower standards that foreign workers were used to in their home countries (von Oswald and Schmidt 1999, 184–191; Herbert 2001, 214–216).

The rules governing guest-worker immigration thus ensured that, in the early years of immigrant arrival, competition with natives over housing, which had been so contentious in some British cities, generally did not take place. Additionally, the fact that guest workers' stay in the host country was contingent on holding a job, which in turn was subject to Germany's comparatively generous labor and welfare laws, further limited the incidence of economic hardship and

---

[6] B134/37467: Draft of a memo, "Foreign Workers; Increased Support for Housing Construction and Infrastructure," February 12, 1973.

deprivation among the immigrant population. When the Federal Employment Office commissioned a report to investigate how political and economic conditions in West European destination countries might affect foreign workers' migration decisions, the analysis concluded that "in the area of social benefits, Germany clearly presents the best option" for migrants.[7] Compared with other countries, Germany not only provided the most expansive unemployment and pension benefits, but it also was the most inclusive in incorporating foreign workers into its labor market and welfare institutions. Most foreigners seemed to share this assessment. According to the report, when a survey asked foreigners what they could learn from Germans, the majority (63 percent) put the country's social welfare system in first place.

Although the report praised the benefits of Germany's inclusive welfare laws, it conceded that "opportunities for political involvement have hardly developed." It went on to note, though, that "due to the dominance of economic motives, this lack in opportunities for political involvement has thus far surely only played a secondary role." Some localities had started including guest-worker representatives in advisory bodies, but few voices called for an expansion of immigrant political power at the local, let alone the *Land* or national, level. The report doubted that "dissatisfaction with political or social conditions" would lead any foreign worker to leave the country, but nevertheless suggested that guest workers who intended to stay in Germany for a prolonged period should be given the opportunity to have a say in deciding matters that were of concern to them.[8]

The call to extend the local franchise to non-Germans would be repeated many times over the course of the next few decades, but it never bore fruit. In the meantime, the great majority of guest workers and their dependents faced restrictive citizenship laws and remained excluded politically. This lack of local and national political leverage meant that politicians were generally predisposed to place the needs of their native constituents ahead of those of the newcomers. Just as in Great Britain, where we have seen that national policy makers and local politicians had been painfully aware that "doing too much" for immigrants would anger natives, German officials were careful not to cater too much to immigrant needs. While the provision of housing and employment did not prove contentious during the boom years of the 1950s and early 1960s, in later years, economic slowdowns and tighter housing markets in the larger cities prompted a more cautious approach to guest workers' economic integration.

In sum, the state, employers, and organized labor designed the guest-worker regime in ways that would limit competition over economic resources between the newcomers and the indigenous population. Relatively generous social

---

[7] B106/69849: Report by Anke Peters, Institute for Labor Market and Occupational Research, Federal Employment Office, entitled "The economic and political conditions in the Federal Republic as determinants for the choice of destination country," April 1972.

[8] Ibid.

benefits in turn guaranteed an adequate standard of living for migrant labor. Economic integration was, however, not matched by political inclusion; access to citizenship and electoral participation were mostly denied.

Immigrant Economic Integration in Hard Times: Germans First

Though the regulations of the guest-worker regime aimed to integrate migrant workers into Germany's labor market and welfare state, the same immigration regime made sure that Germans would be given priority in the distribution of jobs and housing once economic conditions deteriorated. This logic substantially reduced the scope for intergroup competition over economic resources.

Employment and Housing: Germans First

During the 1970s, with the era of full employment and economic expansion having come to an end, official policy making toward immigrants became more stringent. The most obvious outward signal of this new orientation came in 1973, when the government put a stop to any further labor migration. The ban coincided with the oil crisis and its anticipated economic repercussions, but employers and the government had become less interested in the continued inflow of foreign workers even prior to the oil shock. Employers began to view the future employment of low-skilled guest workers as an impediment to their interests in modernizing production, while the government was forced to revise its ideas about the anticipated fiscal benefits of the guest-worker scheme. The arrival of spouses and children had made the initial cost–benefit calculations obsolete. As one newspaper put it in 1971, "the non-integrated guest worker, vegetating on a very low standard of living, generates relatively minor costs of about DM 30,000. But in the case of full integration, claims on services totaling DM 150,000 to 200,000 per worker have to be assessed."[9]

In light of this new set of circumstances, the government began to pursue a more restrictive approach to migrant labor. While the principle of equal treatment in social and labor matters still applied to foreign workers in possession of a work permit, unemployed guest workers were now at a clear disadvantage. The Federal Employment Office and its local branches throughout the country were obligated to allocate jobs to foreign workers only if native labor was unavailable.[10] In 1974, when the national unemployment rate had more than doubled in the span of one year (see Table 7.2), the president of the Federal Employment Office sent a letter to all local offices insisting that the

---

[9] *Das Handelsblatt*, "Mehr Auslandsinvestitionen – weniger Gastarbeiter," January 23, 1971; cited in Herbert (2001, 227). On the changing cost–benefit calculations of employers and the state, see Herbert (2001, 226–229).

[10] B149/54450: Letter by the Federal Employment Office to all offices, November 13, 1974. This decree did not apply to the employment of workers from the European Community. Of the sending countries, only Italy belonged to the European Community at the time.

TABLE 7.2. *Foreign Population and Unemployment Rates in Germany, 1960–2000*

Year	Foreign Population (in thousands)	Share of Foreigners in the Overall Population (%)	Unemployment Rate	
			Foreign Population (%)	Overall Population (%)
1960	686	1.2	—	—
1968	1,924	3.2	1.5[a]	2.1[a]
1969	2,381	3.9	0.2	0.9
1970	2,977	4.9	—	—
1971	3,439	5.6	0.6	0.8
1972	3,527	5.7	—	—
1973	3,966	6.4	0.8	1.2
1974	4,127	6.7	2.9	2.8
1975	4,09	6.6	6.8	4.7
1976	3,948	6.4	5.1	4.6
1977	3,948	6.4	4.9	4.5
1978	3,981	6.5	5.3	4.3
1979	4,144	6.7	4.7	3.8
1980	4,453	7.2	5.0	3.8
1981	4,63	7.5	8.2	5.5
1982	4,667	7.6	11.9	7.5
1983	4,535	7.4	14.7	9.1
1984	4,364	7.1	14.0	9.1
1985	4,379	7.2	13.9	9.3
1986	4,513	7.4	13.7	9.0
1987	4,241	6.9	14.3	8.9
1988	4,489	7.3	14.4	8.7
1989	4,846	7.7	12.2	7.9
1990	5,343	8.4	10.9	7.2
1991	5,882	7.3	10.7	6.3
1992	6,496	8.0	12.2	6.6
1993	6,878	8.5	15.1	8.2
1994	6,991	8.6	16.2	9.2
1995	7,174	8.8	16.6	9.3
1996	7,314	8.9	18.9	10.1
1997	7,366	9.0	20.4	11.0
1998	7,320	8.9	19.6	9.4
1999	7,344	8.9	18.4	8.8
2000	7,297	8.9	16.4	7.8

[a] Figures are for 1967. Figures refer to the area covering the former West Germany.

Source: Herbert (2001, 238) and Beauftragte (2002, 441; 2005, 574).

guidelines were to be implemented by "applying strict standards in every single case." Local officials were not only ordered to give preference to Germans with similar qualifications as guest workers, but they were also instructed to encourage the placement of German individuals whose employment was seen to be of particular interest to national labor market policy (*arbeitsmarktpolitisches Interesse*); German part-time and older workers, as well as ex-convicts, were to be given priority over guest workers.[11] In the case of rising unemployment, then, the principle of equal treatment was replaced by the principle of "Germans first" (*Vorrang deutscher Arbeitnehmer*).

In the housing field, German households also generally fared better than their immigrant counterparts. By the 1970s, it had become apparent that the initial plans for accommodating guest workers had outlived their usefulness. Employers were obligated to provide housing for migrants they had recruited from abroad, but no such regulation existed for the employment of guest workers already residing in Germany who had moved on to another job.[12] As many migrants reunited with their families, they moved out of employer-provided hostels and sought housing, which, amid a general relaxation of the housing market, was a scarce resource in some of Germany's larger cities.

In the private rented market, the availability of older, substandard housing that had been abandoned by German households reduced competition between native and migrant families. On the basis of nationwide patterns, public officials concluded in 1975 that immigrant families generally rented older apartments that were no longer desired by German tenants as a result of the high rate of new building construction in the private and social housing sector.[13] The *Deutsche Städtetag*, an organization representing the interests of Germany's cities and towns, similarly noted that older housing stock that would have otherwise been scheduled for redevelopment was now occupied by guest workers (cf. Luft 2006, 125). Access to government-subsidized social housing[14] – the source of so much immigrant–native strife in Great Britain – was, in turn, virtually closed off to guest workers and their families. A government survey of the housing situation of immigrants in North Rhine Westphalia, the *Land* with the largest guest-worker population, showed that 85 percent of migrant households lived in prewar buildings and concluded that "immigrants hardly stand a chance

---

[11] Ibid.

[12] B134/37467: Draft of a memorandum, "Foreign Workers; Increased Support for Housing Construction and Infrastructure," February 12, 1973.

[13] B106/69849: Letter by the Federal Ministry of Land Use Planning, Building Industry and Urban Development (*Bundesminister für Raumordnung, Bauwesen und Städtebau*) to several federal ministries, August 15, 1975. The literature repeatedly mentions that immigrants moved into housing that had been deserted by natives. See, e.g., Pagenstecher (1994, 45) and Eberle (2007), whose work is entitled, "'If Someone Moved Out, Turks Moved In.'"

[14] Social housing in Germany refers to housing built with state subsidies but often not owned by the state. Local authorities either assign this type of housing directly to tenants or may give out permits that prospective tenants have to present to landlords. Rents as well as tenant incomes cannot exceed a designated ceiling (Häussermann 1994).

of obtaining social housing."[15] Another survey conducted in 1971 confirmed this assessment: It revealed that only 1 percent of guest workers lived in social housing.[16]

Officials had become aware of the disadvantaged position that the newcomers occupied in the housing market. As a result of foreign workers' language barriers and inexperience, guest workers often paid rents above market value in undesirable locations. To avoid the development of immigrant "ghettos" and the ensuing "decline in reputation" of this group, over the course of the 1970s, a larger number of social housing units would be opened up to guest workers and their families.[17] Though official guidelines prevented the explicit enactment of a policy that would assign guest-worker households apartments in the social housing stock that had been freed up by German tenants who moved into newly built units, such a practice, referred to as "tenant rotation" or "apartment exchange" (*Mieterrotation* or *Wohnungsaustausch*), was nevertheless unofficially endorsed and carried out locally.[18]

On the whole, housing did not represent a major source of grievance for the great majority of immigrants who had moved out of employer-provided accommodation. A representative survey, carried out by employment offices in 1972, found that of the 60 percent of guest workers who no longer lived in employer-provided housing, 80 percent were satisfied with their accommodation.[19]

To further alleviate some of the pressures on housing and other public resources such as education and social services, the federal government and the *Länder* decided to restrict the areas where guest workers could settle. The immigration ban had put a stop to new labor migrants' entering the country, but the government also wanted to regulate the movement of migrants within Germany. Some local governments had already banned immigrants from moving into their most overcrowded areas. In Berlin, for example, migrants were not allowed to settle in three districts where they were said to have put an

---

[15] B106/45161. This file contains BT Drs 6/3085, January 31, 1972, on which these numbers are based.

[16] See Mehrländer (1974, 183). This survey draws on the responses of 1,678 Italian, Greek, Spanish, Yugoslav, and Turkish guest workers residing in North Rhine Westphalia and Baden-Württemberg. At the time of the survey, 56 percent of guest workers hailing from these countries were employed in these two *Länder*.

[17] B119/5017: "Note for the Meeting with the European Community Commission – Social Affairs Directorate – Held May 9, 1974."

[18] Ibid. The Federal Employment Office said it welcomed such a policy, but could not provide financial assistance to facilitate tenant rotation, since its mandate was limited to the construction of new housing units.

[19] According to the survey, 60 percent of respondents were "content" (*zufrieden*) and 20 percent were "more or less content" (*einigermaßen zufrieden*) with their housing situation. The remainder was "not content" (*nicht zufrieden*). Information on guest workers living in employer-provided housing is not supplied. See B134/37467: Draft of a memorandum, "Foreign Workers; Increased Support for Housing Construction and Infrastructure," February 12, 1973. The author noted, however, that the presumed lower standards of guest workers as well as potential response biases should be borne in mind when interpreting the findings.

"increased burden" on social services.[20] Munich's city council had enacted a similar measure. The Ministry of Labor, along with representatives of the *Länder*, followed suit by banning guest workers from settling in areas where large inflows of immigrants had put a strain on public resources. In these so-called overburdened settlement areas (*überlastete Siedlungsgebiete*), which included cities and towns where the share of immigrants exceeded twice the national average of 6 percent, employment offices were prohibited from allocating jobs to immigrants for at least one year. Future allocations would only be allowed if the number of immigrants fell below a designated threshold. Individual *Länder* could, however, make use of one exception: Unmarried immigrants (whose use of local public services tended to be limited) were allowed to be assigned to jobs, even in overburdened areas – provided no Germans qualified for the position.[21]

The ban (*Zuzugssperre*) showed some signs of success. The Bavarian Minister of Labor praised the settlement restrictions for having halted a further rise in areas of guest-worker concentration and noted that the share of immigrants in Munich, where housing and public services had been stretched thin, had fallen by close to 7 percent.[22] Still, the program was eventually phased out in 1977, when employer associations and companies complained that constraints on immigrants' mobility had left many positions unfilled.[23]

To summarize, a system of rules and regulations operated to keep Germans from losing out in the competition over employment, housing, and public resources once these goods threatened to become scarce. While these resources had not been in short supply during the initial period of guest-worker recruitment when the German economy flourished and families had not yet reunited, local, state, and federal officials increasingly favored natives in the allocation of economic goods once economic conditions worsened and the immigrant population expanded to include spouses and children.

Immigrant Policy and the Prevention of Immigrant–Native Conflict

At the federal level, the preferential treatment of Germans was quite deliberately seen as a means to keep hostility against immigrants in check. For instance, when policy makers and organizations dealing with guest-worker questions recommended expanding special housing programs for guest-worker households in the early 1970s, government officials were wary of allocating increased funds

---

[20] B134/37467: Undated letter of the Berlin Senate to the Berlin House of Representatives.

[21] B 119/5136: Memorandum by the Federal Ministry of Labor, "Regulation of Migration of Foreign Workers into Overburdened Settlement Areas," October 22, 1974.

[22] B136/12893: Letter of the Bavarian Minister of Labor to the Chancellor's Office and other Ministries, February 12, 1976.

[23] In addition, the 1976 association treaty between the European Community and Turkey, which allowed Turkish guest workers who had been legally employed in Germany for at least five years to have free movement within the country, limited the effectiveness of the ban. The treaty did, however, contain an escape clause, whereby such movement could be restricted as a result of labor market considerations. Meier-Braun (1988, 14, 83) therefore claims that pressure on the part of business in the affected regions was the main reason for the ban's demise.

to these newcomers. "In light of the scarce housing supply among natives," an official noted, "any special program for guestworkers would not appeal to the native population and could possibly even lead to increased hostility against foreigners."[24] Even though officials acknowledged that existing housing programs were "insufficient," and had to be "subsidized to a greater extent," they nevertheless seemed to agree that "funds should preferably be raised without incurring additional charges on the federal budget and... should not be specially administered or distributed, if only so that the apartment-seeking domestic population were not given support for the allegation that foreigners were treated more favorably than Germans."[25] To achieve this end, the fees that employers paid for the recruitment of guest workers were to cover housing expenses and increased from DM 350 to DM 1,000. As a result, the monies that were set aside in the federal budget for additional housing specifically targeted at immigrants were either paltry or nonexistent.[26] Similarly, when confronted with the fact that many guest workers did not move into social housing because rents were considered too high, the federal government rejected a proposal to single out individual guest workers with a means-tested housing allowance that would go beyond the benefits received by the general population.[27] Finally, placing restrictions on the areas of immigrant settlement had also been conceived by the Ministry of the Interior as one of the "potential measures for the prevention of the emergence of xenophobia."[28]

The federal government, the *Länder*, and cities were thus certainly aware of the potential for conflict between immigrants and natives that could arise in a tense economic environment. Officials at the Ministry of the Interior, for

---

[24] B134/37467: "Memo Regarding the Construction of Apartments for Foreign Workers; Establishment of a Special Fund," November 21, 1972. Even in 1960, federal ministries rejected a proposal that would have housed guest workers in newly built terraced houses or higher-quality hostels, rather than in the eventual barrack-style accommodations, because they felt that funding for such housing should first go to benefit the German population (von Oswald and Schmidt 1999, 187).

[25] A handwritten comment remarked that such a strategy would be problematic, for "the 'underprivileged' can only be pulled up through 'privilege'." See B134/37467: "Memo Regarding Foreign Workers; Increased Subsidies for Housing and Services," February 12, 1973.

[26] In 1974, the Federal Employment Office had cut its funding for hostels, apartments, and day care centers for immigrant families and children from a planned DM 70.3 million to DM 28 million; see B119/5017: "Note for the Meeting with the European Community Commission – Social Affairs Directorate – Held May 9, 1974." In 1975, the Federal Employment Office received no funds to subsidize hostels or apartments for foreign workers in North Rhine Westphalia, where nearly 30 percent of all foreign workers lived; see B134/37467: Minutes of the Fifth Meeting of the Working Group "Apartments and Hostels," held March 12, 1975 at the Ministry of the Interior, Düsseldorf.

[27] B134/37467: Minutes of the Fifth Meeting of the Working Group "Apartments and Hostels," held March 12, 1975 at the Ministry of the Interior, Düsseldorf.

[28] B106/45159: "Foreign Workers in the Federal Republic of Germany – Possibilities and Limits of Their Integration in the Area of Interior Administration," January 23, 1973. The author did not think that such a measure would pass. He was concerned that restricting guest workers' geographic mobility would also impede their upward mobility and therefore violate the "widely accepted" principle of equal treatment.

example, collected local press clippings that dealt with latent intergroup tensions that had been building in cities like Munich, Frankfurt, and Berlin where the share of immigrants had risen from close to zero in the early 1960s to 18, 17, and 9 percent, respectively, by the mid-1970s.[29] But unlike Great Britain, where anti-immigrant candidates had run in local elections, large-scale violent confrontations between immigrants and natives had occurred, and a government task force was charged with investigating *existing* "racial strife," the emphasis in Germany was on the *prevention* of such conflict. As Schönwälder (2001) states in her comprehensive history of guest-worker migration and settlement, though isolated scuffles between migrant labor and German workers had occurred as the economy showed signs of weakening in the late 1960s, such conflicts "took place exclusively at the workplace and did not spill into cities" (174–175). Furthermore, despite increased negative coverage of immigration in the press, anti-immigration campaigns (*'Ausländer raus' Kampagnen*) did not materialize (204).[30]

By 1973, the government had not been aware of sustained local confrontations between immigrants and natives in Germany. Nonetheless, officials deemed it important to "avoid any undesirable developments" in this area and commissioned research projects to investigate the causes of potential hostility directed against immigrants.[31] Archival records show, then, that similar to deliberations in Britain, officials in Germany felt that competition over resources and the preferential treatment of immigrants in the allocation of economic goods would be the main source of intergroup clashes. In contrast to the situation in Britain, however, guest workers could not use electoral means to steer local resources their way. When economic conditions deteriorated, the government refrained from implementing programs that were seen to target immigrants directly with benefits, gave Germans priority in the allocation of jobs, and prevented migrant workers from settling in areas where public services were considered overloaded.

National Salience amid Local Inaction
By the early 1980s, as unemployment figures kept on climbing, so did the national politicization of immigration. In 1983, when 60 percent of Germans nationwide thought that the "foreigner problem" was "very important," conservative Chancellor Kohl stated categorically that "the number of foreign citizens must be reduced" and designated immigrant policy as one of his administration's central priorities (Mehrländer 1986, 104; Papalekas 1986, 8).

---

[29] See newspaper clippings, mostly from 1973, in B106/45166; see also B106/45167: "Share of Foreigners in the Residential Population of the Federal Republic," Bonn, February 27, 1976.

[30] Electoral campaigns of the far-right National Democratic Party (NPD) gained momentum in some localities in the late 1960s, but one cannot attribute these successes to immigration, since the party's main theme was the reestablishment of the Greater German Reich and the rejection of communism (e.g., Schönwälder 2001, 184).

[31] B106/45159: Internal letter, Ministry of the Interior, "Research Projects of the Federal Office for Population Research; Announcement of Research Contracts in the Areas of Foreigner and Citizenship Law," July 24, 1973.

To what extent, though, was the population's rising concern over immigration reflected in local-level mobilizations or violent confrontations? Many have argued that politicians, and especially the Kohl campaign, manipulated opinions toward immigrants for electoral reasons, rather than taking their cues from local protests over guest workers in the cities and towns where these migrants had in fact settled (e.g., Meier-Braun 1988, 26–27; Thränhardt 1995).

The few available local polls on the topic seem to confirm the notion that local intergroup relations were not riddled with conflict. Surveys conducted between 1978 and 1980 show that in Dortmund, an industrial city with a large Turkish population that had been severely affected by economic restructuring, two-thirds of respondents thought that German and immigrant families "lived well together." This finding was replicated in Berlin. These results not only applied to the cities as a whole but also held in the more derelict areas in need of redevelopment (*Sanierungsgebiete*) where immigrants had settled disproportionately (Arendt 1982, 134). Larger-scale violent confrontations between immigrants and natives also do not appear to have occurred in Germany during this time.

Local anti-immigrant movements received hardly any support from the native population, in spite of the publicity they attracted. In Hamburg, for example, a local party emerged in 1982 with the sole purpose to stop immigration (*Hamburger Liste für Ausländerstopp*). Even though its campaign had been covered by the national press,[32] the party's vote share never reached above 1 percent.[33] In the northern city of Kiel, a party dedicated to limiting the number of immigrants garnered 3.8 percent of the local poll in 1982, a result that some considered a success.[34] Indeed, it appears that the growing salience of immigration at the national level was not mirrored in town halls across the country. Anti-immigrant parties had not been elected. This lack of electoral success is particularly striking given that local electoral rules in Germany are based on proportional representation, which generally makes it easier for smaller parties to gain seats and should give anti-immigrant movements an edge over their counterparts in Great Britain, where candidates are elected according to plurality in single or multimember districts. But, as one observer noted, the "anti-immigrant climate" in Germany did not produce "organizational forms... [as] in England."[35] The few organizational manifestations of the anti-immigrant climate that did exist received little support.

[32] See *Der Spiegel*, "Ausländer: 'Das Volk hat es satt'," May 3, 1982.

[33] This result does not mask within-city strongholds; among Hamburg's 100 districts, the party scored over 2 percent only once, attracting 3.1 percent of all votes (local election results are available at http://www.statistik-nord.de/fileadmin/wahldb/index.php?site=votedb_tables).

[34] *Der Spiegel*, "Ausländer: 'Das Volk hat es satt'," May 3, 1982.

[35] See Tsiakalos (1983, 21). The author rightly goes on to say that it is difficult to quantify the clearly rising anti-immigrant climate in Germany (22). I do not question that sentiments against immigrants rose during the early 1980s, but when we consider measurable instances of immigrant–native conflict, such as electoral results or large-scale violence, we observe that Germany scores much lower on these indicators than does Great Britain.

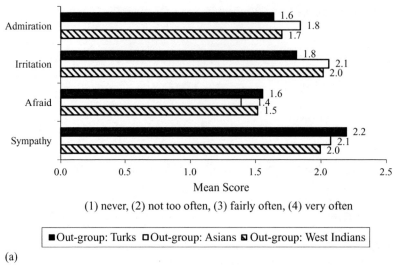

(1) never, (2) not too often, (3) fairly often, (4) very often

| ■Out-group: Turks □Out-group: Asians ◩Out-group: West Indians |

(a)

Now, I would like to ask whether you have ever felt the following ways about (out-group) and their families living here. For each feeling that I ask you about, please tell me whether you have felt that way very often, fairly often, not too often, or never.

Admiration   How often have you felt admiration for (out-group) living here?

Irritation   How often have you felt irritation at (out-group) living here?

Afraid   How often have you felt afraid of (out-group) living here?

Sympathy   How often have you felt sympathy for (out-group) living here?

FIGURE 7.1. Germany and Great Britain: (a) feelings toward the out-group; (b) reasons why immigrants don't do as well; (c) immigration policy opinion; (d) opinions about the out-group. *Source:* Eurobarometer 30 (see Reif and Melich 1992).

The lack of success of organized racism is not due to higher levels of tolerance among the German public, perhaps brought about in reaction to their country's shameful Nazi past. Opinion polls from the late 1980s reveal that prejudice against the Turkish minority was widespread and at least as pronounced as Britons' negative attitudes toward West Indians and Asians. Figures 7.1(a)–7.1(d) show responses to the same questions we encountered in Chapter 3. In the German case, the only out-group in question is the Turks (British results, pertaining to Asians and West Indians, are presented again to facilitate comparison). While Germans are slightly less likely than British respondents to blame racial and cultural characteristics for socioeconomic disadvantage, they are more likely than Britons to consider the out-group's values problematic for achieving success. Levels of social acceptance, such as those related to marriage and work, see Figure 7.1(d), are lower compared to British responses, and answers to other questions tap approximately similar levels of subtle and not-so-subtle prejudice.

Furthermore, it is worthwhile noting that the local electoral failures occurred *before* the government had enacted legislation to promote the return of

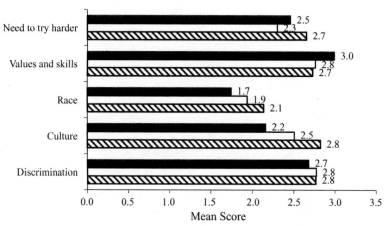

(1) Disagree strongly, (2) Disagree somewhat, (3) Agree somewhat,
(4) Agree strongly

■Out-group: Turks □Out-group: Asians ▣Out-group: West Indians

(b)

Please tell me whether you agree strongly, agree somewhat, disagree somewhat, or disagree
strongly with each of the following reasons why (out-group) living here may not do as well as
the German/British people in Germany/Great Britain.

Need to try harder	It is just a matter of some people not trying hard enough; if (out-group) would only try harder they could be as well off as German/British people.
Values and skills	(Out-group) living here teach their children values and skills different from those required to be successful in Germany/Great Britain.
Race	(Out-group) come from less able races and this explains why they are not as well off as most German/British people.
Culture	The cultures of the home countries of (out-group) are less well developed than that of Germany/Great Britain.
Discrimination	There is a great deal of discrimination against (out-group) living here today that limits their chances to get ahead.

FIGURE 7.1 (*continued*)

immigrants (see the subsequent text). Nationwide opinion, by contrast, seemed
to track government action. By late 1984, when return migration had reached
its peak, only 35 percent considered the "foreigner problem" to be very important (a drop of 25 points in the span of one year) and the topic ranked twenty-
ninth on the list of political problems confronting Germans (Papalekas 1986,
8). While national preoccupation with immigration decreased once the Kohl
government moved on to other policy areas, we again notice that circumstances
on the ground in the areas of immigrant settlement failed to compel natives to
support opposition movements even when immigration policy was nationally
salient. Immigrants and their families simply were not actual competitors in

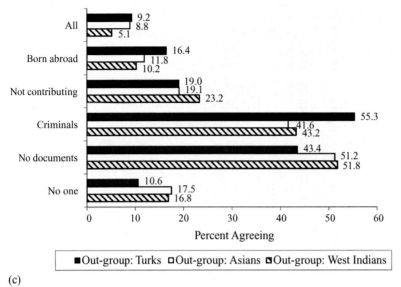

All

Born abroad

Not contributing

Criminals

No documents

No one

Percent Agreeing

■Out-group: Turks □Out-group: Asians ▨Out-group: West Indians

(c)

There are a number of policy options concerning the presence of (out-group) immigrants living here. In your opinion which is the one policy that the government should adopt in the long run?

All	Send all (out-group), even those born in Germany/Great Britain, back to their own country.
Born abroad	Send only those (out-group) who were not born in Germany/Great Britain back to their own country.
Not contributing	Send only those (out-group) back who are not contributing to the economic livelihood of Germany/Great Britain.
Criminals	Send only those (out-group) who have committed severe criminal offenses back to their own country.
No documents	Send only those (out-group) who have no immigration documents back to their own country.
No one	The government should not send back to their own country any of the (out-group) now living in Germany/Great Britain.

FIGURE 7.1 (*continued*)

the market for jobs, housing, and public services and therefore did not warrant organized or large-scale violent resistance at the local level.

To review, I have argued that organized mobilization against immigrants did not occur in Germany because natives did not lose out in the competition over material resources. In the early years of immigrant arrival, such resources were generally abundant. Once the supply of jobs, housing, and public resources tightened, government officials followed allocation rules that placed the needs of natives ahead of those of immigrants. The question that arises, then, is this: Why did politically disenfranchised immigrants not turn against the state when their economic situation became more precarious and state policies effectively discriminated against them?

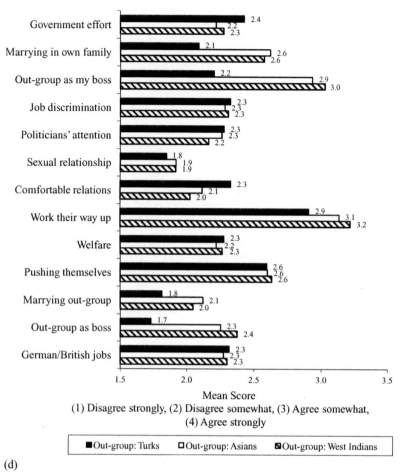

Mean Score
(1) Disagree strongly, (2) Disagree somewhat, (3) Agree somewhat,
(4) Agree strongly

| ■ Out-group: Turks | □ Out-group: Asians | ◩ Out-group: West Indians |

(d)

Now, I would like to ask you a few more questions about (out-group) and their families living here. Tell me as I read each of the following statements whether you agree strongly, agree somewhat, disagree somewhat, or disagree strongly.

Government effort	The government should make every effort to improve the social and economic position of (out-group) living in Germany/Great Britain.
Marrying in own family	I would not mind if an (out-group) person who had a similar family economic background as mine joined my close family by marriage.
Out-group as my boss	I would not mind if a suitably qualified (out-group) person was appointed as my boss.
Job discrimination	(Out-group) get the worst jobs and are underpaid in Germany/Great Britain largely because of discrimination.
Politicians' attention	Most politicians in Germany/Great Britain care too much about (out-group) and not enough about the average German/British person.

FIGURE 7.1 (*continued*)

Sexual relationship	I would be willing to have sexual relationships with a (out-group) person.
Comfortable relations	German/British people and (out-group) can never be really comfortable with each other, even if they are close friends.
Work their way up	Many other groups have come to Germany/Great Britain and overcome prejudice and worked their way up. (Out-group) should do the same without any special favor.
Welfare	Most (out-group) living here who receive support from welfare could get along without if they tried.
Pushing themselves	(Out-group) living here should not push themselves where they are not wanted.
Marrying out-group	Most German/British people would not mind if a (out-group) person with a similar family economic background as their own joined their close family by marriage.
Out-group as boss	Most German/British people would not mind if a suitably qualified (out-group) person was appointed as their boss.
German/British jobs	(Out-group) have jobs that the German/British should have.

FIGURE 7.1 (*continued*)

Between Exit and Integration: State Responses to Immigrant Economic Disadvantage

The absence of immigrant–state conflict during times of increased economic scarcity is a result of the economic foundations of Germany's immigration regime. In essence, when economic conditions worsened, the rules of the guest-worker program ensured a minimum standard of well-being on the part of migrants living in Germany by ordering or inducing the economically least successful foreigners to leave the country, while the principle of equal treatment stipulated that the remaining guest workers were covered by Germany's comparatively extensive social welfare benefits. The state took additional steps to ensure that this logic would operate, on the one hand, by providing incentives for dissatisfied immigrants to exit, and, on the other, by attempting to economically integrate those migrants who had decided to stay.[36] The fear of future social unrest in case of large-scale immigrant unemployment and socioeconomic marginalization was a central motive for economic integration policies.[37] At the same time, as we have seen, politicians were not often inclined to allocate resources to a nonvoting constituency, especially if such measures appeared to put voting natives at a disadvantage. As a result, integration policies that were specifically targeted at immigrants remained rather modest in nature. Nevertheless, for most of the 1970s and 1980s, balancing immigrant and native needs in this fashion proved sufficiently effective in limiting economic hardship and

---

[36] Joppke (1998) argues that legal as well as moral constraints prevented the government from pursuing the nonvoluntary return of foreigners.

[37] Guiraudon (2002) also identifies the maintenance of social peace as an important policy consideration and further argues for the relevance of the judicial system in the granting of migrant social rights.

keeping discontent among the country's migrant population at bay – even in the face of political exclusion.

The Absence of Immigrant–State Conflict

In Great Britain, archival evidence has shown that, by the early 1970s, migrant hostility against state actors had alarmed policy makers and politicians. In the 1980s, this opposition would erupt into large-scale riots. In Germany, by comparison, first- and later-generation guest workers did not engage in such violent confrontations with the state.

Official reports of smaller-scale clashes or peaceful resistance – widespread in British official correspondence – that the secondary literature might have missed failed to turn up as well in archival materials, in spite of the numerous documented occasions of discussions concentrating on the nature and effects of immigrant settlement in Germany. During the 1960s and 1970s the interior ministers of the *Länder* met frequently at conferences to discuss, among other things, the domestic security implications of the growing immigrant presence. In addition, *Länder* representatives responsible for immigration questions (*Ausländerreferenten*) met to exchange information several times a year. The reports of these conferences and meetings do not mention instances of low-level or large-scale confrontations between immigrants and state actors (nor do they mention clashes between immigrants and natives).[38] This absence was not for lack of surveillance; at the National Archives an entire folder is dedicated to the monitoring of immigrants' political activities by the Ministry of the Interior.[39] The political activities of immigrants were closely watched, if only to avoid the "infiltration of communists" (Pagenstecher 1994, 29). When officials expressed concern with violent protest on the part of immigrants, it was limited to crimes committed against institutions or individuals of the foreigners' home countries. Croatian and Turkish nationalists or militant supporters of the Greek and Palestinian resistance movements, and their intentions to "carry out their differences illegally on German soil," were considered a danger to the country's security, but no mention was made of activities directed against the German state.[40]

It is unlikely that migrants' residence status in Germany (which was generally less secure than that of their counterparts in Britain) prevented them from engaging in antistate behavior, for fear of deportation. The clashes that had been documented in Britain in the 1970s were still minor in nature and

---

[38] For the contents of these conferences and meetings, I examined the following files: B106/39995, B106/39996, B106/60299, and B106/60300, which cover the years 1965 to 1976 (for conferences of the interior ministers) and 1971 to 1973 (for meetings of the *Ausländerreferenten*). Schönwälder (2001) draws on files from previous *Ausländerreferenten* meetings, and does not mention instances of immigrant–state conflict either.

[39] See file B106/69888, entitled "Organizations of Migrant Workers in the Federal Republic of Germany, 1956–1980."

[40] B106/45159: Report, "Foreign Workers in the Federal Republic of Germany – Possibilities and Limits of Their Integration in the Area of Interior Administration," January 23, 1973.

fell short of criminal activity that would have warranted arrest or, in the German case, deportation. Moreover, by the late 1970s, German authorities had enacted administrative guidelines that severely circumscribed the possibility of deporting second-generation migrant youth who had grown up in Germany based on criminal conduct and even multiple convictions. Finally, while immigrants could not participate in elections, German law allowed non-Germans to voice their grievances through organizations, petitions, and demonstrations.[41]

Exit, Economic Integration, and the Threat of Unrest

The absence of immigrant–state conflict is due to the economic features of the guest-worker regime. As the term suggests, the overriding rationale of the guest-worker scheme was to employ migrants temporarily in jobs that natives would not or could not do. As a result, foreign workers who were unemployed, had used up their unemployment benefits, and did not receive a renewed work permit were supposed to leave the country. The assumed flexibility of imported labor to adjust to economic fluctuations had, after all, been a major selling point of the guest-worker program (Piore 1979). In the mid-1970s, when surveys showed that 60 to 70 percent of guest workers intended to stay for a prolonged period of time or even for good, these restrictive measures were still in place.[42] Guest workers who were not able to find work once their unemployment benefits had expired had to draw on social assistance (*Sozialhilfe*) and were subject to deportation once these payments exceeded a period of three months. A proposal suggested relaxing this rule, so that these workers would remain available to employers once the economy picked up again, but it failed to gain support.[43] The exportation of unwanted labor was to remain a policy objective and, according to the Ministry of Labor, a substantial number of guest workers were leaving thanks to the "restrictive execution" (*restriktive Handhabung*) of existing law.[44] Such stringency was considered "justified, because the danger of radicalization of unemployed immigrants was very large."[45]

Return migration was extensive. Millions of foreigners left the Federal Republic during the 1970s, and between 1974 and 1977, when the employment outlook was gloomy, net migration to Germany was negative.[46] According to

---

[41] See Huber and Unger for a discussion of deportation practices and migrants' political rights (1982, 143–144, 181–182).

[42] B134/37467: "Memo Regarding the Construction of Apartments for Foreign Workers; Establishment of a Special Fund," November 21, 1972. Guest workers who had obtained a "special work permit" (*besondere Arbeitserlaubnis*) were exempt from these measures.

[43] B149/54451: "Report of a Meeting of the Government and *Länder* Representatives Responsible for Matters Related to Immigration," April 22–23, 1975 (*Ausländerreferentenbesprechung*).

[44] B149/54452, prepared document for the presidents' meeting (*Sprechunterlage für die Präsidentenbesprechung*), July 14, 1975.

[45] B149/54451: Internal letter, Ministry of Labor, January 29, 1975, referring to a proposal that would have offered immigrants half of their unemployment benefits in one lump-sum payment to provide incentives for return.

[46] Author's calculations, based on Herbert (2001, 384).

a high-ranking official at the Ministry of Labor, the large-scale departure of unemployed migrants had provided "noticeable relief for the German labor market and contributed to the Federal Republic being spared major social and economic conflicts" (Bodenbender 1982, 52). Indeed, for most of the 1970s, the unemployment rate among immigrants was not significantly higher, and initially even lower, than that of their native counterparts (see Table 7.2).

Despite these developments, politicians and policy makers followed the inauspicious trends in foreigners' economic status and became anxious that some of those who stayed would decide to voice their discontent with their deteriorating economic situation. The guiding principles of foreigner policy (*Ausländerpolitik*) were thus to maintain the immigration ban, encourage guest workers to leave, and integrate those who stayed behind.[47] The socioeconomic integration of second-generation immigrant youth had already emerged as an important issue in the early 1970s.[48] Having surveyed the generally unfavorable educational and economic performance of guest-worker children, public officials began to contemplate the potential law-and-order implications of an entrenched immigrant underclass. Similar to Great Britain, officials in Germany looked to the "grave instances of civil strife" in the United States with concern and concluded that Germany would also have to face "serious social conflicts" if migrants were to be permanently disadvantaged economically.[49] Some likened the continuation of immigration and the associated emergence of an underprivileged, low-skilled second generation to the "import of social explosives" that would eventually threaten the state.[50]

Actors outside of government had also recognized the potential social costs that could arise if immigrant youth were not integrated economically. In a letter to the Ministry of Labor, the Federation of German Trade Unions (DGB) urged the government to institute policies that would allow immigrant youth greater access to the labor market. The "dangers" associated with a failure to do so, not only "for immigrants themselves, but for the state and society as a whole," the DGB warned, would far outweigh the perceived labor market benefits that resulted from the exclusion of the second generation.[51] In 1978, the Christian Democratic Party (CDU/CSU) called on the government to make the improvement of the economic opportunities of immigrant youth a policy priority. Children of guest workers, now numbering close to 1 million, lagged behind their German counterparts in education, employment, and occupational

---

[47] BT Drs 9/1629, May 5, 1982.

[48] When one is speaking of the 1970s, it would be more accurate to speak of the "1.5" generation, as is common in studies of immigrants in the United States. Individuals of this generation are born in the sending countries, but largely grew up in the host country.

[49] This was the assessment of a 1972 study based on conditions in Munich. Its findings were summarized by the Federal Ministry of the Interior in an undated document; see B106/45167.

[50] The Bavarian Ministry of the Interior expressed this opinion; see B119/5135 (the letter is undated but is most likely from late 1972 or early 1973).

[51] B149/54452: Letter from the DGB national executive board (*Bundesvorstand*) to the Ministry of Labor, February 2, 1976.

mobility. If no significant changes occurred, immigrant youth would "one day organize and rebel against their approaching fate."[52] Local officials similarly perceived the "masses of school dropouts as a 'ticking time bomb'" and press coverage spoke of the danger to domestic security if immigrant ghettos and "Harlem-like" conditions were allowed to develop (cf. Pagenstecher 1994, 45–46).

In view of these alarming forecasts, the federal government made the economic and social incorporation of the second generation the "overriding goal" of its overall integration framework.[53] Social support centers that had been originally established to offer guest workers advice and support on a temporary basis were to be continued and expanded. "[I]n light of the current difficult employment situation" these institutions would "show immigrants ways to overcome their problems while at the same time counteract the development of dissatisfaction and aggression."[54] Under the leadership of Social Democratic Party (Sozialdemokratische Partei Deutschlands, or SPD) Chancellor Helmut Schmidt, more liberal rules in the area of youth employment were enacted.[55] The government also encouraged the Länder to institute integration measures in the area of schooling and youth supervision (e.g., German language courses, homework assistance, and teacher training). Starting in 1976, the Ministry for Youth, Family and Health ran additional programs to promote the supervision and support of youth in inner cities and the government implemented measures that provided practical and pedagogical help to ease the transition from school to work.[56] Finally, in addition to the federal government's integration agenda, the late 1970s witnessed a lot of activity in many Länder, which proposed and instituted integration plans alongside federal programs (Meier-Braun 1988).

However, the emphasis on integration soon gave way to a renewed focus on return migration. During the second half of the 1970s, unemployment rates had fallen steadily but, by 1981, following the second oil crisis, numbers were on the rise again (see Table 7.2). Moreover, the unemployment rate among immigrants started diverging from that of the population as a whole. With the great majority of immigrants employed in blue-collar work in sectors that were generally on the decline (see Table 7.3), policy makers did not expect this trend

---

[52] BT Drs 8/811, May 17, 1978.
[53] BT Drs 8/2716, March 29, 1979.
[54] B106/69849: Excerpt from an unsourced document entitled "Integration Measures" (Integrierende Massnahmen) contained in a 1975 file on the "Overall Concept for Immigrant Policies, Integration and Incorporation" (Gesamtkonzeption für die Ausländerpolitik, Integration, Eingliederung).
[55] Initially, children of guest workers were only granted work permits if they had entered Germany before 1975, but this date was later extended by two years and eventually replaced by a two-year waiting period, which could also be shortened in the case of educational and language training. Spouses who joined their partners in Germany were required to wait four years until they could apply for a work permit. See Meier-Braun (1988, 13) and BT Drs 8/2875, June 13, 1979.
[56] BT Drs 9/1629, May 5, 1982, pp. 8–13. See also Faist (1995).

TABLE 7.3. *Selected Sectors with a High Share of Foreign Employees, 1981*

Sector	No. of Foreign Employees	Foreign Employees as Share of All Employees (%)
Sectors with a high share of foreign employees		
Foundries	31,785	26.8
Fishing, fish farming	820	23.0
Restaurants and lodging	87,411	22.1
Textile processing	61,770	19.5
Plastics processing	63,955	18.8
Steelworks, cold forming	48,909	17.9
Iron and sheet metal goods	67,595	17.4
Paper conversion, book binding	17,377	16.4
Road vehicle manufacturing	150,053	16.0
Pulp	9,884	15.7
Glass	11,978	15.5
Iron and steel manufacturing	49,875	15.1
Electrical engineering	149,753	14.6
Construction	173,464	14.5
Mining	31,715	12.9
Mechanical engineering	104,289	10.2
Most common economic sectors among foreign employees		
Construction	173,464	9.0
Road vehicle manufacturing	150,053	7.8
Electrical engineering	149,753	7.8
Retail	123,521	6.4
Mechanical engineering	104,289	5.5
Restaurants and lodging	87,411	4.5

Note: In 1981, foreigners constituted 9.2 percent of all employees.
Source: BT Drs 9/1629, May 5, 1982.

to abate in the near future. As a result, the SPD-led government reordered its priorities and now officially placed the "strengthening of the willingness to return" ahead of the integration of immigrants.[57]

Helmut Kohl's Christian Democratic Party–Free Democratic Party (CDU–FDP) coalition government also pursued return policies vigorously. It passed legislation that would award "return bonuses" (*Rückkehrprämien*) to immigrant workers who had become unemployed as a result of factory closures or who had been ordered to work shorter hours as a result of falling demand (*Kurzarbeit*). Though this law applied to a relatively small number of guest

[57] BT Drs 9/1629, May 5, 1982.

workers, it targeted those who had been employed in the sectors of the economy that were not expected to recover in the near future, such as steel, mining, and shipbuilding. In the state of North Rhine Westphalia, for example, every third application for return bonuses came from workers in the ailing steel industry. Companies themselves also offered financial compensation for departing guest workers (Körner 1986, 69; Motte 1999, 179; Kühne 2000, 47; Herbert 2001, 256). Other regulations allowed guest workers to buy out their pension contributions, provided they left the country with their dependents – a policy that also proved beneficial for Germany's treasury.[58] The government also provided financial support for the reintegration of migrants into their home countries.[59] To reduce barriers to return further and assist with the adjustment in the countries of origin, home-bound guest workers would be allowed to carry over home savings and loan agreements signed in Germany without financial penalties.[60]

The Federal Employment Office attributed the reduction in the unemployment rate among immigrants in 1984 to return legislation.[61] Indeed, 15 percent of all Turkish citizens residing in Germany (the group who had been hardest hit by unemployment) left the country that year alone.[62] Moreover, just as had occurred a decade earlier, the Federal Employment Office sent a circular to all local branches, reminding them to strictly follow existing guidelines that gave Germans preference in the allocation of jobs over unemployed migrants, who, in turn, would become reliant on social assistance, which remained grounds for deportation. Critics considered this policy a deliberate government tactic to bring about an "involuntary return via administrative pressure."[63]

To sum up, immigrant–state conflict did not hit German streets even when economic conditions declined as a result of the economic foundations of the guest-worker regime. The state encouraged or coerced foreign workers that

---

[58] In previous years, guest workers had to wait two years before they could claim these contributions. The share that had been paid in by the employer remained, however, in Germany's coffers. The government estimated that its return policies had produced short-term savings of DM 320 million in unpaid unemployment and child benefits. The projected net savings for the state's pension system amounted to DM 2.5 billion; see BT Drs 10/2497, November 26, 1984.

[59] Previous administrations had already made financial assistance for this purpose available. Legislation providing for specific incentives for return had been delayed because the government feared wasting resources by targeting foreign workers with return bonuses who intended to return anyway; see BT Drs 9/1629, May 5, 1982.

[60] BT Drs 10/4450, December 4, 1985.

[61] BT Drs 10/2497, November 26, 1984. While the number of returnees is not in dispute, some have challenged the government's assertion that the legislation was the immediate cause for the rise in out-migration (cf. Motte 1999).

[62] According to one estimate, approximately half of all Turks who lived in Germany between 1960 and 1983 had returned by 1984 (Jamin 1999, 157).

[63] The Hamburg Senate expressed this opinion. This time, however, this ruling disadvantaged a smaller share of immigrants. Approximately 60 percent of foreign workers had been in Germany long enough to have obtained a "special work permit" (*besondere Arbeitserlaubnis*), which excluded this group from the discriminatory practice; see Hamburg Drs 11/1887, January 3, 1984.

were no longer of use to the German economy to exit, while targeting integration measures at those who stayed behind. Electoral disenfranchisement, meanwhile, remained the norm.[64] The Kohl government rejected legislative proposals to ease naturalization requirements for second-generation immigrants and explicitly ruled out the notion that Germany had become a country of immigration (*Einwanderungsland*) (Mehrländer 1986, 103).

The Guest-Worker Regime in Context

Balancing economic integration with coerced or voluntary exit and political exclusion worked for a while to prevent both types of immigrant conflict from emerging, but it did not become a sustainable approach. In the coming decades, the second- and third-generation immigrant-origin population rose steadily and would have to be integrated into German labor market institutions and local public infrastructures. Improvements in the residence status of immigrants who had long resided in Germany meant that return would no longer apply to the majority of guest workers.

Immigrant Economic Integration in Germany and Great Britain
An over-time and cross-country comparison illustrates the initial effectiveness of the guest-worker regime in keeping economic disadvantage in check and also depicts the effects of this system's demise. Figure 7.2 plots the unemployment rates of immigrants in Germany (i.e., the non-German population) and ethnic minorities in Great Britain, while Figure 7.3 charts the ratio of these groups' unemployment rates to overall unemployment rates (data based on ethnicity are unavailable in Germany, though the low naturalization rate of immigrants should capture most of this population).[65] Initially, unemployment rates among immigrants in Germany were very low, even below overall rates. Over time, the number of jobless immigrants in Germany increased, as did the unemployment gap between natives and immigrants. The large-scale exit of many guest workers during the difficult 1980s coincided with a temporary

---

[64] Throughout the late 1970s and 1980s, various voices (the Greens and the Social Democrats, welfare organizations, unions, the Protestant church, as well as the government's appointee for immigrant matters) had lobbied the government to extend the local franchise to immigrants. In the late 1980s, two states, Schleswig-Holstein and Hamburg, had tried to enact local voting rights for non-Germans, but these measures were ruled unconstitutional: Immigrants were not considered part of the German people (*Volk*) and hence not entitled to vote. See, e.g., Huber and Unger (1982, 172), Meier-Braun (1988, 15–16) and Kühne (2000, 48–49).

[65] Germany: Unemployment rates refer to the non-German population for all years. Great Britain: Unemployment rates up to 1971 refer to persons born in the New Commonwealth; between 1971 and 1972, figures refer to persons born or whose parents were born in the New Commonwealth. Starting in 1973, unemployment rates cover the population of West Indian, African, Indian, Pakistani, and Bangladeshi origin. Between 1973 and 1983, figures refer to the average of the male and female unemployment rates. For all others years, original sources contained overall ethnic minority unemployment rates. British unemployment rates for the years up to 1971 exclude youth unemployment, i.e., school leavers.

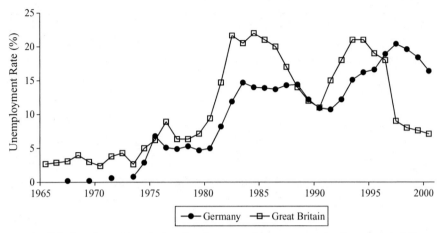

FIGURE 7.2. Immigrant or ethnic minority unemployment rates in Germany and Great Britain, 1965–2000. (*Sources:* Field et al. 1981, 22; Office for National Statistics 1997, 300; Herbert 2001, 238; Leslie, Lindley, and Thomas 2001, 377, 379; Beauftragte 2002, 441; and Labour Force Survey 2006. See footnote 65 for more information.)

reduction in immigrant unemployment and brought rates closer to those of German citizens. Since the late 1980s, unemployment rates of immigrants in Germany have tracked those of the German workforce, but at considerably higher levels (see also Table 7.2).

Turning to Great Britain, we observe substantially higher unemployment rates among ethnic minorities during most of the 1980s as well as a much larger gap between ethnic minority and overall unemployment. In 1984, for

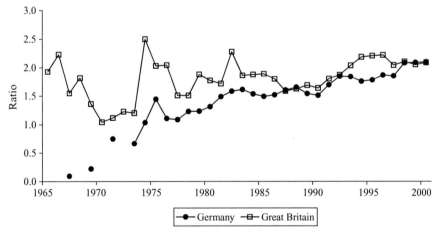

FIGURE 7.3. Ratio of immigrant or ethnic minority unemployment rates to overall unemployment rates in Germany and Great Britain, 1965–2000. (*Notes* and *sources:* See Figure 7.2.)

example, when overall unemployment rates in Germany and Britain were 9.1 and 11.7 percent, respectively, the difference between immigrant and overall unemployment rates was 4.9 percentage points in Germany, compared to 10.3 points in Britain, illustrating that the recession was even more disproportionately borne by Britain's ethnic minorities. Economic integration and large-scale return had resulted in a smaller gap in Germany, even when over 70 percent of foreign workers in Germany were blue-collar workers at the time.[66] The ratio of immigrant unemployment to overall unemployment in Britain almost always exceeds the ratio we observe in Germany (Figure 7.3). Yet, as time has passed, return migration faded, and later generations of migrants have joined the workforce, this difference has narrowed.

Finally, the decision to open up German labor market institutions, including vocational training, to descendants of guest workers also had *comparatively* favorable effects on youth unemployment. In both Germany and Britain, ethnic minority youth unemployment rates have been approximately twice as high as overall youth rates; but in Germany, this rate was 15.4 percent among immigrant (non-German) youth, compared to 28.1 percent among ethnic minority youth in Britain.[67] In sum, during times of overall economic decline, Germany's immigration regime performed better in reducing levels of economic disadvantage among immigrants than did its British counterpart, where immigration had largely eluded state and economic planners.

In addition to ethnic minorities' relatively better labor market integration in Germany – and hence reduced economic needs at the local level – when compared to Great Britain, Germany's more expansive welfare state also reduced economic pressures in cities and towns where immigrant-origin minority communities had settled. As is well known, social expenditures (covering, among other things, benefits to families, the elderly, the unemployed, or those in need of housing) have been more generous in Germany (Esping-Andersen 1990). Though both countries aggressively cut back on these expenditures in the 1980s, overall spending levels always remained substantially higher in Germany. Whereas the logic of the guest-worker regime kept unemployment at relatively lower levels, more wide-ranging welfare support ensured that economically disadvantaged immigrant-origin minorities in Germany – as well as the indigenous population – were at lower risk of encountering economic scarcity compared with these populations in Britain. These differences have had significant impacts on the incidence of immigrant conflict.

---

[66] In 1987, over 70 percent of economically active immigrants were "workers" (*Arbeiter*), whereas less than 20 percent were white-collar employees (*Angestellte*); see BT Drs 12/6960, March 11, 1994.

[67] These figures refer to 1987 (for Germany) and to 1991 (for Great Britain). In 1987, the unemployment rate of non-British (as opposed to ethnic minority) youth was 15.9 percent. This figure is less useful for our purposes since the great majority of immigrants and their descendants in Britain are British citizens. For 1987 figures, see Werner and König (2001, 12–13); 1991 figures are available at www.nomisweb.co.uk.

TABLE 7.4. *Housing Amenities: German and Foreign Households (%)*

Amenity	German Nationals			Foreign Nationals		
	1984	1989	1998	1984	1989	1998
Toilet	97	97	98	84	89	98
Bath	97	98	98	76	85	97
Central heating	81	84	93	53	58	84

Source: Beauftragte (2005, 103).

The Demise of the Guest-Worker Logic

Nevertheless, with the demise of the guest-worker scheme, the labor market position of first- and later-generation immigrants in the economy has become more vulnerable, residential concentration in low-income neighborhoods has taken hold, and overall developments have been mixed. In the housing field, immigrants have seen gradual improvements over the decades and, as Table 7.4 shows, the level of amenities in housing occupied by immigrants is close to the standards enjoyed by their German neighbors. These improvements are partly due to immigrants' increased access to social housing. Many of these apartments are, however, in large housing estates at the outskirts of cities that had been vacated by Germans. While the quality of housing has thus increased, the immigrant-origin population tends to cluster in areas with a higher concentration of economic deprivation and joblessness. Studies have also shown that discrimination still persists in the private market. Immigrant households still pay higher rents for less space and have to allocate a larger share of their incomes to housing as a result (Beauftragte 2005, 101–111). Though immigrant-origin minorities have thus been more likely than the indigenous population to live in economically deprived neighborhoods, a government report concluded that the state's social safety measures "in case of unemployment, sickness and disability as well as the state's involvement in housing construction have so far prevented... [the type of] social exclusion described in American cities" from occurring in Germany (Beauftragte 2005, 107).

In the area of education and labor market entry, improvements have taken place amid continued disadvantage. Over the decades, immigrants have become less likely to drop out of high school, but in 2002, 19 percent still had no high school degree, in contrast to 8 percent of Germans. The share of immigrants with advanced high school degrees (*Hochschulreife, Realschulablschluss*, and *Fachhochschulreife*) rose from 35 to 40 percent over the course of the 1990s, but was still well below German levels, which remained at 68 percent. The share of immigrant youths employed in apprenticeships and vocational training had increased considerably over the course of the 1980s and early 1990s (from a low of 14 percent in 1979–1980 to 44 percent in 1994), but this development has stalled (Beauftragte 2005, 38, 44, 590, 592; Bundesministerium für Bildung und Forschung 2006, 179). Surveys among Germany's Turkish-origin residents further revealed that this group often experienced "unequal treatment" and that such discrimination has more frequently been perceived by the second generation (Goldberg and Sauer 2003, 118).

Similar to their counterparts in Great Britain, then, ethnic minorities in Germany in the new millennium are increasingly exposed to economic downturns and gradual advancements in education, employment, and housing are overshadowed by disadvantage. Coupled with electoral disenfranchisement, this experience has contributed to the emergence of immigrant–state conflict. According to the head of Germany's police union, the police have encountered tense relations with immigrant-origin youths in several deprived inner-city areas in Germany. In Berlin, where overall as well as minority unemployment rates have been above the national average, confrontations between the forces of law and order and members of the city's Turkish-origin youth have taken place at the beginning of the twenty-first century.[68]

As has been pointed out throughout this chapter, the characteristic feature of the guest-worker regime was its economically driven rationale and design. While cracks in this system had started emerging as even guest workers did not represent the promised flexible "reserve army of labor," a system of economically driven rules and administrative regulations had nevertheless greatly shaped their migration to Germany, the nature of their settlement, and, in many cases, their return. The resulting reduced intergroup resource competition between immigrants and natives and relatively low (but rising) economic disadvantage among migrants kept the development of immigrant conflict in check. By implication, the demise of the guest-worker logic has been associated with increased ethnic minority economic disadvantage as well as with a greater potential for conflict.

New Types of Immigrants, New Types of Conflict

In the late 1980s Germany was confronted with an entirely different type of immigration with profound consequences for intergroup conflict. Though the chief goal of this chapter has been to explain how the economic and political features of Germany's guest-worker regime account for the relative absence of local immigrant conflict involving the guest-worker population, one cannot discuss immigration and conflict in postwar Germany without making reference to the outburst of xenophobia that accompanied the inflow of *Aussiedler* and asylum-seekers beginning in the late 1980s. This section provides an analytical discussion of these immigration regimes and how they relate to conflict outcomes.[69]

---

[68] On confrontations with the police, see, e.g., Gesemann (2001, 364) and *DDP Basisdienst*, "'Frust und Hass' – Polizisten in Berlin bei Festnahme attackiert," November 15, 2006. For Berlin labor market data, see Hillmann (2001).

[69] For more extensive treatments, see, e.g., Bade (1994), Bade and Oltmer (1999), and Blahusch (1999).

In essence, I argue that the key to understanding immigrant–native conflict involving the new arrivals – especially when compared with the absence of collective local resistance targeting guest workers in previous decades – lies in the new immigrants' capacity to claim scarce economic goods, often at the expense of natives. I have previously stated that this ability tends to rest on immigrants' electoral clout. In the case of *Aussiedler* and asylum-seekers, by contrast, it was enshrined in laws and regulations giving these groups preferential treatment in the allocation of economic goods. These rules were a product of the immediate postwar period, when the mass migration associated with the fall of communism had not been conceived. But since the new migrant groups lacked local as well as national political power, politicians were relatively unconstrained in making substantial changes in the laws guiding immigration as well as the distribution of goods to ethnic German *Aussiedler* and refugees. Once legal reforms curtailed the capacity of immigrants to obtain economic resources, the incidence of local immigrant–native conflict declined.

The Immigration Regimes of Aussiedler *and Asylum-Seeker Migration*
Over the decades, Germany had received a steady stream of *Aussiedler* or so-called ethnic Germans from Eastern Europe and the former Soviet Union. These migrants were persons who had lived in Germany's former eastern territories and had not migrated westward immediately after World War II, but the group also included those who had lived in Eastern Europe and the former USSR for generations but could still claim German ancestry. As German minorities, *Aussiedler* often suffered expulsion, repression, and discrimination and the Federal Republic consequently granted this group the right of return and immediate access to German citizenship. Between 1950 and 1987, 1.4 million ethnic Germans arrived in Germany, but annual figures averaged less than 40,000.[70] With the end of the Cold War and the collapse of the Soviet Union, the number of ethnic Germans arriving in Germany rose precipitously. Between 1988 and 2005, over 3 million *Aussiedler* came to Germany, with an annual intake of almost 400,000 in 1990. The same geopolitical events that had encouraged the emigration of *Aussiedler* also led thousands of asylum-seeking Eastern Europeans to leave their homelands; in 1988, 70 percent of political refugees hailed from Eastern Europe. In addition, by the early 1990s, the violent conflict in the former Yugoslavia caused large waves of refugees to flee the war-torn region, and many arrived in Germany. Unlike the guest-worker regime, then, the arrival of ethnic Germans and refugees was neither a product of technocratic planning nor dictated by the country's economic

---

[70] *Aussiedler* statistics are based on Bundesverwaltungsamt (2006). During this time, these settlers constituted "model immigrants" with relatively high occupational qualifications. The federal government assigned *Aussiedler* families to cities and towns across Germany and smaller towns actually competed for this group: *Aussiedler* generally did not represent a burden on local finances and by increasing the total population they often entitled smaller towns to additional federal population-based funding (Thränhardt 1999, 232).

needs. Moreover, the xenophobic backlash that would ensue targeted migrants of predominantly German and European descent.

In addition to their German or European heritage, one of the crucial features that distinguished the new arrivals from the guest-worker population was their favorable position in the distribution of material resources. As codified by the 1953 Federal Law on Refugees and Expellees (*Bundesvertriebenengesetz*), as a result of their experience of discrimination in the Soviet bloc, *Aussiedler* had access to a range of entitlements upon arrival, such as unemployment benefits, language and educational training, financial "integration assistance," and subsidies to promote homeownership; they were also paid a full state pension.[71] Critically, ethnic Germans were also the "most privileged group in the housing market... they are immediately eligible for an apartment in the social housing stock. Indeed, they have the highest priority. Aussiedler can get access to an apartment earlier than local families who have been looking for housing for some years" (Faist and Häussermann 1996, 87–88). Similar to their obligations to ethnic Germans, local authorities are also required to find housing for asylum-seekers in various forms of accommodation, including social housing, hotels, private apartments, public buildings, and hostels, albeit on a temporary basis and at generally lower costs. Local authorities also provide asylum-seekers with cash or in-kind benefits, but this group does not receive preferential treatment in the job market.[72] In short, by law, *Aussiedler* and asylum-seekers had access to state resources that sometimes exceeded that of the indigenous population.

These entitlements coincided with preexisting housing shortages and high unemployment. During the 1980s, the Kohl government had steadily cut federal subsidies for the construction of new social housing and instead enacted policies that would promote home ownership. When the supply of housing appeared to exceed demand in the mid-1980s, the government eliminated funding for social housing altogether.[73] As a consequence, in 1988 – when the number of *Aussiedler* had suddenly nearly tripled compared to the previous year – the construction of social housing had reached its lowest level since at least 1950 (see Figure 7.4).[74] The same year, the shortage of dwellings was estimated at 1 million and cities like Stuttgart, Munich, Frankfurt, and Mannheim counted

---

[71] For a discussion of *Aussiedler*, their social rights and integration, see Faist and Häussermann (1996), essays in Bade and Oltmer (1999), and Blahusch (1999, 137–138).

[72] See Faist and Häussermann (1996, 90) and Dörr and Faist (1997). Asylum-seekers can obtain a job-specific work permit one year after arrival, provided no German or EU citizen is available to fill the position.

[73] BT Drs 10/5810, July 1, 1986.

[74] Figures on social housing indicate housing that was approved for construction. Figures include all asylum-seekers entering Germany, but the majority of applications were not accepted: The average annual acceptance rate from 1971, when these data were first published, to 2000 is 14.4 percent; for the 1990s it is 5.4 percent; author's calculations. After 1990, data on inflows of *Aussiedler* and asylum-seekers as well as on new social housing include the new eastern states.

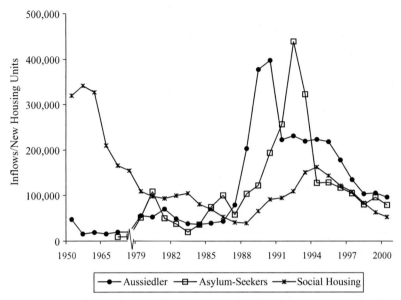

FIGURE 7.4. Inflows of *Aussiedler*, asylum-seekers, and the construction of social housing, 1950–2000. (*Sources:* For social housing data, see Statistisches Bundesamt 1983–1984, 135; 2002, 146; 2004, 156; for inflows of *Aussiedler*, see Bundesverwaltungsamt 2006; and for inflows of asylum-seekers, see Schwarze 1999, 31 and Statistisches Bundesamt 2004, 51. See footnote 74 for more information.)

thousands of residents on their waiting lists for social housing.[75] In Hamburg, citizens organized demonstrations to protest the to protest the government's housing policy and the lack of affordable housing, as older buildings were torn down without new constructions filling the gap. In the meantime, the federal government had announced that it would spend DM 1.1 billion on new housing specifically for *Aussiedler*.[76] In previous years, the government had been much more reluctant to target guest workers with specific spending measures, let alone to announce such initiatives publicly.

Before such housing was completed, however, ethnic Germans vied for the same pool of limited social housing as did long-settled German residents. Given their privileged status and their more urgent housing need, *Aussiedler* households often had a competitive advantage in the state-run housing sector. Local authorities, who were responsible for finding as well as paying for the accommodation of ethnic Germans, preferred to house *Aussiedler* in the social housing stock rather than the far more costly alternative of hotel accommodations. As a result, low-income households, who had long waited for an apartment in cities' social housing stock, lost out to *Aussiedler* families who were considered "housing emergencies" (*Wohnungsnotstandsfälle*) and the participation

[75] *Der Spiegel*, "Wohnungsnot im Wohlstands-Deutschland," December 12, 1988.
[76] *Der Spiegel*, "Mieten: Urängste werden wach," September 18, 1989.

rate in social housing among the latter exceeded the rate among the settled local population (Faist and Häussermann 1996, 95). Special measures to house asylum-seekers would also gain much local and national attention. Finally, the preferential treatment of the new migrants in the areas of housing and the assistance measures targeted at these groups came at the heels of the 1980s' record unemployment levels. Scarcity of goods thus coexisted alongside increased economic need.

Native Backlash

The combination of local economic scarcity and immigrants' capacity to obtain valued resources generated a native backlash. When the far-right *Republikaner*, a party that had emerged in the early 1980s and styled itself after the French *Front National*, ran on an anti-immigrant platform in early 1989 in Berlin, where rents had increased by nearly 30 percent in three years, its success sent shock waves through the political establishment. Having garnered 7.5 percent of the vote and eight seats in the city state's parliament, the party performed particularly well in precincts with high shares of low-skilled workers and social housing units (Falter 1994, 57).

This success was soon repeated elsewhere. In Munich, where rents had increased by 27 percent in three years and the waiting list for social housing counted 18,000 applicants, six *Republikaner* were elected. Frankfurt, which saw rents rise by a whopping 39 percent, elected seven candidates of the extreme-right National Democratic Party (NPD), while Düsseldorf, where 4,000 "emergency housing cases" had already been recorded in mid-1988 and rents had climbed by 14 percent, returned two *Republikaner*.[77] In total, by late 1989, thirty-three cities and towns had elected 108 candidates of the extreme-right, anti-immigrant *Republikaner* or NPD.[78]

According to election surveys, voters who supported the *Republikaner* were more likely to complain about high rents, prompting Social Democratic critics of the CDU's cuts in social housing to comment that "every additional apartment means one vote less for the *Republikaner*."[79] More generally, compared with other voters, supporters of the NPD and the *Republikaner* were more likely to live in deprived areas, occupy run-down housing, and more often expressed doubts that the major parties were able to solve unemployment, immigration, and housing problems (Jaschke 1993, 133–136). Finally, a 1989 survey showed that when asked which group was to blame for exacerbating

---

[77] See *Der Spiegel*, "Praktisch leergefegt," June 13, 1988 and *Der Spiegel*, "Mieten: Urängste warden wach," September 18, 1989.

[78] Election results are based on my examination of city and town council compositions in *Deutscher Städtetag* (1990 edition). This publication does not list vote shares. If one calculates vote shares by simply dividing the number of seats won by the *Republikaner* or the NPD by the total number of seats, vote shares of the extreme right amount to 7.5 percent in Munich and Frankfurt but only to 2.4 percent in Düsseldorf (where rent increases had been much lower and the waiting list for social housing counted fewer applicants).

[79] *Der Spiegel*, "Mieten: Urängste werden wach," September 18, 1989.

the housing shortage, Germans were most likely to single out *Aussiedler*, ahead of asylum-seekers and guest workers.[80]

Xenophobic electoral mobilization was followed by a massive rise in racist violence. Violent attacks against asylum-seekers and immigrants had only accounted for 5 and 15 percent, respectively, of all right-wing violence in 1990 (the remainder constituting assaults on left-wing groups, the homeless, the disabled, as well as anti-Semitic attacks). By 1992, though, perpetrators directed almost two-thirds of such crime against asylum-seekers and approximately 20 percent against other immigrants (Koopmans and Olzak 2004, 218). The president of the Federal Office for the Protection of the Constitution, which deals with such crime, echoed this shift, stating that – despite decades of guest-worker migration and settlement – violence against foreigners was "a relatively new manifestation of right-wing extremism" (cited in Gessenharter 1999, 18). The anti-immigrant wave that had begun as an electoral protest against the "competition . . . over housing, jobs, and social benefits" (Blahusch 1999, 148) associated with *Aussiedler* and asylum-seekers thus began to disproportionately target asylum-seekers, the group that had also invited excessive political and media coverage.[81] Some of the most heinous acts, such as the firebombing of hostels housing these refugees, had begun in the new *Länder* in the eastern parts of Germany, where racist violence occurred at a much higher rate than in the western *Länder*.[82]

The majority of victims of violent and nonviolent hostility were asylum-seekers and not the guest-worker population and their descendents (Pagen-stecher 1994, 151), yet long-settled immigrants had also become victims. That these migrants had been targeted was often greeted with indignation and confusion on the part of Germans and guest workers (Bade 1994, 84). Moreover, these assaults did not necessarily map onto long-standing local conflicts. In the towns of Solingen and Mölln, for example, where the two most gruesome arson attacks had occurred, together causing the deaths of eight Turkish-origin residents, no far-right councilors had been elected. In Mölln, German and Turkish residents had described intergroup relations as peaceful before the attack while Solingen had recently been praised for its achievements in integrating its predominantly Turkish immigrant population.[83]

---

[80] *Der Spiegel*, "Arbeitslose Ausländer abschieben?," April 14, 1989.

[81] In this sense, public discourse may have also caused the spread of racist violence, as Koopmans and Olzak (2004) persuasively argue. But see Karapin (2002) for an account that focuses on the local dimension of such violence in East German towns. For a discussion of research on right-wing violence in Germany, see, e.g., Ohlemacher (1999) and Green and colleagues (2001).

[82] Between 1990 and 1999, "Per million inhabitants, the average yearly number of radical right violent events ranged from 29 in the Eastern states of Brandenburg and Mecklenburg-Vorpommern to three in Bavaria in the West" (Koopmans and Olzak 2004, 213).

[83] See *Der Spiegel*, "'So müsst' die Welt untergehen,'" November 30, 1993 and *Süddeutsche Zeitung*, "Solingen: Nach dem Brandanschlag eskaliert die Gegengewalt," June 1, 1993. The attacks and the following media attention did uncover a greater amount of clandestine extremist activity than such descriptions would lead one to believe.

The *spread* of highly publicized racist violence during the very unusual (postunification) period of the early 1990s thus suggests that the correlation between other indicators of local-level immigrant–native conflict and racist attacks – demonstrated in Chapter 4 – did not hold everywhere in Germany. Moreover, the proliferation and later entrenchment of racist violence in East Germany does not map on entirely to the logic of immigrant–native conflict proposed in this book. While some have shown that the high incidence of racist crime in the east is a function of economic conditions (e.g., Falk and Zweimüller 2005), the relatively low share of migrants and their lacking electoral clout does not support the theory advanced here. Others have argued that "the rapid, chaotic transitions to both representative democracy and a market economy . . . [and] the collapse of state authority over an ethnically diverse population" underpinned the local dynamics causing racist violence in the eastern *Länder* (Karapin 2002, 161). The East German case thus may suggest the limits of this book's argument when applied to postcommunist, democratizing settings.

To sum up, though it is not my intention to argue that a desire to protest against unfair treatment in the allocation of economic goods guided every arsonist in the eastern or western *Länder*, I do claim that the mobilization against immigrants and the success of local anti-immigrant parties that had started in West Germany in early 1989 – thirty-four years after the first guestworker treaty had been signed – is tied directly to the sudden inflow of migrants whose preferential access to state resources threatened to leave many natives without these goods at a time of resource scarcity.

Changes in Immigration Regimes and the Decline in Immigrant–Native Conflict

In 1992, 611 xenophobic arson attacks were registered in Germany; two years later, the number had dropped to 80, and by 1997 such attacks were down to 25. During this time, the ratio of anti-immigrant arson attacks relative to other right-wing extremist arson attacks also declined, from approximately seven to one in 1992, to two to one in 1997 (Neubacher 1999, 267). This reduction coincided with a general downturn in racist violence as well as with the decline of far-right parties in many cities and towns.

Local-level immigrant–native conflict diminished as immigrants increasingly lost their ability to claim scarce economic resources. Politicians reacted to the electorates' "concerns over distributive justice" (Bade 1994, 171) and the ensuing intergroup conflicts by successively curtailing immigrant entry and access to economic goods. In its official justification for these measures targeted at fellow ethnic Germans, the government explicitly referred to the prevention of further social conflicts and expressed hopes that a reduced inflow of *Aussiedler* would help the public with its lacking acceptance (*Akzeptanzprobleme*) of this group.[84] Prospective *Aussiedler* were now required to apply for entry to

---

[84] See BT Prt 11/214, May 31, 1990 and BR Drs 763/92, November 11, 1992, cited in Blahusch (1999, 127, 141).

Germany while still in the origin country and only those whose ethnic German status had been confirmed received an entry permit. Furthermore, seeking to limit immigration to overburdened localities – and reminiscent of its handling of guest workers in the 1970s – the government assigned *Aussiedler* without adequate housing options to areas where accommodations were not in short supply. The receipt of benefits would later become conditional on *Aussiedler's* staying in these designated municipalities. New legislation also substantially reduced the financial and social assistance paid out to ethnic Germans, and the group of persons qualifying for *Aussiedler* status was further restricted with the implementation of a quota system. Moreover, applicants from democratizing Eastern European countries had to provide (increasingly missing) evidence that their German heritage was cause of present discrimination.[85] A series of laws further limited asylum-seekers' social benefits and, after heated and emotional debate, the government went so far as to change the constitution to enact radical restrictions to Germany's asylum laws.[86]

The motivation driving restrictive immigration laws and allocation procedures was thus similar to legislation targeted at guest workers and their families. When it came to the latter, however, the stated aim had been on the *prevention* of future conflict and the maintenance of social peace – especially during times when the economy could afford to lose guest workers. This time, the government reacted to an unforeseen outbreak of public hostility that expressed itself not only at the ballot box.

Conclusion

The rules and regulations that shape immigrants' arrival, settlement, and access to economic goods crucially influence the incidence of both types of immigrant conflict in local immigrant destinations. Balancing immigrant economic integration with the maintenance of native privilege, Germany's guest-worker regime instituted procedures that reduced immigrant economic disadvantage as well as intergroup competition over local resources. In doing so, policy makers applied strategies that were both coercive and integrationist. But integrative measures remained largely economic in nature; citizenship and local political power would remain elusive for most of the guest-worker population.

The German state treated guest workers as cogs in a greater economic machine that were easily replaced, restricted, and returned. The prevention of immigrant–native and immigrant–state conflict also became one of the leading principles supporting this approach. For the first three decades of guest-worker immigration, the twin logics of integration and exit did indeed work to ensure a minimum standard of economic well-being among guest workers and

---

[85] For a more detailed discussion of these changes, see Blahusch (1999, 126–145) and Bundesministerium des Inneren (2001, 178–180).

[86] According to the revised law, only those asylum-seekers who had not arrived via a member state of the European Union, or other "safe states" to be designated by Germany, could apply for asylum. In practice, these stipulations ruled out the majority of refugees.

their families in Germany. Moreover, they did so without impinging on the economic welfare of the indigenous population. But by the end of the twentieth century, the initial rules and regulations governing guest-worker migration no longer applied and the labor market position of many former guest workers and their descendants reflected their often lower skill profile. Finally, the contrast between the relative absence of local immigrant conflict involving the guest-worker population and the xenophobic mobilization against *Aussiedler* and asylum-seekers further underscores the significance of the immigration regime in allocating economic resources across groups and hence structuring immigrant conflict.

That the incidence of sustained intergroup conflict had been comparatively muted with regard to the guest-worker population was not a product of Germans' tolerant attitudes toward the newcomers, especially when measured against British views. Rather, Germans never felt the need to mobilize against immigrants because their migrant neighbors did not threaten natives' access to resources.

There is, of course, a flip side to immigrants' lacking capacity to obtain scarce material resources. With the demise of the guest-worker regime, many first- and later-generation immigrants have suffered from the consequences of disadvantage rather than privilege. While the economic integration of all migrants who had arrived in Germany via the guest-worker scheme has lagged behind that of natives, it is the experience of Germany's Turkish residents – the largest nationality group at both the country level and in most localities – that tends to be marked by disadvantage and thus conducive to immigrant–state conflict.[87] These developments take place as local authority budgets have fallen steadily over the years and legislation has substantially scaled back welfare state expenditures.

At the same time, important changes in the potential political influence of Germany's ethnic minority population might pull these tendencies in the direction of increased intergroup conflict rather than immigrant–state conflict. In 1999, the government officially recognized the obsolescence of the guest-worker system. It ratified legislation that relaxed naturalization requirements for many long-settled immigrants and granted automatic citizenship to children born in Germany. If the hundreds of thousands of Turks who have chosen to become German citizens translate their numbers into political leverage and successfully demand economic resources, then the integrative intent of the legislation might come at the cost of a "German" backlash. Much will depend, however, on how Germany's Turks, who are themselves divided along religious, regional, and ideological lines, will represent themselves politically.[88]

---

[87] In 1996, in sixty-four out of the eighty-four cities with a population of over 100,000, Turkish residents constituted the largest group of non-Germans; see *Deutscher Städtetag* (1996 edition), author's calculations.

[88] Moreover, since the Maastricht Treaty came into effect in 1993, all EU-origin residents have been able to vote in local elections. However, these nationality groups rarely constitute more than 10 percent of a city's non-German population. At the present time, it is doubtful that EU migrants will represent a pivotal voting bloc at the polls.

Furthermore, as a result of the less economically based recent immigration and the fading of the national regulatory mechanisms that had guided guest-worker settlement, local authorities play an increasingly important role in shaping immigrant integration and conflict (see also Ireland 2004). During the 1970s, local governments could rely on federal ministries to impose settlement bans in areas where public services were considered overburdened. More recently, local officials follow the actions that some of their British counterparts took decades earlier. For instance, in cities and towns across Germany, including Berlin and Hamburg, more stringent residency requirements have been implemented to reduce the pool of immigrants who may qualify for social housing. Frankfurt enacted a quota system, whereby the share of non-Germans as well as of ethnic Germans living in state-subsidized housing could not exceed designated thresholds.[89] Alongside these restrictive measures, however, many cities have been experimenting with their own integration models and promote local efforts by giving out "integration prizes" to organizations that are seen to further interethnic understanding. In light of these cross-cutting developments, immigrant conflict in Germany will likely take on more variegated patterns in the years to come.

[89] See Thränhardt (1999, 238) on residency requirements and Klopp (2002, 138–139) on Frankfurt. Thränhardt states that no systematic research exists on these decisions and notes that the *Deutsche Städtetag*, the official body representing German cities and towns, has refused to commission a systematic survey.

8

Immigration and Conflict across Countries

The previous chapters have shown how national immigration frameworks can shape and interact with local political economies and immigrant political behavior to determine patterns of immigrant conflict. Comparing across countries, we have seen that Germany's postwar guest-worker regime was structured in ways that limited competition over material resources between immigrants and natives at the local level. Comparatively stringent immigration and settlement regulations meant that immigrants were less likely to confront resource shortages upon arrival while the economic rationale of guest-worker migration prompted the state to encourage or force the departure of those migrants whose labor was no longer needed. As the initial rules that had guided postwar migration gradually faded, relative economic integration without political incorporation became the norm. In Great Britain, by contrast, the state played a far less interventionist role in recruiting and settling immigrant labor. As a result, economic competition between immigrants and natives as well as economic deprivation on the part of immigrants has been more common.

Variation in the economic conditions in the local areas of settlement interacts with immigrants' capacity to obtain valued economic goods, and these are the two central variables that explain the incidence of both immigrant–native and immigrant–state conflict. Indeed, differences in conflict outcomes across cities and over time within Great Britain have been as significant as variation across Germany and Great Britain.

How does the theory of immigrant conflict developed in this book travel to other immigrant destinations? Virtually all Western European countries have been receiving large shares of immigrants for quite some time now. Some countries (such as France, the Netherlands, Austria, Denmark, or Belgium) opened their doors to labor migration many decades ago, while others (such as Spain, Ireland, or Italy) have only more recently switched roles from net exporters to net importers of migrants. Questions surrounding immigrant integration have become highly salient in most of these countries as publics and policy makers increasingly worry about the social, economic, and political consequences of domestic ethnic and religious diversity.

The purpose of this chapter is to demonstrate how the model of immigrant conflict proposed in the foregoing chapters can be applied beyond Great Britain and Germany. My goal here is not to provide a full empirical test of this book's theory of immigrant conflict in additional settings. Rather, I want to show how the identification of key macrolevel and microlevel variables driving immigrant conflict can help us understand and predict such strife in other countries and cities.

The chapter is divided into two parts. In the first part, I examine the substantively and analytically important case of France. The macro-institutions guiding postwar migration in France depart from those adopted by Germany but resemble those of Great Britain: a weakly coordinated immigration regime coincided with a relatively liberal citizenship framework. Unlike in Great Britain, however, France's newest citizens encountered electoral micro-institutions less amenable to immigrant local political mobilization. Immigrant–state conflict has thus been characteristic of many immigrant destinations in France, while a native backlash has tended to occur when immigrant-origin minorities have been able to break through the rather inhospitable electoral landscape.

Confrontations between immigrants and state actors have long characterized many of France's deprived suburban areas; the well-publicized riots that broke out in the fall of 2005 (and again in 2007) only differed in scope and in scale from previous incidents of a similar kind. Moreover, many localities have not escaped sustained conflicts between longer-settled French natives and immigrant communities. As I will show, an examination of the economic features of France's postwar immigration regime helps us understand the country's relatively high overall incidence of immigrant conflict. Over-time and across-space differences in local economic conditions and the ways in which immigrants have navigated the local electoral system in turn explain why some towns have been more likely to experience immigrant–native conflict, while others have encountered sustained immigrant–state conflict.

In the second part of the chapter, I take up contemporary developments that bear on the nature and incidence of immigrant conflict across Europe. Put simply, labor migration has given way to noneconomic forms of migration that more easily escape the deliberate planning of policy makers and that tend to place greater burdens on municipal infrastructures. This shift in immigration regimes has been accompanied by a rise in immigrant-origin citizens. Over the course of the 1990s, significant increases in naturalization and net migration rates took place across Europe, developments that have paved the way for greater electoral potential among the continents' new citizens. Moreover, as more and more first- and later-generation immigrants have become citizens, many countries received additional migrants as family reunification and political asylum – rather than labor migration – became the predominant immigration regimes. These types of migrant inflows tend to result in lower labor market integration and can also be more challenging for local authorities when compared to labor migration. Finally, the decentralization of service delivery has endowed many municipalities with enhanced decision-making authority over the allocation of goods. When this decentralization has coincided with high levels economic scarcity, the potential for immigrant conflict has expanded. These political and economic dynamics likely account for variation in conflict patterns in many of Europe's cities.

Immigrant Conflict in France

France has been the site of both types of immigrant conflict for a number of decades now. Confrontations between immigrant-origin youths and state actors have taken place here since the 1970s, while organized resistance against ethnic minorities took root in the 1980s. Minorities of North African descent have been the main targets of such antagonism, but they have also been prominent participants in immigrant–state conflict. This section will demonstrate how the economic and political foundations of France's immigration regime explain the high rate of overall conflict we observe here: A postwar immigration regime that has brought together inflows of poorly cared for guest workers with (post-)colonial war-induced immigration and waves of family reunification has largely escaped the control of France's technocrats. As a result of lacking economic integration and a general economic slowdown, many areas of immigrant settlement have become synonymous with urban deprivation and decay. On the political side, a relatively open *ius soli* citizenship regime combines with a more closed local political system to lead to a checkered pattern of immigrant electoral power at the municipal level.

In what follows, I will argue that the different ways in which ethnic minorities have penetrated the local electoral arena in a context of economic scarcity explains the variegated outcomes of immigrant conflict in France. Assessing the prevalence of immigrant conflict in French towns is, however, difficult because there are significant data limitations. Measuring ethnic difference – as well as the consequences that may flow from it – is especially problematic in the French case, where an assimilationist, republican ethos shuns data-collection efforts that take ethnic markers into account, leading to the "statistical invisibility" of ethnic ancestry (Kastoryano 2004, 69). Such restrictions have obvious implications for the collection of data on racist violence. As one review concluded, "the subject ... remains poorly developed.... The lack of qualitative and quantitative studies demonstrates the sensitivity of this issue in a context characterised by the overwhelming influence of a republican model that refuses the categorisation of individuals based on origin, racial belonging, or religion" (Agency for the Development of Intercultural Relations 2004, 39). Moreover, the data on racist incidents that are being collected by government agencies or nongovernment monitoring bodies are often not made available to the public (European Monitoring Centre on Racism and Xenophobia 2005, 94–95). As a result, my examination of general tendencies in local immigrant–native conflict in France will track and explain variation in the performance of the

Front National at the municipal level, across time and localities. I discuss broad patterns of immigrant–state conflict, and, where available, more detailed accounts of both types of conflict at the local level by drawing on secondary sources dealing with cognate issues. Before doing so, I outline the broad features of France's immigration regime[1] – a topic that has been covered more extensively by the literature.

Immigration Regime

By the early 1960s, after close to 3 million postwar immigrants had arrived in France, observers concluded that "the government had lost control over immigration" (DeLey 1983, 199). This assessment came despite ambitious designs by French planners to make immigration an integral part of the country's state-led economic growth and recovery. Faced with high war casualties, low birthrates, and the need to jump-start industrial expansion, demographic and economic planners called for immigration to fill labor shortages and restore France's population.

Between 1946 and 1965, the French government thus signed labor recruitment treaties with Italy, Greece, Spain, Portugal, Yugoslavia, Turkey, Morocco, Mali, Mauritania, Senegal, and Turkey. But in stark contrast to the ways in which Germany drafted and settled its guest workers, France's handling of labor recruitment was rather lax. By the mid-1950s migrants were able to enter without proof of employment and policy makers increasingly favored "spontaneous" migration whereby the movement of labor was presumed to follow market signals. As a result, in the second half of the 1950s, 50 percent of migrants attained legal status only after they had already entered the country; by 1968, more than 80 percent of foreign workers had arrived without a permit.

In addition to the relatively unguided immigration of these labor migrants, colonial ties and warfare led to large inflows of Algerian migrants, who constituted nearly 20 percent of all migrants in 1970.[2] North African migrants had, on average, the fewest transferable skills among the migrant population and were the first ones to suffer the consequences of the economic recession that was to end the so-called *Trente Glorieuses* of rapid economic growth in the mid-1970s (De Ley 1983, 199; Hollifield 1992, 52; Sturm-Martin 2001, 98–99). As in many other European countries, the end of economic expansion also heralded the end of *official* immigration. France enacted a ban on immigration in 1974, but enforcement of the legislation was not too stringent, especially when compared to Germany: "the French ban on new immigration was less categorical than the German. French authorities, recognizing foreign labor to

---

[1] This overview draws on more detailed analyses, including those by Tapinos (1975), Freeman (1979), Verbunt (1985), Hollifield (1992), Gastaut (2000), Sturm-Martin (2001), Lequin (2006b), and Dancygier (2007b).

[2] Algerians who had fought with the French army or supported the French during the Algerian war, so-called *harkis*, were no longer welcomed in Algeria, and many of them fled to the metropolis.

be a structural component of labor supply, were willing to grant exemptions to the new regulations." In a further difference with Germany, family immigration was also encouraged through the granting of work permits to spouses and family members (Hollifield 1986, 118).

Summing up these developments from the perspective of municipalities, we see that the predominance of initially undocumented, undirected migration resulted in local infrastructures adjusting to the significant population increases in a rather ad hoc fashion, if at all. Moreover, the low-skill and low-income profile of many migrants, coupled with the arrival of their family members, meant that the additional pressures on local public resources induced by a growing population were not necessarily matched by a rise in tax revenues, especially once the recession caused many migrants to lose their jobs.

Economic Integration
The central state's measures to integrate migrants economically and to alleviate resource shortages in the areas of settlement were, on the whole, inadequate. While many originally undocumented immigrants had been granted work permits (*régularisation*) and thus gained legal status, integration into France's housing market often did not follow, as the state's various housing policies exacerbated an already inhospitable situation: By the early 1980s, three-fourths of officially classified slums (*logements insalubres*) were occupied by migrants and their descendents (Frey and Lubinski 1987, 86). In yet another contrast to developments in Germany, attempts by the French state to require employers to help provide accommodations for migrant workers were met with resistance on the part of employer associations as well as labor unions (Hollifield 1986, 117). In the early years of immigrant settlement, when postwar France experienced an acute shortage of housing, the state built cheap, provisional accommodation for immigrants, located in the industrial zones of larger conurbations. These tended to be of extremely low quality and soon began to resemble slums and shantytowns (*bidonvilles*).[3] Other substandard housing consisted of shabbily built hostels for single male workers (*foyers*), where deplorable living conditions caused 16,000 *foyer* residents to protest with rent and hunger strikes in the mid-1970s.[4]

The state eventually destroyed many of these housing structures and placed some of their former residents, mainly North Africans, in transitional complexes (*cités de transits*) "before a social worker would certify that they were socially prepared to live in 'modern' housing" (Hein 1991, 594). These social housing projects (*Habitat à Loyer Modéré*, or HLM), built by the state and

---

[3] In 1970, there were 113 *bidonvilles* in the Paris region alone, housing 75,000 residents; the largest *bidonville* was to be found in Nanterre, where 23,000 residents, mostly hailing from Algeria, were housed (Lequin 2006a, 410).

[4] A series of deaths that had been caused by unsafe *foyer* living conditions also caused a public outcry. Nevertheless, in the early 1980s close to 130,000 individuals still occupied these dwellings (Hein 1991, 594; Lequin 2006a, 425).

partly financed by employers, consisted mainly of high-rise developments that had been abandoned by upwardly mobile French nationals. Throughout the 1980s, immigrants joined native working-class tenants that had remained; by 1990, 28 percent of households headed by foreign nationals (compared with 14 percent of their French counterparts) ended up living in HLMs, often located in disadvantaged, "end-of-work" suburban neighborhoods (*banlieues*) and largely cut off from the economic opportunities of France's larger cities.[5]

For many immigrants and their descendents, inadequate housing has thus been matched by economic dislocation. Policies to induce unemployed migrants to return to their home countries had backfired, as most remained; of the returnees, fewer than one-third had actually been unemployed (Ireland 1994, 49). The French public increasingly blamed immigrants for the country's deteriorating employment situation, a development that was aided by politicians who "made sure that people understood that there was a connection between the presence of two million immigrant workers and the unemployment of one million French workers."[6] Immigrants were often portrayed as burdens on an overstretched welfare state; by the mid-1980s, 53 percent of those surveyed thought that immigrants illegitimately benefited from social assistance (Gastaut 2000, 301). The prolonged economic downturn and industrial restructuring of the 1980s and 1990s indeed severely affected the immigrant-origin population. In 1983, the unemployment rate among foreign nationals, a disproportionate number of whom had been employed in blue-collar, low-skill jobs, stood at over 14 percent, compared to 7.5 percent among their French counterparts. As overall unemployment rates rose over the course of the 1980s and 1990s, so did the unemployment gap between foreign and French nationals. By 1999, 11 percent of French citizens were jobless, compared with 22 percent of foreign nationals. Among non-EU nationals, this figure rose to 30 percent, while a staggering 42 percent of non-EU youths were out of work. Comparable figures for EU nationals stood at 11 and 16 percent, respectively.[7]

Political Incorporation
While France's uncoordinated immigration regime and steep recession helped to economically marginalize many immigrants, the country's citizenship laws have been more inclusive. In contrast to Germany's restrictive provisions at the time, immigrants could naturalize after having lived in France for five years; children born on French soil to foreign parents could claim French citizenship

[5] See Hargreaves (1995, 66–76) for a brief discussion of housing and HLMs. See also Body-Gendrot (2002) and Mucchielli and Aït-Omar (2006, 24–29) for a short summary of the "processus de ghettoïsation" in many immigrant neighborhoods.

[6] See Verbunt (1985, 154). Jacques Chirac, as prime minister in 1976, articulated this view on television: "Un pays dans lequel il y a 90000 chômeurs, mais où il y a 2 millions d'immigrés, n'est pas un pays dans lequel le problème de l'emploi est insoluble" (cited in Gastaut 2000, 252).

[7] These figures reflect a generally high youth unemployment rate, amounting to 26.5 percent in France compared to an EU average of 18.3 percent (in 1999). See Werner and König (2001, 8–13).

at majority; and dual nationality has been tolerated. In addition to relatively open citizenship laws, successive amnesty provisions led to the legalization of clandestine migrants and thus paved the way for future naturalizations.[8]

The legal framework thus gave some first-generation and many later-generation immigrants formal access to the electoral arena; by the mid-1980s, an estimated 800,000 potential voters of North African origin lived in France (Hargreaves 1991, 362). In practice, though, many encountered a closed local political system that has been unwelcoming to newcomers. In French municipalities, at-large elections – no electoral units exist below the municipality – combine with electoral rules that favor winning parties by allocating a disproportionate share to them and thus make it difficult for smaller parties or independent candidates to upset the electoral balance.[9] Moreover, party elites play a very important role in the placement of candidates on electoral lists but have often been unwilling to assign spots, let alone highly ranked ones, to ethnic minority candidates.

The office of the mayor is endowed with extensive political powers, but it is difficult to penetrate by outsiders. When mayors and "local power barons" have selected immigrant-origin candidates to run for local office, these newcomers have seldom held key positions that would allow them to influence policy (Bird 2005, 438). This situation contrasts with the local electoral configuration in Great Britain, where small wards can swing citywide elections, membership in the ward party is easy to obtain, and local party members (often of immigrant origin) select candidates of their choosing. Finally, at the local level, France's ethos of republicanism and assimilationism clashes with ideas of communal or ethnically based political mobilization. Playing the "ethnic card" has thus not been a commonly used recruitment device; notwithstanding a set of common interests, Muslims, for instance, "do not vote as a bloc."[10]

Although the potential for immigrant local political power has existed from a purely formal, citizenship-rights perspective, its realization has varied greatly across time and space as a result of these micro-institutions of the municipal political system. Yet, local elites' generally poor record of incorporating the country's ethnic minority electorate did help spawn a movement demanding change. Unwilling to accept effective disenfranchisement, members of the North African second generation (so-called *Beurs*) joined with an organization called *France Plus* in 1985 to campaign for the extension of local voting

---

[8] In 1999, out of 4.3 million foreign-born immigrants, 1.56 million had naturalized (Garbaye 2005, 65–66); see also DeLey (1983) on legalization. In the mid-1980s, the Chirac government tried but failed to make access to French citizenship more restrictive. See Brubaker (1992) for an examination of citizenship laws in France and Germany.

[9] Under the semiproportional system, a party that wins, for example, 60 percent of the vote then receives 50 percent of all council seats, plus 60 percent of the remaining seats; that is, a total of 80 percent of seats (Bird 2005, 461).

[10] Laurence and Vaisse (2006, 203). See also Bowen (2007). See Bird (2005) and Garbaye (2005) for examinations of the ways in which the local political system tends to work against the incorporation of ethnic minority candidates.

rights to nonnationals and to lobby for the selection of Maghrebi candidates. The movement also organized mobilization drives, as registration rates among those North Africans who had naturalized were estimated to have been as low as 20 percent in the parliamentary and regional elections of 1986.[11] Although the former demand had not been met, the movement's goal to field immigrant-origin candidates at the 1989 municipal elections proved much more successful. Labeled *Objectif 300*, this campaign's goal was to elect at least 300 councilors across the towns and cities of France. In its negotiations with local party elites, *France Plus* stressed two demands: First, ethnic minority candidates could not be relegated to the bottom of party lists as symbolic tokens (*beurs de service*), but had to be placed on winnable list positions; second, lists that fielded such candidates were not to enter into coalitions with the anti-immigrant *Front National*.[12] The latter had not been very successful during the previous local elections in 1983, but it threatened to become an electoral force in 1989. In sum, during a time of stagnant growth, rising unemployment, housing decay, and increasing strains on public resources, France's immigrant-origin electorate pushed for greater political incorporation.

The enhanced electoral engagement of France's Maghrebi population coincided not only with an economic downturn but also with a considerable transfer of distributive responsibilities to the local level. As pressures on state-provided goods multiplied, administrative reforms beginning in 1982 determined that important domains, such as housing and education policies, social assistance programs, and town planning, came within the purview of local elected officials. Furthermore, mass layoffs in the private sector were accompanied by an expansion of public employment. This trend was particularly pronounced at the local level, which in 1996 employed 32.1 percent of all public employees, up from 20.4 percent in 1969 (Négrier 1999, 125; Loughlin 2007). Access to local government, or at least to those who did, thus became increasingly important and desirable.

The Two Faces of Immigrant Conflict

Given the stylized facts of France's postwar immigration regime – economic exclusion and disadvantage coupled with political marginalization giving way to gradual, but not uniform, incorporation – we should observe both types of immigrant conflict here. Indeed, by the 1970s (well before efforts for enhanced electoral representation took root), confrontations between immigrant-origin

---

[11] The second generation's push for voting rights and local political representation is of particular interest here, but the *Beur* movement that had preceded it campaigned on a wide range of issues, including economic disadvantage, restrictive immigration laws, societal racism, and judicial discrimination. On the *Beur* movement as well as *France Plus*, see, e.g., Hargreaves (1991), Geisser (1997), and Wihtol de Wenden and Leveau (2001).

[12] On the mobilization of ethnic minority candidates, see articles in *Le Monde*, "Parallèllement à une mobilisation contre la loi 'Pasqua'; Des beurs en piste pour les municipales," December 12, 1989; and "La candidature du docteur Salem Kacet à Roubaix; Un beur au centre," January 20, 1989. See also Geisser (1997).

youths and the forces of law and order had become increasingly common in the country's *banlieues*, the suburbs often marked by decay and urban blight, where immigrants were most densely concentrated. As early as 1973, local police chiefs attributed this type of violence to the disadvantaged social and economic situation in which most North African youths found themselves.[13] These less publicized small-scale confrontations between the police and immigrant youths were harbingers of the more massive antistate disturbances that erupted at the end of the decade and, more forcefully, during the "hot summer" of 1981.

Here we notice direct parallels with events in Britain, where I used archival records and local histories to trace minor instances of conflict between West Indian youths and the police throughout the 1970s, before the major unrest of 1981 took place. In another similar development, urban renewal funds were promised after violent disturbances had occurred on a larger scale. The 1981 riots in France were the catalyst for the policies embodied in the *Développement Social des Quartiers*, launched in 1982. Based on reports (dating back to the 1970s) on the high and rising incidence of poverty, urban deprivation, and housing decay, this development strategy was to address the failings of the social, economic, and educational policies at the local level. It soon became evident, however, that these measures (as well as others that followed) were wholly inadequate given the scale of the problems (Cannan 1995; Loughlin 2007, 106).

Confrontations between immigrant-origin youths and the police have taken place in many impoverished suburbs, but the rising salience of ethnic minority demands throughout the 1980s also contributed to a growing backlash against the immigrant presence. In 1983, when immigrant–state conflict, large and small, had become an entrenched feature of everyday life in many de facto disenfranchised immigrant areas, Le Pen's *Front National* only garnered 0.1 percent of the municipal vote. This was soon to change. While many areas of immigrant concentration were marked by economic disadvantage, it was variation in the patterns of political inclusion that explains what type of conflict came to dominate.

Secondary sources dealing mainly with local immigrant political incorporation in France provide us with some indications that support this claim. Focusing on differences in immigrants' political integration in the towns of La Courneuve (a suburb northeast of Paris) and Roubaix (a northern industrial city), Ireland (1994, 101–145) finds that immigrants tended to be co-opted by local elites in the former, whereas candidates of North African descent were

---

[13] See Zancarini-Fournel (2004, 121–126), whose investigation of national archives and municipal records of suburbs around Lyon establishes the first recorded incident in 1971 in Vaulx-en-Velin (specifically, in the cité de la Grapnière where, in 1976, 83 percent of workers were unskilled and 63 percent of families earned less than the government-specified minimum). Vaulx-en-Velin witnessed the country's first large-scale immigrant–state riot in 1979. It is here that Algerian-origin Urban Affairs Minister Fadela Amara unveiled first details of the Sarkozy government's "Marshall Plan" for the *banlieues* (see *The Guardian*, "Sarkozy Unveils Plan for Deprived Housing Estates," January 22, 2008).

elected and given prominent positions in the latter. In La Courneuve, the politically dominant Communist Party was openly hostile to autonomous immigrant mobilization, and it was not until second-generation youths had repeatedly clashed with the police that some immigrant demands were grudgingly accommodated. While the *Front National* tried to exploit these confrontations for its own purposes, the party tended to perform below average here.[14]

In Roubaix, by contrast, a more competitive electoral environment "gave immigrants more leverage, and the political parties and trade union locals . . . accepted the foreign workers' specific demands"; elected officials "regularly brought up the immigrants' problems and demands at municipal council meetings . . . [and] immigrants had a direct pipeline to the municipality" (Ireland 1994, 127–129). Local politicians reached out to immigrants of European and of North African origin. Such early and extensive incorporation coincided with massive economic dislocation: Between 1974 and 1984 the textile town lost 30 percent of its jobs (Manfrass 1991, 49). As a result of these twin dynamics of immigrant political incorporation and economic scarcity, Roubaix produced its own grassroots anti-immigrant party (*Roubaix aux Roubaisiens*) in the early 1980s and later became a stronghold of the *Front National* (FN). The FN's 1989 campaign leaflets explicitly attacked the governing Socialist Party for including ethnic minority candidates on their lists, and they condemned the party for allegedly "granting voting rights to immigrants, and, with your [the local taxpayers'] money, funding social services for immigrants" (Garbaye 2005, 207). As for confrontations with the forces of law and order, "most of Roubaix's second generation never participated in such violent events" (Ireland 1994, 138).

Turning our attention to the city of Lille, just a few miles distance from Roubaix, Garbaye (2005, 144–186) documents the "persistent political exclusion" of immigrants, the municipality's "unresponsive[ness] to issues pertaining to minority disadvantage" (145–146), and the absence of effective ethnic minority leaders. Faced with this unreceptive political configuration and ensuing neglect of their needs, immigrant-origin youths in Lille reflected a common French pattern, being "caught in a perverse cycle of submission and antagonism with the municipality that rested on trading off law and order against petty benefits" (Garbaye 2005, 179–180). In the process, social centers were torched and violent unrest became chronic, while the *Front National* was not able to make considerable electoral headway.

In contrast to Lille, the southern port city of Marseille came to be known for its anti-immigrant mobilization and welcomed Le Pen's xenophobic party in the late 1980s and 1990s. Immigrant-origin youths in Marseille have not been known to engage in large-scale violent battles with representatives of the

---

[14] Ireland notes that the FN's vote share fell below the departmental average during the 1989 European elections, but it nevertheless obtained 16 percent of the vote. The party did not run on its own slate during the 1983 and 1989 local elections, but its candidates competed as part of the *Union de la Droite* slate (1994, 118–122).

state, despite several incidents that could have triggered such clashes, including the death of a young motorcyclist who was killed in a police chase. Marseille also did not experience immigrant–state violence during the 2005 riots. Some have attributed this relative calm to the efforts the city has undertaken to establish contacts between ethnic minorities and the local administration (Body-Gendrot 2000, 196). Indeed, Marseille was "the only city in France to ... institutionalise relations with ethnic minorities by naming a local civil servant officially responsible for them" (Moore 2001, 130). Moreover, after the 1989 election, Marseille had elected three Maghrebi councilors. In the following elections, the *Front National* increased its vote share from 13.6 to 22 percent – double the share it had attained in Lille.

These cases illustrate how the mechanisms that produce the two faces of immigrant conflict, grounded in economic scarcity and immigrant local electoral power, have been at work in the French context. Taking a step back, we also observe how the general tendencies of immigrant conflict map onto wider economic and political institutions and dynamics. Immigrant–state conflict first appeared in the 1970s, on the heels of an immigration regime characterized by poorly managed resource provision and coinciding with growing immigrant socioeconomic disadvantage as well as pervasive local electoral exclusion. By the late 1980s, as the second generation's push for political incorporation began to bear some fruits at the local level, the native backlash gained momentum. Between 1989 and 1995, the *Front National* was able to triple its overall share of the local vote (Messina 2007, 59).

Economic issues loomed large in the FN's electoral appeals. According to a survey of fifty-eight of the party's manifestos during the 1995 municipal contests, the FN's rhetoric focused predominantly on the costs that immigrants imposed on France's welfare state and the party's proposed solution – *Préférence Nationale* – which envisioned a system whereby French nationals would receive preferential treatment in the allocation of all state-provided services.[15] *Préférence Nationale* was mentioned fifty-four times, compared to "Identité et immigrés" or "Déliquance immigrée," themes that appeared only seven and two times, respectively.[16]

In the national debate, the assault on immigrants by the *Front National*, as well as by more mainstream politicians and the media, also began to highlight the issue of Islam and the faith's perceived incompatibility with traditional French values. While Le Pen spoke of the "Muslim invasion," the conservative newspaper *Le Figaro* accompanied its front-page headline "Will the French ever be French again?" with a picture of Marianne, historic symbol of the

---

[15] This policy proposal was an ingenious attempt to make two of the party's main demands – cutting expenditures while improving services for socially marginalized natives – compatible. Excluding immigrants from public services would, according to the FN, drastically cut government expenditures and thereby make resources available to native French. See Le Gallou and Club de l'Horloge (1985) and Front National (1993) for a detailed discussion of the party's ideas and proposals.

[16] The survey is based on campaign information from 107 communes; see Oriol (1998).

French Republic, wearing a chador.[17] The Rushdie Affair, heated controversies surrounding the wearing of the headscarf, and public debates about North African immigrants' loyalties during the 1991 Gulf War further thrust the apparent culture clash into the national spotlight.

Identity-based fear or rejection of Muslim immigrants cannot, however, explain patterns of anti-immigrant backlash in France. The towns just mentioned here are all home to substantial numbers of Muslim immigrants. Moreover, even though they all witnessed the expansion of Islamic associational life and the establishment of prayer rooms or mosques, they experienced different patterns of immigrant conflict. Rather, the nascent immigrant local political clout in economically deprived settings lies at the heart of the xenophobic success during the 1990s.

A quantitative examination of the *Front National*'s 1995 electoral performance at the municipal level supports this claim. The main purpose of the analysis that follows is to test whether Muslim political power is associated with a rise in the extremist party's vote share and, if so, whether this effect is conditional on municipalities' economic fortunes. Before discussing the findings, it should be noted that data limitations make these results suggestive rather than conclusive. First, since the collection of data based on ethnicity or religion is prohibited in France, I have to rely on citizens' nationality to estimate their religious background. The Muslim population share (in which I include Algerian, Moroccan, Tunisian, and Turkish nationals) will thus underestimate the true share, although the two should be correlated if we assume that naturalized children tend to stay in the same municipality as their (non-French) parents and that naturalization does generally not prompt moving to a different municipality. Second, I use local unemployment rates as a proxy measure for competition over economic resources. As we have seen previously, unemployment figures are a rather crude measure of competition over state-provided goods. While they indicate the need for such resources, they do not measure their availability in a given locality. Data on Maghrebi councilors rely on a survey conducted by Geisser (1997). Newspaper and secondary sources allowed me to cross-check the accuracy of the results for several municipalities, but I must assume that this variable is subject to some error. Overall, the measurement error in these independent variables is likely to attenuate their effects. Lastly, while it would have been ideal to additionally compare the effects of immigrant electoral power among immigrants of North African and Turkish origin with such effects among those of European origin to better isolate the effect of ethnic background, to the best of my knowledge only information on the election of the former is available.[18]

---

[17] *Le Monde* "Permier Pas," February 28, 1989; Simmons (1996, 159).

[18] I was also not able to locate sources that list councilors by municipality, which would have allowed the coding of names by ethnicity. However, even if such data were easily available, the fact that the employment situation of EU nationals is far more favorable than that of their non-EU counterparts, in turn producing differential needs for state-provided resources across groups, would make a comparison that failed to control for these differences not very informative.

TABLE 8.1. *Determinants of Local Anti-Immigrant Party Success in France, 1995*

Variable	1. Maghrebi Councilors	2. Muslim Population	3. Maghrebi Councilors and Muslim Population
Maghrebi councilor	−13.407*** (4.69)		−13.441*** (4.49)
Muslim population		−1.207 (.735)	.341 (.216)
Unemployment	.297*** (.110)	−.029 (.172)	.249** (.108)
Maghrebi Councilor × Unemployment	.788*** (.270)		.538* (.275)
Muslim Population × Unemployment		.105** (.042)	
Maghrebi Councilor × Muslim Population			.729* (.390)
Population (log)	−.905 (.720)	−.266 (.681)	−.286 (.709)
FN vote share in previous local election	.896*** (.080)	.788*** (.085)	.830*** (.086)
Constant	9.588 (8.090)	6.359 (7.599)	2.613 (7.961)
N	119	119	119
Adj. R^2	.59	.61	.63

Notes: Ordinary least squares coefficients are given with standard errors in parentheses. Results using Tobit are very similar (the data only contain eight left-censored observations). The Muslim population consists of individuals with an Algerian, Moroccan, Tunisian, or Turkish nationality. $*p < .10; **p < .05; ***p < .01$.
Source: http://elections.figaro.net/popup_2004/accueil.html; *Le Monde* (various issues), Geisser (1997), and the National Institute of Statistics and Economic Studies (2002).

Table 8.1 presents the determinants of the FN's 1995 vote share in the country's 100 largest municipalities, including Paris (which consists of twenty *arrondissements*, each electing local councilors).[19] The party's vote share in these municipalities ranges from zero (the FN did not compete in eight local contests) to 32.7 percent, with a mean value of 11.1 percent. Before I address the findings, it is interesting to note that the correlation between the share of Muslim residents in a municipality and the number of Maghrebi councilors amounts to $r = .28$ – a much weaker correlation than the nearly perfect

[19] I restrict myself to these municipalities for two reasons. First, I assume that data on ethnic minority councilors are more reliable for larger municipalities than for France's many smaller *communes* (the country contains over 36,000 municipalities and even the larger ones are quite small; aside from the Paris *arrondissements*, 30 municipalities in my sample are home to fewer than 60,000 residents; the smallest municipality numbers just over 50,000.) Second, much of the data had to be entered by hand. Finally, the regressions exclude one outlier, Roubaix. Roubaix' unemployment rate (31.8 percent) is the highest in the sample and far exceeded the next highest observation (24.7 percent). Even though the FN receives 24.4 percent of the vote in Roubaix and elects a councilor of Maghrebi background – thus corresponding to the theory of immigrant–native conflict advanced in this book – given its extraordinarily high unemployment rate, its citizens "should have" supported the FN in even greater numbers.

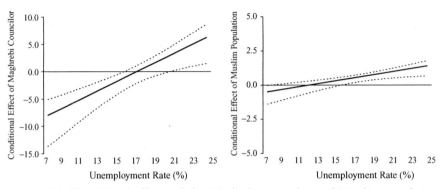

FIGURE 8.1. Conditional effects of the Maghrebi councilor and Muslim population variables on the local *Front National* vote.

correspondence between the presence of Muslims and their local political representation in Great Britain today (see Chapter 1), reflecting the different electoral micro-institutions that organize relationships between ethnic minority electorates, local officeholders, and the voting booth.

Turning to the results, we see that the main quantity of interest in Column 1 is the effect of having elected a Maghrebi councilor (a dummy variable; only Roubaix and Marseille elected two and three Maghrebi candidates, respectively), interacted with a municipality's unemployment rate, Maghrebi Councilor × Unemployment. This effect is positive and statistically significant, suggesting that as unemployment increases, so does the positive impact of Maghrebi political power on the 1995 FN vote. Put differently, economic scarcity magnifies the electoral backlash associated with immigrant political power. The negative coefficient of the Maghrebi councilor variable indicates that the election of local politicians of North African origin is associated with a decrease in the FN's vote share if unemployment were at the fictional value of zero, while the positive effect of the unemployment variable suggests that Le Pen's party can score victories in high-unemployment areas that do not contain Maghrebi councilors. Figure 8.1 reveals that electing Maghrebi representatives in low-unemployment areas is in fact associated with lower electoral support for the anti-immigrant party. Immigrant electoral representation only appears to provoke a xenophobic response in municipalities where large shares of residents are out of a job. Note that since I control for the party's vote share in the previous 1989 election, it is not the case that the FN's success in 1995 is simply driven by its earlier showing and subsequent institutionalization (the results are very similar when the variable measuring the 1989 vote share is dropped).

In Model 2, Muslim population shares do have an impact on the FN vote, but they produce much smaller effects and are further mediated by economic conditions. It would take a very large increase in the local Muslim population to approximate the impact that one or two elected councilors of North African origin has on the FN's electoral success (in high-unemployment areas).[20]

Figure 8.1 displays these findings visually (note that the two charts use different scales on the y axis; the solid lines trace the effect and the dashed lines indicate the 95 percent confidence intervals). While the share of the Muslim population does not appear to have a substantively large impact on the *Front National*'s vote, we should nevertheless expect it to matter. Specifically, the election of Maghrebi councilors might be more threatening to French voters as the size of the Muslim constituency – and hence the amount of state resources to be distributed to this group – increases. Model 3, where I test for this possibility by means of a Maghrebi Councilor × Muslim Population interaction, suggests that this might well be the case.[21]

In sum, these results do not suggest that the presence of Muslim immigrants is unrelated to the success of anti-immigrant campaigns in France, but rather that this relationship is significantly mediated by economic and electoral variables that a culturalist account would miss. The present local-level findings are also compatible with research identifying the socioeconomic characteristics that have led individual French voters to turn to the FN.[22] Lastly, the quantitative results also mesh with the aforementioned qualitative accounts that point to a connection between the electoral ascendance of minorities with a North African background on the one hand and a strong backlash against their potential political clout at the polls on the other.

Partly as a result of the intensity of the xenophobic protest, the local electoral strength of France's immigrant-origin population was not long-lived. In contrast to developments in Great Britain, where South Asian political leverage was based both on consistent mobilization and comparatively open local electoral institutions, Maghrebi electoral strength abated in the following elections as elites became less willing to nominate ethnic minority candidates and low minority turnout rates returned. The FN's vote share dropped to 2.0 percent in

---

[20] Including the Maghrebi population variable in the Maghrebi councilors regressions (not shown) does not alter the substantive effect of Maghrebi Councilor × Unemployment, which now has a coefficient of $\beta = .763$ and a standard error of $SE = .270$. The effect of Maghrebi population is strong (with a coefficient of $\beta = .601$, and a standard error of $SE = .187$) but again turns insignificant and negative when Maghrebi Population × Unemployment is added. Including this interaction also weakens the effect of Maghrebi Councilor × Unemployment, which now has a coefficient of $\beta = .565$ and a standard error of $SE = .300$.

[21] Further calculations (not shown) show this effect to be statistically significant across the majority of values of the Muslim population variable.

[22] Using 1995 survey data, Lubbers and Scheepers (2002) find, e.g., that unemployed voters are more likely to support the xenophobic party, when one controls for unfavorable attitudes toward Muslims and Islam. See also Mayer (2002). At the contextual level, Lubbers and Scheepers do find that the share of Muslim immigrants at the level of the *département* has a positive effect on FN support, but Kestilä and Söderlund (2004) find no evidence that the share of non-EU nationals matters in explaining the FN vote across *départements*. (Neither study interacts the share of immigrants with other contextual variables.)

the 2001 local elections, its seats plummeting from a high of 1,075 to a low of 106.[23] The incidence of antistate violence has not experienced a similar decline.

In short, these qualitative and quantitative findings show that major features of the French case are consistent with the logic of immigrant conflict proposed here. The present conceptualization of the *Front National* vote is surely somewhat superficial. It does not measure, for example, if and how the party's strategic adaptation from a one-issue, anti-immigrant party to a more encompassing movement at the national level filtered down to municipal elections (cf. Dancygier 2007b). Importantly, at the national level, the law-and-order stance of the party's platform must have been in part a reaction to the phenomenon of immigrant–state conflict, suggesting dynamics of immigrant conflict over time and across spatial units that are not captured here. Although the FN's 1995 manifestos at the municipal level hardly mentioned the issue of law and order (Oriol 1998), a more thorough investigation of immigrant–native conflict would have to take more careful measure of the party's platform and furthermore collect data on additional indicators of intergroup clashes, such as anti-immigrant rallies and violence.

Although more detailed studies of the interactions between economic shortages and immigrant political behavior on the one hand, and anti-immigrant and antistate responses on the other (as well as improved data on immigrant-origin minorities) are thus needed, the evidence presented here demonstrates that the explanatory power of the book's main theoretical propositions travels to the French setting, where an immigration regime that did not adequately address the economic needs of migrants coalesced with a liberal citizenship code, but also with local electoral institutions that have only sometimes been conducive to the effective representation of immigrant-origin citizens.

Citizenship, Immigration, and Economic Developments across Europe

Though postwar mass migration has been taking place from the 1960s onward, it is since the 1990s that immigration and immigrant integration have been highly salient topics in public debates across many European countries. In most instances where immigration has been politicized, the tone has been hostile to immigrants and has been accompanied by electoral advances of the far right. Over the course of the 1990s and early 2000s, parties that have made anti-immigration platforms central to their campaigns have garnered over 10 percent of the vote in national parliamentary elections in Austria, Belgium, Denmark, France, Italy, Norway, and Switzerland (Dancygier 2008). At the local level, these parties have also made significant gains, though, as is to be expected, support for xenophobic parties has varied across cities and towns. The rest of this chapter argues that changes in immigration regimes, immigrant

---

[23] See Messina (2007, 59). The true anti-immigrant vote share is slightly higher, since the xenophobic *Mouvement National Républicain*, a breakaway from the FN, also scored some successes.

political incorporation, and developments in the supply of and demand for local economic resources across countries explain the rising conflict potential.

Trends in Citizenship and Immigrant Political Power

The rest of this chapter argues that changes in immigration regimes, immigrant political incorporation, and developments in the supply of and demand for local economic resources across countries explain this rising conflict potential. Figure 8.2 provides a broad overview of immigration and naturalizations across countries since the 1970s (or later, depending on data availability).[24] Several interesting patterns stand out. First, a set of small European countries (notably Austria, Belgium, Sweden, and Switzerland) have witnessed especially high naturalization rates. Between 1970 and 2005, Sweden naturalized over 900,000 residents, or what would amount to approximately 10 percent of its overall population (as measured in 2005). In Austria, Belgium, and Switzerland, this figure stands at 5.9, 7.1, and 8.7 percent, while in the United Kingdom, Germany, and France those who naturalized between 1970 and 2005 represent approximately 3.7, 4.7, and 4.6 percent of the population, respectively.[25] In local areas of immigrant concentration, these shares are bound to be much higher. Second, almost all countries witnessed upward trends in citizenship acquisitions starting in the 1990s. In some, such as Germany and Belgium, these increases were in part due to liberalizations of the nationality code. In others, the requirements for obtaining citizenship have remained stringent (as in Austria and Switzerland) but immigrants and their descendents have resided in the host countries long enough to meet them. In new immigration countries such as Spain and Ireland, citizenship acquisitions still trail inflows.

In addition to the ease with which immigrant denizens can become citizens, access to local voting rights can also function as an important determinant of immigrants' electoral clout in the cities and towns in which they locate. In France and Germany, the extension of the local franchise to nonnationals has been highly controversial. In Belgium, where nonnationals were given the right to participate in local elections in 2004, the issue had also been extremely divisive since at least the 1980s. Vienna's attempt to enfranchise its non-EU nationals in 2002 was promptly banned by Austria's highest court and similar endeavors launched by German states in the late 1980s were declared unconstitutional (Bauer 2007). That members of the nonimmigrant electorate are suspicious of incorporating a new set of voters who will make claims that may impinge on their welfare is of course very much in line with the theory put forth in this book. But overall, countries have nevertheless expanded nonnationals' access to the ballot box at the municipal level. The majority of West European

---

[24] I collected naturalization data from a variety of sources, including national statistical yearbooks and Clarke, van Dam, and Gooster (1998). I thank Raymond Hicks for helping me gather these data. For net migration rates, see OECD (2007).

[25] These calculations assume that those who have naturalized are, by 2005, still alive and resident in the respective countries where they naturalized.

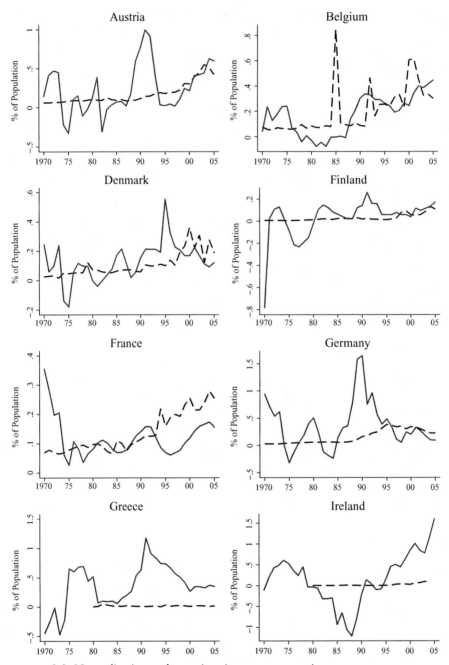

FIGURE 8.2. Naturalization and net migration across countries.

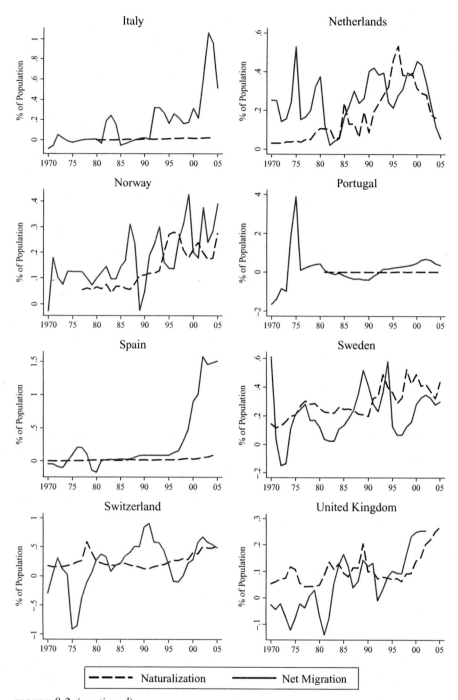

FIGURE 8.2 *(continued).*

(EU-15) countries today grant local voting rights to noncitizens originating outside of the EU.[26] Summing up these developments, when considered from a purely institutional perspective, the rise in citizenship acquisitions and the extension of the local franchise have enhanced the potential for local immigrant electoral power.

Immigrant-origin political actors have indeed become more prominent, particularly at the local level. In Austria, more than three-fourths of those who acquired citizenship in the 1990s and 2000s have reached voting age, prompting political parties, especially in larger cities, to seek their votes (Hutter and Perchinig 2008, 18–19). The political representation of minorities of immigrant background has also risen considerably in the Netherlands. In just over a decade, the number of Turkish and Moroccan councilors increased close to five-fold and tenfold, respectively. By 2006, ethnic minority candidates constituted 25 percent of elected councilors in Amsterdam and 20 percent in Rotterdam (Dekker and Fattah 2006).

In neighboring Belgium, candidates with immigrant origins have also made significant advances in the 1990s, following changes in the citizenship code and ensuing steep naturalization spikes in 1985 and beyond. In Brussels alone, 150,000 foreign residents and more than half of the capital's Moroccan and Turkish population acquired Belgian citizenship between 1988 and 2002. Nonetheless, electoral advances have been uneven. When Antwerp elected its first councilor of non-EU origin – a Moroccan woman – in 1988, not a single one of Brussels' nineteen ethnically diverse municipalities had elected ethnic minority candidates. Since then, however, the number of minority representatives, most of whom are of Moroccan and Turkish origin, has grown rapidly: There were 14 elected in 1994, 90 in 2000, and 138 (or 20 percent of all councilors) in 2006 (Rea 2000; D. Jacobs 2007, 28). The number of ethnic minority councilors has also climbed steadily in Denmark, increasing fivefold between 1985 and 2001. Today, "Ethnic minorities are surprisingly well represented in local councils in Denmark" (Togeby 2008, 331).

What unites the Netherlands, Belgium, and Denmark are both local voting rights for nonnationals and rising naturalizations, as well as local electoral systems that combine proportional representation with preferential voting rules. These systems allow voters to cast additional ballots for specific candidates and thus facilitate ethnically based mobilization. Such electoral laws are more likely to result in the election of ethnic minority politicians than France's more majoritarian, anti-communal system (Bird 2005; ter Wal 2007, 256–257; Togeby 2008).

---

[26] Studying why political actors would extend these rights in the face of native opposition is an interesting question that merits further research. Such a move can be expected if politicians think that immigrant voters will cast their ballots for parties and politicians that helped enact local voting rights legislation and that these new votes exceed the votes cast in opposition to migrant enfranchisement. But given the likely ex ante uncertainty about noncitizen turnout, we might also expect parties and politicians who enjoy wide margins of support, and who can thus afford to absorb potential losses that are due to native desertions, to back such laws.

Changing Immigration Regimes and the Economic Characteristics of Immigrants

Returning to Figure 8.2, we observe that the rise in immigrant citizens has coincided with a rise in immigration. Even though many European countries enacted official immigration bans in the first half of the 1970s, the inflow of migrants has tended to outpace their outflows: Since the early 1990s net migration has been positive in all countries in nearly all years. In contrast to earlier waves, however, more recent migration has not been primarily guided by economic forces (especially in countries that have long received immigrants). Rather, family reunification and formation, as well as political asylum, have continued to boost the migrant populations in cities and towns across Europe. In 1992, as much as 50 percent of immigration to Europe was due to family reunification and by 1998 this figure had shot up to 70 percent. Thus, in Sweden, for example, 76 percent of migrants entered on the basis of family reunification or asylum in 1997, and only 2 percent arrived as a result of their status as workers (Brücker et al. 2002, 18–19). In Denmark, the yearly shares of resident permits issued as a result of employment also averaged just 11 percent between 1988 and 1997, never exceeding 15 percent (Pedersen 1999, 170; author's calculations).

As I have laid out in Chapter 2, and as the comparison across immigration regimes in the previous chapters has made plain, the prevalence of noneconomic immigration regimes is, all else equal, likely to have negative effects on the labor market integration of migrants, which in turn may influence local resource scarcity. Studies have in fact found significant cohort effects, whereby migrants arriving in the late 1980s and 1990s have fared worse in the labor market than previous arrivals of similar national backgrounds.[27] The patchy economic integration of second- and third-generation immigrants thus coincides with new immigrant populations whose linguistic and skill profiles may prove difficult fits for local labor markets. The underrepresentation of labor migrants is especially marked among migrants with origins outside of the EU. For instance, though labor migrants constituted 23 percent of all migrants in the Netherlands in 2003, among "non-Western" arrivals this figure stood at a mere 8 percent, compared with 40 percent among Western migrants (ter Wal 2007, 253; author's calculations). This skewed composition represents a shift even for the Netherlands, whose postwar immigration regime had consisted of both noneconomic and economic inflows. Similar discrepancies can be found across Europe.

Migrants who tend to be most culturally distinct from Europe's native-born citizenry thus also tend to be least likely to arrive as economic migrants – a development that is quite different from earlier guest-worker migration and one that cultural accounts of immigrant conflict need to wrestle with. Figure 8.3 reveals that unemployment rates differ dramatically across citizenship groups,

---

[27] See Schultz-Nielsen and Constant (2004, 132–135) for a discussion of these effects in Denmark and Sweden.

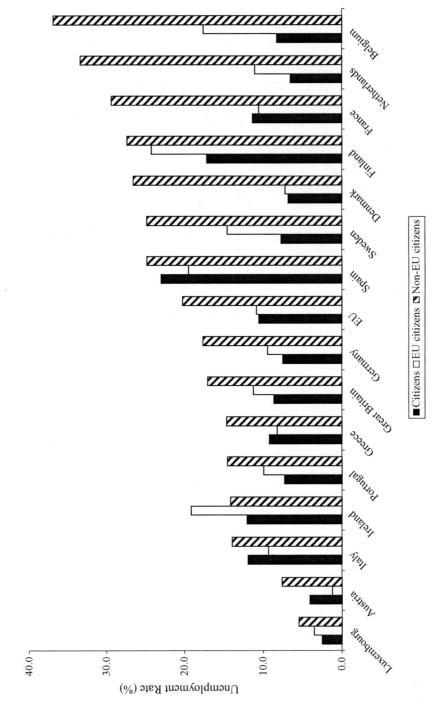

FIGURE 8.3. Unemployment rate by citizenship, 1995. (*Source:* Werner and König 2001.)

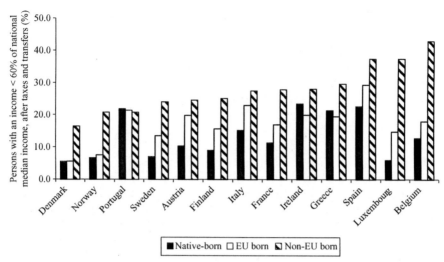

FIGURE 8.4. Risk of poverty by country of birth, 2004. (*Source:* Lelkes 2007.)

with non-EU citizens being less likely to be employed than EU or host country citizens in all countries (except for Ireland). Non-EU citizens fare especially poorly in Denmark, Finland, France, the Netherlands, and Belgium, where more than one in four were jobless in 1995. On the basis of the naturalization rates presented earlier, we can assume that substantial numbers of these economically disadvantaged migrants have by now become citizens – some of whom will make their economic needs heard in the cities in which they have settled.

Cross-national unemployment rates only paint a partial picture of economic need, since countries vary in the extent to which they even out income differentials through taxes and transfers. Figure 8.4 therefore depicts the "at risk of poverty" rate in 2004 – the share of persons with a disposable income below 60 percent of national median income – for European countries where data were available.[28] The data show that persons born outside of the European Union have consistently lower incomes than those born in the EU or individuals born in the host country, though differences in the expansiveness of national transfer systems have caused the levels of economic need among immigrants to vary across countries. Disposable incomes among migrants in Denmark and Sweden – where taxes and transfers are extensive – are therefore higher than unemployment rates would suggest and might therefore also reduce demand for scarce economic resources locally. But even here, non-EU migrants are at substantially higher risk of poverty. Transfers thus lessen *local* poverty to a

---

[28] It is important to keep in mind that median incomes differ across countries. The high differential in Luxembourg is therefore in part due to the country's high median income. I thank Orsolya Lelkes for providing me with these data.

degree, but the size of welfare spending targeted at migrant communities has been a salient topic in *national* debates.

In sum, as noneconomic migration motives predominated at the end of the twentieth century, the economic integration of immigrants has been difficult in many countries. Migrants originating outside of the European Union have tended to arrive on the basis of political asylum or family reunification. Their level of economic need consistently and often drastically exceeds national averages, though levels of unemployment and income deprivation vary across nations and, most likely, across cities within countries.

In many cases, these developments represent substantial changes from the immigration regimes that were prevalent in the 1960s and 1970s. Countries that used to have coordinated, labor-based immigration regimes have become less coordinated while citizenship acquisitions and the associated potential for local electoral clout have risen. Though the degree to which policy makers devised recruitment plans for migrant inflows and coordinated immigration with municipalities varied across Europe (Hammar 1985), primary migrants tended to find employment in local labor markets. Moreover, governments in several countries, such as in Sweden, the Netherlands, and Germany, enacted policies that would manage the delivery of goods and services in the local areas of settlement (Soysal 1994). In more recent years, the predominance of noneconomic forms of migration, the often ad hoc nature of such inflows, and the declining labor market fortunes of first-generation labor migrants and their offspring have made it more difficult to sustain adequate supplies of local resources. The next section places these institutional changes in the context of broader economic developments that have influenced local resource provision.

Economic Developments and Local Resource Scarcity

Addressing the material needs of noneconomic immigrants – along with those of the immigrant-origin minority populations now in their second and third generation – should have thus proved more challenging for local governments. But much depends on levels of central government support in settling and integrating immigrants, social spending trends, as well as on the supply of preexisting municipal infrastructures. More generally, and as we have observed in previous chapters, societal needs and demands (influenced by poverty and unemployment rates) interact with public spending decisions in areas of local service delivery to jointly affect the level of resources available to individuals at the municipal level. Although levels of social spending vary across countries, the growth of total government expenditures (the costs of the goods and services produced by the public sector) slowed down in the first half of the 1990s in all OECD countries, even as social needs tended to rise. In the EU-15 countries, social spending (as a share of gross domestic product) declined in the late 1980s and late 1990s, before picking up again in the early 2000s.[29]

---

[29] See Clayton and Pontusson (1998) and OECD (2007). As Clayton and Pontusson state, however, a measure of actual welfare effort should take into account not only the supply of services but also societal need.

Moreover, as the size of the overall government pie has been shrinking, many countries have been devolving rights and responsibilities from the center to lower tiers of government and the subnational portion of public spending has grown as a result. Conflicts over resources should therefore implicate the local state to a greater degree than in the past, holding all else constant. Though details vary across countries, as a general trend, decentralization has been salient in the areas of education, health, and welfare services (OECD 1997; Joumard and Kongsrud 2003; Ireland 2004). In terms of public housing, which often falls within the purview of local government, reduced levels of new constructions, stagnant market shares, and increasing housing costs have been common across Western Europe. By 2003, housing expenditures constituted over one-fourth of all spending in households in five EU-15 countries (Priemus and Dieleman 1997; National Board of Housing, Building and Planning, 2005).

Similarly, as the case of France illustrates, public employment exemplifies the trend of decentralization amidst spending cuts. In the United Kingdom, where public sector employment was slashed by nearly 30 percent from peak levels in the late 1980s, over 50 percent of the public workforce was employed by local government in 1994. In Sweden and Denmark, where public employment cutbacks occurred as the number of jobless climbed, the share of workers employed by local government increased from 46 percent in 1985 to 58 percent in 1994 (Sweden) and from 69 to 73 percent (Denmark). These developments have persisted into the twenty-first century for a range of European countries (OECD 1997, 37; Clayton and Pontusson 1998; Joumard and Kongsrud 2003, 11).

In brief, as both economic needs and local government control over state resources have expanded, the overall supply of such resources has declined. The ability to influence local government decision making and resource allocation has consequently become ever more valuable. Synthesizing these trends from the perspective of immigrant conflict, decentralization in the face of shrinking overall spending represents an ominous development: Local political actors have gained increasing control over a decreasing pool of resources at a time when noneconomic immigration motives were dominant, economic needs of immigrants were high as a result, and citizenship acquisitions have gone up. Keeping in mind that the political and economic developments outlined herein represent general tendencies and that details will necessarily vary by locality, these broad trends nevertheless shed light on the environment in which immigrants and natives confront one another as well as the state in Europe's towns and cities.

Implications for Immigrant Conflict

According to the logic of immigrant conflict advanced in this book, a rise in ethnic minorities' local electoral power, continued inflows of economically disadvantaged migrants – especially when these occur in an ad hoc fashion and are not part of coordinated immigration regimes – as well as contractions in spending amid gains in local government discretion over resources should be associated with an increase in the incidence of immigrant–native conflict. Though many of Europe's anti-immigrant parties have made strong showings since the 1990s, much of the media coverage and public debate has concentrated less on the electoral and economic consequences of immigration, and has instead focused on the cultural threats associated with the inflow and long-term settlement of Muslims. The political salience of immigration and the divisive rhetoric surrounding immigrant integration has without a doubt been fueled by concerns about Islam and the religion's compatibility with Western norms and values. Islamist extremism, the role of Imams, Muslims' treatment of women (including domestic violence, forced marriages, and honor killings), and the wearing of headscarves in public institutions are just some of the issues that have filled the headlines. The Swiss public's vote to ban the construction of minarets in the Fall of 2009 appears to embody Europe's trepidation with Islam.

The dilemma between multiculturalism and religious pluralism on the one hand and the toleration of illiberal values and practices on the other thus appears to have dominated public discourse about immigration and ethnic diversity over the past decade. But can this clash of cultures explain patterns of immigrant–native and immigrant–state conflict in Europe's cities and towns? As mentioned at the outset of this book, those who posit that ethnic and religious difference has been at the heart of such conflicts need to at the very least account for the correlation between immigrants' cultural backgrounds and their socioeconomic status; the figures presented herein have shown clear patterns between migrants' non-EU (and often Muslim) backgrounds and their socioeconomic disadvantage.

As this book has sought to make clear, cultural distance cannot explain patterns of local immigrant conflict in Great Britain, Germany, and France. It is also difficult to make the case that religious practices or cultural norms are responsible for sustained immigrant conflict in cities of other European countries. Take Amsterdam and Rotterdam, for example, where minorities of Turkish and Moroccan descent have entered city halls in growing numbers since the 1990s. Few cities have experienced the type of highly visible and threatening events associated with Islam as has Amsterdam, where the filmmaker Theo van Gogh was murdered by an Islamist extremist in broad daylight.[30] The killer, a Moroccan-origin Dutchman, first shot and then stabbed his victim repeatedly with a knife, before skewering a threatening letter to his chest. In Rotterdam, Muslim public figures have also caused controversies, but the city has not witnessed a similarly dramatic event.[31]

---

[30] Van Gogh's film "Submission" addresses the mistreatment of women by Muslim men in a provocative fashion. In the film, the text of the Koran is projected onto the naked body of a Muslim woman in prayer.

[31] For instance, in 2001, a "Moroccan imam in Rotterdam, Khalil el-Moumni, condemned homosexuals as 'worse than dogs' and was taken to court on charges of discrimination" (Ireland 2004, 130). On van Gogh's murder, see Buruma (2006).

Yet, conflict outcomes have been much more pronounced in Rotterdam than they have been in Amsterdam. In Amsterdam, support for the populist, anti-immigrant *Leefbaar* party (formerly headed by Pim Fortuyn) dropped from 5 percent in 2002 to 1 percent in 2006 and 2010. The extremist murder thus did not inspire the city's residents to mobilize against Muslims at the polls. Though mosques and Muslim schools in several cities had been targeted with arson attempts after the horrific van Gogh murder, these did not tend to be supported by local grass-roots movements and widespread attacks against Muslims did not take place.[32] In spite of incessant and heated press coverage, "The 'civil war' that some feared, the pogroms on Muslim areas, the retaliations by newly recruited jihadis, none of this actually happened. Most people kept their cool" (Buruma 2006, 7). By contrast, in Rotterdam (where the door of a mosque had been scorched after the murder) *Leefbaar* ended more than fifty years of Social Democratic rule in 2002, winning over one-third of the vote in 2002 and 29 percent in 2006 and 2010. Geert Wilder's anti-Muslim Party for Freedom has also scored successes in local elections, though not in multicultural Amsterdam.

It is also not immediately apparent how cultural clashes can explain support for the xenophobic Danish People's Party (DPP). At the national level, the DPP has been an outspoken opponent of immigration, a stance which earned it over 13 percent of the vote in parliamentary elections in 2005 and 2007. One of the national party's main themes has been its criticism of the size of the welfare benefits that native Danes transfer to the immigrant population (as displayed in Figures 8.3 and 8.4, Denmark residents born outside of the EU are at lowest risk of poverty but have among the highest unemployment rates). But equally prominent in its rhetoric has been the party's insistence that Muslim immigration represents a grave threat to Denmark's ethnic identity and cultural heritage (Rydgren 2004). At the local level, though, support for the DPP has hovered only around 5 percent since the party first ran in 1997. Moreover, as Figure 8.5 shows, the immigrant presence, which is correlated with immigrants' political power (Togeby 2008), tends to lead voters to the DPP as local economic conditions worsen; in municipalities where unemployment is low, the presence of immigrants and support for the DPP show no relationship (note that these correlations are not a result of immigrants living in high-unemployment areas).[33]

The mediating role of economic conditions – and the relatively low overall local share of DPP votes – arises even when cultural issues were highly salient. Just before the November 2005 municipal elections, the so-called cartoon controversy shook the country. Muslims in Denmark (and later on throughout

---

[32] *Trouw,* "Moskeeen in brand gestoken; Binnenlandse Zaken: Het gaat om losse incidenten," November 8, 2004.

[33] Figure 8.6 displays correlations between the share of first- and second-generation immigrants and unemployment rates in ninety-four (out of a total of ninety-eight) Danish municipalities in 2005 where the DPP ran. The correlation between the share of (nonwestern) immigrants and local unemployment is $r = -.047$ $(-.003)$. Data are available at www.statistikbanken.dk.

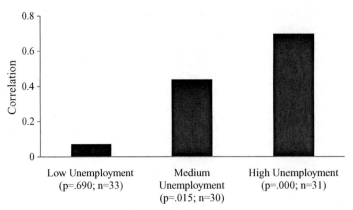

FIGURE 8.5. Correlation between the 2005 Danish People's Party vote share and the share of the local immigrant population, by local unemployment.

the world) protested against the publication of caricatures of the prophet Mohammed by a conservative Danish newspaper. Even though the DPP used this incident in its 2007 parliamentary campaign, at the local level the controversy apparently failed to mobilize voters. In Copenhagen, where Muslims had taken to the streets in protest, the DPP attained average results of 5.9 percent (within Copenhagen, precincts in the area of the first public protests – Nørrebro – showed the DPP polling below 4 percent; see Hussain 2007, 48; Københavns Kommune 2008). Overall, the comparatively unimpressive success of the anti-immigrant party at the local level must be evaluated in light of the fact that unemployment is modest, welfare provision remains high, and, as a result, local economic scarcity is relatively low, especially in comparison with a set of other European countries.

One such country is Belgium. Though Belgium has undergone similar trends – a rise in economically disadvantaged immigrants along with decentralization and cutbacks of service provision – immigrant conflict has been much more pronounced here. The xenophobic *Vlaams Blok* (VB; later reborn as the *Vlams Belang* after being outlawed for having violated antiracism laws) attained an average of 15 percent of the vote in the 224 municipalities (out of a total of 308) in which the party competed.[34] Racist violence has also plagued some Belgian cities (Centre for Equal Opportunities and Opposition to Racism 2004). Figures 8.3 and 8.4 again provide some clues that may drive these developments: Immigrant unemployment as well as poverty risk rates in Belgium are the highest in the sample. Figure 8.2 in turn shows that economic disadvantage has been accompanied with dramatic increases in naturalization and, as already mentioned, substantial gains in ethnic minority political power.

[34] My calculations, based on data available at www.binnenland.vlaanderen.be/verkiezingen/verkiezingen2006/.

Furthermore, over the course of the 1980s and 1990s, Belgian government service delivery has been decentralized as "the rather austere Belgian welfare state made huge...budget cuts in all policy domains, turning a blind eye to new needs.... [I]nvestments were frozen, as were the wages of civil servants, teachers, [and] nurses.... In Flanders...the construction of social housing dropped dramatically and in Wallonia and the Brussels Capital Region it was stopped altogether" (De Decker, Kesteloot, Maesschalck, and Vranken 2005, 161). Antwerp cut its city workforce by more than one-fourth between 1982 and 1994 while Brussels had lost 80,000 manual jobs – many of them held by ethnic minorities – between 1974 and 1995. Urban renewal projects were marked by their absence (Swyngedouw 2000, 124, 131–132; de Decker et al. 2005, 160). By 1991, the male unemployment rate among Moroccans and Turks of the second generation had jumped to well over 30 percent in Flanders, Brussels, and Wallonia (Phalet and Swyngedouw 2003, 789).

In light of these economic developments, Belgian cities have experienced both types of immigrant conflict. Antwerp has been the site of extreme and sustained intergroup conflict. In 1988, the VB made its strongest showing here, gaining 18 percent of the vote, a success that coincided with the election of the first Moroccan-origin councilor in the city, followed by affirmative action in the selection of city employees (Bousetta 1998, 167). In the following years, the number of ethnic minority councilors would increase along with an escalation in immigrant–native conflict. The VB became the biggest party on the council in 1994, garnering close to 30 percent of the vote, and xenophobic violence was taken to new heights as racist murders shook the city in the following years.[35]

In Brussels, by contrast, where immigrant-origin councilors had yet to be elected, confrontations between ethnic minority youths and state actors took center stage in the late 1980s and early 1990s. Following a minor altercation between second-generation immigrants and the police, rioting broke out in several Brussels municipalities with a high share of ethnic minorities where, after three decades of immigrant settlement, not a single councilor of Moroccan or Turkish background had been elected. The confrontations "were exclusively between youths and the police, and not at all between 'immigrants' and native Belgians...[they were an] expression of a desire for citizenship in Brussels and in Belgium.... Resistance to powerlessness was manifested in violence, the only way for these young people to make their voices heard and to deliver their unexpected message" (Martiniello 1997a, 293, 298–299; see also Rea 2001).[36]

More recently, however, the growing number of naturalized Belgians has helped boost immigrant political power. As the number of ethnic minority councilors in Brussels municipalities has risen, so has the representation of

---

[35] See *Süddeutsche Zeitung*, "Belgier demonstrieren gegen Rassismus," May 26, 2006.

[36] Similar violence would break out again in 1997 in three Brussels municipalities (Molenbeek, Anderlecht, and St. Gilles). Writing about these immigrant–state disturbances, Lambert (1997) points out that the *Parti Socialiste* – the major left-of-center party – did not field any ethnic minority candidates here in the previous elections.

councilors of the far-right wing. Indeed, several authors have mentioned in passing a correlation between the successes and failures of ethnic minority representatives on the one hand, and the fortunes of the far-right parties in Antwerp (Bousetta 1998), Brussels (Martiniello 1998, 134), Charleroi (Ireland 2004, 183), and Liège (Martiniello 1997b, 117) on the other. The theory of immigrant conflict put forth in this book helps us make sense of these local relationships.

Though the logic of immigrant conflict proposed here appears to travel to settings across Europe, there are also instances that, at first glance, do not seem to fit its theoretical predictions. For instance, Austria's Freedom Party has performed well locally since at least the early 1990s, when the party had made anti-immigration themes prominent, but before naturalizations had gained momentum. Yet, it is unclear to what extent a local vote for the Freedom Party is indeed a vote against immigrants. In national elections between 1986 and 1999, only between 3 and 15 percent of Haider's voters supported the populist's party based on its views on immigration (Luther 2007, 249). (By comparison, immigration motivated the vote choice among close to 60 percent of Le Pen supporters in the presidential election of 2002; see Dancygier 2007b, 262.)

In Switzerland, xenophobic electoral advances appear to outpace ethnic minority political representation, though it is unclear to what extent cultural clashes drive local anti-immigrant agitation here. The controversial referendum banning the construction of minarets did not grow out of confrontations with local Muslim neighbors. Calculations across cantons and smaller-sized districts (*Bezirke*) reveal that the share of Muslims in the population is not correlated with the share of voters approving the ban.[37] Instead, voters in more ethnically homogeneous rural areas, some of which contained not a single Muslim resident, were more likely than those living in urban centers to vote against the building of minarets.[38]

Though the electoral clout of Switzerland's immigrants may not be the central determinant of local interethnic conflict here, aspects of the Swiss case nevertheless provide an interesting extension to this book's theory of immigrant–native conflict. Consistent with its tradition of local autonomy and direct democracy, Switzerland grants municipalities a large degree of discretion in naturalization decisions, and local electorates sometimes vote on these processes. In one Swiss town, for example, a "Committee for the maintenance of the Swiss race" was successful in urging its citizens to vote against the extension of citizenship to immigrants from the former Yugoslavia.[39] More generally, in

---

[37] The correlation between the Muslim population and the "yes" vote is $r = .05$ at the canton level and $r = .02$ at the district level (my calculations, based on vote statistics available at http://www.bfs.admin.ch/bfs/portal/de/index/themen/17/03/blank/key/2009/05.html, accessed March 9, 2010; data on religious affiliation were sent to me by the Swiss Federal Statistical Office).

[38] *Neue Zürcher Zeitung*, "Geografie des Protests," December 2, 2009.

[39] *Der Spiegel*, "Rote Pässe, braune Hände," May 26, 2008.

municipalities where the anti-immigrant Swiss People's Party is strong, voters are also more likely to turn down naturalization requests.[40]

In Switzerland, native voters can thus engage in preemptive xenophobia by preventing immigrants from becoming citizens, a precondition for local electoral influence. As I have tried to convey throughout this book, opposition against immigrants' gaining political power and, with it, leverage over the distribution of resources, is one central feature of immigrant conflict.

---

[40] This relationship holds in a sample of larger municipalities, between 1990 and 2002 (Helbling and Kriesi 2004).

9

Conclusion

According to recent population projections, positive net migration will be the only source of population increase in Europe by 2015 (Eurostat 2008). Even at the end of the twentieth century, immigration outpaced emigration in most advanced democracies, with most arrivals settling in urban areas. Cities across Europe, already culturally and ethnically diverse, will become even more so as immigration continues and native fertility rates remain low. In the United States, where non-Hispanic whites are poised to lose their majority status in the next several decades, one in three households residing in larger cities reported speaking a language other than English at home in 2006.[1]

Reviewing the Argument

This diverse reality underscores the urgency of answering the central question that I have pursued in this book: What explains conflict between immigrants and natives and between immigrants and the state in local areas of settlement? Though scholarship has addressed the domestic consequences of immigration from various angles, few have tackled this question systematically. This book has sought to fill this void by clarifying when, where, and why sustained clashes between immigrants and natives and between immigrants and the state emerge. Throughout this book, I have illuminated the economic bases of both types of conflict. Simply put, natives are much more likely to turn against their immigrant neighbors, and immigrants are much more prone to engage in confrontations with state actors, when each group faces economic shortages. Resource scarcity – not ethnic difference – is the key driver of immigrant conflict.

---

[1] Larger cities are those with populations exceeding 100,000. See http://www.census.gov/compendia/statab/cats/population/ancestry_language_spoken_at_home.html, accessed February 6, 2009.

But economic conditions only tell half the story. As I have demonstrated in the preceding chapters, immigrants' capacity to actually obtain scarce resources determines which *type* of conflict will ensue. When immigrant communities wield local political power, and they use this clout to acquire limited economic resources from local government, immigration will impinge on the economic well-being of natives. Natives are likely to protest this resource allocation by engaging in anti-immigrant behavior. Voting for xenophobic candidates lets local politicians know that catering to immigrant needs may carry a hefty electoral price, while targeting immigrants with harassment and violence sends a message to the new settlers that the indigenous population will fight to retain their access to important goods.

Natives will not resort to such measures when they do not have to give up scarce resources in the face of immigration. Specifically, when immigrants do not possess the local political clout to induce local politicians to distribute valued material goods to this new constituency, natives will not engage in anti-immigrant behavior. This neglect of immigrant needs by local politicians, however, inspires opposition against state actors on the part of immigrants. Conflicts between immigrants and the state will thus arise when immigrants lack electoral clout and material goods in economically hard times. These propositions, in a nutshell, form the core argument of this book.

If economic conditions and immigrant electoral behavior are the twin forces that shape immigrant conflict, I identified a number of institutional arrangements that in turn affect these variables. In doing so, I have drawn attention to the significance of immigration regimes in influencing resource shortages in the cities and towns where immigrants settle. Immigrants' ability to work, their skills, and their demographic composition will affect the level and types of demands they make on local resources, while rules that make immigration conditional on the availability of local resources and that prepare municipal infrastructures for the arrival of newcomers will have impacts on the supply of goods available to immigrants and natives. Immigration regimes will then interact with broader economic swings to produce variation in economic scarcity across cities within and across countries. On the electoral side, citizenship laws and electoral institutions determine the ease with which immigrant residents can turn into pivotal voters. But immigrants' capacity to mobilize their fellow migrants also critically shapes the extent to which local politicians will want to represent this new voting bloc.

I have demonstrated how this logic plays out in different group, local, and national contexts. I have shown that South Asian migrants in Britain have more often gained local electoral leverage than their West Indian counterparts and have connected this variation in political power to differences in conflict outcomes: South Asians have been more likely than West Indians to be involved in immigrant–native conflict, while West Indian migrants have been more likely to be involved in clashes with the state when compared to their South Asian counterparts. Furthermore, the incidence of both types of conflict rose during economically trying times and was especially pronounced in cities hard hit by deprivation and recession. I also established that dynamics of racist violence across Greater London are consistent with these patterns. Finally, these broad relationships between economic scarcity and immigrant electoral behavior find more precise expression in the in-depth study of specific locales over time. Here, I have been able to more directly trace and observe the processes that tie immigrants' political behavior and local resource shortages to conflict outcomes.

Stepping outside the context of Great Britain brings the significance of national immigration regimes in configuring the supply of and demand for local resources into sharper relief. In Britain, initial postwar immigration occurred as a by-product of an expansive citizenship code. Immigration thus took place in the absence of policies guiding migrant arrival and settlement, thereby exacerbating resource shortages in some cities and towns. In Germany, by contrast, I have shown how regulations directing guest-worker migration explicitly linked immigration to employment; made arrival provisional on the availability of local resources; and made migrants' stay dependent on their employment status. The economically focused logic and implementation of guest-worker migration, I have argued, reduced local resource pressures, especially when compared to the local economic repercussions of immigration in Great Britain. Though immigrants were largely deprived of electoral power, their relative economic integration in Germany held both kinds of immigrant conflict in check, even as attitudes toward ethnically distinct immigrants were no friendlier here than they were in Great Britain. Indeed, this book has shown that the unplanned inflow of ethnic brethrens (the German-heritage *Aussiedler*) and asylum-seekers – many of whom of European origin – engendered a backlash that was much more severe than native responses to guest workers. The former did not flex their electoral muscle, but a set of laws enabled them to claim scarce local resources, causing native opposition.

Once we appreciate how the economic dimensions of immigration regimes combine with immigrant political behavior to contribute to immigrant conflict, we also begin to understand cross-national differences in subnational conflict outcomes. In France, for instance, the absence of managed migration; the lacking provision of adequate resources to immigrant-receiving locales; and the variable capacity of immigrant-origin minorities to have their demands met by city halls explains why both immigrant–native and immigrant–state conflict are frequent occurrences across municipalities. The French case has also illustrated how economic developments seemingly unrelated to immigration and interethnic relations may nevertheless shape patterns of immigrant conflict: the expansion of local government discretion over the allocation of economic goods – such as public employment or social services – just when such goods became increasingly valuable, put a premium on local government access. Lastly, a bird's-eye view across countries of economic decentralization, as well as trends in the economic features of recent immigration waves and the rising rates at which immigrant residents turn into voting citizens, puts contemporary immigrant conflict in perspective.

Concluding Implications

A number of theoretical and policy implications flow from the book's central argument. First, if conflict between immigrants and natives breaks out when immigrants are in a position to acquire resources, intergroup clashes are in fact a sign of immigrant *integration*, albeit of a type that is resisted by many. Native hostility to successful immigrant claims making during times of economic scarcity suggests the rejection of possible *outcomes* of immigration and ethnic diversity, rather than hostility against population change and diversity per se. What natives are reacting against are the consequences of immigrants' exercising their rights as full-fledged citizens. Viewed in this light, sustained intergroup confrontations actually signal immigrant progress toward incorporation.

This interpretation is compatible with analyses of intergroup conflict between immigrants and natives and blacks and whites in the United States, which have found that majority groups attack minority groups "to maintain their dominance and control ... the *breakdown* of a rigid system of discrimination and the racial queue sparks ethnic collective action" (Olzak 1992, 209, 216; emphasis added). Lynching violence against blacks in the U.S. South hence rose as the interracial Populist Movement challenged white political supremacy at the end of the nineteenth century *and* as economic conditions deteriorated (Olzak 1992). Minority access to goods previously held by the majority population thus generates intergroup conflict. Conversely, that the maintenance of racial discrimination and the resulting protection of majority interests does not yield violent intergroup clashes is compatible with the theory and findings presented in this book. Even in a context where racial prejudice is rife, such as in the nineteenth-century U.S. South, the expression and organization of racist behavior varies with the actual threat that minority groups pose to the majority's control over material resources.

On the flip side, the absence of intergroup conflict does not necessarily indicate the integration of minority groups or the enlightened tolerance of majority populations. In this book, calm relations between immigrants and natives have come about when economic conditions have been comparatively favorable, or when immigrants have lacked the capacity to back up their demands for needed economic goods with pivotal votes. This latter scenario has in turn been associated with confrontations between immigrants and the state as politically excluded groups press for their fair share of resources by registering their dissatisfaction with state neglect. The occurrence of immigrant–state conflict thus indicates the stubborn maintenance, rather than the disintegration, of discriminatory barriers. When immigrants do not posses sufficient political power, local politicians face few electoral incentives that would prompt them to challenge these barriers. In these ways, immigrant–native and immigrant–state conflict may indicate different stages of immigrant integration within and across countries.

A second theoretical implication relates to the role of the state in shaping intergroup conflict. One assumption that this book has put forth is that resource allocation by the state – rather than the market – widens the scope for *effective* anti-immigrant actions. Though grievances related to the loss of market goods, such as nonpublic employment or privately owned housing, are probably just as strongly felt as grievances related to the loss of publicly distributed goods, state actors are likely to be more vulnerable to anti-immigrant activity than market actors. We have seen, for instance, that realtors who benefit from the rising house prices that immigration may bring about cannot be easily swayed to limit allocating their properties to natives. Local officials, by contrast, may just do so, especially if failure to give in to native demands leads to their ouster on election day. Though the distinction between market and state goods in engendering intergroup conflict is not absolute – prolonged native boycotts against immigrant labor or stores, for instance, may achieve the desired results – this book has argued that xenophobes have an easier time effecting policy change if they target elected officials as opposed to private employers or landlords.

If it is true that sustained intergroup conflict is more likely to emerge when the state is in charge of distributing scarce economic goods, then several implications follow. Conflict outcomes should vary across countries and time periods based on national and over-time differences in, first, the level of local government involvement in the allocation of economic goods and, second, the demand for and supply of such resources. As explored in Chapter 8, economic decentralization, especially amid resource cuts, should be associated with higher levels of conflict, all else equal. By contrast, privatization should be related to a decreased incidence of conflict, holding supply and demand constant. In Great Britain, the sell-off of large shares of council housing thus might have lowered the probability of conflict, had it not occurred during a steep recession when access to affordable housing was critical for many families and slum clearance had displaced millions.[2] In a country like Sweden, by comparison, state provision of resources is much more pervasive, but a generous welfare state ensures that these resources are generally more widely available. In France, the role of the state in providing economic goods is also significant, but the level of resources it disburses falls short of that expended in Sweden, and it is this difference that may have helped to generate a higher incidence of immigrant conflict in French municipalities when compared to Swedish locales. One could further investigate whether the relatively less prominent position of the state in distributing resources in the United States has shaped patterns of local immigrant–native relations here.

But the American case also hints at the possibility of endogenizing state involvement in the production of intergroup conflict. In other words, groups that are economically threatened by immigration may attempt to bring market goods under state control. Anticipating that they cannot win economic battles in the marketplace, these groups may instead try to enlist local officials in

---

[2] According to Yelling, "Between 1955 and 1985 some 1.48 million houses were demolished or closed as a result of slum clearance in England and Wales, displacing more than 3.66 million people" (2000, 234).

the fight against immigrant competitors. Local anti-immigrant ordinances that require employers and landlords to verify the legal status of their workers and tenants, or attempts to limit the opening of immigrant-owned stores through the implementation of licensing and zoning restrictions, implicate the state in market-based competition.

These conjectures have implications for our study of intergroup and group–state conflicts. Though the latter have, for obvious reasons, paid more explicit attention to the role of the state in allocating goods, analyses of intergroup conflict should also benefit from taking the state more seriously. In the context of developing countries and less advanced democracies, state actors have indeed played a more prominent role in facilitating ethnic conflict (e.g., Wilkinson 2004). However, with regard to studying conflicts between migrant or racial minority groups on the one hand and native or racial majority groups on the other in developed democracies, more explicit attention to the role of the state in structuring conflict outcomes is still needed.[3]

Lastly, the occurrence of immigrant conflict can be viewed as a product of a series of policy trade-offs. Relative calm in Germany, for instance, was premised on the departure of migrants who did not perform economically. Failures of anti-immigrant campaigns in British cities, such as Birmingham, were less a result of natives' tolerant attitudes and were instead attributable to immigrants' inability to make advances in schooling, housing, and employment. The neglect of immigrant needs, in turn, may engender conflictual relations between immigrant-origin minorities and the state. As policy makers in Britain had recognized, the prevention of one type of conflict may come at the cost of inviting the other type of conflict. The surest way out of this trap is also likely to be one of the most difficult: providing sufficient economic resources to all.

Though enlarging the pie of material goods available to immigrant and natives locally is challenging, especially when economies undergo downturns, immigration regimes can be designed in ways that address local resource shortages prior to immigrants' arrival. Resource conflicts may be mitigated, for instance, if the sudden inflow of refugees is channeled to municipalities with fewer preexisting resource pressures. The expansion of housing and social services in time for immigrant arrival also lowers the probability of supply shortages in the local areas of settlement. Skill-based migration regimes can alleviate some of the pressures associated with migration, while shifting the burden of immigration-related spending from municipalities to the national stage may also help to diminish local conflicts.

Still, the prevention of immigrant conflict cannot be the sole guiding principle of immigration policy. Immigrants may prefer to live in areas where they can rely on the support of social networks, regardless of the resource constraints that these locales confront. Similarly, most democratic states will allow family reunification of long-settled migrants, even if the arrival of spouses and children

---

[3] For accounts of intergroup conflict in Europe that do take the state seriously, see Karapin (2002) and Koopmans et al. (2005).

puts strains on local infrastructures. Lax regulation of inflows and outflows, while presenting municipalities with uncertainty, may be welcomed from the standpoint of economic efficiency. Quickly developing humanitarian crises can thwart the careful planning of immigration regimes. Immigrants themselves may more highly value living close to friends and family, rather than escaping native hostility. They also most likely prefer to be allowed to enter countries where their needs could be neglected by an unresponsive state, rather than to live in regimes or war zones that threaten their lives. In short, immigration will – and often should – occur regardless of its implications for local immigrant conflict.

Yet, that immigrant conflict is fundamentally based on economic realities and that immigrants' political behavior matters in the production of conflict types yields entirely different policy implications than do accounts that accord primacy to ethnic and cultural difference. Many ethnically diverse cities have been and remain free of sustained conflict, while effective economic policies can in turn alleviate the pressures that have caused immigrant conflict in others.

Appendix A

Coding Large-Scale Instances of Immigrant–Native and Immigrant–State Violence

I adopted the following rules for deciding which events should count as instances of large-scale immigrant–native and immigrant–state violence:

1. The event has to be mentioned in at least one of Britain's two major national newspapers, *The Times* or *The Guardian*.
2. The event has to be discussed in the quite extensive social science secondary literature.
3. London witnessed more violent events in July 1981 than Table 3.1 indicates, but not all of these events should be characterized as large-scale violence. Keith (1993) has devised an intensity ranking of "all serious incidents of public disorder" occurring in London in July 1981, drawing on a list compiled by the Home Office. These rankings are based on a "quantitative measure of the type and extent of damage suffered by property at the scene of disorder . . . a quantitative measure of the type and extent of violent conflict at the scene of disorder," and the existence and use of petrol bombs as "one particular element of the 'rioting armoury' as symptomatic of the escalation of violence" (Keith 1993, 111). I am including those events that ranked in the top ten (out of twenty-seven), according to Keith's index (only nine appear in the table since Keith counts events in Southall as two consecutive incidents).
4. The London riots also sparked a number of copycat events throughout the country that are not listed in this table. These events tend not to be discussed in the secondary literature or in national newspapers, and it is therefore difficult to assess their nature and intensity. For consistency, I excluded these events from this table. I only include the riots in Handsworth, Birmingham, Moss Side, Manchester, and Toxteth, Liverpool, as these are singled out by both *The Times* or *The Guardian* and

are covered in more detail by the secondary literature. When I expand the list to incorporate events about which there is sufficient information regarding the type of immigrant conflict and the identity of participants, the differences relating to the varied involvement of immigrant groups in immigrant–native and immigrant–state violence remain.

Appendix B

Data and Variables: Immigrant Turnout

The 2003 Home Office Citizenship Survey: People, Families and Communities contains a nationally representative sample of around 10,000 people over sixteen years of age living in England and Wales and an oversample of ethnic minorities of around 5,000 respondents.

Sample Used in Models

Respondents are British citizens born outside of the United Kingdom.

The (unweighted) sample contains 1,004 South Asian and 898 black respondents.

Dependent Variables

Local election turnout: "Can I check, did you vote in the last local council election?"

An answer of "yes" was coded as 1, and "no" was coded as 0.

General election turnout: "Can I check, did you vote in the last general election?"

An answer of "yes" was coded as 1, and "no" was coded as 0.

Independent Variables

The self-reported ethnic origins of the respondents (dummy variables) are listed here.

South Asian	Indian, Pakistani, or Bangladeshi
Black Caribbean	Black Caribbean
Black African	Black African
White	White British, white Irish, any other white background
Chinese	Chinese
Mixed ethnicity	Mixed white and black Caribbean, mixed white and black African, mixed white and Asian, mixed other
Other Asian	Asian not from Indian subcontinent or China
Other black	Black not from Caribbean or Africa
Other ethnicity	Any other ethnic group
Ethnic neighborhood	"What proportion of people in your neighborhood is from the same ethnic group as you?" Less than half (1), about half (2), more than half (3)
Age	Respondent's age in years
Gender	Female (1), male (0)
Income	Respondent's income, grouped into 15 categories, ranging from no income (0) to £100,000 or more (14)
Low-skilled	Respondent employed in routine and semiroutine occupations (1), otherwise (0)
Read local paper	"Do you regularly read any local newspaper about your area? By regularly I mean at least once a week." Yes (1), No (0)
Read national paper	"Do you regularly read any national newspaper? By regularly I mean at least once a week." Yes (1), No (0)

TABLE B.1. *Summary Statistics: Immigrant Turnout (Respondents Born Outside of the United Kingdom)*

		Unweighted		Weighted			
Variable	Observations	M	SD	M	SD	Min.	Max.
South Asian	2850	0.35	0.48	0.20	0.40	0	1
Black Caribbean	2850	0.15	0.36	0.06	0.24	0	1
White	2850	0.10	0.31	0.51	0.50	0	1
Chinese	2850	0.03	0.17	0.02	0.16	0	1
Black African	2850	0.16	0.37	0.08	0.28	0	1
Mixed ethnicity	2850	0.04	0.19	0.02	0.15	0	1
Other ethnicity	2850	0.09	0.28	0.05	0.23	0	1
Other Asian	2850	0.07	0.25	0.05	0.21	0	1
Other black	2850	0.01	0.08	0.00	0.05	0	1
Ethnic neighborhood	2581	1.46	0.74	1.57	0.83	1	3
Voted local election	2520	0.55	0.50	0.55	0.50	0	1
Voted general election	2520	0.70	0.46	0.64	0.48	0	1
Age	2851	46.75	16.06	46.71	17.00	16	93
Female	2851	0.43	0.50	0.37	0.48	0	1
Income	2714	4.11	2.60	4.98	3.04	0	14
Low skill	2747	0.33	0.47	0.28	0.45	0	1
Read local paper	2841	0.63	0.48	0.65	0.48	0	1
Read national paper	2842	0.68	0.47	0.76	0.43	0	1

Source: Home Office (2005), author's calculations.

TABLE B.2. Immigrant Turnout: Local and General Elections

Variable	Local Election		General Election	
South Asian	.137 (.214)	.298 (.224)	.176 (.224)	.410* (.243)
Ethnic neighborhood	−.044 (.108)	.001 (.102)	−.105 (.105)	−.077 (.112)
Ethnic Neighborhood × South Asian	.262** (.130)	.233* (.127)	.101 (.132)	.104 (.140)
White British	.203 (.226)	.294 (.237)	.006 (.240)	.231 (.263)
White Irish	.411* (.250)	.478* (.247)	−.097 (.259)	−.089 (.259)
White other	−.021 (.225)	.218 (.227)	−1.04*** (.219)	−.888*** (.240)
Other Asian	.345** (.159)	.598*** (.181)	−.066 (.172)	.248 (.184)
African	−.226* (.134)	.056 (.163)	−.679*** (.143)	−.353** (.166)
Other black	−.220 (.370)	−.115 (.391)	.591 (.560)	.524 (.589)
Chinese	−.741*** (.266)	−.490* (.281)	−.726*** (.277)	−.341 (.268)
Other ethnic group	−.296** (.159)	−.128 (.187)	−.612*** (.164)	−.337* (.184)
Mixed ethnicity	−.193 (.194)	−.009 (.203)	−.582*** (.212)	−.296 (.225)
Age		.024*** (.004)		.030*** (.004)
Gender		−.273** (.120)		−.059 (.130)
Income		−.023 (.021)		−.005 (.022)
Low-skilled		−.039 (.117)		.069 (.125)
Local or national paper		.153 (.122)		.260** (.125)
Constant	−.026 (.170)	−1.21 (.347)	.731*** (.173)	−1.04*** (.347)
N	2271	2085	2271	2086
Log likelihood	−1500.83	−1275.45	−1342.91	−1105.21

Notes: Black Caribbean is the reference category. Probit coefficients with robust standard errors in parentheses are given. Models use sampling weights to correct for ethnic minority oversampling.
* p < .10; ** p < .05; *** p < .01.
Source: 2003 Home Office Citizenship Survey (Home Office 2005).

References

Agency for the Development of Intercultural Relations. 2004. National Analytical Study on Racist Violence and Crime – RAXEN Focal Point for France. Retrieved July 14, 2008, from http://fra.europa.eu/fra/material/pub/RAXEN/4/RV/CS-RV-NR-FR.pdf.

Alesina, Alberto, Reza Baqir, and William Easterly. 1999. "Public Goods and Ethnic Divisions." *Quarterly Journal of Economics* 114 (4):1243–1284.

Anwar, Muhammad. 1979. *The Myth of Return: Pakistanis in Britain*. London: Heinemann.

———. 1986. *Race and Politics: Ethnic Minorities and the British Political System*. London: Tavistock.

———. 1998. *Between Cultures: Community and Change in the Lives of Young Asians*. London: Routledge.

Arendt, Peter. 1982. "Ausländische Arbeitnehmer und das soziale Umfeld." In *Gastarbeiterpolitik oder Immigrationspolitik* (pp. 129–136), eds. F. Ronneberger and R. Vogel. München: Günter Olzog Verlag.

Back, Les, and Michael Keith. 1999. "'Rights and Wrongs': Youth, Community and Narratives of Racial Violence." In *New Ethnicities, Old Racisms?* (pp. 131–162), ed. P. Cohen. London: Zed Books.

Back, Les, and Anoop Nayak. 1999. "Signs of the Times? Violence, Graffiti and Racism in the English Suburbs." In *Divided Europeans: Understanding Ethnicities in Conflict* (pp. 243–283), eds. T. Allen and J. Eade. The Hague: Kluwer Law International.

Back, Les, and John Solomos, eds. 2000. *Theories of Race and Racism*. New York: Routledge.

Bade, Klaus J. 1994. *Ausländer, Aussiedler, Asyl: eine Bestandsaufnahme*. München: C. H. Beck.

Bade, Klaus J., and Jochen Oltmer, eds. 1999. *Aussiedler: Deutsche Einwanderer aus Osteuropa*. Osnabrück: Rasch.

Bagguley, Paul, and Yasmin Hussain. 2003. "The Bradford 'Riot' of 2001: A Preliminary Analysis." Paper presented at the Ninth Alternative Futures and Popular Protest Conference, Manchester Metropolitan University, April 22–24.

Ballard, Roger, ed. 1994. *Desh Pardesh: The South Asian Presence in Britain*. London: Hurst & Company.

Bates, Robert H. 1983. "Modernization, Ethnic Competition, and the Rationality of Politics in Contemporary Africa." In *State versus Ethnic Claims: African Policy Dilemmas* (pp. 152–171), eds. D. Rothchild and V. A. Olunsorola. Boulder, CO: Westview Press.

Bauer, Thomas K., Magnus Lofstrom, and Klaus F. Zimmermann. 2000. "Immigration Policy, Assimilation of Immigrants and Natives' Sentiments towards Immigrants: Evidence from 12 OECD-Countries." IZA Discussion Paper No. 187.

Bauer, Werner T. 2007. "Das kommunale AusländerInnenwahlrecht im europäischen Vergleich." Vienna: Österreichische Gesellschaft für Politikberatung und Politikentwicklung. Retrieved September 26, 2007, from http://www.hlavac.spoe.at/presse_detail.siteswift?so=all&do=all&c=download&d=s%3A13%3A%22article%3A155%3A1%22%3B.

Baumann, Gerd. 1996. *Contesting Culture: Discourses of Identity in Multi-ethnic London*. Cambridge: Cambridge University Press.

Beauftragte der Bundesregierung für Ausländerfragen. 2002. *Bericht über die Lage der Ausländer in der Bundesrepublik Deutschland*. Berlin and Bonn.

Beauftragte der Bundesregierung für Migration, Flüchtlinge und Integration. 2005. *Bericht über die Lage der Ausländerinnen und Ausländer in Deutschland*. Berlin.

Begum, Halina, and John Eade. 2005. "All Quiet on the Eastern Front? Bangladeshi Reactions in Tower Hamlets." In *Muslim Britain: Communities under Pressure* (pp. 179–193), ed. T. Abbas. London: Zed Books.

Beissinger, Mark. 2008. "A New Look at Ethnicity and Democratization." *Journal of Democracy* 19 (3):85–97.

Ben-Tovim, Gideon, John Gabriel, Ian Law, and Kathleen Stredder, eds. 1986. *The Local Politics of Race*. Houndmills: Macmillan.

Benyon, John. 1986. "Spiral of Decline: Race and Policing." In *Race, Government, and Politics in Britain* (pp. 227–277), eds. Z. Layton-Henry and P. B. Rich. Basingstoke: Macmillan.

————, ed. 1984. *Scarman and after*. Oxford: Pergamon Press.

Benyon, John, and John Solomos, eds. 1987. *The Roots of Urban Unrest*. Oxford: Pergamon Press.

Bhachu, Parminder. 1985. *Twice Migrants: East African Sikh Settlers in Britain*. London: Tavistock.

Bird, Karen. 2005. "The Political Representation of Visible Minorities in Electoral Democracies: A Comparison of France, Denmark, and Canada." *Nationalism and Ethnic Politics* 11 (4):425–465.

Björgo, Tore. 1993. "Terrorist Violence against Immigrants and Refugees in Scandinavia: Patterns and Motives." In *Racist Violence in Europe* (pp. 29–45), eds. T. Björgo and R. Witte. London: Macmillan.

Blahusch, Friedrich. 1999. *Zuwanderungspolitik im Spannungsfeld ordnungspolitischer und ethnisch-nationalistischer Legitimationsmuster*. Frankfurt: Peter Lang.

Blalock, Hubert. 1967. *Toward a Theory of Minority-Group Relations*. New York: Wiley.

Bleich, Erik. 2003. *Race Politics in Britain and France: Ideas and Policymaking since the 1960's*. Cambridge: Cambridge University Press.

————. 2007. "Hate Crime Policy in Western Europe." *American Behavioral Scientist* 51 (2):149–165.

Bloemraad, Irene. 2006. *Becoming a Citizen: Incorporating Immigrants and Refugees in the United States and Canada*. Berkeley: University of California Press.

Bodenbender, Wolfgang. 1982. "Die politischen und gesellschaftlichen Rahmenbedingungen der Ausländerpolitik." In *Gastarbeiterpolitik oder Immigrationspolitik* (pp. 33–55), eds. F. Ronneberger and R. Vogel. München: Günter Olzog Verlag.

Body-Gendrot, Sophie. 2000. *The Social Control of Cities.* Oxford: Blackwell.

———. 2002. "Living Apart or Together with our Differences? French Cities at a Crossroads." *Ethnicities* 2 (3):367–385.

Bonilla-Silva, Eduardo. 1997. "Rethinking Racism: Toward a Structural Interpretation." *American Sociological Review* 62 (3):465–480.

Boothroyd, David. n.d. Tower Hamlets Borough Council Election Maps. Retrieved May 7, 2006, from http://www.election.demon.co.uk/thbc/thbcmap.html.

Borjas, G. J. 1994. "The Economics of Immigration." *Journal of Economic Literature* 32 (4):1667–1717.

Bousetta, Hassan. 1998. "Le paradoxe anversois. Entre racisme politique et ouvertures multi-culturelles." *Revue européenne de migrations internationales* 14 (2):151–172.

Bowen, John. 2007. *Why the French Don't Like Headscarves.* Princeton: Princeton University Press.

Bowling, Benjamin. 1993. "Racial Harassment and the Process of Victimization: Conceptual and Methodological Implications for the Local Crime Survey." *British Journal of Criminology* 33 (2):231–250.

———. 1998. *Violent Racism: Victimisation, Policing and Social Context.* Oxford: Oxford University Press.

Bowyer, Benjamin T. 2009. "The Contextual Determinants of Whites' Racial Attitudes in England." *British Journal of Political Science* 39 (3):559–586.

Bradford Congress. 1996. *The Bradford Commission Report.* London: The Stationery Office.

Brambor, Thomas, William Roberts Clark, and Matt Golder. 2006. "Understanding Interaction Models: Improving Empirical Analyses." *Political Analysis* 14 (1):63–82.

Brass, Paul R. 1997. *Theft of an Idol.* Princeton: Princeton University Press.

Bristow, Mike. 1976. "Britain's Response to the Uganda Asian Crisis: Government Myths versus Political and Resettlement Realities." *New Community* 5 (3):265–279.

Brown, Colin. 1984. *Black and White Britain: The Third PSI Survey.* London: Heinemann.

Brubaker, Rogers. 1992. *Citizenship and Nationhood in France and Germany.* Cambridge, MA: Harvard University Press.

Brubaker, Rogers, Margit Feischmidt, Jon Fox, and Liana Grancea. 2006. *Nationalist Politics and Everyday Ethnicity in a Transylvanian Town.* Princeton: Princeton University Press.

Brubaker, Rogers, and David Laitin. 1998. "Ethnic and Nationalist Violence." *Annual Review of Sociology* 24:423–452.

Brücker, Herbert, Gil S. Epstein, Barry McCormick, Gilles Saint-Paul, Allesandra Venturini, and Klaus Zimmermann. 2002. "Part I. Managing Migration in the European Welfare State." In *Immigration Policy and the Welfare System* (pp. 1–167), eds. T. Boeri, G. Hanson, and B. McCormick. New York: Oxford University Press.

Bundesministerium des Inneren. 2001. *Bericht der Unabhängigen Kommission 'Zuwanderung'.* Berlin.

Bundesministerium für Bildung und Forschung. 2006. *Berufsbildungsbericht.* Berlin.

Bundesverwaltungsamt. 2006. Aussiedlerstatistik seit 1950. Retrieved July 23, 2007, from http://www.bmi.bund.de/cln_012/Internet/Content/Common/Anlagen/Themen/

Vertriebene__Spaetaussiedler/Statistiken/Aussiedlerstatistik__seit__1950,
templateId=raw,property=publicationFile.pdf/Aussiedlerstatistik_seit_1950.pdf.

Burney, Elizabeth. 1967. *Housing on Trial*. London: Oxford University Press.

Burns, Danny, Robin Hambleton, and Paul Hoggett. 1994. *The Politics of Decentralisation*. London: Macmillan.

Buruma, Ian. 2006. *Murder in Amsterdam*. New York: Penguin.

Calavita, Kitty. 2005. *Immigrants at the Margins: Law, Race, and Exclusion in Southern Europe*. Cambridge: Cambridge University Press.

Campaign Against Racialism and Fascism. 1981. *Southall: The Birth of a Black Community*. London: Institute of Race Relations and Southall Rights.

Candappa, Mano, and Danièle Joly. 1994. *Local Authorities, Ethnic Minorities and 'Pluralist Integration': A Study in Five Local Authority Areas*. Coventry: Centre for Research in Ethnic Relations.

Cannan, Crescy. 1995. "Urban Social Development in France." *Community Development Journal* 30 (3):238–247.

Card, David. 2005. "Is the New Immigration Really so Bad?" *The Economic Journal* 115 (507):300–321.

———. 2007. "How Immigration Affects US Cities." Center for Research and Analysis of Migration, Discussion Paper No. 11/07.

Carter, Elisabeth. 2005. *The Extreme Right in Western Europe*. Manchester: Manchester University Press.

Centre for Equal Opportunities and Opposition to Racism. 2004. National Analytical Study on Racist Violence and Crime: RAXEN Focal Point for Belgium. Retrieved April 14, 2005, from http://fra.europa.eu/fra/material/pub/RAXEN/4/RV/CS-RV-NR-BE .pdf.

Cesari, Jocelyn. 2005. Ethnicity, Islam and les banlieues: Confusing the Issues. Retrieved June 9, 2006, from http://riotsfrance.ssrc.org/Cesari/.

Chamberlain, Mary. 2001. "Migration, the Caribbean and the Family." In *Caribbean Families in Britain and the Trans-Atlantic World* (pp. 32–47), eds. H. Goulbourne and M. Chamberlain. London: Macmillan Caribbean.

Chandra, Kanchan. 2001. "Ethnic Bargains, Group Instability, and Social Choice Theory." *Politics and Society* 29 (3):337–362.

———. 2004. *Why Ethnic Parties Succeed: Patronage and Ethnic Headcounts in India*. Cambridge: Cambridge University Press.

Chessum, Lorna. 2000. *From Immigrants to Ethnic Minority*. Aldershot: Ashgate.

Chiswick, Barry. 2006. "The Worker Next Door." *New York Times*, June 3.

Chua, Amy. 2004. *World on Fire*. New York: Anchor Books.

Citrin, Jack, Donald P. Green, and Cara Wong. 1997. "Public Opinion toward Immigration Reform: The Role of Economic Motivations." *Journal of Politics* 59 (3):858–581.

Clare, John. 1984. "Eyewitness in Brixton." In *Scarman and after: Essays Reflecting on Lord Scarman's Report, the Riots and their Aftermath* (pp. 46–53), ed. J. Benyon. Oxford: Pergamon Press.

Clarke, James, Elsbeth van Dam, and Liz Gooster. 1998. "New Europeans: Naturalisation and Citizenship in Europe." *Citizenship Studies* 2 (1):43–67.

Clayton, Richard, and Jonas Pontusson. 1998. "Welfare-State Retrenchment Revisited: Entitlement Cuts, Public Sector Restructuring, and Inegalitarian Trends in Advanced Capitalist Societies." *World Politics* 51 (1):67–98.

Coleman, David. 1994. "The United Kingdom and International Migration: A Changing Balance." In *European Migration in the Late Twentieth Century: Historical Patterns,*

Actual Trends, and Social Implications (pp. 37–66), eds. H. Fassmann and R. Münz. Aldershot: E. Elgar.

Collier, Paul, and Anke Hoeffler. 2004. "Greed and Grievance in Civil War." *Oxford Economic Papers* 56 (4):563–595.

Commission for Racial Equality. 2005. National Analytical Study on Racist Violence and Crime. RAXEN Focal Point for the UK. Retrieved May 7, 2006, from http://eumc .eu.int/eumc/material/pub/RAXEN/4/RV/CS-RV-NR-UK.pdf.

Cornwell, Elmer E. 1964. "Bosses, Machines, and Ethnic Groups." *Annals of the American Academy of Political and Social Science* 353:27–39.

Craig, Kellina M. 1999. "Retaliation, Fear, or Rage: An Investigation of African American and White Reactions to Racist Hate Crimes." *Journal of Interpersonal Violence* 14 (2):138–151.

Dancygier, Rafaela. 2007a. *Immigration and Conflict.* Ph.D. Dissertation, Department of Political Science, Yale University, New Haven.

———. 2007b. "Immigration and the Political Institutionalization of Xenophobia in France." In *Racism, Xenophobia, and Redistribution* (pp. 237–264), eds. J. E. Roemer, W. Lee, and K. van der Straten. Cambridge, MA: Harvard University Press.

———. 2008. "Mobilizing against Citizenship: Party and Voter Responses to Naturalization." Paper presented at the Annual Meeting of the American Political Science Association, Boston, August 28–31.

Dancygier, Rafaela, and Donald P. Green. 2010. "Hate Crime." In *Handbook of Prejudice, Stereotyping, and Discrimination*, eds. J. F. Dovidio, M. Hewstone, P. Glick, and V. M. Esses. Thousand Oaks, CA: Sage Publications.

Dancygier, Rafaela, and Elizabeth Saunders. 2006. "A New Electorate? Comparing Preferences and Partisanship Between Immigrants and Natives." *American Journal of Political Science* 50 (4):962–981.

De Decker, Pascal, Christian Kesteloot, Filip de Maesschalck, and Jan Vranken. 2005. "Revitalizing the City in an Anti-Urban Context: Extreme Right and the Rise of Urban Policies in Flanders, Belgium." *International Journal of Urban and Regional Research* 29 (1):152–171.

Dekker, Lisette, and Brahim Fattah. 2006. *Meer Diversiteit in de Gemeenteraden.* Amsterdam: Instituut voor Participatie en Politiek.

DeLey, M. 1983. "French Immigration Policy since May 1981." *International Migration Review* 17 (2):196–211.

Department for Communities and Local Government. 2004. Indices of Deprivation 2004. Retrieved July 22, 2006, from http://www.communities.gov.uk/index.asp?id= 1128448.

Desai, Rashmi. 1963. *Indian Immigrants in Britain.* London: Oxford University Press.

Deutscher Städtetag. Various years. *Statistisches Jahrbuch Deutscher Gemeinden.* Köln: Deutscher Städtetag.

Dhondy, Mala. 1977. "East End Notes." *Race Today* 9 (3):66–68.

Dickson, Eric S., and Kenneth Scheve. 2006. "Social Identity, Political Speech, and Electoral Competition." *Journal of Theoretical Politics* 18 (1):5–39.

Documentation and Advisory Centre on Racial Discrimination. 2005. National Analytical Study on Racist Violence and Crime: RAXEN Focal Point for Denmark. Retrieved May 7, 2006, from http://fra.europa.eu/fra/material/pub/RAXEN/4/RV/ CS-RV-NR-DA.pdf.

Dörr, Silvia, and Thomas Faist. 1997. "Institutional Conditions for the Integration of Immigrants in Welfare States: A Comparison of the Literature on Germany, France,

Great Britain, and the Netherlands." *European Journal of Political Research* 31 (4):401–426.

Dunbar, Edward. 2003. "Symbolic, Relational, and Ideological Signifiers of Bias-Motivated Offenders: Toward a Strategy of Assessment." *American Journal of Orthopsychiatry* 73 (2):203–211.

Dustmann, Christian, Francesca Fabbri, and Ian Preston. 2005. "The Impact of Immigration on the British Labour Market." *The Economic Journal* 115 (507):324–341.

Eade, John. 1989. *The Politics of Community*. Aldershot: Avebury.

———. 1990. "Nationalism and the Quest for Authenticity: The Bangladeshis in Tower Hamlets." *New Community* 16 (4):493–503.

———. 1996. "Nationalism, Community, and the Islamization of Space in London." In *Making Muslim Space in North America and Europe* (pp. 217–233), ed. B. D. Metcalf. Berkeley: University of California Press.

Eberle, Sebastian. 2007. *'Wenn jemand auszog, zogen Türken ein'. Migration und soziostruktureller Wandel in einer deutschen Grosstadt am Beispiel Berlin-Kreuzbergs zwischen 1969 und 1973*, Philosophische Fakultät I. Berlin: Berlin Institut für Geschichtswissenschaften, Humboldt-Universität.

Edwards, John, and Richard Batley. 1978. *The Politics of Positive Discrimination*. London: Tavistock.

Equality Authority & National Consultative Committee on Racism and Interculturalism. 2005. National Analytical Study on Racist Violence and Crime: RAXEN Focal Point for Ireland. Retrieved May 7, 2006, from http://fra.europa.eu/fra/material/pub/RAXEN/4/RV/CS-RV-NR-IE.pdf.

Esping-Andersen, Gøsta. 1990. *The Three Worlds of Welfare Capitalism*. Princeton: Princeton University Press.

European Monitoring Centre on Racism and Xenophobia. 2005. Racist Violence in 15 EU Member States. Retrieved May 7, 2006, from http://eumc.eu.int/eumc/material/pub/comparativestudy/CS-RV-main.pdf.

Eurostat. 2008. From 2015, Deaths Projected to Outnumber Births in the EU27. Retrieved February 6, 2009, from http://epp.eurostat.ec.europa.eu/pls/portal/docs/PAGE/PGP_PRD_CAT_PREREL/PGE_CAT_PREREL_YEAR_2008/PGE_CAT_PREREL_YEAR_2008_MONTH_08/3–26082008-EN-AP.PDF.

Faist, Thomas. 1995. *Social Citizenship for Whom?* Aldershot: Avebury.

Faist, Thomas, and Hartmut Häussermann. 1996. "Immigration, Social Citizenship and Housing in Germany." *International Journal of Urban & Regional Research* 20 (1):83–98.

Falk, Armin, and Josef Zweimüller. 2005. "Unemployment and Right-Wing Extremist Crime." CEPR Discussion Paper No. 4997.

Falter, Jürgen W. 1994. *Wer wählt rechts?: Die Wähler und Anhänger rechtsextremischer Parteien im Vereinigten Deutschland*. München: C. H. Beck.

Farrar, Max. 2002. "The Northern 'Race Riots' of the Summer of 2001 – Were They Riots, Were They Racial? A Case-study of the Events in Harehills, Leeds." Paper presented at the BSA Race and Ethnicity Study Group Seminar on 'Parallel Lives and Polarisation', City University, London, May 18.

Fearon, James D. 2006. "Ethnic Mobilization and Ethnic Violence." In *The Oxford Handbook of Political Economy* (pp. 852–868), eds. B. R. Weingast and D. A. Wittman. Oxford: Oxford University Press.

Fearon, James D. 1999. "Why Ethnic Politics and 'Pork' Tend to Go Together." Mimeo, Stanford University, Palo Alto.

Fearon, James, and David Laitin. 1996. "Explaining Interethnic Cooperation." *American Political Science Review* 90 (4):715–735.

———. 2000. "Violence and the Social Construction of Ethnic Identity." *International Organization* 54 (4):845–877.

———. 2003. "Ethnicity, Insurgency, and Civil War." *American Political Science Review* 97 (1):75–90.

Fennema, Meindert, and Jean Tillie. 1999. "Political Participation and Political Trust in Amsterdam. Civic Communities and Ethnic Networks." *Journal of Ethnic and Migration Studies* 25 (4):703–726.

———. 2001. "Civic Community, Political Participation and Political Trust of Ethnic Groups." *Connections* 24 (1):26–41.

Fetzer, Joel S. 2000. *Public Attitudes toward Immigration in the United States, France, and Germany*. Cambridge: Cambridge University Press.

Field, Simon, George Mair, Tom Rees, and Philip Stevens. 1981. *Ethnic Minorities in Britain*. London: Home Office.

Fishman, William J. 1997. "Allies in the Promised Land: Reflections on the Irish and the Jews in the East End." In *London: The Promised Land?* (pp. 38–49), ed. A. J. Kershen. Aldershot: Avebury.

Fitzgerald, Marian. 1988. "Different Roads? The Development of Afro-Caribbean and Asian Political Organisation in London." *New Community* 14 (3):385–396.

Flett, Hazel. 1982. "Dimensions of Inequality: Birmingham Council Housing Allocations." *New Community* 10 (1):46–56.

Foot, Paul. 1965. *Immigration and Race in British Politics*. Harmondsworth: Penguin Books.

Ford, Robert. 2008. "Is Racial Prejudice Declining in Britain?" *British Journal of Sociology* 59 (4):609–636.

Fording, Richard C. 1997. "The Conditional Effect of Violence as a Political Tactic: Mass Insurgency, Welfare Generosity, and Electoral Context in the American States." *American Journal of Political Science* 41 (1):1–29.

Forman, Charlie. 1989. *Spitalfields: A Battle for Land*. London: Hilary Shipman.

Foster, Janet. 1999. *Docklands: Cultures in Conflict, Worlds in Collision*. London: UCL Press.

Fraga, Luis R., and Gary M. Segura. 2006. "Culture Clash? Contesting Notions of American Identity and the Effects of Latin American Immigration." *Perspectives on Politics* 4 (2):279–287.

Freeman, Gary P. 1979. *Immigrant Labor and Racial Conflict in Industrial Societies: The French and British Experience, 1945–1975*. Princeton: Princeton University Press.

———. 1986. "Migration and the Political Economy of the Welfare State." *Annals of the American Academy of Political and Social Science* 485:51–62.

———. 1995. "Modes of Immigration Policies in Liberal Democratic States." *International Migration Review* 29 (4):881–902.

———. 2004. "Immigrant Incorporation in Western Democracies." *International Migration Review* 38 (3):945–969.

Freeman, Gary P., and Alan K. Kessler. 2008. "Political Economy and Migration Policy." *Journal of Ethnic and Migration Studies* 34 (4):655–678.

Front National. 1993. *300 mesures pour la renaissance de la France: Front national, programme de gouvernement: l'alternative nationale*. Paris: Editions nationales.

Frey, Martin, and Volker Lubinski. 1987. *Probleme infolge hoher Ausländer-konzentration in ausgewählten europäischen Staaten.* Wiesbaden: Bundesinstitut für Bevölkerungsforschung.

Fryer, Peter. 1984. *Staying Power: The History of Black People in Britain.* London: Pluto Press.

Frymer, Paul. 2005. "Racism Revised: Courts, Labor Law, and the Institutional Construction of Racial Animus." *American Political Science Review* 99 (3):373–387.

Gamm, Gerald H. 1989. *The Making of New Deal Democrats: Voting Behavior and Realignment in Boston, 1920–1940.* Chicago: University of Chicago Press.

Garbaye, Romain. 2005. *Getting into Local Power: The Politics of Ethnic Minorities in British and French Cities.* Oxford: Blackwell.

Gardner, Katy, and Abdus Shukur. 1994. "'I'm Bengali, I'm Asian, and I'm Living Here': The Changing Identity of British Bengalis." In *Desh Pardesh: The South Asian Presence in Britain* (pp. 142–164), ed. R. Ballard. London: Hurst & Company.

Garofalo, James. 1991. "Racially Motivated Crimes in New York City." In *Race and Criminal Justice* (pp. 161–173), eds. M. J. Lynch and E. B. Patterson. New York: Harrow & Heston.

Gastaut, Yvan. 2000. *L'immigration et l'opinion en France sous la Ve République.* Paris: Seuil.

Gay, Claudine. 2006. "Seeing Difference: The Effect of Economic Disparity on Black Attitudes toward Latinos." *American Journal of Political Science* 50 (6):982–999.

Geisser, Vincent. 1997. *Ethnicité Républicaine.* Paris: Presses de Sciences Po.

George, Alexander L., and Andrew Bennett. 2005. *Case Studies and Theory Development in the Social Sciences.* Cambridge, MA: MIT Press.

Gesemann, Frank. 2001. "'Wenn man den Polizisten nicht vertrauen kann, wem dann?' Zur gegenseitigen Wahrnehmung von Migranten und Polizisten." In *Migration und Integration in Berlin* (pp. 363–384), ed. F. Gesemann. Opladen: Leske & Budrich.

Gessenharter, Wolfgang. 1999. "Rechtsextremismus, Neue Radikale Rechte und Intellektuelle Neue Rechte. Begriffliche Klärungen und empirische Befunde." In *Rechtsextremismus und Fremdenfeindlichkeit* (pp. 17–52), eds. F. Dünkel and B. Geng. Mönchengladbach: Forum Verlag.

Gilens, Martin. 1999. *Why Americans Hate Welfare: Race, Media, and the Politics of Antipoverty Policy.* Chicago: University of Chicago Press.

Gimpel, James G., and James R. Edwards. 1999. *The Congressional Politics of Immigration Reform.* Boston: Allyn & Bacon.

Gish, Oscar. 1968. "Color and Skill: British Immigration, 1955–1968." *International Migration Review* 3 (1):19–37.

Givens, Terri. 2005. *Voting Radical Right in Western Europe.* New York: Cambridge University Press.

Givens, Terri, and Adam Luedtke. 2005. "European Immigration Policies in Comparative Perspective: Issue Salience, Partisanship and Immigrant Rights." *Comparative European Politics* 3 (1):1–22.

Glass, Ruth. 1961. *London's Newcomers.* Cambridge, MA: Harvard University Press.

Godley, Andrew. 1997. "Leaving the East End: Regional Mobility among East European Jews in London, 1880–1914." In *London: The Promised Land?* (pp. 50–65), ed. A. J. Kershen. Aldershot: Avebury.

Göktürk, Deniz, David Gramling, and Anton Kaes, eds. 2007. *Germany in Transit: Nation and Migration, 1955–2005.* Berkeley: University of California Press.

Goldberg, Andreas, and Martina Sauer. 2003. *Perspektiven der Integration der türkischstämmigen Migranten in Nordrhein-Westfalen*. Münster: Lit Verlag.

Golder, Matt. 2003. "Explaining Variation in the Success of Extreme Right Parties in Western Europe." *Comparative Political Studies* 36 (4):432–466.

Goodey, Jo. 2007. "Racist Violence in Europe: Challenges for Official Data Collection." *Ethnic and Racial Studies* 30 (4):570–589.

Goulbourne, Harry. 1990. "The Offence of the West Indian: Political Leadership and the Communal Option." In *Black and Ethnic Leaderships* (pp. 296–322), eds. P. Werbner and M. Anwar. London: Routledge.

Graef, Rogers. 1989. *Talking Blues: The Police in their Own Words*. London: Collins Harvill.

Greaves, George. 1984. "The Brixton Disorders." In *Scarman and after: Essays Reflecting on Lord Scarman's Report, the Riots and their Aftermath* (pp. 63–72), ed. J. Benyon. Oxford: Pergamon Press.

Green, Donald P., Abelson R. P., and M. Garnett. 1999. "The Distinctive Political Views of Hate-Crime Perpetrators and White Supremacists." In *Cultural Divides: Understanding and Overcoming Group Conflict* (pp. 429–464), eds. D. A. Prentice and A. D. T. Miller. New York: Russell Sage Foundation.

Green, Donald P., Jack Glaser, and Andrew Rich. 1998. "From Lynching to Gay Bashing: The Elusive Connection between Economic Conditions and Hate Crime." *Journal of Personality and Social Psychology* 75 (1):82–92.

Green, Donald P., Laurence H. McFalls, and Jennifer K. Smith. 2001. "Hate Crime: An Emergent Research Agenda." *Annual Review of Sociology* 27:479–504.

Green, Donald P., and Andrew Rich. 1998. "White Supremacist Activity and Cross-burnings in North Carolina." *Journal of Quantitative Criminology* 14 (3):263–282.

Green, Donald P., and Rachel Seher. 2003. "What Role Does Prejudice Play in Ethnic Conflict?" *Annual Review of Political Science* 6:509–531.

Green, Donald P., Dara Z. Strolovitch, and Janelle S. Wong. 1998. "Defended Neighborhoods, Integration, and Racially Motivated Crime." *American Journal of Sociology* 104 (2):372–403.

Green, Hazel, and Christine Farmer. 2004. *2003 Home Office Citizenship Survey: People, Families and Communities – Technical Report*. London: Office for National Statistics.

Guiraudon, Virginie. 2002. "Including Foreigners in National Welfare States: Institutional Venues and Rules of the Game." In *Restructuring the Welfare State: Political Institutions and Policy Change* (pp. 129–156), eds. B. Rothstein and S. Steinmo. New York: Palgrave.

Gurr, Ted. 1970. *Why Men Rebel*. Princeton: Princeton University Press.

Habyarimana, James, Macartan Humphreys, Daniel N. Posner, and Jeremy M. Weinstein. 2009. *Coethnicity: Diversity and the Dilemmas of Collective Action*. New York: Russell Sage Foundation.

Hainmueller, Jens, and Michael J. Hiscox. 2007. "Educated Preferences: Explaining Attitudes toward Immigration in Europe." *International Organization* 61 (2):399–442.

Hall, Peter A. 1986. *Governing the Economy: The Politics of State Intervention in Britain and France*. New York: Oxford University Press.

Hall, Peter A., and David Soskice. 2001. *Varieties of Capitalism: The Institutional Foundations of Comparative Advantage*. Oxford: Oxford University Press.

Hammar, Tomas. 1985. *European Immigration Policy*. Cambridge: Cambridge University Press.

Handley, James Edmund. 1947. *The Irish in Modern Scotland*. Cork: Cork University Press.

Hansen, Randall. 1999. "The Kenyan Asians, British Politics, and the Commonwealth Immigrants Act, 1968." *The Historical Journal* 42 (3):809–834.

———. 2000. *Citizenship and Immigration in Post-War Britain: The Institutional Origins of a Multicultural Nation*. Oxford: Oxford University Press.

Hanson, Gordon. 2007. "The Economic Logic of Illegal Immigration." Council on Foreign Relations, Council Special Report No. 26.

Hanson, Gordon, Kenneth F. Scheve, and Matthew J. Slaughter. 2007. "Public Finance and Individual Preferences over Globalization Strategies." *Economics and Politics* 19 (1):1–33.

Hardin, Russell. 1995. *One for All: The Logic of Group Conflict*. Princeton: Princeton University Press.

Hargreaves, Alec G. 1991. "The Political Mobilization of the North African Immigrant Community in France." *Ethnic and Racial Studies* 14 (3):350–367.

———. 1995. *Immigration, 'Race' and Ethnicity in Contemporary France*. New York: Routledge.

Häussermann, Hartmut. 1994. "Social Housing in Germany." In *Social Rented Housing in Europe* (pp. 53–75), eds. B. Danermark and I. Elander. Delft: Delft University Press.

Hawkes, Barbara. 1990. *Southall: An Ethnography of Change*. B.Sc. Dissertation, Department of Human Sciences, The University of West London, Brunel.

Heath, Anthony, and Shamit Saggar. 2000. British General Election Study: Ethnic Minority Survey, 1997 [Computer file]. 2nd ICPSR version. London, England: Social and Community Planning Research [Producer], 1998. Colchester, England: The Data Archive/Ann Arbor, MI: Interuniversity Consortium for Political and Social Research [Distributors].

Hechter, Michael, and Dina Okamoto. 2001. "Political Consequences of Minority Group Formation." *Annual Review of Political Science* 4:189–215.

Hein, Jeremy. 1991. "Immigrants, Natives and the French Welfare State: Explaining Different Interactions with a Social Welfare Program." *International Migration Review* 25 (3):592–609.

Heineman, Benjamin W. 1972. *The Politics of the Powerless*. London: Oxford University Press.

Heitmeyer, Wilhem. 1993. "Hostility and Violence towards Foreigners in Germany." In *Racist Violence in Europe* (pp. 17–28), ed. R. Witte. New York: St. Martin's Press.

Helbling, Marc, and Hanspeter Kriesi. 2004. "Staatsbürgerverständnis und politische Mobilisierung: Einbürgerungen in Schweizer Gemeinden." *Swiss Political Science Review* 10 (4):33–58.

Henderson, Jeff, and Valerie Karn. 1984. "Race, Class and the Allocation of Public Housing in Britain." *Urban Studies* 21 (2):115–128.

———. 1987. *Race, Class, and State Housing: Inequality and the Allocation of Public Housing in Britain*. Brookfield, VT: Gower Publishing.

Herbert, Ulrich. 2001. *Geschichte der Ausländerpolitik in Deutschland: Saisonarbeiter, Zwangsarbeiter, Gastarbeiter, Flüchtlinge*. München: C. H. Beck.

Herek, Gregory M., Jeanine C. Cogan, and J. Roy Gillis. 2002. "Victim Experiences in Hate Crimes Based on Sexual Orientation." *Journal of Social Issues* 58 (2):319–339.

Hesse, Barnor, Rai K. Dhawant, Christine Bennett, and Paul McGilchrist, eds. 1992. *Beneath the Surface: Racial Harassment.* Avebury: Aldershot.

Hewitt, Roger L. 1996. *Routes of Racism.* Stoke-on-Trent: Trentham Books.

———. 2005. *White Backlash and the Politics of Multiculturalism.* Cambridge: Cambridge University Press.

Hill, Michael J., and Ruth M. Issacharoff. 1971. *Community Action and Race Relations: A Study of Community Relations Committees in Britain.* London: Oxford University Press.

Hillmann, Felicitas. 2001. "Struktur und Dynamik der Arbeitsmarktintegration der ausländischen Bevölkerung in Berlin." In *Migration und Integration in Berlin* (pp. 185–208), ed. F. Gesemann. Opladen: Leske & Budrich.

Hiro, Dilip. 1991. *Black British White British: A History of Race Relations in Britain.* London: Grafton.

Hollifield, James F. 1986. "Immigration Policy in France and Germany." *Annals of the American Academy of Political and Social Science* 485:113–128.

———. 1992. *Immigrants, Markets, and States.* Cambridge, MA: Harvard University Press.

Holman, Robert. 1970. "Handsworth/Soho: An Area of Multiple Deprivation." In *Race in the Inner City* (pp. 36–42), ed. A. John. London: Runnymede Trust.

Home Office. 2001a. *Crime, Policing and Justice: The Experience of Ethnic Minorities – Findings from the 2000 British Crime Survey.* London.

———. 2001b. *Community Cohesion: A Report of the Independent Review Team chaired by Ted Cantle.* London.

———. 2005. The Citizenship Survey. Research Development Statistics. Retrieved December 13, 2005, from http://www.homeoffice.gov.uk/rds/citizensurvey.html.

Hopkins, Daniel J. 2009. "The Diversity Discount: When Increasing Ethnic and Racial Diversity Prevents Tax Increases." *Journal of Politics* 71 (1):160–177.

———. 2010. "Politicized Places: Explaining Where and When Immigrants Provoke Local Opposition." *American Political Science Review* 104 (1): 40–60.

Hornsby-Smith, Michael P., and Angela Dale. 1988. "The Assimilation of Irish Immigrants in England." *The British Journal of Sociology* 39 (4):519–544.

Horowitz, Donald L. 1985. *Ethnic Groups in Conflict.* Berkeley: University of California Press.

———. 2001. *The Deadly Ethnic Riot.* Berkeley: University of California Press.

Howard, Marc Morjé. 2006. "Comparative Citizenship: An Agenda for Cross-National Research." *Perspectives on Politics* 3 (4):443–455.

Howe, Darcus. 1985. *Darcus Howe on Black Sections in the Labour Party.* London: Race Today Publications.

Huber, Bertold, and Klaus Unger. 1982. "Politische und rechtliche Determinanten der Ausländerbeschäftigung in der Bundesrepublik Deutschland." In *Ausländer in der Bundesrepublik Deutschland und in der Schweiz* (pp. 124–194), eds. H.-J. Hoffmann-Nowotny and K.-O. Hondrich. Frankfurt: Campus Verlag.

Husbands, Christopher T. 1982. "East End Racism 1900–1980." *The London Journal* 8 (1):3–25.

———. 1983. *Racial Exclusionism and the City: The Urban Support of the National Front.* London: Allen & Unwin.

Hussain, Asifa. 2001. *British Immigration Policy under the Conservative Government.* Aldershot: Ashgate.

Hussain, Mustafa. 2007. *Muslims in the EU – Cities Report – Denmark.* New York: Open Society Institute and EU Monitoring and Advocacy Program.

Hussain, Yasmin, and Paul Bagguley. 2005. "Citizenship, Ethnicity and Identity: British Pakistanis after the 2001 'Riots'." *Sociology* 39 (3):407–425.

Hutter, Karl, and Bernhard Perchinig. 2008. Partizipation und Mehrheitsgesellschaft – Partizipation braucht Voraussetzungen. Retrieved January 22, 2008, from http://www.integration.at/forum/viewforum.php?f=3.

Iganski, Paul. 2001. "Hate Crimes Hurt More." *American Behavioral Scientist* 45 (4):626–638.

Ireland, Patrick. 1994. *The Policy Challenge of Ethnic Diversity: Immigrant Politics in France and Switzerland.* Cambridge, MA: Harvard University Press.

———. 2004. *Becoming Europe: Immigration, Integration, and the Welfare State.* Pittsburgh, PA: University of Pittsburgh Press.

Jacobs, Andrew. 2007. "With 40-Year Prism, Newark Surveys Deadly Riot." *New York Times*, July 8.

Jacobs, Brian D. 1986. *Black Politics and Urban Crisis in Britain.* Cambridge: Cambridge University Press.

Jacobs, Dirk. 2007. "Représentation politique et vote ethnique à Bruxelles." *Echos* (57):27–31.

Jamin, Mathilde. 1999. "Fremde Heimat: Zur Geschichte der Arbeitsmigration aus der Türkei." In *50 Jahre Bundesrepublik – 50 Jahre Einwanderung* (pp. 145–164), eds. J. Motte, R. Ohliger and A. v. Oswald. Frankfurt: Campus Verlag.

Jaschke, Hans-Gerd. 1993. *Die "Republikaner": Profile einer Rechtsaussen-Partei* (2nd ed.). Bonn: J. H. W. Dietz.

Jenness, Valerie, and Ryken Grattet. 2001. *Making Hate a Crime: From Social Movement to Law Enforcement.* New York: Russell Sage Foundation.

John, Augustine. 1970. *Race in the Inner City: A Report from Handsworth.* London: Runnymede Trust.

John, DeWitt. 1969. *Indian Workers' Association in Britain.* London: Oxford University Press.

Joly, Danièle. 1995. *Britannia's Crescent: Making a Place for Muslims in British Society.* Aldershot: Avebury.

Jones-Correa, Michael. 2001a. "Comparative Approaches to Changing Interethnic Relations in Cities." In *Governing American Cities* (pp. 1–14), ed. M. Jones-Correa. New York City: Russell Sage Foundation.

———. 2001b. "Structural Shifts and Institutional Capacity: Possibilities for Ethnic Cooperation and Conflict in Urban Settings." In *Governing American Cities* (pp. 183–209), ed. M. Jones-Correa. New York: Russell Sage Foundation.

Joppke, Christian. 1998. "Why Liberal States Accept Unwanted Immigration." *World Politics* 50 (2):266–293.

Joseph Rowntree Reform Trust Ltd. 2005. "The Far Right in London: A Challenge for Local Democracy?" York: Joseph Rowntree Reform Trust Ltd.

Joshua, Harris, Tina Wallace, and Heather Booth. 1983. *To Ride the Storm: The 1980 Bristol Riot and the State.* London: Heinemann.

Joumard, Isabelle, and Per M. Kongsrud. 2003. "Fiscal Relations across Government Levels." OECD Economics Department Working Paper No. 375.

Kalyvas, Stathis. 2006. *The Logic of Violence in Civil War.* Cambridge: Cambridge University Press.

Karapin, Roger. 1999. "The Politics of Immigration Control in Britain and Germany: Subnational Politicians and Social Movements." *Comparative Politics* 31 (4):423–444.

———. 2002. "Antiminority Riots in Unified Germany – Cultural Conflicts and Mischanneled Political Participation." *Comparative Politics* 34 (2):147–167.

Kastoryano, Riva. 2004. "Race and Ethnicity in France." In *Social Inequalities in Comparative Perspective* (pp. 66–88), eds. F. Devine and M. C. Waters. Malden, MA: Blackwell.

Katznelson, Ira. 1973. *Black Men, White Cities: Race, Politics, and Migration in the United States, 1900–30 and Britain, 1948–68*. London: Published for the Institute of Race Relations by Oxford University Press.

Keith, Michael. 1987. "'Something Happened': The Problems of Explaining the 1980 and 1981 Riots in British Cities." In *Race and Racism: Essays in Social Geography* (pp. 275–303), ed. P. Jackson. London: Allen & Unwin.

———. 1993. *Race, Riots and Policing: Lore and Disorder in a Multi-Racist Society*. London: UCL Press.

———. 1995. "Making the Street Visible: Placing Racial Violence in Context." *New Community* 21 (4):551–65.

———. 2005. *After the Cosmopolitan? Multicultural Cities and the Future of Racism*. London: Routledge.

Kerner Commission. 1968. "Kerner Report on Civil Disorders: Supplemental Studies for the National Advisory Commission on Civil Disorders." New York: Praeger.

Kestilä, Elina, and Peter Sönderlund. 2007. "Subnational Political Opportunity Structures and the Success of the Radical Right: Evidence from the March 2004 Regional Elections in France." *European Journal of Political Research* 46 (6):773–796.

Key, V. O. 1949. *Southern Politics in State and Nation*. New York: Knopf.

Kimber, Richard, and Ian Outlaw. 2004. UK General Election Results. Retrieved April 21, 2005, from http://www.psr.keele.ac.uk/psr.htm.

King, Charles. 2004. "The Micropolitics of Social Violence." *World Politics* 56 (3):431–455.

King, Gary. 1989. *Unifying Political Methodology: The Likelihood Theory of Statistical Inference*. Cambridge: Cambridge University Press.

King, Mike, and David Waddington. 2004. "Coping with Disorder? The Changing Relationship between Police Public Order Strategy and Practice – A Critical Analysis of the Burnley Riot." *Policing & Society* 14 (2):118–137.

Kirp, David L. 1979. *Doing Good by Doing Little*. Berkeley: University of California Press.

Kirwan, Paul. 1965. *Southall: A Brief History*. Southall: Borough of Southall.

Kitschelt, Herbert. 1996. *The Radical Right in Western Europe: A Comparative Analysis*. Ann Arbor: University of Michigan Press.

———. 2000. "Linkages between Citizens and Politicians in Democratic Polities." *Comparative Political Studies* 33 (6–7):845–879.

Klopp, Brett. 2002. *German Multiculturalism*. Westport, CT: Praeger.

Københavns Kommune. 2008. Emnevalg. Retrieved December 27, 2008, from http://www.sk.kk.dk/data2005/orientering/Ori0511.xls.

Koch-Arzberger, Claudia. 1985. *Die Schwierige Integration: Die bundesrepublikanische Gesellschaft und ihre 5 Millionen Ausländer*. Opladen: Westdeutscher Verlag.

Koopmans, Ruud. 1996. "Explaining the Rise of Racist and Extreme Right Violence in Western Europe: Grievances or Opportunities." *European Journal of Political Research* 30 (2):185–216.

Koopmans, Ruud, and Susan Olzak. 2004. "Discursive Opportunities and the Evolution of Right-Wing Violence in Germany." *American Journal of Sociology* 110 (1):198–230.

Koopmans, Ruud, and Paul Statham, eds. 2000. *Challenging Immigration and Ethnic Relations Politics: Comparative European Perspectives.* New York: Oxford University Press.

Koopmans, Ruud, Paul Statham, Marco Giugni, and Florence Passy. 2005. *Contested Citizenship: Immigration and Cultural Diversity in Europe.* Minneapolis: University of Minnesota Press.

Körner, Heiko. 1986."Das Gesetz zur Förderung der Rückkehrbereitschaft von Ausländern vom 28. November 1983 – Eine kritische Bilanz." In *Die "neue" Ausländerpolitik in Europa in den Aufnahme- und Entsendeländern* (pp. 65–72), eds. H. Körner and U. Mehrländer. Bonn: Verlag Neue Gesellschaft.

Krueger, Alan B., and Jorn-Steffen Pischke. 1997. "A Statistical Analysis of Crime against Foreigners in Unified Germany." *The Journal of Human Resources* 32 (1):182–209.

Kuepper, William, G. Lynne Lackey, and E. Nelson Swinerton. 1975. *Ugandan Asians in Britain.* London: Croom Helm.

Kühne, Peter. 2000. "The Federal Republic of Germany: Ambivalent Promotion of Immigrants' Interests." In *Trade Unions, Immigration, and Immigrants in Europe, 1960–1993* (pp. 39–63), eds. R. Penninx and J. Roosblad. New York: Berghahn Books.

Kwong, Peter. 2001. "Ethnic Subcontracting as an Impediment to Interethnic Coalitions: The Chinese Experience." In *Governing American Cities* (pp. 71–90), ed. M. Jones-Correa. New York: Russell Sage Foundation.

Labour Force Survey. 2006. Labour Force Survey (LFS) Historical Quarterly Supplement Table 10 – Economic activity by ethnic group. Office for National Statistics. Retrieved July 9, 2007, from http://www.statistics.gov.uk/STATBASE/ssdataset.asp?vlnk=7910.

Labour Party (Great Britain). 1990. *The Archives of the British Labour Party pt. 1, National Executive Committee Minutes of the Labour Representation Committee, 1900–06 and Labour Party since 1906.* Reading, England: Research Publications. Microform.

Lahav, Gallya. 2004. *Immigration and Politics in the New Europe.* New York: Cambridge University Press.

Laitin, David. 1986. *Hegemony and Culture: Politics and Religious Change among the Yoruba.* Chicago: University of Chicago Press.

————. 1998. *Identity in Formation: The Russian-Speaking Populations in the Near Abroad.* Ithaca, NY: Cornell University Press.

Lambert, Pierre-Yves. 1997. 1991, 1997: mêmes causes, mêmes effets. Retrieved January 3, 2008, from http://www.suffrage-universel.be/be/bemipylsoir.htm#cureghem.

Laurence, Jonathan, and Justin Vaisse. 2006. *Integrating Islam: Political and Religious Challenges in Contemporary France.* Washington, DC: Brookings Institution Press.

Lawrence, Daniel. 1974. *Black Migrants: White Natives.* London: Cambridge University Press.

_____. 1987. "Racial Violence in Britain." *New Community* 14 (1/2):151–160.

Layton-Henry, Zig. 1977. "Race and Politics in Ladywood – 1. The Parties and the Campaign." *New Community* 6 (1 & 2):130–135.

_____. 1986. "Immigration and Race Relations: Political Aspects – No. 14." *New Community* 13 (1):119–125.

_____. 1992. *The Politics of Immigration: Immigration, 'Race' and 'Race' Relations in Post-war Britain*. Oxford: Blackwell.

Leather, Philip. 2000. "Grants to Home-owners: A Policy in Search of Objectives." *Housing Studies* 15 (2):149–168.

Le Gallou, Jean-Yves, and Club de l'Horloge. 1985. *La préférence nationale: réponse à l'immigration*. Paris: A. Michel.

Lelkes, Orsolya. 2007. "Poverty among Migrants in Europe." Vienna: European Centre for Social Welfare Policy and Research.

Lequin, Yves. 2006a. "Immigrés en ville." In *Histoire des Étrangers et de l'Immigration en France* (pp. 408–427), ed. Y. Lequin. Paris: Larousse.

_____. 2006b. "Les Vagues d'Immigrations successives." In *Histoire des Étrangers et de l'Immigration en France* (pp. 385–406), ed. Y. Lequin. Paris: Larousse.

Leslie, Derek, Joanne Lindley, and Leighton Thomas. 2001. "Decline and Fall: Unemployment among Britain's Non-White Ethnic Communities." *Journal of the Royal Statistical Society. Series A (Statistics in Society)* 164 (2):371–387.

Lieberman, Evan. 2003. *Race and Regionalism in the Politics of Taxation in Brazil and South Africa*. Cambridge: Cambridge University Press.

Lieberman, Robert. 2005. *Shaping Race Policy: The United States in Comparative Perspective*. Princeton: Princeton University Press.

Lieberson, Stanley. 1985. "Unhyphenated Whites in the United States." *Ethnic and Racial Studies* 9 (1):159–180.

Lomas, Glenys Barbara Gillian. 1975. *The Coloured Population of Great Britain: A Comparative Study of Coloured Households in Four County Boroughs*. London: Runnymede Trust.

Long, Scott. 1997. *Regression Models for Categorical and Limited Dependent Variables*. Thousand Oaks, CA: Sage Publications.

Loughlin, John. 2007. *Subnational Government: The French Experience*. New York: Palgrave Macmillan.

Lubbers, Marcel, and Peer Scheepers. 2002. "French Front National Voting: A Micro and Macro Perspective." *Ethnic and Racial Studies* 25 (1):120–149.

Luft, Stefan. 2006. *Abschied von Multikulti*. Gräfelfing: Resch Verlag.

Luther, Kurt Richard. 2007. "Wahlstrategien und Wahlergebnisse des österreichischen Rechtspopulismus, 1986–2006." In *Wechselwahlen: Analysen zur Nationalratswahl 2006* (pp. 231–254), eds. F. Plasser and P. A. Ulram. Vienna: Facultas WUV.

Luttmer, Erzo F. P. 2001. "Group Loyalty and the Taste for Redistribution." *Journal of Political Economy* 109 (3):500–528.

Macpherson, Sir William. 1999. "The Stephen Lawrence Inquiry: Report of an Inquiry by Sir William Macpherson of Cluny." London: The Stationery Office.

MacRaild, Donald M. 1999. *Irish Migrants in Modern Britain, 1750–1922*. New York: St. Martin's Press.

Manfrass, Klaus. 1991. *Türken in der Bundesrepublik – Nordafrikaner in Frankreich*. Bonn: Bouvier.

Mansbridge, Jane. 1999. "Should Blacks Represent Blacks and Women Represent Women? A Contingent 'Yes'." *Journal of Politics* 61 (3):628–657.

Marrett, Valerie. 1989. *Immigrants Settling in the City*. Leicester: Leicester University Press.

———. 1993. "Resettlement of Ugandan Asians in Leicester." *Journal of Refugee Studies* 6 (3):248–259.

Marrow, Helen B. 2005. "New Destinations and Immigrant Incorporation." *Perspectives on Politics* 3 (4):781–799.

Marsh, Peter. 1967. *Anatomy of a Strike: Unions, Employers and Punjabi Workers in a Southall Factory*. London: Institute of Race Relations.

Martin, John, and Gurharpal Singh. 2002. *Asian Leicester*. Phoenix Mill: Sutton.

Martiniello, Marco. 1997a. "Ethnic Conflict within a Fractured Belgian Nation-State." *International Journal on Minority and Group Rights* 4 (3–4):289–300.

———. 1997b. "Quelle Participation Politique?" In *La Belgique et ses Immigrés* (pp. 101–120), ed. P. Blaise. Brussels: De Boeck Université.

———. 1998. "Les élus d'origine étrangère à Bruxelles: une nouvelle étape de la participation politique des populations d'origine immigrée." *Revue européenne des migrations internationales* 14 (2):123–149.

Martiniello, Marco, and Andrea Rea. 2003. Belgium's Immigration Policy Brings Renewal and Challenges. Retrieved September 3, 2008, from http://www.migrationinformation.org/Profiles/print.cfm?ID=164.

Mason, Gail. 2005. "Hate Crime and the Image of the Stranger." *British Journal of Criminology* 45 (6):837–859.

Massey, Douglas S. 2007. "Understanding America's Immigration 'Crisis'." *Proceedings of the American Philosophical Society* 151 (3):309–327.

Mateos, Pablo. 2007. "Classifying Ethnicity Using People's Names." Paper presented at the Social Statistics and Ethnic Diversity Conference, University of Montreal (Canada), December 6–8.

Maxwell, Rahsaan. 2008. *Tensions and Tradeoffs: Ethnic Minority Migrant Integration in Britain and France*. Ph.D. Dissertation, Department of Political Science, University of California at Berkeley.

Mayda, Anna Maria. 2006. "Who Is Against Immigration? A Cross-Country Investigation of Individual Attitudes toward Immigrants." *The Review of Economics and Statistics* 88 (3):510–530.

Mayer, Nonna. 2002. *Ces Français qui votent Le Pen*. Paris: Flammarion.

McAdam, Douglas, Sidney Tarrow, and Charles Tilly. 2001. *Dynamics of Contention*. Cambridge: Cambridge University Press.

McDevitt, Jack, Jennifer Balboni, Luis Garcia, and Joann Gu. 2001. "Consequences for Victims: A Comparison of Bias – and Non-Bias-Motivated Assaults." *American Behavioral Scientist* 45 (4):697–713.

McDevitt, Jack, Jack Levin, and Susan Bennett. 2002. "Hate Crime Offenders: An Expanded Typology." *Journal of Social Issues* 58 (2):303–317.

McEvoy, David, and Howard Aldrich. 1986. "Survival Rates of Asian and White Retailers." *International Small Business Journal* 4 (3):28–37.

McPhail, Clark. 1994. "The Dark Side of Purpose: Individual and Collective Violence in Riots." *The Sociological Quarterly* 35 (1):1–32.

Mehrländer, Ursula. 1974. *Soziale Aspekte der Ausländerbschäftigung*. Bonn: Verlag Neue Gesellschaft.

———. 1986. "Auswirkungen der "neuen" Ausländerpolitik auf Situation und Verhalten der ausländischen Wohnbevölkerung im Aufnahmeland – Beispiel Bundesrepublik Deutschland." In *Die "neue" Ausländerpolitik in Europa: Erfahrungen in den*

Aufnahme- und Entsendeländern (pp. 103–119), eds. H. Körner and U. Mehrländer. Bonn: Verlag Neue Gesellschaft.

Meier-Braun, Karl-Heinz. 1988. *Integration und Rückkehr? Zur Ausländerpolitik des Bundes und der Länder, insbesondere Baden-Württembergs.* Mainz: Grünewald.

Messina, Anthony M. 1989. *Race and Party Competition in Britain.* Oxford: Oxford University Press.

———. 2007. *The Logics and Politics of Post-WWII Migration to Western Europe.* New York: Cambridge University Press.

Metropolitan Police Service. 2000. "The Investigation of Racist, Domestic Violence and Homophobic Incidents: A Guide to Minimum Standards." London: MPS.

———. n.d. *Community Safety Units.* Metropolitan Police Service. Retrieved May 4, 2006, from http://www.met.police.uk/csu/whatcsu.htm.

Milner, Helen, and Dustin Tingley. 2009. "Preferences toward Openness: The Economic and Political Influences on Immigration Policy in the US." Unpublished manuscript, Princeton University.

Migration Policy Institute. 2008. Global City Migration Map. Retrieved June 10, 2008, from http://www.migrationinformation.org/DataHub/gcmm.cfm#map4list.

Modood, Tariq, Richard Berthoud, Jane Lakey, James Nazroo, Patten Smith, Satnam Virdee, and Sharon Beishon. 1997. *Ethnic Minorities in Britain: Diversity and Disadvantage.* London: Policy Studies Institute.

Mohammed, Marwan. 2009. "Youth Gangs, Riots and the Politicisation Process." In *Rioting in the UK and France: A Comparative Analysis* (pp. 157–172), eds. D. Waddington, F. Jobard, and M. King. Cullompton: Willan Publishing.

Money, Jeanette. 1997. "No Vacancy: The Political Geography of Immigration Control in Advanced Industrial Countries." *International Organization* 51 (4):685–720.

Moore, Damian. 2001. "Marseille: Institutional Links with Ethnic Minorities and the French Republican Model." In *Multicultural Policies and Modes of Citizenship in European Cities* (pp. 123–141), eds. A. Rogers and J. Tillie. Aldershot: Ashgate.

Motte, Jan. 1999. "Gedrängte Freiwilligkeit: Arbeitsmigration, Betriebspolitik und Rückkehrförderung 1983/84." In *50 Jahre Bundesrepublik – 50 Jahre Einwanderung* (pp. 165–184), eds. J. Motte, R. Ohliger and A. v. Oswald. Frankfurt: Campus Verlag.

Mucchielli, Laurent, and Véronique Le Goaziou, eds. 2006. *Quand les banlieues brûlent...* Paris: La Découverte.

Mucchielli, Laurent, and Abderahim Aït Omar. 2006. "Introduction générale. Les émeutes de novembre 2005: les raisons de la colère." In *Quand les banlieues brûlent...* (pp. 5–30), eds. L. Mucchielli and V. Le Goaziou. Paris: La Découverte.

Mudde, Cas. 2007. *Populist Radical Right Parties in Europe.* Cambridge: Cambridge University Press.

Mughan, Anthony and Pamela Paxton. 2006. "Anti-Immigrant Sentiment, Policy Preferences and Populist Party Voting in Australia." *British Journal of Political Science* 36 (2):341–358.

Mullins, David. 1986. "Events and Trends in Race Relations: July to December 1986." *New Community* 13 (1):111–118.

Myers, Daniel J. 1997. "Racial Rioting in the 1960s: An Event History Analysis of Local Conditions." *American Sociological Review* 62 (1):94–112.

Nally, Michael. 1984. "Eyewitness in Moss Side." In *Scarman and after: Essays Reflecting on Lord Scarman's Report, the Riots and their Aftermath* (pp. 54–62), ed. J. Benyon. Oxford: Pergamon Press.

Nandy, Dipak. 1970. "Some Concluding Comments." In *Race in the Inner City* (pp. 48–53), ed. A. John. London: Runnymede Trust.

Nash, David, and David Reeder, eds. 1993. *Leicester in the Twentieth Century*. Phoenix Mill: Sutton.

National Insititute of Statistics and Economic Studies (INSEE). 2002. *Communes... Références – Bases de Données*. Paris: INSEE Information Service.

National Board of Housing, Building and Planning, Sweden. 2005. "Housing Statistics in the European Union 2004." Karlskrona.

Négrier, Emmanuel. 1999. "The Changing Role of French Local Government." *West European Politics* 22 (4):120–140.

Neubacher, Frank. 1999. "Fremdenfeindliche Brandanschläge – Kriminologisch-empirische Befunde zu Tätern, Tathintergründen und gerichtlicher Verarbeitung in Jugendstrafverfahren." In *Rechtsextremismus und Fremdenfeindlichkeit* (pp. 265–287), eds. F. Dünkel and B. Geng. Mönchengladbach: Forum Verlag.

Newton, Kenneth. 1976. *Second City Politics: Democratic Processes and Decision-Making in Birmingham*. Oxford: Clarendon Press.

Norris, Pippa. 2005. *Radical Right: Voters and Parties in the Electoral Market*. New York: Cambridge University Press.

Oakley, Robin. 2005. "Policing Racist Crime and Violence: A Comparative Analysis." Vienna: European Monitoring Centre on Racism and Xenophobia.

Office for National Statistics. 1997. "Trends in Labour Market Participation of Ethnic Groups: 1984–1996." *Labour Market Trends* 105 (8):295–303.

Office of the Deputy Prime Minister. 2006. Review of the Evidence Base on Faith Communities, London.

Ohlemacher, Thomas. 1999. "'Wechselwirkungen nicht ausgeschlossen': Medien, Bevölkerungsmeinung und fremdenfeindliche Straftaten 1991–1997." In *Rechtsextremismus und Fremdenfeindlichkeit* (pp. 53–68), eds. F. Dünkel and B. Geng. Mönchengladbach: Forum Verlag.

Oliver, J. Eric, and Tali Mendelberg. 2000. "Reconsidering the Environmental Determinants of White Racial Attitudes." *American Journal of Political Science* 44 (3):574–589.

Olzak, Susan. 1992. *The Dynamics of Ethnic Competition and Conflict*. Palo Alto, CA: Stanford University Press.

Olzak, Susan, and Suzanne Shanahan. 1996. "Deprivation and Race Riots: An Extension of Spilerman's Analysis." *Social Forces* 74 (3):931–961.

Organisation for Economic Co-Operation and Development. 1997. *Managing across Levels of Government*. Paris: OECD.

———. 2007. *International Migration Outlook – SOPEMI*. Paris: OECD.

———. 2008. *A Profile of Immigrant Populations in the 21st Century*. Paris: OECD.

Oriol, Paul. 1998. "Les Immigrés et les Élections Municipales de 1995." *Migrations Société* 56 (March/April):5–17.

Ottaviano, Gianmarco I. P., and Giovanni Peri. 2006. "Wages, Rents and Prices: The Effects of Immigration on U.S. Natives." Center for Research and Analysis of Migration, Discussion Paper No 13/07.

Ouseley, Herman. 2001. "Community Pride not Prejudice: Making Diversity Work in Bradford." Bradford: Bradford Vision.

Pagenstecher, Cord. 1994. *Ausländerpolitik und Immigrantenidentität*. Berlin: Bertz.

Papalekas, Johannes Chr. 1986. "Statt einer Einleitung: Über das Umschlagen des Ausländerproblems zur Eigengesetzlichkeit." In *Strukturwandel des*

Ausländerproblems (pp. 7–16), ed. J. C. Papalekas. Bochum: Studienverlag Brockmeyer.

Patterson, Sheila. 1963. *Dark Strangers*. London: Tavistock.

———. 1969. *Immigration and Race Relations in Britain, 1960–1967*. London: Published for the Institute of Race Relations by Oxford University Press.

Paul, Kathleen. 1997. *Whitewashing Britain: Race and Citizenship in the Postwar Era*. Ithaca, NY: Cornell University Press.

Pedersen, Søren. 1999. "Migration to Denmark during the Period 1960–97." In *Immigration to Denmark* (pp. 148–190), eds. D. Coleman and E. Wadensjö. Aarhus: Aarhus University Press.

Petersen, Roger. 2002. *Understanding Ethnic Violence: Fear, Hatred, and Resentment in Twentieth-Century Eastern Europe*. Cambridge: Cambridge University Press.

Peterson, Paul. 1981. *City Limits*. Chicago: University of Chicago Press.

Peggie, A. 1979. "Minority Youth Politics in Southall." *New Community* 7 (2):170–177.

Phalet, Karen, and Marc Swyngedouw. 2003. "Measuring Immigrant Integration: The Case of Belgium." *Studi Emigrazione/Migration Studies* 40 (152):773–803.

Phillips, Christopher. 2000. *Birmingham Votes 1911–2000*. Plymouth: Local Government Chronicle Elections Centre, University of Plymouth.

Phillips, Deborah. 1981. "The Social and Spatial Segregation of Asians in Leicester." In *Social Interaction and Ethnic Segregation* (pp. 101–121), eds. P. Jackson and S. J. Smith. London: Academic Press.

———. 1987. "The Rhetoric of Anti-Racism in Public Housing Allocation." In *Race and Racism: Essays in Social Geography* (pp. 212–237), ed. P. Jackson. London: Allen & Unwin.

———. 1988. "Race and Housing in London's East End: Continuity and Change." *New Community* 14 (3):356–369.

Pilkington, Edward. 1988. *Beyond the Mother Country: West Indians and the Notting Hill White Riots*. London: Tauris.

Pinderhughes, Howard L. 1993. "The Anatomy of Racially Motivated Violence in New York City: A Case Study of Youth in Southern Brooklyn." *Social Problems* 40 (4):478–492.

Piore, Michael J. 1979. *Birds of Passage: Migrant Labor and Industrial Societies*. Cambridge: Cambridge University Press.

Pischke, Jörn-Steffen, and Johannes Velling. 1997. "Employment Effects of Immigration to Germany: An Analysis Based on Local Labor Markets." *Review of Economics and Statistics* 79 (4):594–604.

Pitkin, Hanna. 1969. *The Concept of Representation*. Berkeley: University of California Press.

Piven, Frances Fox, and Richard A. Cloward. 1971. *Regulating the Poor*. New York: Pantheon Books.

Posner, Daniel P. 2005. *Institutions and Ethnic Politics in Africa*. Cambridge: Cambridge University Press.

Priemus, Hugo, and Frans Dieleman. 1997. "Social Rented Housing: Recent Changes in Western Europe – Introduction." *Housing Studies* 12 (4):421–425.

Putnam, Robert D. 2007. "*E Pluribus Unum*: Diversity and Community in the Twenty-first Century." *Scandinavian Political Studies* 30 (2):137–74.

Race Today. 1978a. "Can BHAG Fight Back?" *Race Today* 10 (5):106–110.

———. 1978b. "Law & Order Hoo! Hoo!" *Race Today* 10 (4):76–77.

Rakindo, Adil. 1975. "Indonesia: Chinese Scapegoat Politics in Suharto's 'New Order'." *Journal of Contemporary Asia* 5 (3):345–352.

Rallings, Colin, and Michael Thrasher. 2003. *Local Elections in Britain: A Statistical Digest* (2nd ed.). Plymouth: Local Government Chronicle Elections Centre, Polytechnic South West.

Rallings, Colin, Michael Thrasher, and Lawrence Ware. 2006. SN: 5319: British Local Election Database, 1889–2003 [Computer file]. Colchester: UK Data Archive [Distributor].

Ratcliffe, Peter. 1981. *Racism and Reaction: A Profile of Handsworth*. London: Routledge & Kegan Paul.

Ravetz, Allison. 2001. *Council Housing and Culture: The History of a Social Experiment*. London: Routledge.

Ray, Larry, and David Smith. 2001. "Racist Offenders and the Politics of 'Hate Crime'." *Law and Critique* 12 (3):203–221.

_____. 2004. "Racist Offending, Policing and Community Conflict." *Sociology* 38 (4):681–699.

Ray, Larry, David Smith, and Liz Wastell. 2004. "Shame, Rage and Racist Violence." *British Journal of Criminology* 44 (3):350–368.

Rea, Andrea. 2000. "La participation politiques des Belges d'origine étrangère." In *Politique multiculturelle et modes de citoyenneté à Bruxelles* (pp. 56–72), eds. A. Rea and N. Ben Mohammed. Brussels: GERME.

_____. 2001. *Jeunes immigrés dans la cité*. Brussels: Éditions Labor.

Reeves, Frank. 1989. *Race and Borough Politics*. Aldershot: Avebury.

Reif, Karheinz, and Anna Melich. 1992. Eurabarometer 30: Immigrants and Out-groups in Western Europe, October-November 1988 [Computer file]. Conducted by Faits et Opinoins. Ann Arbor, MI: Inter-University Consortium for Political and Social Research [Producer and Distributor].

Rex, John. 1982. "The 1981 Urban Riots in Britain." *International Journal of Urban and Regional Research* 6 (1):99–113.

Rex, John, and Robert Moore. 1967. *Race, Community, and Conflict*. London: Oxford University Press.

Rex, John and Yunus Samad. 1996. "Multiculturalism and Political Integration in Birmingham and Bradford." *Innovation: The European Journal of Social Sciences* 9 (1):11–31.

Rex, John, and Sally Tomlinson. 1979. *Colonial Immigrants in a British City: A Class Analysis*. London: Routledge & Kegan Paul.

Ritchie, David. 2001. *Panel Report*. Oldham: Oldham Independent Review Team.

Robinson, Vaughn. 1981. "The Development of South Asian Settlement in Britain and the Myth of Return." In *Ethnic Segregation in Cities* (pp. 149–169), eds. C. Peach, V. Robinson, and S. Smith. Athens: The University of Georgia Press.

_____. 1993. "Marching into the Middle Classes: The Long-Term Resettlement of East African Asians in the UK." *Journal of Refugee Studies* 6 (3):230–247.

_____. 1995. "The Migration of East African Asians to the UK." In *The Cambridge Survey of World Migration* (pp. 331–336), ed. R. Cohen. Cambridge: Cambridge University Press.

Roemer, John E., Woojin Lee, and Karine Van der Straeten. 2007. *Racism, Xenophobia and Redistribution: A Study of Four Democracies*. Cambridge, MA: Harvard University Press.

Rose, E. J. B. 1969. *Colour and Citizenship: A Report on British Race Relations.* London: Oxford University Press.

Rowe, Michael. 1998. *The Racialisation of Disorder in Twentieth Century Britain.* Aldershot: Ashgate.

Rydgren, Jens. 2004. "Explaining the Emergence of Radical Right-Wing Populist Parties: The Case of Denmark." *West European Politics* 27 (3):474–502.

Saggar, Shamit. 1991. *Race and Public Policy: A Study of Local Politics and Government.* Aldershot: Avebury.

———. 2000. *Race and Representation: Electoral Politics and Ethnic Pluralism in Britain.* Manchester: Manchester University Press.

———. 2009. *Pariah Politics: Understanding Western Radical Islamism and What Should Be Done.* Oxford: Oxford University Press.

Saggar, Shamit, and Joanne Drean. 2001. "British Public Attitudes and Ethnic Minorities." Cabinet Office: Performance and Innovation Unit.

Saiz, Albert. 2007. "Immigration and Housing Rents in American Cities." *Journal of Urban Economics* 61 (2):345–371.

Scarman, Leslie George. 1982. *The Brixton Disorders, 10–12 April 1981: The Scarman Report.* Harmondsworth: Penguin Books.

Scott, Duncan. 1972–1973. "West Pakistanis in Huddersfield: Aspects of Race Relations in Local Politics." *New Community* 2 (1):38–43.

Scheve, Kenneth, and Matthew J. Slaughter. 2001. "Labor Market Competition and Individual Preferences over Immigration Policy." *The Review of Economics and Statistics* 83 (1):133–145.

Schneider, Cathy Lisa. 2007. "Police Power and Race Riots in Paris." *Politics and Society* 35 (4):523–549.

Schönwälder, Karen. 2001. *Einwanderung und ethnische Pluralität: Politische Entscheidungen und öffentliche Debatten in Grossbritannien und der Bundesrepublik von den 1950er bis zu den 1970er Jahren.* Essen: Klartext.

Schultz-Nielsen, Marie-Louise, and Amelie Constant. 2004. "Employment Trends for Immigrants and Natives." In *Migrants, Work, and the Welfare State* (pp. 119–146), eds. T. Trances and K. F. Zimmermann. Odense: University Press of Southern Denmark.

Schwarze, Susan. 1999. *Das Arenen-Verhandlungsmodell – Deutsche Asylpolitik im europäischen Kontext von 1989 bis 1993.* Politische Wissenschaften, Freie Universität Berlin.

Seawright, Jason, and John Gerring. 2008. "Case Selection Techniques in Case Study Research: A Menu of Qualitative and Quantitative Options." *Political Research Quarterly* 61 (2):294–308.

Seliga, Joseph. 1998. "A Neighborhood Transformed: The Effect of Indian Migration on the Belgrave Area of Leicester, 1965–1995." *The Local Historian* 28 (4):225–241.

Senior, Clarence. 1957. "Race Relations and Labor Supply in Britain." *Social Problems* 4 (4):302–312.

Sharpe, L. J. 1965. "Brixton." In *Colour and the British Electorate 1964* (pp. 12–30), ed. N. Deakin. New York: Praeger.

Sherif, Muzafer. 1966. *In Common Predicament: Social Psychology of Intergroup Conflict and Cooperation.* Boston: Houghton Mifflin.

Sherman, Alfred. 1965. "Deptford." In *Colour and the British Electorate* (pp. 106–119), ed. N. Deakin. New York: Praeger.

Shipley, Peter. 1981. "The Riots and the Far Left." *New Community* 9 (2):194–198.

Shively, Michael. 2005. "Study of Literature and Legislation on Hate Crime in America." Washington, DC: United States Department of Justice.

Shuttleworth, Alan. 1965. "Sparkbrook." In *Colour and the British Electorate 1964* (pp. 54–76), ed. N. Deakin. New York: Praeger.

Sibbit, Rae. 1997. "*The Perpetrators of Racial Harassment and Violence.*" London: Home Office.

Sides, John, and Jack Citrin. 2007. "European Opinion about Immigration: The Role of Identities, Interests and Information." *British Journal of Political Science* 37 (3):477–504.

Sikh Human Rights Group. 2002. *Southall Report.* SWRT-SHRG Conference. Retrieved May 3, 2005, from http://www.shrg.net/events/20021109%20Southall/southall_conf_report.pdf.

Sills, Andrew, Gillian Taylor, and Peter Golding. 1988. *The Politics of the Urban Crisis.* London: Hutchinson.

Sills, Andrew, M. Tarpey, and Peter Golding. 1983. "Asians in an Inner City." *New Community* 11 (1 & 2):34–41.

Simmons, Harvey G. 1996. *The French National Front: The Extremist Challenge to Democracy.* Boulder, CO: Westview Press.

Simon, Julian L. 1999. *The Economic Consequences of Immigration.* Ann Arbor: University of Michigan Press.

Singer, Daniel. 1991. "The Resistible Rise of Jean-Marie Le Pen." *Ethnic and Racial Studies* 14 (3):368–381.

Singh, Gurharpal. 2003. "Multiculturalism in Contemporary Britain: Reflections on the 'Leicester Model'." *IJMS: International Journal on Multicultural Societies* 5 (1):40–54.

Smith, David J. 1977. *Racial Disadvantage in Britain: The PEP Report.* Harmondsworth: Penguin Books.

Sniderman, Paul M., and Louk Hagendoorn. 2005. *When Ways of Life Collide.* Princeton: Princeton University Press.

Sniderman, Paul M., Louk Hagendoorn, and Markus Prior. 2004. "Predisposing Factors and Situational Triggers: Exclusionary Reactions to Immigrant Minorities." *American Political Science Review* 98 (1):35–49.

Sniderman, Paul M., Pierangelo Peri, Rui J. P. de Figueiredo Jr., and Thomas Piazza. 2000. *The Outsider: Prejudice and Politics in Italy.* Princeton: Princeton University Press.

Solomos, John, and Les Back. 1995. *Race, Politics, and Social Change.* London: Routledge.

Solomos, John, and Gurharpal Singh. 1990. "Racial Equality, Housing and the Local State." In *Race and Local Politics* (pp. 95–114), eds. W. Ball and J. Solomos. Basingstoke: Macmillan Education.

Soysal, Yasemin Nuhoglu. 1994. *Limits of Citizenship: Migrants and Postnational Membership in Europe.* Chicago: University of Chicago Press.

Spencer, Sarah. 2006. "Social Integration of Migrants in Europe: A Review of the European Literature 2000–2006." Oxford: Center on Migration, Policy and Society.

Spiers, Maurice. 1965. "Bradford." In *Colour and the British Electorate 1964* (pp. 120–156), ed. N. Deakin. New York: Praeger.

Spilerman, Seymour. 1970. "The Causes of Racial Disturbances: A Comparison of Alternative Explanations." *American Sociological Review* 35 (4):627–649.

————. 1976. "Structural Characteristics of Cities and the Severity of Racial Disorders." *American Sociological Review* 41 (5):771–793.

Statistisches Bundesamt. 1983–1984. *Datenreport 1983/48.* Bonn.

————. 2002. *Datenreport 2002.* Bonn.

————. 2004. *Datenreport 2004.* Bonn.

————. 2007. Ausländer: Bundesländer, Stichtag, Geschlecht, Ausgewählte Staaten der Welt. Statistisches Bundesamt. Retrieved July 8, 2007, from www.destatis.de.

Steinert, Johannes-Dieter. 1995. *Migration und Politik: Westdeutschland – Europa – Übersee 1945–1961.* Osnabrück: Secolo Verlag.

Stoker, Gerry, Sean Baine, Susan Carlyle, Steve Charters, and Tony Du Sautoy. 1991. "Reflections on Neighbourhood Decentralisation in Tower Hamlets." *Public Administration* 69:373–384.

Straubhaar, Thomas. 1992. "Allocational and Distributional Aspects of Future Immigration to Western Europe." *International Migration Review* 26 (2):462–483.

Sturm-Martin, Imke. 2001. *Zuwanderungspolitik in Grossbritannien und Frankreich.* Frankfurt: Campus Verlag.

Sullaway, Megan. 2004. "Psychological Perspectives on Hate Crime Laws." *Psychology, Public Policy, and Law* 10 (3):250–292.

Sugrue, Thomas J. 1996. *The Origins of the Urban Crisis: Race and Inequality in Postwar Detroit.* Princeton: Princeton University Press.

Sugrue, Thomas J., and Andrew P. Goodman. 2007. "Plainfield Burning: Black Rebellion in the Suburban North." *Journal of Urban History* 33 (4):568–601.

Swyngedouw, Marc. 2000. "Belgium: Explaining the Relationship between Vlaams Blok and the City of Antwerp." In *The Politics of the Extreme Right* (pp. 121–143), ed. P. Hainsworth. London: Pinter.

Tajfel, Henri. 1982. "Social Psychology of Intergroup Relations." *American Review of Psychology* 33:1–39.

Tapinos, Georges Photios. 1975. *L'immigration étrangère en France: 1946–1973.* Paris: Presses universitaires de France.

Tarrow, Sidney. 1998. *Power in Movement: Social Movements and Contentious Politics* (2nd ed.). Cambridge: Cambridge University Press.

Taylor, Stan. 1978. "Race, Extremism and Violence in Contemporary British Politics." *New Community* 7 (1):56–67.

————. 1981. "Strategy Changes on the Ultra-right." *New Community* 9 (2):199–202.

ter Wal, Jessica. 2007. "The Netherlands." In *European Immigration: A Sourcebook* (pp. 249–261), eds. A. Triandafyllidou and R. Gropas. Aldershot: Ashgate.

Thatcher, Margaret. 1993. *The Downing Street Years.* London: HarperCollins.

Thompson, Eric J. 1972. *Demographic, Social and Economic Indices for Wards in Greater London.* London: Greater London Council, Department of Planning and Transportation.

Thompson, Heather Ann. 2000. "Understanding Rioting in Postwar Urban America." *Journal of Urban History* 26 (3):391–402.

Thränhardt, Dietrich. 1999. "Integration und Partizipation von Einwanderergruppen im lokalen Kontext." In *Aussiedler: Deutsche Einwanderer aus Osteuropa* (pp. 229–246), eds. K. J. Bade and J. Oltmer. Osnabrück: Rasch.

————. 1995. "The Political Uses of Xenophobia in England, France, and Germany." *Party Politics* 1 (3):323–345.

Tilly, Charles. 1978. *From Mobilization to Revolution.* New York: Random House.

Togeby, Lise. 2008. "The Political Representation of Ethnic Minorities: Denmark as a Deviant Case." *Party Politics* 14 (3):325–343.

Tompson, Keith. 1988. *Under Siege: Racism and Violence in Britain Today.* New York: Penguin.

Trounstine, Jessica. 2008. *Political Monopolies in American Cities.* Chicago: University of Chicago Press.

Trounstine, Jessica, and Melody E. Valdini. 2008. "The Context Matters: The Effects of Single-Member versus At-Large Districts on City Council Diversity." *American Journal of Political Science* 52 (3):554–569.

Troyna, Barry, and Robin Ward. 1982. "Racial Antipathy and Local Opinion Leaders: A Tale of Two Cities." *New Community* 9 (3):454–466.

Tsiakalos, Georgios. 1983. *Ausländerfeindlichkeit.* München: C. H. Beck.

Usher, Dan. 1977. "Public Property and Effects of Migration upon Other Residents of the Migrants' Countries of Origin and Destination." *Journal of Political Economy* 85 (5):1001–1026.

Van Der Brug, Wouter, Meindert Fennema, and Jean Tillie. 2005. "Why Some Anti-Immigrant Parties Fail and Others Succeed: A Two-Step Model of Electoral Support." *Comparative Political Studies* 38 (5):537–573.

van Donselaar, Jaap. 1993. "The Extreme Right and Racist Violence in the Netherlands." In *Racist Violence in Europe* (pp. 46–61), eds. T. Björgo and R. Witte. London: Macmillan.

Varshney, Ashutosh. 2002. *Ethnic Conflict and Civic Life: Hindus and Muslims in India.* New Haven, CT: Yale University Press.

Verbunt, Gilles. 1985. "France." In *European Immigration Policy: A Comparative Study* (pp. 127–164), ed. T. Hammar. Cambridge: Cambridge University Press.

von Oswald, Anne, and Barbara Schmidt. 1999."Nach Schichtende sind sie immer in ihr Lager zurückgekehrt." In *50 Jahre Bundesrepublik – 50 Jahre Einwanderung* (pp. 184–213), eds. J. Motte, R. Ohliger, and A. v. Oswald. Frankfurt: Campus Verlag.

Waddington, David, Fabien Jobard, and Mike King, eds. 2009. *Rioting in the UK and France: A Comparative Analysis.* Cullompton: Willan Publishing.

Wahl, Klaus, ed. 2003. *Skinheads, Neonazis, Mitläufer: Täterstudien und Prävention.* Opladen: Leske & Budrich.

Waldinger, Roger. 2005. "Networks and Niches: The Continuing Significance of Ethnic Connections." In *Ethnicity, Social Mobility and Public Policy: Comparing the US and the UK* (pp. 342–362), eds. G. Loury, T. Modood, and S. Teles. New York: Cambridge University Press.

Walker, Martin. 1977. *The National Front.* London: Fontana.

Watts, Meredith W. 2001. "Aggressive Youth Cultures and Hate Crime: Skinheads and Xenophobic Youth in Germany." *American Behavioral Scientist* 45 (4):600–615.

Weil, Patrick. 2001. "Access to Citizenship: A Comparison of Twenty-Five Nationality Laws." In *Citizenship Today: Global Perspectives and Practices* (pp. 17–35), eds. A. T. Aleinikoff and D. Klusmeyer. Washington, DC: Brookings Institution Press.

Weiner, Myron. 1978. *Sons of the Soil.* Princeton: Princeton University Press.

Werner, Heinz, and Ingeborg König. 2001. "Integration ausländischer Arbeitnehmer in die Arbeitsmärkte der EU-Länder." Diskussionsbeiträge des Instituts für Arbeitsmarkt – und Berufsforschung der Bundesanstalt für Arbeit 10.

West Midlands County Council. Race Relations and Equal Opportunities Committee Review Panel. 1986. *A Different Reality: An Account of Black People's Experiences and their Grievances before and after the Handsworth Rebellion of September 1985: Report of the Review Panel*. Birmingham: West Midlands County Council.

Wieviorka, Michel. 1999. *Violence en France*. Paris: Seuil.

_____. 2005. Violence in France. Retrieved May 15, 2006, from http://riotsfrance.ssrc.org/Wieviorka/.

Wilkinson, Steven. 2004. *Votes and Violence: Electoral Competition and Ethnic Riots in India*. Cambridge: Cambridge University Press.

Willems, Helmut. 1995. "Development, Patterns and Causes of Violence against Foreigners in Germany." *Terrorism and Political Violence* 7 (1):162–181.

Willems, Helmut, Roland Eckert, Stefanie Würtz, and Linda Steinmetz, eds. 1993. *Fremdenfeindliche Gewalt: Einstellungen, Täter, Konflikteskalation*. Opladen: Leske & Budrich.

Winant, Howard. 2000. "Race and Race Theory." *Annual Review of Sociology* 26:169–185.

Wisconsin v. Mitchell. 1993. United States Supreme Court.

Wihtol de Wenden, Catherine, and Rémy Leveau. 2001. *La Beurgeoisie: Les Trois Âges de la Vie Associative Issue de l'Immigration*. Paris: CNRS.

Witte, Rob. 1995. "Racist Violence in Western Europe." *New Community* 21 (4):489–500.

Woolcott, David. 1965. "Southall." In *Colour and the British Electorate 1964* (pp. 31–58), ed. N. Deakin. New York: Praeger.

Yashar, Deborah J. 2005. *Contesting Citizenship in Latin America*. Cambridge: Cambridge University Press.

Yelling, Jim. 2000. "The Incidence of Slum Clearance in England and Wales, 1955–85." *Urban History* 27 (2):234–254.

Zancarini-Fournel, Michelle. 2004. "Généalogie des Rébellions Urbaines en Temps de Crise (1971–1981)." *Vingtième Siècle. Revue d'histoire* 84 (4):119–127.

Zolberg, Aristide, and Long Litt Woon. 1999. "Why Islam is like Spanish: Cultural Incorporation in Europe and the United States." *Politics and Society* 27 (5):5–38.

Index